PERSPECTIVES ON MUSIC

Leroy Ostransky

Professor of Music and
Composer in Residence
University of Puget Sound

Englewood Cliffs, N.J./1963
PRENTICE-HALL, INC.

PERSPECTIVES
ON
MUSIC

PRENTICE-HALL INTERNATIONAL, INC., *London*
PRENTICE-HALL OF AUSTRALIA, PTY., LTD., *Sydney*
PRENTICE-HALL OF CANADA, LTD., *Toronto*
PRENTICE-HALL FRANCE, S.A.R.L., *Paris*
PRENTICE-HALL OF JAPAN, INC., *Tokyo*
PRENTICE-HALL DE MEXICO, S.A., *Mexico City*

Library of Congress Catalog card number 63-9750
Printed in the United States of America
60824 C

PERSPECTIVES ON MUSIC by Leroy Ostransky

to *Sonya*

Foreword

THIS COLLECTION OF WRITINGS ON MUSIC IS INtended for college students who elect a two-semester music course as part of an Arts or a Humanities requirement. The majority of these students enter into this course with little or no formal musical training. The course—often called "Introduction to Music Literature" or "Survey of Music" or "Music 101" or something else similar to these titles—is frequently the student's first encounter with a college music course and (according to the way in which his curriculum is planned) is likely to be a terminal course as well.

It is with this knowledge in mind, and with the experience that comes from fifteen years of teaching such a course to non-music majors, that these writings were brought together. Although each contributing writer is a specialist with his own particular musical discipline—Aaron Copland, composer; Leonard Bernstein, composer and conductor; Oscar Thompson, encyclopedist; Abram Chasins, pianist; to mention but a few—there is one factor that binds them together. Each of these professional musicians makes a strong plea to the non-professional musician, the layman, to try to understand what music is about.

It is safe to assume that a certain number of beginning students will have had some experience with, and enjoyment of, various phases of serious music and will continue to do so throughout their lives. For these students this collection offers the kind of information that we believe will lead not only to a better understanding, but also we trust, to an even greater enjoyment of all music.

The special value of this collection, however, lies in the way it can be made to fascinate and interest the intelligent student with a minimum of experience in serious music. Our collection starts where the student is; it does not assume knowledge and experience that the student is not likely to have. The writings explain clearly and lucidly, and, for the most part, in non-technical language, the ramifications of music in a way calculated to draw the student to the great music itself.

It is our belief that each instructor prefers to explain such things as scale construction, chord construction, note values, and other fundamentals in his own way and in his own time, if he wishes to discuss these questions at all. For this reason we have excluded our own explanation of these matters. Again, we cannot presume to suggest that one particular symphony—the *Jupiter,* for example—is a more useful or more valuable musical illustration for the section on *the symphony,* than, say, Beethoven's *First.* The instructor will no doubt introduce his favorite pieces of music to coincide with the appropriate essay, and that is as it should be.

Although some of the essays are historically oriented, it has not been our intention in collecting these essays to provide a history of music. It has been our intention, rather, to take the student logically from one aspect of music to another aspect of music, according to his current frame of reference.

For example, we believe that the subject of *program music* may be introduced to the class without first discussing the question of *form* in music. Most program music, as we know, may be followed intelligently and understood by simply making the student aware of the composer's program. On the other hand, it is difficult to make students understand the special appeals of *absolute music* without first presenting them with the elements of form. Therefore, it seemed logical to present these three subjects in this order: program music; form; absolute music.

To look back for a moment: Since the orchestra is the principal medium for performing program music, it seemed logical to have the subject of *the orchestra* precede program music. The section on absolute music is given to chamber music, because this kind of music—absolute music—is the principal province of the small chamber ensemble. The transition from absolute music to the symphony is an easy one; the most significant example of absolute music for orchestra is the symphony.

Though related to the symphony, the concerto takes us temporarily away from the ensemble and enables us to focus our attention on *the concert soloist.* The subjects of *music for piano* and *music for voice* logically follow close behind. Discussions of vocal music bring us inexorably to the *opera,* which in turn leads us to the *ballet.* The origins of opera must be sought in the music of the church, and here, we confess, it seemed as logical to have the church music precede opera as to follow it. The final choice will no doubt remain with the individual instructor.

At this stage in the student's training, we have found it useful to provide him with a degree of historical perspective. To this end, we have selected essays characterizing the musical life of the chief historical periods—the Middle Ages, the Renaissance, the Baroque Era, the Classical Period, the Romantic Period, and the Twentieth Century—through their composers. These essays may either be used in the order we have presented them or individually as the necessity presents itself.

We have concluded with essays on musical comedy and jazz—types of music with which the student has had wide experience and with which he is at once familiar. We believe that the intelligent student will now be able to place these familiar types of music, as well as all music, in their proper context.

Each essay is preceded by a short introduction giving the background and information necessary to an understanding of the essay's intention. Each essay is then followed by a series of what we believe to be interesting and provocative questions of a serious nature. These questions may be used for class discussion, as subjects for short papers, or as examination questions. Wherever possible, the questions have been phrased in concrete terms and deal with ideas on which students feel capable of expressing themselves.

Finally, in selecting the various essays, we have tried to point out that music exists because human beings have composed music for others who have performed it for others who have listened, and that this vital, essential activity is still going on.

L.O.

Acknowledgments

I WISH TO ACKNOWLEDGE THE ASSISTANCE OF Warren Perry, librarian of the University of Puget Sound, and his associates, Elspeth Pope and Desmond Taylor. My deepest thanks I owe to my wife, who suffered through the selection of each essay, except my own.

I wish to express my appreciation for permission to use the following materials:

HOW WE LISTEN, with permission of the publishers, from *What to Listen for in Music* by Aaron Copland. Copyright © 1939, 1957 by the McGraw-Hill Book Company, Inc.

IMAGE PROCESSES AND CONNOTATION, reprinted from *Emotion and Meaning in Music* by Leonard B. Meyer by the permission of the University of Chicago Press. Copyright 1956 by the University of Chicago Press.

THE LANGUAGE OF MUSIC, from *How to Understand Music* by Oscar Thompson. Copyright 1936 by Oscar Thompson. Reprinted by permission of the Estate of Oscar Thompson.

THE NATIONAL SCHOOLS, reprinted from *Symphonic Music* by Homer Ulrich by permission of the Columbia University Press. Copyright 1952 by the Columbia University Press.

A DIGEST OF FORM, reprinted from the Naval Training Course *Basic Music,* published by the Bureau of Naval Personnel, Department of the Navy, 1961; used by permission.

CHAMBER MUSIC by Donald Francis Tovey, reprinted from *Cobbett's Cyclopedic Survey of Chamber Music,* Volume 1, by permission of the publishers, the Oxford University Press, Inc. Copyright 1929-1930 by Oxford University Press, Inc.

FOUR RUSSIANS CALLED BUDAPEST by Philip Hart, from *High Fidelity* Magazine, May 1961. Reprinted by permission. Copyright 1961 by *High Fidelity* Magazine.

JASCHA HEIFETZ, reprinted from *The Other Side of the Record* by Charles O'Connell, by permission of Alfred A. Knopf, Inc. Copyright 1947 by Charles O'Connell.

VLADIMIR HOROWITZ, reprinted from *Speaking of Pianists* by Abram Chasins, by permission of Alfred A. Knopf, Inc. Copyright 1957 by Abram Chasins.

THE AMATEUR PIANIST, reprinted from *The Literature of the Piano* by Ernest Hutcheson, by permission of Alfred A. Knopf, Inc. Copyright 1948 by Alfred A. Knopf, Inc. Permission in the British Commonwealth and Empire by Hutchinson & Co. Ltd.

CHOPIN AT 38, reprinted from *Chopin* by Herbert Weinstock, by permission of Alfred A. Knopf, Inc. Copyright 1949 by Herbert Weinstock.

THE HEYDAY OF OPERA, reprinted from *Going to the Opera* by Lionel Salter, by permission of Lionel Salter. Copyright 1955 by Phoenix House Ltd.

THE GRAND ROMANTIC BALLETS, reprinted from *Ballet Music: An Introduction* by Humphrey Searle, by permission of Cassell and Company Ltd. Copyright 1958 by Humphrey Searle.

THE CHORALE IN THE CHURCH SERVICE, reprinted with the permission of The Macmillan Company from *J. S. Bach* by Albert Schweitzer, Volume 1, tr. by Ernest Newman. First published in English in 1911 by Breitkopf and Härtel. Permission outside the United States of America by A. & C. Black Ltd.

BACH, from: *The Stream of Music* by Richard Anthony Leonard. Copyright 1943 by Richard Anthony Leonard. Reprinted by permission of Doubleday and Company, Inc.

THE WEATHER AT MOZART'S FUNERAL by Nicolas Slonimsky, from *The Musical Quarterly*, January, 1960. Copyright 1960 by G. Schirmer, Inc. Reprinted by permission.

THE IMPRESSIONISTS, from *Music of the World* by Kurt Pahlen. Copyright 1949 by Crown Publishers, Inc. Used by permission of the publisher.

BARTOK IN AMERICA, reprinted from *The Life and Music of Béla Bartók* by Halsey Stevens, by permission of the publishers, the Oxford University Press, Inc. Copyright 1953 by the Oxford University Press, Inc.

WHATEVER HAPPENED TO THAT GREAT AMERICAN SYMPHONY? from *The Joy of Music* by Leonard Bernstein. Reprinted by permission of Simon and Schuster, Inc. Copyright © 1954-1959 by Leonard Bernstein. Permission in the British Commonwealth and Empire by M/s George Weidenfeld and Nicolson Ltd.

JAZZ: SOME EARLY DIFFICULTIES, reprinted from *The Anatomy of Jazz* by Leroy Ostransky, by permission of the University of Washington Press. Copyright © 1960 by the University of Washington Press.

Table of Contents

MUSIC FOR THE CHURCH

COMPOSERS IN THEIR TIMES

MUSIC OF SHOW BUSINESS

THE MEANING OF MUSIC / 1

Aaron Copland was born in Brooklyn, New York, in 1900, and is one of America's best known composers of serious music. Among his most popular works are Appalachian Spring, *the ballet* Billy the Kid, *and* El Salón México. *A tireless and devoted teacher and lecturer, Copland has written many articles on music for the layman. Concerned with raising the level of musical understanding of the average listener, he wrote his book,* What to Listen for in Music. *However, before we can know what to listen for, we must first know how to listen; Copland's essay deals with that subject.*

how we listen

AARON COPLAND

WE ALL LISTEN TO MUSIC ACCORDING TO OUR separate capacities. But, for the sake of analysis, the whole listening process may become clearer if we break it up into its component parts, so to speak. In a certain sense we all listen to music on three separate planes. For lack of a better terminology, one might name these: (1) the sensuous plane, (2) the expressive plane, (3) the sheerly musical plane. The only advantage to be gained from mechanically splitting up the listening process into these hypothetical planes is the clearer view to be had of the way in which we listen.

The simplest way of listening to music is to listen for the sheer pleasure of the musical sound itself. That is the sensuous plane. It is the plane on which we hear music without thinking, without considering it in any way. One turns on the radio while doing something else and absent-mindedly bathes in the sound. A kind of brainless but attractive state of mind is engendered by the mere sound appeal of the music.

You may be sitting in a room reading this book. Imagine one note struck on the piano. Immediately that one note is enough to change the atmosphere of the room—proving that the sound element in music is a powerful and mysterious agent, which it would be foolish to deride or belittle.

The surprising thing is that many people who consider themselves qualified music lovers abuse that plane in listening. They go to concerts in order to lose themselves. They use music as a consolation or an escape. They enter an ideal world where one doesn't have to think of the realities of everyday life. Of course they aren't thinking about the music either. Music allows them to leave it, and they go off to a place to dream, dreaming because of and apropos of the music yet never quite listening to it.

Yes, the sound appeal of music is a potent and primitive force, but you must not allow it to usurp a disproportionate share of your interest. The sensuous plane is an important one in music, a very important one, but it does not constitute the whole story.

There is no need to digress further on the sensuous plane. Its appeal to every normal human being is self-evident. There is, however, such a thing as becoming more sensitive to the different kinds of sound stuff as used by various composers. For all composers do not use that sound stuff in the same way. Don't get the idea that the value of music is

---

commensurate with its sensuous appeal or that the loveliest sounding music is made by the greatest composer. If that were so, Ravel would be a greater creator than Beethoven. The point is that the sound element varies with each composer, that his usage of sound forms an integral part of his style and must be taken into account when listening. The reader can see, therefore, that a more conscious approach is valuable even on this primary plane of music listening.

The second plane on which music exists is what I have called the expressive one. Here, immediately, we tread on controversial ground. Composers have a way of shying away from any discussion of music's expressive side. Did not Stravinsky himself proclaim that his music was an "object," a "thing," with a life of its own, and with no other meaning than its own purely musical existence? This intransigent attitude of Stravinsky's may be due to the fact that so many people have tried to read different meanings into so many pieces. Heaven knows it is difficult enough to say precisely what it is that a piece of music means, to say it definitely, to say it finally so that everyone is satisfied with your explanation. But that should not lead one to the other extreme of denying to music the right to be "expressive."

My own belief is that all music has an expressive power, some more and some less, but that all music has a certain meaning behind the notes and that that meaning behind the notes constitutes, after all, what the piece is saying, what the piece is about. This whole problem can be stated quite simply by asking, "Is there a meaning to music?" My answer to that would be "Yes." And "Can you state in so many words what the meaning is?" My answer to that would be, "No." Therein lies the difficulty.

Simple-minded souls will never be satisfied with the answer to the second of these questions. They always want music to have a meaning, and the more concrete it is the better they like it. The more the music reminds them of a train, a storm, a funeral, or any other familiar conception the more expressive it appears to be to them. This popular idea of music's meaning—stimulated and abetted by the usual run of musical commentator—should be discouraged wherever and whenever it is met. One timid lady once confessed to me that she suspected something seriously lacking in her appreciation of music because of her inability to connect it with anything definite. That is getting the whole thing backward, of course.

Still, the question remains, How close should the intelligent music lover wish to come to pinning a definite meaning to any particular work? No closer than a general concept, I should say. Music expresses, at different moments, serenity or exuberance, regret or triumph, fury or delight. It expresses each of these moods, and many others, in a numberless variety of subtle shadings and differences. It may even express a state of meaning for which there exists no adequate word in any language. In that case, musicians often like to say that it has only a purely musical meaning. They sometimes go farther and say that *all* music has only a purely musical meaning. What they really mean is that no appropriate word can be found to express the music's meaning and that, even if it could, they do not feel the need of finding it.

But whatever the professional musician may hold, most musical novices still search for specific words with which to pin down their musical reactions. That is why they always find Tchaikovsky easier to "understand" than Beethoven. In the first place, it is easier to pin a meaning-word on a Tchaikovsky piece than on a Beethoven one. Much easier. Moreover, with the Russian composer, every time you come back to a piece of his it almost always says the same thing to you, whereas with Beethoven it is often quite difficult to put your finger right on what he is saying. And any musician will tell you that that is why Beethoven is the greater composer. Because music which always says the same thing to you will necessarily soon become dull music, but music whose meaning is slightly different with each hearing has a greater chance of remaining alive.

Listen, if you can, to the forty-eight fugue themes of Bach's *Well-Tempered Clavichord*. Listen to each theme, one after another. You will soon realize that each theme mirrors a different world of feeling. You will also soon realize that the more beautiful a theme seems to you the harder it is to find any word that will describe it to your complete satisfaction. Yes, you will certainly know whether it is a gay theme or a sad one. You will be able, in other words, in your own mind, to draw a frame of emotional feeling around your theme. Now study the sad one a little closer. Try to pin down the exact quality of its sadness. Is it pessimistically sad or resignedly sad; is it fatefully sad or smilingly sad?

Let us suppose that you are fortunate and can describe to your own satisfaction in so many words the exact meaning of your chosen theme. There is still no guarantee that anyone else will be satisfied. Nor need they be. The important thing is that each one feel for himself the specific expressive quality of a theme or, similarly, an entire piece of music. And if it is a great work of art, don't expect it to mean exactly the same thing to you each time you return to it.

Themes or pieces need not express only one emotion, of course. Take such a theme as the first main one of the *Ninth Symphony*, for example. It is clearly made up of different elements. It does not say only one thing. Yet anyone hearing it immediately gets a feeling of strength, a feeling of power. It isn't a power that comes simply because the theme is played loudly. It is a power inherent in the theme itself. The extraordinary strength and vigor of the theme results in the listener's receiving an impression that a forceful statement has been made. But one should never try to boil it down to "the fateful hammer of life." That is where the trouble begins. The musician, in his exasperation, says it means nothing but the notes themselves, whereas the nonprofessional is only too anxious to hang on to any explanation that gives him the illusion of getting closer to the music's meaning.

Now, perhaps, the reader will know better what I mean when I say that music does have an expressive meaning but that we cannot say in so many words what that meaning is.

The third plane on which music exists is the sheerly musical plane. Besides the pleasurable sound of music and the expressive feeling that it gives off, music does exist in terms of the notes themselves and of their manipulation. Most listeners are not sufficiently conscious of this third plane.

Professional musicians, on the other hand, are, if anything, too conscious of the mere notes themselves. They often fall into the error of becoming so engrossed with their arpeggios and staccatos that they forget the deeper aspects of the music they are performing. But from the layman's standpoint, it is not so much a matter of getting over bad habits on the sheerly musical plane as of increasing one's awareness of what is going on, in so far as the notes are concerned.

When the man in the street listens to the "notes themselves" with any degree of concentration, he is most likely to make some mention of the melody. Either he hears a pretty melody or he does not, and he generally lets it go at that. Rhythm is likely to gain his attention next, particularly if it seems exciting. But harmony and tone color are generally taken for granted, if they are thought of consciously at all. As for music's having a definite form of some kind, that idea seems never to have occurred to him.

It is very important for all of us to become more alive to music on its sheerly musical plane. After all, an actual musical material is being used. The intelligent listener must be prepared to increase his awareness of the musical material and what happens to it. He must hear the melodies, the rhythms, the harmonies, the tone colors in a more conscious fashion. But above all he must, in order to follow the line of the composer's thought, know something of the principles of musical form. Listening to all of these elements is listening on the sheerly musical plane.

Let me repeat that I have split up mechanically the three separate planes on which we listen merely for the sake of greater clarity. Actually, we never listen on one or the other of these planes. What we do is to correlate them—listening in all three ways at the same time. It takes no mental effort, for we do it instinctively.

Perhaps an analogy with what happens to us when we visit the theater will make this instinctive correlation clearer. In the theater, you are aware of the actors and actresses, costumes and sets, sounds and movements. All these give one the sense that the theater is a pleasant place to be in. They constitute the sensuous plane in our theatrical reactions.

The expressive plane in the theater would be derived from the feeling that you get from what is happening on the stage. You are moved to pity, excitement, or gaiety. It is this general feeling, generated aside from the particular words being spoken, a certain emotional something which exists on the stage, that is analogous to the expressive quality in music.

The plot and plot development is equivalent to our sheerly musical plane. The playwright creates and develops a character in just the same way that a composer creates and develops a theme. According to the degree of your awareness of the way in which the artist in either field handles his material will you become a more intelligent listener.

It is easy enough to see that the theatergoer never is conscious of any of these elements separately. He is aware of them all at the same time. The same is true of music listening. We simultaneously and without thinking listen on all three planes.

In a sense, the ideal listener is both inside and outside the music at the same moment, judging it and enjoying it, wishing it would go one way and watching it go another—almost like the composer at the moment he composes it; because in order to write his music, the composer must also be inside and outside his music, carried away by it and yet coldly critical of it. A subjective and objective attitude is implied in both creating and listening to music.

What the reader should strive for, then, is a more *active* kind of listening. Whether you listen to Mozart or Duke Ellington, you can deepen your understanding of music only by being a more conscious and aware listener—not someone who is just listening, but someone who is listening *for* something.

QUESTIONS

1. When you play a record or turn your radio on while studying, on what level are you listening to the music? Are you listening at all? What do you hear?

2. Which would you say has a more sensuous appeal: a piano playing, a trumpet playing, an orchestra playing? Why? What are your reasons? What are the contributing factors?
3. Name a piece of music that expresses something special for you. Do you think other people find the same expressiveness, the same meaning in the music as you do? Why?
4. Is it necessary to understand a piece of music in order to enjoy it? On what listening level is "understanding?" On what level is pure "enjoyment?"
5. Why is the life of an average popular hit song only about three months? What, exactly, makes a standard work standard?

THE MEANING OF MUSIC / 2

The meaning of a musical composition depends on the individual listener, his education, his tastes, his experience, his memory. Leonard Meyer, who teaches music at the University of Chicago and has done considerable research and writing on the effect of music on people, presents us with some interesting points of view. In his authoritative book, Emotion and Meaning in Music, *Meyer tells us that music sets up images in the listener's mind; the music we hear evokes moods and memories, which then arouse these images. The following essay helps us to understand how music moves us, how it affects our feeling toward music, and why we may prefer certain kinds of music.*

Image processes and connotation

LEONARD B. MEYER

THE AFFECTIVE EXPERIENCES THUS FAR DISCUSSED result from a direct interaction between a series of musical stimuli and an individual who understands the style of the work being heard. Because the forces shaping such an experience are exclusively musical, the form of the affective experience will be similar to the form of the musical work which brought it into being.

Not all affective experiences are as direct as this. Often music arouses affect through the mediation of conscious connotation or unconscious image processes. A sight, a sound, or a fragrance evokes half-forgotten thoughts of persons, places, and experiences; stirs up dreams "mixing memory with desire"; or awakens conscious connotations of referential things. These imaginings, whether conscious or unconscious, are the stimuli to which the affective response is really made. In short, music may give rise to images and trains of thought which, because of their relation to the inner life of the particular individual, may eventually culminate in affect.

But if such image processes are really unconscious, we can never know them. . . . Only feeling penetrates into awareness, a feeling aroused by something of which the subject is quite ignorant. Self-conscious minds seem to have a repugnance for such isolated disembodied mental phenomena: they are felt to be morbid and eerie. Consequently a process of rationalization is undertaken at once. Whatever is in the focus of attention at the moment when the affect arises is held to be the direct cause of it. Thus many affective experiences attributed directly to musical stimuli may in point of fact be the products of unconscious image processes. Because neither we nor the subject himself can know anything about such unconscious image processes any discussion of such an experience is clearly impossible.

Often, however, image processes are conscious. The listener is aware of the associations which he makes while listening. Conscious image processes may be either private, relating only to the peculiar experiences of a particular individual, or they may be collective, in the sense that they are common to a whole group of individuals within a culture. The image processes of a whole community will be referred to here as connotations.

Private images, even when they are brought to consciousness with-

---

IMAGE PROCESSES AND CONNOTATION from *Emotion and Meaning in Music* by Leonard B. Meyer; copyright 1956 by the University of Chicago Press. Reprinted by permission.

out psychic distortion, are problematical because it is almost impossible to trace the relationships existing either between the musical stimulus and the image processes aroused or between the image processes and the resultant affect. The peculiar experience of an individual may, for example, cause a "happy" tune to be associated with images of a sad occasion.

Even where the original association appears to be relevant and appropriate to the character of the music being played, affective experience may be a result of the private meaning which the image has for the particular listener. For example, the image of a triumphal procession might within a given culture be relevant to the character of a piece of music; but the association might for private reasons arouse feelings of humiliation or defeat. Thus while the image itself is relevant to the music, the significance which it has for the particular individual is purely personal.

Image processes, whether private or collective, are tremendous temptations toward extramusical diversion. For an image, even though originally relevant to a particular passage, may itself initiate further image processes. The development and proliferation of these may, however, proceed without reference to the subsequent successions of musical stimuli. That is, one image may follow another, not because of the associations which obtain between the images and the progress of the music, but because of the associations in the mind of the listener between the images themselves.

Neither the form nor the referential content of such experiences, however affective they may be, have any necessary relationship to the form and content of the musical work which presumably activated them. The real stimulus is not the progressive unfolding of the musical structure but the subjective content of the listener's mind.

Yet, in spite of the many and cogent objections which can be leveled against the relevance of such responses, it seems probable that conscious or unconscious image processes play a role of great importance in the musical affective experiences of many listeners. Indeed, it is often difficult for even the most disciplined and experienced listeners to escape the deepseated power of memory over affective experience.

It should be noted in this connection that not only do memories frequently result in affective experience but affective experiences themselves tend to evoke memories and arouse image processes appropriate to the character of the affective experience, whether sad or gay, noble or tender, as determined by the objective situation. In other words, even the most purely musical affective experiences may give rise to image processes which, developing their own series of associations, may become independent of the musical succession itself.

By connotations, as distinguished from image processes, are meant those associations which are shared in common by a group of individuals within the culture. Connotations are the result of the associations made between some aspect of the musical organization and extramusical experience. Since they are interpersonal, not only must the mechanism of association be common to the given cultural group, but the concept or image must have the same significance for all the members of the group. The concept must be one that is to some extent standardized in cultural thinking; it must be a class concept that has the same meaning for, and produces the same attitudes in, all the members of the group. In the West, for example, death is usually depicted by slow tempi and low ranges, while in certain African tribes it is portrayed in frenzied musical activity; yet this results from difference in attitudes toward death rather than from differences in the associative processes of the human mind. The particular way in which a connotation is realized or represented in music cannot be understood apart from the beliefs and attitudes of the culture in question.

Some connotations are entirely traditional. Association is by contiguity; i.e., some aspect of the musical materials and their organization becomes linked, by dint of repetition, to a referential image. Certain instruments become associated with special concepts and states of mind. The organ, for example, is associated for Western listeners with the church and through this with piety and religious beliefs and attitudes. The gong is linked by contiguity to the Orient and often connotes the mysterious and the exotic. In fact, even where this association does not seem intended, as in Varèse's *Ionisation,* it tends to modify our response to this music. Certain modes of tonal organization may awaken connotations. The pentatonic mode, for example, is used in the nineteenth century to represent things pastoral. Certain intervals may be used to indicate special concepts or states of mind. For instance, the diminished fifth was closely associated with expressions of grief and anguish during the baroque period. Or specific tunes may be employed to evoke concepts, memories, or image processes. This is a frequent device in the music of Charles Ives.

As a rule such associations are used in combination so that each reinforces the other. If the composer wishes to evoke connotations of piety and those connected with religious beliefs, he will not only employ the appropriate instrument but he will also use techniques of composition —modality, polyphony, and so forth—that have the same associations.

Notice that all these associations are intracultural. The gong will not have a special exotic meaning for the oriental in whose music it is common, though it may have other different associations for him. Nor will the pentatonic mode connote things pastoral to peoples who use this mode for all kinds of music, for cultivated art music as well as for folk music.

Because such associations are completely cultural and in no sense necessary, they are subject to change. Old associations die and new ones come into being. In Western music, for example, the harp is no longer associated, as it was in the Middle Ages, with religious subjects. Because of its use in French music of the late nineteenth century, it is much more likely to be associated with a certain tender vagueness.

A particular epoch may develop quite an elaborate system of connotations in which certain melodic, rhythmic, or harmonic practices become signs of certain states of mind or are used to designate specific emotional states. The composers of the baroque period developed such a system of connotations. Other composers, notably Wagner, have invented their own systems of connotative symbols, in which a specific melody, not just a more or less general figure, indicates and symbolizes a specific idea, concept, or individual.

If our responses to such special systems of connotative or designative symbols are to be really effective, they must become habitual and automatic. This requires time and repeated encounters with a given association. We do not need to learn that an oboe is traditionally a pastoral instrument. By hearing it used in this context time and time again, by reading about pipes and shepherds in literature, and by seeing such instruments depicted in paintings of Pan or Marsyas, we gradually build up a set of powerful associations. Once such an association has become firmly established, our response to it will be just as direct and forceful as if the response were natural.

However important associations made by contiguity may be, they constitute but a small fraction of the total group of connotations evoked by music. Most of the connotations which music arouses are based upon similarities which exist between our experience of the materials of music and their organization, on the one hand, and our experience of the nonmusical world of concepts, images, objects, qualities, and states of mind, on the other.

There is a great deal of evidence, some of it intercultural, which indicates that our experience of musical stimuli is not a separate, special category of experience but that it is continuous with and similar to our experiences of other kinds of stimuli.

Both music and life are experienced as dynamic processes of growth and decay, activity and rest, tension and release. These processes are differentiated, not only by the course and shape of the motions involved in them, but also by the quality of the motion. For instance, a motion may be fast or slow, calm or violent, continuous or sporadic, precisely articulated or vague in outline. Almost all modes of experience, even those in which motion is not directly involved, are somehow associated qualitatively with activity. Spring, revolution, darkness, the pyramids, a circle—each, depending upon our current opinion of it, is experienced as having a characteristic motion. If connotations are to be aroused at all, there will be a tendency to associate the musical motion in question with a referential concept or image that is felt to exhibit a similar quality of motion.

The unity of perceptual experience, regardless of the particular sense employed, is also demonstrated by the fact that in experience even single musical tones tend to become associated with qualities generally attributed to non-aural modes of sense perception. This tendency is apparent not only in Western culture but in the culture of the Orient and in many primitive cultures. In Western culture, for example, tones are characterized with respect to size (large or small), color value (light or dark), position (e.g., a large object is generally associated with a low position), and both size and position are associated with color.

Through such visual and tactile qualities, which are themselves a part of almost all referential experience, tones become associated with our experience of the world. Thus, the associations, if any, evoked by a low tone will be limited, though not defined, by the fact that in Western culture such tones are generally associated with dark colors, low position, large size, and slower motion.

Often referential experiences are themselves partly aural. A city, the wind, solitude, or the expressions of the human voice—all have a peculiar quality of sound which music can imitate with varying success. Such imitation will tend to awaken connotations similar in some respects at least to the experiences which originally conditioned the musical organization.

To what extent the associations arising from similarities between our experience of music and our experience of the nonmusical world are products of cultural conditioning and to what extent they are in some sense natural is difficult to say. The many studies made by psychologists, although they present ample evidence of associative consistency within Western culture, throw little light upon the problem of the naturalness of these responses; for the subjects in such experiments have, almost without exception, already been saturated with the beliefs and attitudes of Western culture.

Evidence from primitive and non-Western cultures is not conclusive. Frequently the associations formed are ones which appear natural to us. But sometimes a connotation strikes us as odd or unusual. In the latter case, however, it must be remembered that the association evoked by a given musical passage depends upon the attitude of the culture toward the concept as well as upon the mechanism of association. In other words, although in a given culture one attitude toward an object or process will usually be dominant, others are possible. For example, although in our culture death is generally considered to be a solemn, fearful, and majestic summoner, it has also been viewed as an old friend or as the sardonic mocker of human pretensions. And obviously each of these attitudes would become associated with very different types of musical presentation.

This much, however, is clear: (1) In most cultures there is a powerful tendency to associate musical experience with extramusical experience. The many musical cosmologies of the Orient, the practice of most primitive cultures, and the writings and practices of many Western composers are striking evidence of this fact. (2) No particular connotation is an inevitable product of a given musical organization, since the association of a specific musical organization with a particular referential experience depends upon the beliefs and attitudes of the culture toward the experience. However, once the beliefs of the culture are understood, most associations appear to possess a certain naturalness because the experiences associated are in some sense similar. (3) No matter how natural a connotation may seem to be, it undoubtedly acquires force and immediacy through cultural experience.

Obviously a complex and subtle connotation is not defined by any single element of the sound organization. Taken individually any one aspect of the musical organization is a necessary but by no means a sufficient cause for defining a given connotation. For instance, while it would not be possible in Western culture to depict the joys of youth in the lowest ranges of the bassoon, high ranges alone would not assure such an association either. Other aspects of the musical organization, such as tempo, dynamics, rhythmic character, and texture, would have to play a part in defining such a connotation.

But the degree of specificity attained in association, the degree to which a given musical disposition will evoke the same or similar connotations in all listeners within the cultural group, is not merely the function of the number of elements defining the connotation. All the elements of music are always present if there is any music at all. That is, there is always texture, whether it be that of a single melodic line or that of a complex polyphonic web; there is always dynamic level, whether it be that of a striking fortissimo or that of a mezzoforte.

The specificity of a connotation depends upon the divergence of the elements of sound from a neutral state. A tempo may be neither fast nor slow; a sound may be neither loud nor soft; a pitch may seem neither high nor low, relative either to over-all range or the range of a particular instrument or voice. From the standpoint of connotation these are neutral states. Connotation becomes specified only if some of the elements of sound diverge from such neutral states.

The elements of sound are interdependent with respect to neutrality and divergence. For instance, changes in pitch are generally accompanied by changes in dynamics, timbre, and sometimes tempo. The relationship is physical as well as psychological. If a 33⅓ r.p.m. phonograph record is played at 78 r.p.m., pitch will get higher, dynamics louder, and timbre more piercing. Thus it is possible to build one divergence upon another. For instance, if tempo is fast and pitches are high, very soft dynamics will be experienced as a divergence, not only from the neutral state of moderate loudness, but also from the "contingent neutrality" in which a rapid tempo and high pitches are generally accompanied by loud dynamics.

In general, the more markedly the elements of a sound pattern diverge from neutrality the more likely they are to evoke connotations and the more specific those connotations are liable to be. Note that this accounts for the fact that many musical works arouse a wide variety of connotations. For the connotations aroused by a piece of music which, on the whole, employs normal ranges, moderate tempi, and so forth will be determined more by the disposition and susceptibility of the particular listener than by the nature of the musical organization itself.

But even where the most complex disposition of the musical materials and the most effective deviations are presented in a piece of music, they function only as necessary causes for the particular connotative experience aroused.

In the first place, unlike literature or the plastic arts, which generally speaking cannot be understood apart from the designative symbols they employ, most musical experience is meaningful without any reference to the extramusical world. Whether a piece of music arouses connotations depends to a great extent upon the disposition and training of the individual listener and upon the presence of cues, either musical or extramusical, which tend to activate connotative responses.

In the second place, unlike verbal symbols or the iconic signs used in the plastic arts, musical sounds are not, save in a few isolated instances, explicit in their denotation. They limit and define the associations possible but, in the absence of either a specific musical symbolism, such as Wagner's, or a definite program furnished by the composer, they cannot particularize connotation. The musical materials and their organization are the necessary causes for a given connotation but, since no summation of necessary causes can ever amount to a sufficient cause, the sufficient cause of any connotation experienced must be supplied by the listener.

The fact that music cannot specify and particularize the connotations which it arouses has frequently been cited as a basic difficulty with any attempt to theorize about the connotative meanings of music. Yet from one point of view, this flexibility of connotation is a virtue. For it enables music to express what might be called the disembodied essence of myth, the essence of experiences which are central to and vital in human existence.

The human mind has an uncanny power of recognizing symbolic forms; and most readily, of course, will it seize upon those which are presented again and again without aberration. The eternal regularities of nature, the heavenly motions, the alternation of night and day on earth, the tides of the ocean, are the most insistent repetitious forms outside our own behavior patterns. . . . They are the most obvious metaphors to convey the dawning concepts of life-functions—birth, growth, decadence, and death.

What music presents is not any given one of these metaphorical events but rather that which is common to all of them, that which enables them to become metaphors for one another. Music presents a generic event, a "connotative complex," which then becomes particularized in the experience of the individual listener.

Music does not, for example, present the concept or image of death itself. Rather it connotes that rich realm of experience in which death and darkness, night and cold, winter and sleep and silence are all combined and consolidated into a single connotative complex.

The interassociations which give rise to such a connotative complex are fundamental in human experience. They are found again and again, not only in the myths and legends of many cultures, but also in the several arts. For example, the connotative complex discussed above is made explicit in Shelley's *Ode to the West Wind:*

> O thou,
> Who chariotest to their dark wintry bed
> The winged seeds, where they lie cold and low
> Each like a corpse within its grave. . . .

Connotative complexes may be more and less specific. Additional divergences in timbre, dynamic level, and so forth may help to limit the quality of the complex. Association by contiguity or the imitation of actual sound processes heard in the extramusical world may also play a part in defining the extent of connotation. Finally, connotation may be specified by the presence of a text, a plot, or a program established by the composer.

Ultimately it is the listener who must make connotation concrete. In so doing the listener may draw upon his stock of culturally established images, including those derived from literature and mythology, or he may relate the connotative complex to his own particular and peculiar experiences. But in either case there is a causal connection between the musical materials and their organization and the connotations evoked. Had the musical organization been different, the connotation would also have been different.

Since, however, connotations are not necessary concomitants of musical experience, a potentially connotative passage may fail to evoke any concrete images whatsoever. Instead the listener may become aware of how the musical passage "feels" in relation to his own designative emotional experiences and the observed emotional behavior of others. The music may, in short, be experienced as mood or sentiment. For not only are connotations themselves intimately associated with moods, in the sense that youth or spring, for instance, are traditionally considered to be times of exuberant and carefree gaiety, but the same psychological and musical processes which arouse specific connotations also evoke definite, though perhaps less specific, mood responses.

In a discussion of the communication of moods and sentiments two important considerations must be kept in mind.

1. The moods and sentiments with which music becomes associated are not those natural spontaneous emotional reactions which are often diffuse and characterless. Rather music depicts those modes of behavior, conventionalized for the sake of more efficient communication, which were called "designative emotional behavior." In Western culture, for example, grief is communicated by a special type of behavior: physical gestures and motor behavior tend to minimal; facial expression reflects the cultural picture of sorrow; the range of vocal expression is confined and often sporadic; weeping is customary; and dress, too, serves as a behavioral sign. It is this special, culturally sanctioned picture of grief which is communicated in Western music. But such designative emotional behavior is not the only possible way of denoting grief. Were the standardized expression of grief in Western culture different, were it, for instance, that of an incessant and violent wailing and moaning, then the "expression" of grief in Western music would be different.

This is important because it allows for and accounts for variation in mood expression between the music of different cultures. That is, different cultures may communicate moods and sentiments in very different ways, not because the psychological mechanism of association is different but because the behavior patterns denoting mood and emotional states are different.

2. Just as communicative behavior tends to become conventionalized for the sake of more efficient communication, so the musical communication of moods and sentiments tends to become standardized. Thus

particular musical devices—melodic figure, harmonic progressions, or rhythmic relationships—become formulas which indicate a culturally codified mood or sentiment. For those who are familiar with them, such signs may be powerful factors in conditioning responses.

Association by contiguity plays a considerable role in the musical definition of mood. A melodic figure, a set of modal relationships, or a harmonic progression is experienced time and time again in conjunction with texts, programs, or extramusical experiences which either designate the mood directly or imply it. In oriental music, for instance, a particular mode or even a particular pitch may become associated with a specific sentiment or humor as well as with connotative concepts such as winter, night, and blackness. Once such associations become habitual, the presence of the proper musical stimulus will, as a rule, automatically evoke the customary mood response. In Western music of the baroque period, to cite only one example, melodic formulas, conventionalized for the sake of communication, attain precision and force through contiguity with texts and programs which fix their meanings within the culture and style.

Mood association by similarity depends upon a likeness between the individual's experiences of moods and his experience of music. Emotional behavior is a kind of composite gesture, a motion whose peculiar qualities are largely defined in terms of energy, direction, tension, continuity, and so forth. Since music also involves motions differentiated by the same qualities, "musical mood gestures" may be similar to behavioral mood gestures. In fact, because moods and sentiments attain their most precise articulation through vocal inflection, it is possible for music to imitate the sounds of emotional behavior with some precision. Finally, since motor behavior plays a considerable role in both designative emotional behavior and in musical experience, a similarity between the motor behavior of designative gestures and that of musical gestures will inforce the feeling of similarity between the two types of experience.

Like connotation, mood or sentiment depend for their definition upon divergence. If the elements of sound are neutral, then the mood characterization, if any, will depend largely upon the disposition of the individual listener. That is, there will be no consistency in the responses of various listeners. But, and this is of paramount importance, the fact that the mood is indefinite does not mean that affect is not aroused. For a lack of divergence in the elements of sound does not preclude significant deviation in those dynamic processes which form our affective responses to music.

It was observed earlier that image processes, whether conscious or unconscious, and connotations often result in affective experience.

Whether mood responses can eventuate in affect is doubtful. Merely because the musical designation of a mood or sentiment is comprehended by the listener does not mean that the listener responds affectively. It is perfectly possible to be aware of the meaning of behavior without responding as though the behavior were our own. But even an empathetic response to the materials delineating mood or sentiment does not require a resultant affective experience. We may sympathize with the mood of another individual without having an emotional experience ourselves. In fact, although such empathetic behavior may create a psycho-physiological condition in which affect is likely to arise, it is difficult to see what direct causal connection could exist between mood and affect. It appears more likely that mood eventuates in affect only through the mediation of image processes or connotations. That is, a mood arouses image processes already associated in the experience of the individual with the particular mood response, and these image processes are the stimuli which actually give rise to affect.

QUESTIONS

1. Have you ever noticed that the background music for all villains in TV Westerns is essentially the same—low sounds, low plucked chords? Why do you suppose the composers of this music all use the same musical ideas?
2. On what wind instrument is an "Oriental" solo usually played? Why? Would the effect be the same on another instrument? Why?
3. When you hear an unaccompanied drum solo, what does it make you think of? Is it the rhythmic pattern that sets your imagination working? Are you moved one way or another simply because it is a drum? Would you feel the same if the rhythmic pattern was repeated on a violin, or a clarinet?
4. Listen to the instructor play several low chords. Of what do these sounds remind you, if anything? Why? Listen to the instructor play high chords. Of what do these remind you, if anything? Listen to ascending and descending scales, and ask yourself the same questions.
5. Do you believe that "sad" music is usually in a minor key? Can you name a "sad" piece of music? Can you name a "gay" piece? Why do you think so?

THE ELEMENTS OF MUSIC / 1

Music is sometimes called the universal language. In the following essay Oscar Thompson, critic, teacher, and editor of the standard reference-work, The International Cyclopedia of Music and Musicians, *uses this idea as his theme. Music, as he points out, is indeed a language; the question, however, is, "How widely is it 'Spoken'?" How widely is it understood or misunderstood? What is the language of music capable of expressing? How does one read and write in this language? Thompson answers these questions, and others, discussing what he calls "the true essentials of the musical language"—sound, motion, and design.*

The Language of Music

OSCAR THOMPSON

MUSIC IS A LANGUAGE IN AND OF ITSELF. AS THE letters of German, or Russian, or Arabic are not the language, so the notes that appear on the staves are not the language. They are the letters of music and, like the letters of all other languages, they came into existence long after the language was spoken, shouted, moaned, whispered, sobbed, and sung. Something like a universal literature in the verbal languages is a relatively recent development in the occidental world. If musical literacy, today, is much more restricted, it yet is more common than verbal literacy was in Chaucer's time in England, less than six centuries ago. Only a little further back and only the priesthood could read and write in those countries of our Western world that today have the least illiteracy. But let us not pursue the musical parallel too far. The practical necessities of daily life are largely responsible for the universal teaching of the three R's. To read, to write, to figure simple sums were essential to the earning of a livelihood, once the world had become a place of barter rather than of spoliation and once the tradesman had replaced the serf and man-at-arms. No such necessity for widespread knowledge of the letters of music has arisen or is likely to arise in our time. Those whose livelihood has depended in any degree on their knowledge of music's symbols have always been few in comparison to the multitude who could eat, sleep, keep a roof over their heads and go about adequately clad, as ignorant of musical notation as they were of Sanskrit or Choctaw.

It would be pleasant to view the world as quite otherwise, with every reasonably well-educated person able to play or sing at sight; and a great many, rather than a scattered few, equipped to peruse a complicated orchestral score and hear it, so to speak, from the examination of the printed page. One feels that the English may take a reasonable pride in those gentlemen and ladies of the late Tudor period who could sit about the table of their host in some manor house and unite their voices in madrigals, ballets, and glees, singing from some manuscript they had never seen before, each with his own part wending its own way, sometimes in a complication of strands that would trouble experienced groups of sight-readers today. A gentleman rode, a gentleman knew the uses of the rapier, and a gentleman sang. He knew notes as he knew the stirrups and as he knew thrust and parry. One may view with like satisfaction a later era in Austria and the German lands when study

---

THE LANGUAGE OF MUSIC from *How to Understand Music* by Oscar Thompson; Fawcett Publications, Inc.

of the string instruments was common enough to provide little ensembles among neighbors or within the family; trios, quartets, miniature orchestras for street and garden serenades. The daughter of a pastry cook and the son of a game warden were as likely to scrape away on fiddle or 'cello as the children of the burgomaster or the count. It was the pleasanter side of an era in which musicians, however gifted, were quite generally regarded as servants. Liveried, or no, they were the literates who taught their masters.

We contrast, a little ruefully, this personal music-making—however raucous much of it must have been—with today's tendency to substitute radio and phonographic music in the home, and realize that not all that has happened in the intervening years has made for greater literacy in music. At the same time we know that there is a much more widespread comprehension of music in its larger and more important forms in the world today than at any time in its past; and note, as one of the reasons for this, that opportunity to hear music has far outstripped opportunity to perform music; and that the average human being can go much further in hearing than he can with performing. His limitations with respect to reading music do not seriously handicap him as a listener. Undoubtedly there are times when any lay listener would be a more intelligent auditor if he could visualize, as some few musicians may visualize, the letters of the language they hear. But we are brought back to the consideration that these letters are not the language. They are the symbols, by means of which the language is made available. They have become necessary in the complicated state of our highly developed art music, but they were not always essential even to the musician. Folk-tunes were passed on from generation to generation, and sung and played through long periods of time, without the symbols existing for their preservation. Mozart, Rossini, and Mendelssohn, in a day when music had been elaborated so as to require a written record, proved that they were able to reproduce what they had heard without ever seeing the notation. The world is full, today, of persons who can play by ear more or less correctly music that is complex enough to trouble a fairly good sight-reader. That many others who do not play at all have ears equally quick to grasp and retain what is heard, also is common experience. To say that such an individual is musically illiterate may be to state the narrow truth. But to deny that he *understands* music on that ground alone would be equivalent to stating that a peasant who could not read or write but could carry on conversation by the hour did not understand his language.

But if it is not a knowledge of the notation of music that determines the understanding of music, what is it? The question becomes the more perplexing when we recall what already has been said of the wide variety of meanings that can be given a single composition; since, after all, it is the meaning of the words that matters in the conversation of the illiterate peasant. It is only when that word "meaning" is bereft of its precise, literal and *unmusical* aspect that it comes properly within the musical scheme. It has to be reconciled with that vague and generalized quality that is the characteristic of music; as a specific representation of an object or an idea is the characteristic of words. Emotional reaction to music does not of itself give that music a meaning. There can be emotional reaction to the beauty of design in music, as in scrollwork or the architecture of a building; a reaction in which the question of meaning can scarcely arise. A single sound, like the clang of a bell or the note of a bird, can stir an emotion and nothing of meaning be implied. The exhilaration of motion may have behind it nothing of meaning and yet be a kind of emotional experience. It is so with the language of music. At one and the same time it may express far less than words and far more. It may stir by profundities and exaltations that words are powerless to utter. It also may stir by mere sound, by mere motion, and by mere design.

In sound, motion, and design we have the true essentials of the musical language. To comprehend the sound, the motion, and the design of a composition is to comprehend much more than the notes, save as the notes are transmuted back into sound, motion, and design. There is no music without these three attributes, unless we are to concede that a single detached sound, like a bell stroke, can stand alone as music. If there are even two successive tones, there is motion, and there is design. To pass from one sound to a second is motion. To follow one tone with another is design. Comprehension of music, then, would seem to resolve itself into a grasp of its combinations of sound, its successions of sound, the patterns into which these combinations and successions are woven. It is by means of these that whatever meaning the music may have (whether it is a meaning intended by the composer or one read into the music by the interpreter or the listener) is evoked or conveyed. This meaning is the *idea* the language has been used to express, but it is *not the language*. The sounds, the motion, the design constitute the language, as words, phrases, and sentences constitute a spoken language, whatever the sense or nonsense uttered in their use.

The language of music is the language of melody, harmony, time values, rhythms, and musical form. All of these are only variations on the theme of sound, motion, and design. A melody is a succession of sounds pleasing to the ear. It cannot escape having motion and design and remain a melody. Harmony is a combination of sounds and acquires motion and design the moment one harmony follows another. Time values and rhythms have to do with motion. A single note may have time but not rhythm. Every melody, whether there is harmony or not, has both time and rhythm. Musical form is another word for design, but of larger scope, in that the design of a single phrase, passage, section, or movement of a work may be only a contributing part to the form of the composition as a whole. There is no more apt expression than the time-honored one which construes form as the bottle into which the composer's music has been poured. Yet the contents have largely shaped the bottles in innumerable instances. In either case, the bottle, of itself, is something of art, or it has been bungled in the making. There is art, unquestionably, in the shaping of a folksong or a country dance; most of what is true of advanced musical forms is true, in some respect, of the most elementary ones. The complex is derived from the simple. The symphony, the opera, the quartet, the sonata, the aria are all growths from the tunes to which early peoples danced or marched; the tunes they used ceremonially in their worship or sang or played for entertainment or consolement in much the same spirit as the music-making of today. Without notation, there has existed from earliest times this language, with its melody, its harmony, its time values, its rhythms, its forms. To grasp the most complex art music of today is thus the same problem that confronted any one who heard the most elementary music in primitive times. The language has been greatly extended, it has an infinitely richer and more varied vocabulary, but its elements are the same.

No distinction can be drawn here between the elements of folk music and art music; or between art music and so-called popular music. The language is the same for all music, good, bad, simple, complex, dull, or palpitant with genius. To understand *some* music is to understand, at least to that extent, *the language of all music*. Some melody is making its effect, some harmony is in some degree comprehended, something of time and rhythm is grasped, some species of musical form is seen for what it is. Sound, motion, and design have spoken, not with the meaning of words, or any other form of factual communication, but in the language that is the language of music and of music alone. The listener who can thus think of music in its own terms, rather than through eternal translation into something of words or mental images, is the one who most readily can approach the greatest of art products in substantially the same spirit of understanding that is brought to the folk dance or the popular song.

QUESTIONS

1. What does a Beethoven symphony have in common with a popular song like *Stardust?* What are the differences between them?
2. Is the importance or significance of a statement affected when it is in a language you don't personally understand? Is its value greater? lesser? the same? What are the special problems in arriving at a satisfactory answer?
3. Is it necessary to be able to read music in order to understand it? Why? Is it necessary to read music to enjoy it? Why?
4. In addition to music, what other subjects use written symbols? Do the symbols of science have anything in common with musical notation? Discuss this question.
5. Did people in previous centuries receive a better musical education than people do now? Are there as many talented amateur musicians today as there were, say, fifty years ago? Give your reasons.

THE ELEMENTS OF MUSIC / 2

Henry Edward Krehbiel (1854-1923) was music critic of the New York Tribune for forty years. During this period he was one of the most distinguished and widely read of all music critics. In addition to his newspaper work, Krehbiel was American editor for the second edition of Grove's Dictionary of Music and Musicians *and the author of a dozen significant books covering a wide range of musical subjects. In his time, Krehbiel championed the cause of the amateur music-lover, the untrained but intelligent listener. To this end he wrote* How to Listen to Music*—a remarkable title for its time (1896). The following essay is from that book.*

Listening to the musical elements

HENRY EDWARD KREHBIEL

THE CAPACITY PROPERLY TO LISTEN TO MUSIC IS better proof of musical talent in the listener than skill to play upon an instrument or ability to sing acceptably when unaccompanied by that capacity. It makes more for that gentleness and refinement of emotion, thought, and action which, in the highest sense of the term, it is the province of music to promote. And it is a much rarer accomplishment. I cannot conceive anything more pitiful than the spectacle of men and women perched on a fair observation point exclaiming rapturously at the loveliness of meadow and valley, their eyes melting involuntarily in tenderness at the sight of moss-carpeted slopes and rocks and peaceful wood, or dilating in reverent wonder at mountain magnificence, and then learning from their exclamations that, as a matter of fact, they are unable to distinguish between rock and tree, field and forest, earth and sky; between the dark-browns of the storm-scarred rock, the greens of the foliage, and the blues of the sky.

Yet in the realm of another sense, in the contemplation of beauties more ethereal and evanescent than those of nature, such is the experience which in my capacity as a writer for newspapers I have made for many years. A party of people blind to form and color cannot be said to be well equipped for a Swiss journey, though loaded down with alpenstocks and Baedekers; yet the spectacle of such a party on the top of the Rigi is no more pitiful and anomalous than that presented by the majority of the hearers in our concert-rooms. They are there to adventure a journey into a realm whose beauties do not disclose themselves to the senses alone, but whose perception requires a co-operation of all the finer faculties; yet of this they seem to know nothing, and even of that sense to which the first appeal is made it may be said with profound truth that "hearing they hear not, neither do they understand."

Of all the arts, music is practiced most and thought about least. Why this should be the case may be explained on several grounds. A sweet mystery enshrouds the nature of music. Its material part is subtle and elusive. To master it on its technical side alone costs a vast expenditure of time, patience, and industry. But since it is, in one manifestation or another, the most popular of the arts, and one the enjoyment of which is conditioned in a peculiar degree on love, it remains passing strange that the indifference touching its nature and elements, and the charac-

---

LISTENING TO THE MUSICAL ELEMENTS from *How to Listen to Music* by Henry Edward Krehbiel; Scribner and Sons; 1896.

ter of the phenomena which produce it, or are produced by it, is so general. I do not recall that anybody has ever tried to ground this popular ignorance touching an art of which, by right of birth, everybody is a critic. The unamiable nature of the task, of which I am keenly conscious, has probably been a bar to such an undertaking. But a frank diagnosis must precede the discovery of a cure for every disease, and I have undertaken to point out a way in which this grievous ailment in the social body may at least be lessened.

It is not an exaggeration to say that one might listen for a lifetime to the polite conversation of our drawing-rooms (and I do not mean by this to refer to the United States alone) without hearing a symphony talked about in terms indicative of more than the most superficial knowledge of the outward form, that is, the dimensions and apparatus, of such a composition. No other art provides an exact analogy for this phenomenon. Everybody can say something containing a degree of appositeness about a poem, novel, painting, statue, or building. If he can do no more he can go as far as Landseer's rural critic who objected to one of the artist's paintings on the ground that not one of the three pigs eating from a trough had a foot in it. It is the absence of the standard of judgment employed in this criticism which makes significant talk about music so difficult. Nature failed to provide a model for this ethereal art. There is nothing in the natural world with which the simple man may compare it.

It is not alone a knowledge of the constituent factors of a symphony, or the difference between a sonata and a suite, a march and a mazurka, that is rare. Unless you chance to be listening to the conversation of musicians (in which term I wish to include amateurs who are what the word amateur implies, and whose knowledge stands in some respectable relation to their love), you will find, so frequently that I have not the heart to attempt an estimate of the proportion, that the most common words in the terminology of the art are misapplied. Such familiar things as harmony and melody, time and tune, are continually confounded. Let us call a distinguished witness into the box; the instance is not new, but it will serve. What does Tennyson mean when he says:

> "All night have the roses heard
> The flute, violin, bassoon;
> All night has the casement jessamine stirr'd
> To the dancers dancing in tune?"

Unless the dancers who wearied Maud were provided with even a more extraordinary instrumental outfit than the Old Lady of Banbury Cross, how could they have danced "in tune?"

Musical study of a sort being almost as general as study of the "three Rs," it must be said that the gross forms of ignorance are utterly inexcusable. But if this is obvious, it is even more obvious that there is something radically wrong with the prevalent systems of musical instruction. It is because of a plentiful lack of knowledge that so much that is written on music is without meaning, and that the most foolish kind of rhapsody, so it show a collocation of fine words, is permitted to masquerade as musical criticism and even analysis. People like to read about music, and the books of a certain English clergyman have had a sale of stupendous magnitude notwithstanding they are full of absurdities. The clergyman has a multitudinous companionship, moreover, among novelists, essayists, and poets whose safety lies in more or less fantastic generalization when they come to talk about music. How they flounder when they come to detail! It was Charles Lamb who said, in his "Chapter on Ears," that in voices he could not distinguish a soprano from a tenor, and could only contrive to guess at the thorough-bass from its being "supereminently harsh and disagreeable"; yet dear old Elia may be forgiven, since his confounding the bass voice with a system of musical short-hand is so delightful a proof of the ignorance he was confessing.

But what shall the troubled critics say to Tennyson's orchestra consisting of a flute, violin, and bassoon? Or to Coleridge's "*loud* bassoon," which made the wedding-guest to beat his breast? Or to Mrs. Harriet Beecher Stowe's pianist who played "with an airy and bird-like touch?" Or to our own clever painter-novelist who, in "Snubbin' through Jersey," has Brushes bring out his violoncello and play "the symphonies of Beethoven" to entertain his fellow canal-boat passengers? The tendency toward realism, or "veritism," as it is called, has brought out a rich crop of blunders. It will not do to have a character in a story simply sing or play something; we must have the names of composers and compositions. The genial gentleman who enriched musical literature with arrangements of Beethoven's symphonies for violoncello without accompaniment has since supplemented this feat by creating a German fiddler who, when he thinks himself unnoticed, plays a sonata for violin and contralto voice; Professor Brander Matthews permits one of his heroines to sing Schumann's *Warum?* and one of his heroes plays "The Moonlight Concerto"; one of Ouida's romantic creatures spends hours at an organ "playing the grand old masses of Mendelssohn"; in "Moths" the tenor never wearies of singing certain "exquisite airs of Palestrina," which recalls the fact that an indignant correspondent of a St. Louis newspaper, protesting against the Teutonism and heaviness of an orchestra conductor's programmes, demanded some of the "lighter" works of "Berlioz and Palestrina."

Alas! these things and the many others equally amusing which Mr.

G. Sutherland Edwards long ago catalogued in an essay on "The Literary Maltreatment of Music" are but evidences that even cultured folk have not yet learned to talk correctly about the art which is practised most widely. There is a greater need than pianoforte teachers and singing teachers, and that is a numerous company of writers and talkers who shall teach the people how to listen to music so that it shall not pass through their heads like a vast tonal phantasmagoria, but provide the varied and noble delights contemplated by the composers.

Ungracious as it might appear, it may yet not be amiss, therefore, at the very outset of an inquiry into the proper way in which to listen to music, to utter a warning against much that is written on the art. As a rule it will be found that writers on music are divided into two classes, and that neither of these classes can do much good. Too often they are either pedants or rhapsodists. This division is wholly natural. Music has many sides and is a science as well as an art. Its scientific side is that on which the pedant generally approaches it. He is concerned with forms and rules, with externals, to the forgetting of that which is inexpressibly nobler and higher. But the pedants are not harmful, because they are not interesting; strictly speaking, they do not write for the public at all, but only for their professional colleagues. The harmful men are the foolish rhapsodists who take advantage of the fact that the language of music is indeterminate and evanescent to talk about the art in such a way as to present themselves as persons of exquisite sensibilities rather than to direct attention to the real nature and beauty of music itself.

Music is dual in its nature; it is material as well as spiritual. Its material side we apprehend through the sense of hearing and comprehend through the intellect; its spiritual side reaches us through the fancy (or imagination, so it be music of the highest class) and the emotional part of us. If the scope and capacity of the art, and the evolutionary processes which its history discloses (a record of which is preserved in its nomenclature), are to be understood, it is essential that this duality be kept in view. There is something so potent and elemental in the appeal which music makes that it is possible to derive pleasure from even an unwilling hearing or a hearing unaccompanied by effort at analysis; but real appreciation of its beauty, which means recognition of the qualities which put it in the realm of art, is conditioned upon intelligent hearing. The higher the intelligence, the keener will be the enjoyment, if the former be directed to the spiritual side as well as the material.

So far as music is merely agreeably co ordinated sounds, it may be reduced to mathematics and its practice to handicraft. But recognition of design is a condition precedent to the awakening of the fancy or the imagination, and to achieve such recognition there must be intelligent hearing in the first instance. For the purposes of this study, design may be held to be Form in its primary stages, the recognition of which is possible to every listener who is fond of music; it is not necessary that he be learned in the science. He need only be willing to let an intellectual process, which will bring its own reward, accompany the physical process of hearing.

Without discrimination it is impossible to recognize even the crude materials of music, for the first step is already a co-ordination of those materials. A tone becomes musical material only by association with another tone. We might hear it alone, study its quality, and determine its degree of acuteness or gravity (its pitch, as musicians say), but it can never become music so long as it remains isolated. When we recognize that it bears certain relationships with other tones in respect of time or tune (to use simple terms), it has become for us musical material. We do not need to philosophize about the nature of those relationships, but we must recognize their existence.

Thus much we might hear if we were to let music go through our heads like water through a sieve. Yet the step from that degree of discrimination to a rudimentary analysis of Form is exceedingly short, and requires little more than a willingness to concentrate the attention and exercise the memory. Everyone is willing to do that much while looking at a picture. Who would look at a painting and rest satisfied with the impression made upon the sense of sight by the colors merely? No one, surely. Yet so soon as we look, so as to discriminate between the outlines, to observe the relationship of figure to figure, we are indulging in intellectual exercise. If this be a condition precedent to the enjoyment of a picture (and it plainly is), how much more so is it in the case of music, which is intangible and evanescent, which cannot pause a moment for our contemplation without ceasing to be?

There is another reason why we must exercise intelligence in listening, to which I have already alluded. . . . Our appreciation of beauty in the plastic arts is helped by the circumstance that the critical activity is largely a matter of comparison. Is the picture or the statue a good copy of the object sought to be represented? Such comparison fails us utterly in music, which copies nothing that is tangibly present in the external world.

It is then necessary to associate the intellect with sense perception in listening to music. How far is it essential that the intellectual process shall go? This essay being for the untrained, the question might be put thus: With how little knowledge of the science can an intelligent listener get along? We are concerned only with his enjoyment of music or, better, with an effort to increase it without asking him to become a musician. If he is fond of the art, it is more than likely that the capacity to discriminate sufficiently to recognize the elements out of which music is made has come to him intuitively.

Does he recognize that musical tones are related to each other in respect of time and pitch? Then it shall not be difficult for him to recognize the three elements on which music rests—Melody, Harmony, and Rhythm. Can he recognize them with sufficient distinctness to seize upon their manifestations while music is sounding? Then memory shall come to the aid of discrimination, and he shall be able to appreciate enough of design to point the way to a true and lofty appreciation of the beautiful in music. The value of memory is for obvious reasons very great in musical enjoyment. The picture remains upon the wall, the book upon the library shelf. If we have failed to grasp a detail at the first glance or reading, we need but turn again to the picture or open the book anew. We may see the picture in a changed light, or read the poem in a different mood, but the outlines, colors, ideas are fixed for frequent and patient perusal. Music goes out of existence with every performance, and must be recreated at every hearing.

Not only that, but in the case of all, so far as some forms are concerned, and of all who are not practitioners in others, it is necessary that there shall be an intermediary between the composer and the listener. The written or printed notes are not music; they are only signs which indicate to the performer what to do to call tones into existence such as the composer had combined into an art-work in his mind. The broadly trained musician can read the symbols; they stir his imagination, and he hears the music in his imagination as the composer heard it. But the untaught music-lover alone can get nothing from the printed page; he must needs wait till some one else shall again waken for him the "Sound of a voice that is still."

This is one of the drawbacks which are bound up in the nature of music; but it has ample compensation in the unusual pleasure which memory brings. In the case of the best music, familiarity breeds ever-growing admiration. New compositions are slowly received; they make their way to popular appreciation only by repeated performances; the people like best the songs as well as the symphonies that they know. The quicker, therefore, that we are in recognizing the melodic, harmonic, and rhythmic contents of a new composition, and the more apt our memory in seizing upon them for the operation of the fancy, the greater shall be our pleasure.

In simple phrase Melody is a well-ordered series of tones heard successively; Harmony, a well-ordered series heard simultaneously; Rhythm, a symmetrical grouping of tonal time units vitalized by accent.

The life-blood of music is Melody, and a complete conception of the term embodies within itself the essence of both its companions. A succession of tones without harmonic regulation is not a perfect element in music, neither is a succession of tones which have harmonic regulation but are void of rhythm. The beauty and expressiveness, especially the emotionality, of a musical composition depend upon the harmonies which either accompany the melody in the form of chords (a group of melodic intervals sounded simultaneously) or are latent in the melody itself (harmonic intervals sounded successively). Melody is Harmony analyzed; Harmony is Melody synthetized.

The fundamental principle of Form is repetition of melodies, which are to music what ideas are to poetry. Melodies themselves are made by repetition of smaller fractions called motives (a term borrowed from the fine arts), phrases, and periods, which derive their individuality from their rhythmical or intervallic characteristics. Melodies are not all of the simple kind which the musically illiterate, or the musically ill-trained, recognize as "tunes," but they all have a symmetrical organization. The dissection of a simple folk-tune may serve to make this plain and also indicate to the untrained how a single feature may be taken as a mark of identification and a holding-point for the memory. Here is the melody of a Creole song called sometimes *Pov' piti Lolotte,* sometimes *Pov' piti Momzelle Zizi,* in the patois of Louisiana and Martinique: (see example below)

It will be as apparent to the eye of one who cannot read music as it will to his ear when he hears this melody played, that it is built up of two groups of notes only. These groups are marked off by the heavy lines across the staff called bars, whose purpose it is to indicate rhythmical subdivisions in music. The second, third, fifth, sixth, and seventh of these groups are repetitions merely of the first group, which is the germ of the melody, but on different degrees of the scale; the fourth and eighth groups are identical and are an appendage hitched to the first group for the purpose of bringing it to a close, supplying a resting-point craved by man's innate sense of symmetry. Musicians call such groups cadences. A musical analyst would call each group a motive, and say that each successive two groups, beginning with the first, constitute a phrase, each two phrases a period, and the two periods a melody. We have therefore in this innocent Creole tune eight motives, four phrases, and two periods; yet its material is summed up in two groups, one of seven notes, one of five, which only need to be identified and remembered to enable a listener to recognize something of the design of a composer if he were to put the melody to the highest purposes that melody can be put in the art of musical composition.

Repetition is the constructive principle which was employed by the folk-musician in creating this melody; and repetition is the fundamental principle in all musical construction. It will suffice for many merely to be reminded of this to appreciate the fact that while the exercise of memory is a most necessary activity in listening to music, it lies in music to make that exercise easy. There is repetition of motives, phrases, and periods in melody; repetition of melodies in parts; and repetition of parts in the wholes of the larger forms.

The beginnings of poetic forms are also found in repetition; in primitive poetry it is exemplified in the refrain or burden, in the highly developed poetry of the Hebrews in parallelism. The Psalmist wrote:

> "O Lord, rebuke me not in thy wrath,
> Neither chasten me in thy hot displeasure."

Here is a period of two members, the latter repeating the thought of the former. A musical analyst might find in it an admirable analogue for the first period of a simple melody. He would divide it into four motives: "Rebuke me not / in thy wrath / neither chasten me / in thy hot displeasure," and point out as intimate a relationship between them as exists in the Creole tune. The bond of union between the motives of the melody as well as that in the poetry illustrates a principle of beauty which is the most important element in musical design after repetition, which is its necessary vehicle. It is because this principle guides the repetition of the tone-groups that together they form a melody that is perfect, satisfying, and reposeful. It is the principle of key-relationship, to discuss which fully would carry me farther into musical science than I am permitted to go. Let this suffice: A harmony is latent in each group, and the sequence of groups is such a sequence as the experience of ages has demonstrated to be most agreeable to the ear.

In the case of the Creole melody the listener is helped to a quick appreciation of its form by the distinct physiognomy which rhythm has stamped upon it; and it is by noting such a characteristic that the memory can best be aided in its work of identification. It is not necessary for a listener to follow all the processes of a composer in order to enjoy his music, but if he cultivates the habit of following the principal themes through a work of the higher class he will not only enjoy the pleasures of memory but will frequently get a glimpse into the composer's purposes which will stimulate his imagination and mightily increase his enjoyment. There is nothing can guide him more surely to a recognition of the principle of unity, which makes a symphony to be an organic whole instead of a group of pieces which are only externally related.

QUESTIONS

1. All trained musicians have had a course in what is called Ear-training. Can you suggest how one "trains" the ear? Can anyone's ears be "trained?" Do you think there is a distinction between listening and hearing? Give your reasons.
2. Discuss the following circumstance: A physician disagreed with a musician over the performance of a symphony they had just heard. The physician held that his opinion was just as valid as the musician's. The musician, in turn, held that his opinion of how a cold should be treated was just as valid as the physician's. Compare both views. What is the case for each side of the argument?
3. Look up "rhythm" and "tempo." Can you suggest how, on occasion, the general public confuses these terms? Give examples, if you can.
4. What does Krehbiel mean when he says, "The language of music is indeterminate and evanescent?" Do you agree? Give your reasons.
5. Do you think there are rules for good melody? What, exactly, does "good" mean, in this context? Give an example of a melody you consider "not good." What are your reasons for this selection? Look up "dissonant." What is its *musical* meaning?

THE ORCHESTRA / 1 *It is rather difficult to discuss one particular aspect of music and its history without encompassing other aspects. The history of the orchestra and orchestration is, of necessity, intimately tied to the history of opera, which in turn is tied to the history of singing. In the following essay Louis Adolphe Coerne (1870-1922) managed to present a survey that is at once broad and penetrating. Coerne was both composer (four operas, concertos, orchestral works, chamber music) and teacher (Harvard, Smith, University of Wisconsin). In 1905, for his studies in the field of orchestration, he received from Harvard the first Ph.D. in music to be awarded by an American university.*

The Beginning of Orchestration

LOUIS ADOLPHE COERNE

THE AWAKENING INTEREST FOR INSTRUMENTAL music received its incentive from two distinctive sources—the organ and accompaniment to solo singing. As a natural corollary to centuries of ecclesiastical supremacy in musical composition, the organ had taken first rank among instruments and was, comparatively speaking, the most advanced, both as to mechanical construction and to correlative technique of its performers. Hence the organ was destined to become a spontaneous yet covert connecting link between pure choral and pure instrumental music.

The initiative in this progression is due to the direct heirs of the Flemish School—the Venetian organists. Both Andreas Gabrieli (1510), pupil of Willaert, and Merulo (1533) had begun to add ornamental embellishments to their accompaniments, and although coherence was lacking, the step once taken led to extended experiments. Thus the treatment of further instruments employed in religious worship instinctively received more careful attention. Little by little composers awoke to the realization that the servile imitation of *a cappella* polyphonic choral writing hitherto employed was unsuited to the characteristics of differentiated individual instruments or combinations of instruments. True, the artistic value of these early attempts was but small, and would almost appear as an incompatibility, taking into consideration the fact that their authors were erudite in the subtleties of canonical device. Nevertheless, several tangible results are to be noted. As has been said, instrumental writing acquired a certain amount of individuality. Through search for balance of tone there was inaugurated a selective process as to the permanent value of each specific *genre* of an instrument. Instrumental adaptation of choral imitation led to contrast. Expansibility of musical thought was quickened. Thus Flemish influence was kept alive in that the incipient forms of their Venetian disciples, inherited by the subsequent violinist-composers, matured into the cyclic sonata.

Conspicuous are the organ works of Frescobaldi (1583-1644), the great predecessor of Bach. His labors also directly influenced subsequent clavier music as developed by Kuhnau in the following century. Credit is due to Giovanni Gabrieli (1587) for systematic attempts at orchestration and a distinctive style of writing for the violin. This latter, however, had to wait for the development of technique, which, as we

---

THE BEGINNING OF ORCHESTRATION from *The Evolution of the Modern Orchestra* by Louis Adolphe Coerne; The Macmillan Co.; 1908.

shall see, was concurrent with the progress of solo singing. And thus the year 1600, epoch-making in the rehabilitation of the drama, can be likewise referred to as a general starting point for independent instrumentation.

The second and more powerful incentive that instrumentation received was from monody, in connection with which its function as accompaniment in simplified form was demonstrated. The *fons et origo* of declamatory recitative are, of course, to be traced to the attempted reforms of the Florentine camerata. Monody was the cradle of opera and oratorio, and became in turn the foster child of her progeny. Now these histrionic roots were diversified and far reaching.

In the first place, during the two centuries preceding the era under discussion, the miracle plays and representations of similar purport had had recourse to musical support, though of a nature disjointed and irrelevant.

Secondly, the efforts of the troubadours, minstrels, and minnesingers embodied solo-singing to instrumental accompaniment, and contained elements of the dramatic.

Lastly, a newly awakened veneration for everything pertaining to classic Greece revealed the nobility of her drama. This was the *causa vera* to be espoused! And the evolution of this renaissance, which reached a climax in 1600, must be traced to the history of the Medici.

Toward the close of the fifteenth century, when three generations of that family had brought Florence to the height of her glory, art had received a new impulse under the fostering care of Lorenzo. Moreover, science had acquired the doctrines of the Greek scholars fleeing from Turkish oppression. And the brief interim of asceticism under the sway of the Dominican monk, Savanarola, was followed by the restoration to power of the Medici. A nonclerical influence in all matters pertaining to art made itself felt, and the founding of the Platonic Academy by Cosimo the Great added fuel to the already existing predilection for the drama as exploited by the Ancients.

Hence the aim of the amateur poet and composer, Bardi, and his coterie was to produce a drama which should faithfully conform to the purity and idealism of classic models. And they sought diligently for a clue to original renditions of Attic tragedy, the Dorian choral lyrics, the song-lyrics of Anacreon, Sappho. But their conception thereof was based on a fallacy, so that were one to judge the fruits of their labors solely for their intrinsic value, the verdict would be disappointing.

On the other hand, the step they took was a gigantic one forward in its revolutionary after-results. For the quintessence of recitative and lyrical solo was contained in Galilei's and Caccini's declamatory recitatives with accompaniment of lute or viol; in Peri's and Caccini's "Dafne" and "Euridice"—the first genuine music dramas in the monodic style; in Cavalieri's allegory or incipient oratorio "L'Anima e Corpo." All these attempts were infinitely more expressive and effective than the sombre selections with which A. Gabrieli and Merulo had been wont to enliven festive secular occasions. Bardi and Corsi, in the face of conservatism and skepticism, had sought to reinstate the principles founded upon the Greek Dithyramb. Inspired by the enthusiasm of these two amateurs, the professionals, Peri and Cavalieri, succeeded simultaneously in discovering two rational operatic designs, capable of sequent dramatic treatment.

Finally, the very nature of the monodic principle was inseparable from instrumental accompaniment, and the primary causes that led to monody, namely, expression and dramatic effect, would in themselves insist upon a keener appreciation for instrumental combination as to selection, distribution of parts, dynamics, color-scheme. This is borne out to a limited extent in the later works of both Peri and Cavalieri, whose instrumentation, though crude, paved the way for their greater contemporary and eventual successor, Monteverde. Even though the bulk of the figured bass accompaniment was assigned to the harpsichord, "Euridice" called into requisition one viol, three flutes, and a triplet of instruments of the lute variety. Cavalieri made use of practically the same combination and even recommended that a violin should duplicate the vocal melody throughout.

In contradistinction to these essays at dramatic scoring should be mentioned the instrumentation of Striggio (1535), whose *intermezzi* or comedies interspersed with music were written in the madrigal style. Nor should the concertante sacred song of Viadana (1564) or the instrumental effects of Gibbons (1583) be overlooked. But Striggio, some thirty-odd years before "Euridice" was produced, had not only forestalled but surpassed his immediate successors by the employment of an orchestra of which more than half were stringed instruments; again, seven of these were played with a bow. So that, considering the primitive methods then in use, the constitution of Striggio's orchestra was unique. It consisted of six lutes, seven viols, two gravicembali, six flutes, eight cornetti and tromboni, all of variated types and sizes.

The above enumeration brings to mind the pre-existence of a rather heterogeneous assortment of now partially obsolete instruments with which we are more or less familiar. Therefore, before proceeding from the subject of instrumentation to that of orchestration proper as inaugurated by Monteverde, a review of the structural and mechanical evolution of instruments themselves would seem in place.

The first serious attention bestowed upon the mechanism of instruments and the selection of those whose qualities should justify permanent retention occurred during the sixteenth century, and, as we have seen, the causes that led up to this were extraneous. In glancing over the names and descriptions of the many varieties of instruments already in existence before this development began, the mind becomes easily confused. Many species of stringed instruments such as lutes, viols, clavichords, harpsichords, not to mention brass instruments, the schalmei, cromornes, abounded on every hand; but the deeper the student of instrumental evolution delves into comparative research, the more he finds authorities at variance. However, the lineage of the three great representatives of stringed instruments as are in use today—instruments played with a bow, the harp, the pianoforte, may fairly be traced simultaneously.

Prehistoric origin of stringed instruments, in spite of extant relics, is a matter of conjecture. History, on the other hand, suggests various sources in various ages. Of greatest recorded antiquity are the Egyptian lute and harp, which were struck with a plectrum or plucked by the fingers. These migrated through Arabia into Spain, thence to Southern Italy, and became diffused over all Europe. The Greek lyra or kithara, having originally but four strings, was also played with a plectrum, and became the heirloom of the Romans. But to discover the origin of instruments played with a bow is a more difficult matter. A number of theories are plausible. Like all other instruments they were probably invented simultaneously by many isolated barbaric races. The bow and arrow were undoubtedly suggestive, and it is to be presumed that primitive types of the lyre family whose strings were originally plucked, were fitted to uncouth sounding-boards and played upon with a bow. The Hindus possessed such instruments, and it is possible that their admission into Europe was concurrent with that of the lute and harp. In defence of this supposition, one might point to the dance of the women attending the Jongleurs. Now the dance is no uncertain revealer of racial characteristics. But not only the dance itself, but also certain features of the accompaniment, as well as the types of instruments peculiar to the Jongleurs bear the impress of Orientalism. As far as is known, neither the Greeks nor the Romans possessed instruments played with a bow.

From the Middle Ages on, the study of instrumental evolution is, of course, based upon authentic history. The most direct line of descent for bowed instruments is probably from either the Celtic crwth or the Oriental rebab to the vielle or viola of the Middle Ages (Spanish vihuela, Latin fidula), of which the last representative was the gamba; and the viola da gamba was the predecessor of the violoncello. The early viols were of manifold types, there being, for instance, as many as seven viole da braccia and six viole da gambe. The violin owes its existence to a gradual metamorphosic development of the early tenor viola, during the latter part of the fifteenth and early sixteenth centuries. Skill in the manufacture of these instruments was of an advanced order in the Netherlands prior to the advent of the great Italian violin makers, whose efforts were eventually crowned by the immutable sovereignty of the Cremonese creations at the commencement of the eighteenth century. The introduction of the contrabasso was likewise of slow growth. For as late as the seventeenth and eighteenth centuries there still existed bass instruments of the lute family, such as the double-necked theorbo and the largest bass lute, the chitarrone, which were struck with a plectrum. But growing appreciation for the wonderful possibilities concealed in the infant violin proper, of technique, tone, color, delicacy, and variety of shading, reacted upon the secondary bowed-instruments, and they in turn were rapidly perfected. Hence, by a judicious selection of the superior and a suppression of the inferior types of viols were the violas and violoncellos evolved; and the theorbo and chitarrone were permanently supplanted by the double-bass, constructed on the same general principles as the violin.

Although the ideal balance of tone and expressive powers as embodied in the modern string orchestra justifies the perspicuity of this selective process in every way, it would seem to be a matter for regret that a certain species of viols, the viola d'amore, should have become practically obsolete. Its seven strings were supplemented by seven concealed understrings, designed to vibrate sympathetically. One might say that this principle has been incorporated in the modern grand pianoforte by means of the "una corda" pedal. But since Meyerbeer resuscitated the viola d'amore in "Les Huguenots" in 1836, the only living composer who has assigned to it a conspicuous rôle is, to the present writer's knowledge, Mr. C. M. Loeffler in his symphonic poem "La Mort de Tintagiles," after Maeterlinck; indeed the original score contained parts for *two* solo viole d'amore though one part has since been rewritten for a violin.

The evolution of the harp is obvious, whereas that of the pianoforte is more complex. The prototype of the modern pianoforte in its embryonic state traces its ancestry to all the various types of stringed instruments taken collectively. Specifically, the primitive acoustic monochord of Pythagoras might be looked upon as a plausible starting point. Add to this a keyboard and its attendant devices as applied to church organs in the earlier centuries of the Christian era, and the prototype is complete. Be that as it may, there was developed during the fourteenth and fifteenth centuries a family of widely known instruments embodying advanced qualities of mechanism, styled "Hackbrett," synonym for cembalo, tympanon, although it is best known as the dulcimer. According to Dr. Riemann, it originated apparently in Germany, since for a time it was called in Italy by the name of Salterio tedesco. The instrument consisted of a flat trapezium-shaped sounding-board on which steel strings were set, and was played upon by two hammers held one in each hand of the performer. In improved form, it is still extant in the hands of the gypsies. But already at the beginning of the sixteenth century was the clavichord established as its successor. The clavichord, according to Hipkins, was derived from the polychord with four strings, which in turn was developed from the monochord "to facilitate the melodic division of the Gregorian tones." Directly appeared still another instrument styled clavicembalo or harpsichord, of which the psaltery, a triangular harp, was undoubtedly the ancestor. The spinet and virginal differed from the harpsichord only as to shape; and in England, virginal was the general term for spinet and harpsichord. The cardinal point of dissimilarity between the mechanical construction of the clavichord and the harpsichord was that the strings of the former were caused to sound by means of metal tangents, which struck against the strings and then pressed them up, whereas the strings of the latter were plucked by hard quills set in wooden jacks. But of far greater importance was the difference of tone-quality. The tone of the clavichord was delicate, subdued—incapable of energetic utterance, but so expressive that it was a favorite with great musicians; that of the harpsichord was crisp, short, uniform. A radical readjustment of mechanism was found necessary in order to combine in one instrument euphony and variation of dynamic force. Therefore in the beginning of the eighteenth century hammer-action was invented, and the pianoforte, derived from the dulcimer, came into existence. Despite this fact, both the clavichord and the harpsichord continued to hold their own beyond the boundaries of that century. And so we see that the perfected modern pianoforte, being but the outcome of a variety of instruments already in existence three hundred years go, was unable to supersede them until the nineteenth century.

Turning our attention again to instruments belonging to the orchestra proper, we find an inexhaustible subject in the evolution of the two other great families, the wood and the brass. Most of the above-advanced hypotheses in respect to origin and migration of strings are equally pertinent to the wind. But the inference that the genesis of these latter instruments antedates that of the lyre and lute is surely justified in that conch shells and the horns of animals must have offered the most natural means for producing artificial musical tones. Again, the construction of stringed instruments suggests a more advanced stage of intellectuality. Finally, there have been preserved to us from antiquity a far more numerous and varied array of comparatively natural instruments such as the Egyptian mem and sebi, respectively vertical and horizontal flutes, of which the former was more common and still exists in the guise of the modern Arab flute. One of the most simple species of horn was the "Schofar" or ram's-horn, used in the temple worship of the Hebrews. The Assyrians as well as the Egyptians possessed trumpets, probably of brass. The war trumpets of the Romans were of bronze. The deep-toned trumpet or tuba was straight; the high-toned lituus was bent; and the buccina, large trumpet or trombone, was curved.

The principle of both single and double reeds was understood by the Greeks. As a result of the researches of Professor A. A. Howard, an accurate description of their representative instruments, the auloi, Latin tibiae, is to be found in "Harvard Studies in Classical Philology," Vol. 4. His article presents strong arguments in favor of the belief that instrumental polyphony was actually practised by the Greeks. Performers upon the auloi played almost invariably upon two pipes at once. The instruments were supplied with finger-holes, were capable of producing both the diatonic and chromatic scales, and may be divided into three classes corresponding, in a general way, to the three types of woodwinds as are in use to-day. All of them had a tube of cylindrical bore, but most of them were supplied with a double mouthpiece like the modern oboe, so that these species of the auloi can be regarded as the prototype of the preferred double-reeds that prevailed during the Middle Ages when they went under the name of schalmei. This nomenclature is confusing; in explanation it should be said that not until after the original schalmei had developed into the pommer, thence to the oboe, was the single-reeded predecessor of the clarinet known by this name. Colloquialism refers to the schalmei in its later application.

Another double-reed that came into temporary existence during the Middle Ages was the variety of cromornes (krummhorn). They differed from the schalmei principally as to form.

The successors of the original schalmei are described in detail by Praetorius, who wrote in the first decade of the seventeenth century. Of the six varieties of pommer mentioned by him, the treble pommer became transformed into the hautbois (high wood); the alto pommer into the cor Anglais (cor anglé, bent horn)—known during the seventeenth and eighteenth centuries as the oboe da caccia; and out of the bass pommer, likewise styled bombarde, emanated the fagotto (bundle of fagots). As a commentary to the above enumeration one should take note of a quite remarkable tendency which was, indeed, already in vogue during the Hellenic age. Namely, that from each parent instrument whether string, wood, or brass, there germinated a complete family representing the four ranges of the human voice. And again from these the process of tribal expansion was carried yet further. Moreover it must be remembered that before the Middle Ages, the art of combining human voices in polyphony was but in a nascent state, and probably existed in classic Greece not at all. Therefore families of instrumental species cannot have been constructed for the purpose of obtaining homogeneous *harmonic* effects. An extensive *range* of con-natural tone-color was then the objective. It will be found that this tendency was uniform throughout the history of instrumental evolution. Of course when we reach the sixteenth century, we find that the advantage of distributing the components of harmony among the members of assimilated instruments began to be appreciated. It is possibly due to this natural evolution that innovators in orchestration at first accustomed themselves to the use of pure tone-color rather than of mixed tints. Thus in the sixteenth century, the flûte à bec, predecessor of the modern flute, was employed in groups of four. Praetorius makes mention of no less than eight different kinds as prevalent in his day. Our chief representative of the single reed, the clarinet, which was not invented until the end of the seventeenth century, owes its origin to a primitive form of instrument with clarinet mouthpiece: the mediaeval chalemiax or chalumeau, whence the phonetic rendition, schalmei. The now obsolete basset-horn belongs properly to this genealogy. It was frequently used during the time of its development by the composers of the latter eighteenth and early nineteenth centuries. From it were devolved the short-lived alto and tenor clarinets, and the better qualities of all three are now embodied in the subsequently perfected bass-clarinet. Mention is also due to the saxophone, invented by Sax in 1840. It should be classed under the heading of wood instruments rather than of brass, since its tone-quality partakes somewhat of the nature of the clarinet. It has a single-reed mouthpiece, and the fingering is akin to that of the clarinet; but the over-blowing produces the octave as in the flute and oboe, whereas in the clarinet the twelfth is produced. Sax made seven different-sized saxophones, of which four are commonly in use, and those particularly in French and American military bands.

The history of brass instruments is extensive; at the same time their development is easy to trace. But it must be remembered that only those instruments possess pedigree from which upper harmonics are produced, i.e., those constructed with long tube and narrow bore. Even this statement must be qualified in that the French horn is of modern extraction. Only trumpets and trombones, therefore, are directly descended from the early Roman instruments with cup-shaped mouthpieces, such as the lituus and buccina. And in the Middle Ages there existed side by side two such families—the Zinken, and the trombe and tromboni. The Zink or cornetto had a wooden tube pierced by sounding holes, and was constructed in different sizes. The larger species was, at the close of the sixteenth century, transformed into the Serpent, which had a bell of brass. This instrument is still in use in some Italian military bands. The Zinken were extant in the hands of the "town musicians" even into the eighteenth century. Akin to them are the simple Alpine Horn and the Lur of Norway.

In the Middle Ages the trumpet was generally made of brass, and the tube was at first unbent. The principle of sliding tubes for the purpose of procuring additional tones to the natural ones of an instrument was of ancient origin. It was applied to trumpets as well as to trombones, a practice still in force in England. The obvious advantage of this device was that a complete chromatic scale could be obtained, impossible for all other brass instruments at a time when crooks and valves were unknown. The earlier name for the trombone, i.e., bass trumpet, was sackbut, but the original appellation, buccina, has been perpetuated in the German Bosaun, now Posaune.

In the sixteenth century, the tromba, synonym for clarino, trumpet, together with the three *genres* of trombones as used by the subsequent great classicists, was already perfected as a sliding-tube instrument. Or one might include both instruments under one heading by speaking of the tromba as a treble trombone. However, in order to obtain more efficient high brass instruments, constant experiments were made. The earlier improvements had obviated the clumsy length of brass instruments by bending and rebending their tubes. Then followed the application to the brass of the finger-hole system of the wooden Zinken. Finally, in the eighteenth century, the introduction of removable crooks improved the trombe as far as quality of tone is concerned. But the highest point of evolution was arrived at early in the nineteenth century, when the perfection of the chromatic valve principle revolutionized not only the mechanism but also the manner of writing for trumpets as well as for horns and bugles.

As has been intimated above, the history of the French horn is short. There is but a slight analogy between it and the *cor de chasse* of the Middle Ages, an instrument that possessed but few tones. The genuine French horn made its appearance in the first half of the seventeenth century, and the stages of its development may be regarded as centennial. In the eighteenth century was added the crook principle; in the nineteenth, the valve system. These improvements were attendant upon those made upon trumpets. Like the trumpet, the "natural" horn was conducive to purity of tone, the chromatic horn to greater practicability without material loss of purity.

The family of bugles belongs more properly to the subject of military bands, but a word is due to their evolution on account of the orchestral importance of one of their members—the bass tuba. The bugle-horn, also known as the saxhorn, is constructed on acoustic principles diametrically opposed to those of the trombe family in that the bore is wider and the tube shorter, whereby the principle of obtaining harmonics is reversed.

The date of Beethoven's birth signalized the first application of key mechanism to wood instruments. Simultaneously, experiments were made upon the now obsolete brass Zinken. The new instrument was called *bugle à clefs,* and was the forerunner of a group of different sized ophicleides, of which the lowest supplanted the sixteenth century Serpent. Subsequently the ophicleide itself was superseded by the bass tuba, a more noble instrument of the same general family.

The evolution of instruments of percussion requires but brief mention. Sound-producing apparatus devoid of definite pitch belongs to the initial attempts of primitive men to assist vocal expression of emotional feeling, to accompany religious orgies, or to encourage their warriors on the march. The modern orchestra includes the best of these primitive species, transformed into perfected types of genuine artistic value, and has also drawn into requisition various instruments originating in countries that are far apart. Most commonly used are the bass drum, the cymbals, and the triangle. The family of drums further includes the long side-drum and the small military drum. With the cymbals and triangle belong the tam-tam or Chinese gong, the Oriental and Spanish tambourine, the Spanish and Neapolitan castanets, and the Turkish crescent or bell-rattle. The use of all such instruments is, of course, the exception rather than the rule. Their mission is primarily to suggest "local" coloring or to emphasize rhythm for dancing.

Instruments of percussion possessing definite and variable pitch are represented primarily by the kettle-drums, which are constant and indispensable members of the orchestra. The early Hackbrett or dulcimer might also be classed under this heading, which further includes the various sets of bells, such as the carillon or Glockenspiel of Chinese origin, together with the Stahlspiel or Lyra, and the Xylophone.

This sketch demonstrates the fact that the early evolution of instruments went hand in hand with that of music in general and is subject to identical hypotheses. With the dawn of secular music, the development of instrumental construction and mechanism is focused upon the sixteenth century, with emphasis upon the anterior practice of employing complete homogeneous groups.

In order to cover the entire ground, this survey of the development of musical instruments has necessarily transgressed the bounds of the sixteenth century perspective. And since we are about to recontinue a critical review of the orchestra as inherited by Monteverde, it will be well to remember that in his day the only orchestral instruments in the modern sense of the word were violins and viols, harps, flutes, pommers, cornetti, trumpets, trombones. In combination with these, lutes, guitars, organs, the clavichord, and the harpsichord were still employed.

Claudio Monteverde (1567-1643) is justly styled the founder of the modern orchestra; but although modern orchestral organization owes its substratum of solidity and balance of tone to him, only indirectly was he led to attain this end, for his paramount objective was artistic expression. Naturally, the employment of artistically grouped instruments appealed to him as the most flexible conveyance for expressive thought. Again, Monteverde was instinctively a dramatic writer, so that as a matter of course the histrionic efforts of the Florentine experimentalists attracted him. Finally, when Monteverde entered upon his dramatic career after having already become celebrated as a writer of madrigals and of other vocal forms, pure choral music as perfected by Palestrina and Lasso was at its zenith, and instrumentation in its elementary state was inseparable from the drama, it being understood that the early attempts at oratorio in the *stilo rappresentativo* were built on the same general principles as the early operas, without differentiation in musical or instrumental treatment. Nor were the incipient efforts at orchestral accompaniment to religious worship of sufficient importance to be taken into consideration. Therefore, *Monteverde's* contribution to the chain of aesthetic and practical musical development consists of his successful search after expressive and dramatic effects and his reconstruction of the orchestra. He also broke away from the Church Modes, employed a system of harmony nearer akin to our own, made free use of the Chord of the Dominant Seventh, and introduced bolder harmonies and unprepared dissonances. These harmonic innovations were already noticeable in his earlier vocal compositions.

As we have seen, Peri contributed much to his successors from a dramatic standpoint, but as for expression, the Florentine *pseudo* music dramas consisted of a monotonous and long-spun succession of primitive and dreary *recitativi* with but little support other than a *basso continuo* and meagre chords, whereas Monteverde, absorbed in the discovery of means by which he might emphasize expression, developed true creative talent in a diversity of ways. For although his chord successions were still crude and his perspective for design but slightly evolved, his realization of the importance of stage effects led him to intensify the dramatic action, to vary the tone-color, to extend the functions of the accompaniment to the voice, and to relieve the monotony of constant *recitativo* by a more liberal and artistic use of the *arioso*.

These innovations were destined to wield far-reaching influence. Though admiration for the earlier pure choral style was soon rekindled in Italy, it was not long before the two styles, the old and the new, were combined, as embodied in the oratorios of Carissimi; and Schütz, who had been taught by Giovanni Gabrieli of Venice, transplanted these Italian methods into Germany. But the direct line of development from Monteverde's dramatic theories is to be traced through Cavalli, and from him through Lulli, into France, thenceforth the permanent home for histrionic displays; for Italy turned to a more careful consideration of melodic beauty and taste for design, whereas the disciples of Schütz, though cultivating the new principles especially in oratorio, still retained their German characteristics.

Turning to Monteverde's labors in the field of instrumentation, we find, in place of the very rudimentary and heterogeneous combinations heretofore employed, a well-defined and fairly logical assortment of instruments, the nuclei of which were strings, and it is the establishment of this nucleus that is epoch making. True, his first dramatic attempt, "Orfeo," was scored for organs, harpsichords, lutes, harps, guitars, trombones, trumpets, flutes, and various members of the viol family, including so-called little French violins, constituting an orchestra of thirty-six men, of whom nearly one third were performers upon brass instruments. On the other hand, it is necessary to take several contingencies into consideration. In the first place, this orchestra, like Cavalieri's, was concealed behind the scenes, instructive in its suggestion for the modern sunken orchestra at Bayreuth. Again, it has been supposed that the loud-voiced trumpets were muted, a device sometimes employed for special effects in modern scoring. (As to this supposition, however, the present writer is of the opinion that the instruments actually employed were the *cornetti muti* or soft-speaking trumpets of wood, and that in translation, the word "muted" has been erroneously applied.) Finally, although Monteverde was not, like Peri and Cavalieri, content to depend entirely upon the performers to supply the necessary chords and embellishments, nevertheless in the art of instrumentation he was but a pioneer, and most of his accompaniments were light and of a primitive nature. The very simplicity of his rudimentary method of scoring is proof that neither he nor his contemporaries could have realized the resonant powers of so formidable an aggregation of brass when properly handled; and just this nonrealization was propitious for the early development of the orchestra, in that, by negative means, noisy trivialities were excluded from the scores of the early masters. But in antithesis to this undue preponderance of metallic tone-quality, the employment of no less than seventeen instruments played with a bow was an immense stride forward, especially when we consider the fact that within the same decade lutes and the harpsichord had constituted the body of embryo orchestras.

At the close of the sixteenth century there were still many varieties of the viol family, but the value of the erroneously styled "little French violin" is said to have been first appreciated by Monteverde, who introduced it into his orchestra where its inestimable value was at once recognized. Profiting by this felicitous innovation, he continued to emphasize the importance of the string band, enlarged it, and, by a judicious suppression of the weaker members of the viol family, established a body of strings that conforms, at least approximately, to the violins, violas, 'cellos, and basses of the present day.

Having once for all instituted a rational and permanent foundation for obtaining solidity of tone combined with facility of execution, it was a matter of course that the brass should ultimately appear in more logical proportion to the strings. The progress of the wood-wind was of slower growth, largely due to technical imperfections and mechanical difficulties of performance. But, considering the means at his disposal, a commendable appreciation for contrasted groups of instruments is embodied in the pages of his later works—indeed, already in "Orfeo" can be traced this tendency to enhance the dramatic situation by means of judicious tone-coloring. Oft-quoted illustrations are the accompaniment of Pluto's songs by four trombones, the lament of Orpheus by bass viols, the chorus of spirits by *organi di legno*. And in his riper works, intelligent instrumentation and characteristic orchestration progress simultaneously. The introduction of the *tremolo, pizzicato,* and other dramatic and expressive devices is attributed to him. He showed some system of scoring, which included more specific instructions for the performers than had hitherto been the custom. And the fact that he distinguished between vocal and instrumental effects is of historic value in that it paved the way for the advent of purely orchestral composition.

It is remarkable that the direct successors of Monteverde should have been more or less blind to the latent powers of this newly vitalized organism, this prototype of the modern orchestra. Even Carissimi (1604) cannot be included among the progressive writers for the orchestra; indeed, his art of scoring stands lower than Monteverde's. Of course, in the development of oratorio, his dramatic influence was of great importance. He caused the monodic style to advance rapidly, by infusing into *recitativo* and the *aria* more spontaneity, into instrumental accompaniment greater interest. Though inferior to Monteverde in originality, Carissimi evinced a keener appreciation for plastic and tonal effects. His eminent pupil, Cesti (1620), is likewise to be remembered less for his instrumentation than for his further development of *recitativo* and the *da capo aria* in connection with the operatic stage.

On the other hand, Cavalli (1600), apart from the fortuitous influence his sojourn at the court of Louis XIV had upon Lulli, inherited a more decided talent for orchestration from Monteverde, whose pupil he was. His interesting experiments in writing accompaniments for two violins and a bass established a precedent that survived the test of many years. Like Monteverde, his instincts were strongly dramatic, but perhaps his connection with St. Mark's Church modified his style of writing for the orchestra. For more especially his *a cappella* sacred works are imbued with considerable warmth of expression, and show sentient regard for melody, rhythm, and form. And thus, even as Carissimi displayed but little feeling for purely instrumental effects, though holding a unique position as a composer of oratorio, so Cavalli must be regarded as primarily a dramatic writer—indeed, among the immediate successors of Monteverde, he alone succeeded in substantially furthering dramatic development in Italy, that is to say, the development of dramatic ideals as had been attempted by the Florentine neophytes of Greek tragedy. For as Langhans expresses it:

> After him Italian opera gradually diverges from the path originally taken, and sacrifices the antique simplicity aimed at by its founders to the ever increasing demand for sensuous charm. The alliance of poetry and music, dissolved in the Middle Ages and renewed but a few decades before, is again broken off, and the equilibrium that had just been acquired is sacrificed anew to the claims of music.

But while the nature of Italian music after Cavalli's time was subject to variable influences, France took up the cause of drama with enthusiasm, and in this field Lulli (1633-1687) looms up as the sole dictator of his age. Favored by the extravagant demands for display and spectacular effects prevalent at the court of Louis XIV, Lulli proceeded to develop dance forms as had been inaugurated by his predecessor, Cambert, whose position he usurped. The *ballet de cour,* already in vogue in France, consisted of dances, dialogues set to music, combined with dramatic episodes. Out of this native form of entertainment, modern French opera was destined to germinate. Having found this a suitable prototype as a basis for his operas, Lulli proceeded to imbue it with exotic principles. Like Monteverde, he discarded the ecclesiastical modes. Again, he adhered strictly to the requirements of his text, and developed declamatory recitative as promulgated by Cavalli. And to the reactive influence of the Italian monodic theorem upon French literature during this brilliant period of Corneille, Molière, Racine, does France owe the excellence of her declamation.

But, considering the versatility of the man, once again a disappointing analogy to the peculiarly prominent deficiency of Carissimi and Cavalli confronts us. For Lulli's orchestration was, like that of Meyerbeer two hundred years later, sensational rather than of enduring worth. By no means is Lulli's universal genius as organizer, composer, and orchestrator to be undervalued, nor is the importance of his influence upon subsequent French music to be lost sight of. But it is evident that the direct evolution of really stable instrumentation was benefited, during this period, more by the crowning achievements of Scarlatti, and by the labors of the secondary Italian composers, who devoted themselves more especially to purely instrumental music, and thereby sowed the seed for subsequent purely orchestral music in Germany. . . . Finally, even though strings formed the basis of his orchestra, augmented by wind instruments both wood and brass, the irrepressible harpsichord, solicitous for the welfare of her flock, and fearful lest emancipation from her protectorate should result in chaos, still closely followed the harmonic delineations of the legitimate orchestral instruments, supporting them, as it were, in concentual leading-strings! Had Lulli and his contemporaries understood the art of judiciously distributing the notes of a chord throughout the orchestra, not to mention the proper choice in number and species of instrument, this custom would have soon fallen into disuse; and, as we know, not until this did take place one hundred years later, was it possible to obtain ideal solidity, balance of tone, contrast, and variety. By a coincidence, the year of Beethoven's birth sounded the death-knell of the orchestral harpsichord, for in the opera "Mitridate," written in that year, Mozart was the last of the great composers to employ it as a regular component of the orchestra.

To Lulli, therefore, orchestration was but a secondary issue, in spite of the importance he attached to it. Form, on the other hand, was permanently benefited by his labors, whereas, in musical history, he occupies the second of the four pedestals sustaining the arch that spans the realm of pure music drama, and retires into the mythical haze of Hellenic tragedy.

As intimated above, further survey of the field of instrumentation in Italy discovers commendable activity, such as was displayed by Legrenzi; by Steffani and Clari; by the violinists Torelli, Vivaldi, and especially Corelli; finally, by the greatest musician both active and creative of the seventeenth century, Scarlatti.

The labors of Legrenzi (1625) are worthy of consideration on account of his logical development of the constituency of the orchestra. As Maestro at San Marco, Venice, he increased the number of instrumentalists at that church to over thirty. It is noteworthy that he employed almost exclusively violins and viols, supported in the bass by four theorbos (i.e., bass instruments of the lute family). The wood-wind was represented by a solitary bassoon, whereas two cornets and three trombones replaced Monteverde's earlier assortment of brass. And thus, already in the seventeenth century was found a man whose perspicuity in the choice of a modest band of loud-voiced instruments commended itself for some of the mightiest climaxes to be found in Beethoven's immortal works.

The significance of chamber music as fostered by Steffani (1655) and Clari (1669) is, of course, well known in musical history. And the wonderful impetus given to the art of violin-making, by stimulating a development of executive technique, brought forth fruit that culminated in the regency of a number of famous violinist-composers. Among these, Torelli (died 1708), for the creation of the *concerto grosso,* Vivaldi (died 1743), for the development of harmonic design and figuration characteristic of his instrument, and Corelli (1653-1713), for combining principles of harmony with contrapuntal devices, rendered invaluable service to the nascent architecture of modern string writing. For by exploring the possibilities of the violin, by establishing its superiority as a solo instrument, by demonstrating not only its potentiality but also its limitations in relation to other instruments, there arose, in consequence, a more delicate perception as to the necessary constitution of an evenly balanced string band. This acquirement was accompanied by improved methods of writing for the strings.

No composer of his time combined these requirements more successfully than Corelli, for the types of composition which occupied his attention were the precursors of the classic sonata, and his contributions thereto mark the starting point of genuinely artistic instrumental music. Corelli's relation to chamber music and the concerto is as that of Monteverde to the orchestra. Neither of them was a radical reformer; they both proceeded along the more conservative lines of evolution, selection, elaboration. The scaffolding of their respective spheres of activity had already been reared by that countless throng of forgotten and unappreciated workers, whose mission it is to make smooth the path for the greater lights, that appropriate and mould into collectaneous form the puny though individual originality of the lesser. But whereas nothing more than a pious interest in an historic heirloom has preserved Monteverde's efforts from falling into oblivion, those of Corelli have been perpetuated by reason of their intrinsic merit.

The highest development of productive musical art during the seventeenth century culminated in Scarlatti (1659-1725). And orchestration was aided by him to no small degree. Of course, his name is primarily coupled with the Neapolitan operatic principles, principles that ultimately led to baneful results, in spite of having enriched the world with sensuous and beautiful melody. Only a cursory review of Scarlatti's expansive activity is permissible as being mostly irrelevant to our subject. Reared in the characteristic atmosphere of Carissimi's cantatas and oratorios, impelled by poetic instinct and fondness for melodic design, he enlarged upon the *da capo aria,* the *recitativo accompagnato,* and in general paid careful attention to the external structure of the separate numbers in his operas. Above all, Scarlatti became the knight errant though eventually the thrall of *il bel canto.* Now highly developed vocal phraseology demands judicious accompaniment, and good orchestral accompaniment requires a nice adjustment of dynamic force combined with skill in writing. It was fortunate, therefore, that Scarlatti possessed both these attributes; and through the channels of this important branch of orchestration, independent orchestration received permanent form. Let us see how this metamorphosis took place.

Retrospection shows us that Peri, initiating a rudimentary dramatic style in place of Flemish polyphony, contributed but slightly to the advancement of instrumental accompaniment. He and his collaborators wrote little more than a figured bass for the harpsichord, and at performance they evoked the aid of the adventitious efforts of a motley aggregation of instrumentalists. The printed scores of Schütz are equally primitive. In France, the lyrical stage piece of Perrin and Cambert, "La Pastorale" (produced in 1659—the year of Scarlatti's birth), showed some slight improvement in the art of scoring; but it has been said that even Lulli composed his operas at the spinet, and at times delegated various details of instrumentation to his secretary. Monteverde established a nucleus of strings. Cavalli developed three-part writing for two violins and a bass. Legrenzi regulated the "distribution" of instruments. Corelli and his contemporaries advanced technique of performance and cultivated instrumentation in the miniature.

The task allotted to Scarlatti was, therefore, not difficult. He accepted the already established supremacy of strings, but soon realized that three-part writing did not produce even balance of tone. Consequently, he adopted a manner of writing which comprised a division of the violins into firsts and seconds. He added, moreover, an individual part for the violas, and thereby established a canon of phonetics that has been accepted by all erudite composers since his time. It is true that these characteristics of orchestration cannot be said to have originated with him, but his persistent use thereof established a precedent of permanent value. In three-part writing, not only the violoncellos and basses progressed simultaneously in unison or octaves, but also the viola, if present, reënforced the bass in slavish delineation. It is obvious that this practice was the result either of sophism or of indifference and ignorance. And the fact that as late as the eighteenth century no less a composer than Haydn or even Mozart should have continued frequently to employ three-part writing for the strings is certainly a paradox and tends to prove how circuitous the process of evolution is. However, Haydn and Mozart had such perfect command of florid counterpoint, that no matter what the distribution of string parts might be, the results were invariably effective.

Four instead of three notes of a chord being now properly dispersed among the strings, Scarlatti proceeded to enrich his orchestra by a logical employment of wind instruments in pairs. The harpsichord, of course, continued to hold its own, but the Händelian principle of long held notes in the wind against more agile string passages is already to be found in his scores, a principle of which Lulli was also cognizant. But Scarlatti's orchestra was more plastic than Lulli's, and his overtures more purely instrumental.

As has been stated, Italian culture of the violin and the increasing regard in which that instrument was held led to the development of execution as well as to an appropriate style of writing for it on a well-defined harmonic basis. These improvements were, moreover, further reflection by a more earnest attention to the progress of other instruments, both as to mechanism and technique. As a result, musical performers improved rapidly, and the isolated, purely instrumental numbers of the opera, heretofore utterly disregarded by the public, began to excite comment. Whereupon Scarlatti, keen to perceive any nascent inclination on the part of his audience, turned to a more careful consideration of the overture. His motives for doing so may not have been of the highest, but the results were directly beneficial in that by eliciting warm approval, these overtures were eventually performed as concert numbers apart from the opera. Though short in form, they consisted of three or four distinct, well-rounded movements, and were destined to become the prototype of the classic symphony.

In specifically instrumental music, Scarlatti paved the way for Bach and Händel by writing for two violins and a violoncello, treated as soli instruments to an accompaniment of a string orchestra.

Finally, the components of his orchestra—represented in his most felicitous scoring by violins, violas, 'cellos, doublebasses, two oboes, two bassoons, two horns—were practically identical with those of the early classicists.

So we see that the orchestra as bequeathed by Scarlatti was based upon a well organized body of strings, supported by a modest array of wood and brass instruments. Differentiated style of choral and instrumental writing was accentuated, and although polyphonic mannerism was still prevalent in orchestration, a tendency for individualistic instrumentation was at least apparent. On the other hand, the latent passion of the violoncello, when emancipated from the double-bass, was as yet unknown; and the harpsichord, by reënforcing the inner harmonies, covered the deficiencies of the wind instruments. That the mechanism of the latter should have remained in so immature a condition at a time when the delicate organism of the ideal string quartet had already been perfected is but the result of natural causes. For when the supremacy of the viols was once for all established, it was of primary importance that *their* efficiency, above all others, should be enhanced; and thus subsidiary instruments were for the time subjected to at least comparative neglect.

QUESTIONS

1. What is monody? Who were some composers of monody? In what ways does monody affect the history of orchestration?
2. Can you suggest reasons why various musical instruments were invented? Do you think the reasons were primarily social? economic? religious? musical?
3. Look up the following instruments. Determine their English equivalents and discuss the possible origin of their names: *hautbois, cor anglais, oboe da caccia, fagotto, krummhorn, saxophone, heckelphone.*
4. Claudio Monteverde has been called the "inventor" of the modern orchestra. What, exactly, did he invent?
5. Look up Stradivari and Guarneri. What is the connection between these families and such composers as Torelli, Vivaldi, and Corelli? Do you think this connection affected the evolution of musical instruments? In what ways?

THE ORCHESTRA / 2 *Hector Berlioz (1803-1869) was one of the master orchestrators of all time. In a period when most composers were still struggling to conquer the normal-sized orchestra, Berlioz was composing works to be performed by thousands. The ideal large orchestra conceived by Berlioz was not a mere fantastic notion; his grasp of the principles of composing for outsized ensembles has still to be matched. In 1884 he wrote his monumental* Traité d'instrumentation et d'orchestration modernes, *a work eventually translated into all European languages. Berlioz's major contributions to music in particular and to the nineteenth century in general are exhaustively treated in Jacques Barzun's two-volume* Berlioz and the Romantic Century.

THE ORCHESTRA & THE CONDUCTOR

HECTOR BERLIOZ

THE ORCHESTRA MAY BE CONSIDERED AS A LARGE instrument capable of uttering at once or successively a multitude of sounds of different kinds; and of which the power is mediocre or colossal according as those means are well or ill chosen and placed in acoustic conditions more or less favorable.

The performers of all kinds whose assemblage constitutes it thus seem to be its strings, its tubes, its pipes, its planes of wood or metal; machines, intelligent it is true, but subject to the action of an immense key-board, played upon by the conductor under the direction of the composer.

I believe I have already said that it seemed to me impossible to indicate how fine orchestral effects are to be found; and that this faculty —developed doubtless by practice and rational observation—is like the faculties of melody, of expression, and even of harmony; and belongs to the number of those precious gifts which the musician-poet, the inspired inventor, must receive from nature herself.

But certainly it is easy to demonstrate, in a manner almost exact, the art of *making orchestras* fit to give a faithful rendering of compositions of all shapes and dimensions.

Theatrical orchestras and concert orchestras should be distinguished the one from the other. The former, in certain respects, are generally inferior to the latter.

The place occupied by the musicians, their disposal on a horizontal plane or on an inclined plane, in an enclosed space with three sides, or in the very centre of a room, with reverberators formed by hard bodies fit for sending back the sound, or soft bodies which absorb and interrupt the vibrations, and more or less near to the performers, are points of great importance. *Reverberators* are indispensable; they are to be found variously situated in all enclosed spaces. The nearer they are to the point whence the sounds proceed, the more potent is their influence.

This is why there is *no such thing* as music in the open air. The most enormous orchestra placed in the middle of an extensive garden open on all sides—like that of the Tuileries—would produce no effect. The reverberation from the palace walls even, were it placed against them, is insufficient; the sound instantaneously losing itself on all the other sides. An orchestra of a thousand wind instruments, with a chorus

---

THE ORCHESTRA & THE CONDUCTOR from *A Treatise on Modern Instrumentation and Orchestration* by Hector Berlioz; Novello and Co. Ltd.; 1907.

of two thousand voices, placed in a plain, would not have a twentieth part of the musical action that an ordinary orchestra of eighty players with a chorus of a hundred voices would have if well disposed in the concert-room at the Conservatoire. The brilliant effect produced by military bands in the streets of great towns comes in support of this statement, which it seems to contradict. But the music is not then in the *open air;* the walls of high houses skirting the streets right and left, avenues of trees, the fronts of grand palaces, neighbouring monuments, all serve as reverberators; the sound revolves and circulates freely in the circumscribed space thus surrounding it, before escaping by the points left open; but let the military band, pursuing its march, and continuing to play, leave the large street for a plain devoid of trees and habitations, and the diffusion of its sounds is immediate, the orchestra vanishes, there is no more music.

The best way of disposing the performers, in a room with dimensions proportioned to their number, is to raise them one above another by a series of steps, arranged in such a way that each row may send out its sounds to the hearer without any intermediate obstacle.

All well-organised concert orchestras should be thus arranged in steps. If the orchestra be erected in a theatre, the stage should be completely closed in at the back, at the sides both right and left, and above, by an enclosure of wooden planks.

If, on the contrary, it be erected in a room dedicated to the purpose, or in a church where it occupies one of the extremities, and if, as it frequently happens in such cases, the back of this space be formed of massive building which reflects with too much force and hardness the sound of the instruments placed against it, the force of the reverberation—and consequently the too great resounding—may easily be mitigated, by hanging up a certain number of draperies, and by bringing together at this point such bodies as will break the motion of the waves of sound.

Owing to the construction of our theatres, and to the exigencies of dramatic representation, this amphitheatrical disposal is not possible for orchestras intended for the performance of operas. The instrumentalists brought together in lyric theatres, in the lowest central point of the building, before the footlights, and on a horizontal plane, are deprived of the majority of the advantages resulting from the arrangement I have just indicated for a concert orchestra; hence, what lost effects, what unperceived delicate gradations in opera bands, in spite of the most admirable execution! The difference is such that composers are almost compelled to bear it in mind, and not to instrument their dramatic scores quite in the same way as symphonies, masses, or oratorios, intended for concert-rooms and churches.

Opera orchestras were always formerly composed of a number of stringed instruments proportioned to the mass of other instruments; but this has not been the case for many years. A comic opera orchestra in which there were only two flutes, two hautboys, two clarinets, two horns, two bassoons, rarely two trumpets, and hardly ever any kettle-drums, was balanced then with nine first violins, eight second violins, six violas, seven violoncellos, and six double-basses; but as four horns, three trombones, two trumpets, a long drum, and cymbals figure there nowadays, without the number of stringed instruments having been increased, the balance is destroyed, the violins are scarcely to be heard, and the result of the whole is detestable. The orchestra of the Grand-Opéra, where there are, besides the wind instruments already named, two cornets-à-pistons and an ophicleide, the instruments of percussion, and sometimes six or eight harps—is not balanced either with twelve first violins, eleven second violins, eight violas, ten violoncellos, and eight double-basses; it should have at least fifteen first violins, fourteen second violins, ten violas, and twelve violoncellos, the extra instruments being left unused in those pieces where the accompaniments are very soft.

The proportions of a comic opera orchestra would suffice for a concert orchestra intended for the performance of Haydn's and Mozart's symphonies.

A larger number of stringed instruments would even be, sometimes, too much for the delicate effects which these masters have usually assigned to the flutes, hautboys, and bassoons.

For Beethoven's symphonies, Weber's overtures, and modern compositions conceived in the grand and impassioned style, there needs, on the contrary, the mass of violins, violas, and basses which I have just indicated for the grand opera.

But the finest concert orchestra, for a room scarcely larger than that of the Conservatoire—the most complete, the richest in gradations, in varieties of tone, the most majestic, the most powerful, and at the same time the most soft and smooth, would be an orchestra thus composed:

21 First Violins.
20 Second do.
18 Violas.
8 First Violoncellos.
7 Second do.
10 Double-Basses.
4 Harps.
2 Piccolo Flutes.
2 Large Flutes.
2 Hautboys.
1 Corno Inglese.
2 Clarinets.
1 Corno di Bassetto, or one Bass-Clarinet.

4 Bassoons.
4 Horns with Cylinders.
2 Trumpets with Cylinders.
2 Cornets à Pistons (or with Cylinders).
3 Trombones—1 Alto, 2 Tenors; or 3 Tenors.
1 Great Bass Trombone.
1 Ophicleide in B♭ (or a Bass-Tuba).
2 Pairs of Kettle-Drums, and 4 Drummers.
1 Long Drum.
1 Pair of Cymbals.

If a choral composition were to be executed, such an orchestra would require:

46 Sopranos—Firsts and Seconds.
40 Tenors—Firsts and Seconds.
40 Basses—Firsts and Seconds.

By doubling or tripling this mass of performers, in the same proportions, and in the same order, a magnificent Festival orchestra might doubtless be obtained. But it is erroneous to believe that all orchestras should be constituted according to a system based on the predominance of stringed instruments; very admirable results may be obtained from a contrary plan. The stringed instruments—too weak to prevail over masses of clarinets and brass instruments—then serve as a harmonious link with the thrilling sounds of the wind instruments; softening their brilliancy in some cases, and animating their effect in others, by means of the tremolo, which, by blending with them, renders musical even the roll of the drums.

Common sense tells the composer—unless he be compelled to a different course by any particular form of orchestra—that he should combine his mass of performers according to the style and character of the work he brings forth, and according to the nature of the principal effects which the subject demands. Thus, in a *Requiem,* and in order to deliver musically the grand images of this *hymn of the dead,* I have employed four small orchestras of brass instruments (trumpets, trombones, cornets, and ophicleides), placed apart from each other, at the four corners of the main orchestra, formed of an imposing body of stringed instruments, of all the other wind instruments doubled and tripled, and of ten drummers playing on eight pairs of kettle-drums tuned in different keys. It is quite certain that the particular effects obtained by this novel form of orchestra were absolutely unattainable by any other.

Here we have an opportunity to remark upon the importance of the various *points of procedure of the sounds.* Certain parts of an orchestra are intended by the composer to interrogate and answer each other; now, this intention can only be made manifest and of fine effect by causing the groups between which the dialogue occurs to be placed at a sufficient distance from one another. The composer should, therefore, in his score, indicate for them the disposition which he judges proper.

The drums, long drums, cymbals, and kettle-drums, if employed to strike certain rhythms all at once—after the common mode of proceeding—may remain together; but if they have to execute an interlocutory rhythm, of which one fragment is struck by the long drums and cymbals, and the other by the kettle-drums and drums, there is no doubt the effect will be made incomparably better, finer, and more interesting, by placing the two masses of instruments of percussion at the extremities of the orchestra, and consequently at a sufficient distance from one another. The constant uniformity of the executive masses is one of the great obstacles to the production of sterling and really new works; it besets composers more from old custom, routine, laziness, and want of reflection than from motives of economy—motives unfortunately but too important, in France especially, where Music is so far from forming a part of the moral being of the nation, where the government does everything for theatres, and nothing at all for music properly so called, where capitalists are ready to give 50,000f. and more for some great master's picture, *because that represents an intrinsic value,* yet would not lay out 50f. to render feasible, once a year, some solemnity worthy of a nation like ours, and fitted to display the very numerous musical resources which it really possesses without the capability of making them of use.

It would nevertheless be curious to try for once, in a composition written *ad hoc,* the simultaneous employment of all the musical forces which might be gathered together in Paris. Supposing that a master had these at his disposal, in a vast space adapted for the purpose by an architect who should be well versed in acoustics and a good musician, he ought, before writing, to determine with precision the plan and arrangement of his immense orchestra, and then to keep them always present to his mind while writing. It is obvious that it would be of the highest importance, in the employment of so enormous a musical mass, to take account of the distance or the nearness of the different groups which compose it. This condition is one of the most essential to deriving the utmost advantage from it, and in calculating with certainty the scope of its effects. Until now, at the Festivals, merely the ordinary orchestra and chorus have been heard, quadrupled or quintupled in their several parts, according to the greater or less number of the performers; but in the case proposed it would be quite another affair; and the composer who should attempt exhibiting all the prodigious and innumerable resources of such an *instrument,* would assuredly have to achieve an entirely new task.

Here, then, is how—with time, care, and the necessary *outlay*—it could be effected in Paris. The disposal of the groups would remain at the will, and subject to the particular intentions, of the composer; the instruments of percussion, which exercise an irresistible influence on the rhythm, and which always lag when they are far from the conductor, should be placed sufficiently near him to be able instantaneously and strictly to obey the slightest variations of movement and measure:

120 Violins, divided into two, or three, and four parts.
40 Violas, divided or not into firsts and seconds; and of which ten at least should be ready to play, when needed, the Viole d'amour.
45 Violoncellos, divided or not into firsts and seconds.
18 Double-Basses with 3 strings, tuned in fifths (G, D, A).
15 other Double-Basses with 4 strings, tuned in fourths (E, A, D, G).
4 Octo-Basses.
6 Large Flutes.
4 Third-Flutes (in E♭), improperly called in F.
2 Octave Piccolo Flutes.
2 Piccolo Flutes (in D♭), improperly called in E♭.
6 Hautboys.
6 Corni Inglesi.
5 Saxophones.
4 Bassons-Quinte.
12 Bassoons.
4 Small Clarinets (in E♭).
8 Clarinets (in C, or in B♭, or in A).
3 Bass-Clarinets (in B♭).
16 Horns (of which six should be with pistons).
8 Trumpets.
6 Cornets à Pistons.
4 Alto-Trombones.
6 Tenor-Trombones.
2 Great Bass-Trombones.
1 Ophicleide in C.
2 Ophicleides in B♭
2 Bass-Tubas.
30 Harps.
30 Pianofortes.
1 very low Organ, provided with stops of at least 16 feet.
8 Pairs of Kettle-Drums (10 Drummers).
6 Drums.
3 Long Drums.
4 Pairs of Cymbals.
6 Triangles.
6 Sets of Bells.
12 Pairs of Ancient Cymbals (in different keys).
2 very low Great Bells.
2 Gongs.
4 *Pavillons Chinois.*

467 Instrumentalists.

40 Children Sopranos (firsts and seconds).
100 Women Sopranos (firsts and seconds).
100 Tenors (firsts and seconds).
120 Basses (firsts and seconds).
360 Chorus-singers.

It will be perceived that in this aggregate of 827 performers the chorus-singers do not predominate; and even thus, there would be much difficulty in collecting in Paris three hundred and sixty voices of any excellence, so little is the study of singing at present cultivated or advanced.

It would evidently be necessary to adopt a style of extraordinary breadth, each time the entire mass is put in action; reserving the delicate effects, the light and rapid movements, for small bands which the author could easily arrange, and make them discourse together in the midst of this musical multitude.

Beside the radiant colours which this myriad of different tone-qualities would give out at every moment, unheard-of *harmonic effects* would be deduced from them.

From the division of the 120 violins into eight or ten parts, aided by the 50 violas, in their high notes, the angelic aërial accent, and the *pianissimo* tint.

From the division of the violoncellos and double-basses below in slow movements, the melancholy religious accent, and the *mezzo forte* tint.

From the union, *in a small band,* of the very low notes of the clarinet family, the gloomy accent, and the *forte* and *mezzo forte* tints.

From the union, *in a small band,* of the low notes of the hautboys, corni inglesi, and bassons-quinte, mingled with the low notes of the large flutes, the religiously mournful accent, and the *piano* tint.

From the union, *in a small band,* of the low notes of the ophicleides, bass-tuba, and horns, mingled with the *pedals* of the tenor-trombones, and of the 16-foot stop (open flute) of the organ, profoundly grave, religious, and calm accents, and the *piano* tint.

From the union, *in a small band,* of the highest notes of the small clarinets, flutes, and piccolo flutes, the shrill accent, and the *forte* tint.

From the union, *in a small band,* of the horns, trumpets, cornets, trombones, and ophicleides, a pompous and brilliant accent, and the *forte* tint.

From the union, *in a large band,* of the 30 harps with the entire mass of bowed instruments playing *pizzicato,* and thus forming together another gigantic harp with *nine hundred and thirty-four* strings, graceful, brilliant, and voluptuous accents, in all tints and gradations.

From the union of the 30 pianofortes with the six sets of bells, the twelve pairs of ancient cymbals, the six triangles (which might be tuned, like the ancient cymbals, in different keys), and the four *pavillons chinois,* constituting a metallic *orchestra* of percussion, joyous and brilliant accents, and the *mezzo forte* tint.

From the union of the eight pairs of kettle-drums with the six drums, and the three long drums, forming a small *orchestra* of percussion, and almost exclusively *rhythmical,* the menacing accent, in all tints.

From the mixture of the two gongs, the two bells, and the three large cymbals, with certain chords of trombones, the lugubrious and sinister accent, in the *mezzo forte* tint.

How can I enumerate all the harmonic aspects under which each of these different groups, associated with other groups either sympathetic or antipathetic with them, would appear!

There might be grand duets between the band of wind instruments and the stringed band; between one of these two bands and the chorus; or between the chorus and the harps and pianofortes only.

A grand trio between the chorus in unison and in octave, the wind instruments in unison and in octave, and the violins, violas, and violoncellos also in unison and in octave.

This trio might be accompanied by a rhythmical form designed by all the instruments of percussion, the double-basses, the harps, and the pianofortes.

A simple chorus, double or triple, without accompaniment.

An air for violins, violas, and violoncellos *together,* or for wooden wind instruments *together,* or for brass instruments *together,* accompanied by a *vocal band.*

An air for sopranos, or tenors, or basses, or all the voices in octave, accompanied by an *instrumental band.*

A small choir singing, accompanied by the large choir, and by some instruments.

A small band playing, accompanied by the large orchestra, and by some voices.

A grand deep melody, executed by all the bowed basses; and accompanied above by the violins divided, and the harps and pianofortes.

A grand deep melody, executed by all the wind basses and the organ; and accompanied above by the flutes, hautboys, clarinets, and the violins divided.

Et cetera, et cetera, et cetera.

The system of rehearsals requisite for this colossal orchestra cannot be doubtful; it is that which must be adopted whenever there is an intention to get up a work of grand dimensions, the plan of which is complex, and certain parts or the whole of which offer difficulties in performance; it is the system of partial rehearsals. This is how the conductor will have to proceed in his analytical operation.

I take for granted that he knows *thoroughly, and in its minutest details,* the score which he is about to have performed. He will first appoint two subconductors, who should—marking the beats of the bar in the general rehearsals—keep their eyes continually upon him, in order to communicate the movement to the masses too far removed from the centre. He will then select rehearsers for each of the vocal and instrumental groups.

He will first make them rehearse themselves, that they may be well instructed in the way in which they will have to direct the portion of study allotted to them.

The first rehearser will rehearse separately the first sopranos, then the seconds, and then the firsts and seconds together.

The second rehearser will practice in the same way the first and second tenors.

The third rehearser will do the same by the basses. After which, three choirs, each composed of a third of the total mass, will be formed; and then lastly, the whole chorus will be practised together.

As an accompaniment to these choral studies, either an organ, or a pianoforte may be used; assisted by a few wind instruments, violins and basses.

The sub-conductors and the orchestral rehearsers will practice separately in the same way:

1stly. The first and second violins separately; then all the violins together.

2ndly. The violas, violoncellos, and double-basses separately; then all together.

3rdly. The entire mass of bowed instruments.

4thly. The harps alone.

5thly. The pianofortes alone.

6thly. The harps and pianofortes together.

7thly. The wooden wind instruments alone.

8thly. The brass wind instruments alone.

9thly. All the wind instruments together.

10thly. The instruments of percussion alone, particularly teaching the kettle-drummers to tune their kettle-drums well.

11thly. The instruments of percussion joined with the wind instruments.

12thly. Lastly, the whole vocal and instrumental mass united, under the direction of the conductor himself.

This method of proceeding will have the result of securing, first, an excellence of execution that never could be obtained under the old system of collective study; and next, of requiring from each performer but four rehearsals at most. It should not be forgotten to have a profusion of tuningforks of the exact pitch among the members of the orchestra; it is the sole means by which the accurate tuning of this crowd of instruments of such various nature and temperament can be ensured.

Vulgar prejudice stigmatizes large orchestras as *noisy:* but if they be well constituted, well practised, and well conducted; if they perform sterling music, they should be called *powerful;* and certainly, nothing is more dissimilar than these two expressions. A trumpery little vaudeville orchestra may be *noisy,* when a large body of musicians properly employed shall be of extreme softness; and shall produce—even in their loudest effects—sounds the most beautiful. Three ill-placed trombones will seem *noisy,* insufferable; and the instant after, in the same room, twelve trombones will strike the public by their noble and *powerful* harmony.

Moreover, unisons acquire real value only when multiplied beyond a certain number. Thus, four violins of first-rate skill playing together the same part will produce but a very poor—nay, perhaps, even detestable effect; while fifteen violins of ordinary talent shall be excellent. This is why small orchestras—whatever the merit of the performers who compose them—have so little effect, and consequently so little value.

But in the thousand combinations practicable with the vast orchestra we have just described would dwell a wealth of harmony, a variety of tone qualities, a succession of contrasts, which can be compared to nothing hitherto achieved in Art; and above all, an incalculable melodic, expressive, and rhythmical power, a penetrating force of unparalleled strength, a prodigious sensitiveness for gradations in aggregate and in detail. Its repose would be majestic as the slumber of ocean; its agitations would recall the tempest of the tropics; its explosions, the outbursts of volcanos; therein would be heard the plaints, the murmurs, the mysterious sounds of primeval forests; the clamours, the prayers, the songs of triumph or of mourning of a people with expansive soul, ardent heart, and fiery passions; its silence would inspire awe by its solemnity; and organizations the most rebellious would shudder to behold its *crescendo* spread roaringly, like a stupendous conflagration!

The Orchestral Conductor

Music appears to be the most exacting of all the Arts, the most difficult to cultivate, and that of which the productions are most rarely presented in a condition which permits an appreciation of their real value, a clear view of their physiognomy, or discernment of their real meaning and true character. Of producing artists, the composer is almost the only one, in fact, who depends upon a multitude of intermediate agents between the public and himself; intermediate agents, either intelligent or stupid, devoted or hostile, active or inert, capable—from first to last—of contributing to the brilliancy of his work, or of disfiguring it, misrepresenting it, and even destroying it completely.

Singers have often been accused of forming the most dangerous of these intermediate agents; but, in my opinion, without justice. The most formidable, to my thinking, is the conductor of the orchestra. A bad singer can spoil only his own part; while an incapable or malevolent conductor ruins all. Happy, also, may that composer esteem himself when the conductor into whose hands he has fallen is not at once incapable and inimical. For nothing can resist the pernicious influence of this person. The most admirable orchestra is then paralysed, the most excellent singers are perplexed and rendered dull; there is no longer any vigour or unity; under such direction the noblest daring of the author appears extravagance, enthusiasm beholds its soaring flight checked, inspiration is violently brought down to earth, the angel's wings are broken, the man of genius passes for a madman or an idiot, the divine statue is precipitated from its pedestal and dragged in the mud. And, what is worse, the public, and even auditors endowed with the highest musical intelligence, are reduced to the impossibility (if a new work be in question, and they are hearing it for the first time) of recognising the ravages perpetrated by the orchestral conductor—of discovering the follies, faults, and crimes he commits. If they clearly perceive certain defects of execution, not he, but his victims, are in such cases made responsible. If he have caused the chorus-singers to fail in taking up a point in a finale, if he have allowed a discordant wavering to take place between the choir and the orchestra, or between the extreme sides of the instrumental body, if he have absurdly hurried a movement, if he have allowed it to linger unduly, if he have interrupted a singer before the end of a phrase, they exclaim: "The singers are detestable! The orchestra has no firmness; the violins have disfigured the principal design; everybody has been wanting in vigour and animation; the tenor was quite out, he did not know his part; the harmony is confused; the author is no accompanist; the voices are . . ." etc., etc., etc.

Except in listening to great works already known and esteemed, intelligent hearers can hardly distinguish the true culprit, and allot to him his due share of blame; but the number of these is still so limited that their judgment has little weight; and the bad conductor—in presence of the public who would pitilessly hiss a *vocal accident* of a good singer—reigns, with all the calm of a bad conscience, in his baseness and inefficiency. Fortunately, I here attack an exception; for the malevolent orchestral conductor—whether capable or not—is very rare.

The orchestral conductor full of goodwill, but incapable, is, on the contrary, very common. Without speaking of innumerable mediocrities directing artists who, frequently, are much their superiors, an author, for example, can scarcely be accused of conspiring against his own works. Yet how many are there who, fancying they are able to conduct, innocently injure their best scores!

Beethoven, it is said, more than once ruined the performance of his symphonies; which he would conduct, even at the time when his deafness had become almost complete. The musicians, in order to keep together, agreed at length to follow the slight indications of time which the concertmeister (first violin-player) gave them; and not to attend to Beethoven's conducting-stick. Moreover, it should be observed, that conducting a symphony, an overture, or any other composition whose movements remain continuous, vary little, and contain few nice gradations, is child's play in comparison with conducting an opera, or like work, where there are recitatives, airs, and numerous orchestral designs preceded by pauses of irregular length.

The example of Beethoven, which I have just cited, leads me at once to say that if the direction of an orchestra appear to me very difficult for a blind man, it is indisputably impossible to a deaf one, whatever may have been his technical talent before losing his sense of hearing.

The orchestral conductor should *see* and *hear;* he should be *active* and *vigorous,* should know the *composition* and the *nature* and *compass* of the instruments, should be able to *read* the score, and possess—besides the especial talent of which we shall presently endeavour to explain the constituent qualities—other almost indefinable gifts, without which an invisible link cannot establish itself between him and those he directs; the faculty of transmitting to them his feeling is denied him, and thence power, empire, and guiding influence completely fail him. He is then no longer a conductor, a director, but a simple beater of the time—supposing he knows how to beat it, and divide it, regularly.

The performers should feel that he feels, comprehends, and is moved: then his emotion communicates itself to those whom he directs, his inward fire warms them, his electric glow animates them, his force of impulse excites them; he throws around him the vital irradiations of musical art. If he be inert and frozen, on the contrary, he paralyses all about him, like those floating masses of the polar seas, the approach of which is perceived through the sudden cooling of the atmosphere.

His task is a complicated one. He has not only to conduct, in the spirit of the author's intentions, a work with which the performers have already become acquainted, but he has also to give them this acquaintance when the work in question is new to them. He has to criticize the errors and defects of each during the rehearsals, and to organise the resources at his disposal in such a way as to make the best use he can of them with the utmost promptitude. For, in the majority of European cities nowadays, musical artisanship is so ill distributed, performers so ill paid, and the necessity of study so little understood, that *economy of time* should be reckoned among the most imperative requisites of the orchestral conductor's art.

Let us now see what constitutes the mechanical part of this art.

The power of *beating the time,* without demanding very high musical attainments, is nevertheless sufficiently difficult to secure, and very few persons really possess it. The signs that the conductor should make—although generally very simple—nevertheless become complicated, under certain circumstances, by the division and even the subdivision of the time of the bar.

The conductor is, above all, bound to possess a clear idea of the principal points and character of the work of which he is about to superintend the performance or study; in order that he may, without hesitation or mistake, at once determine the time of each movement desired by the composer. If he have not had the opportunity of receiving his instructions directly from the composer, or if the *times* have not been transmitted to him by tradition, he must have recourse to the indications of the metronome, and study them well; the majority of composers, nowadays, taking the precaution to write them at the head, and in the course of, their pieces. I do not mean to say by this that it is necessary to imitate the mathematical regularity of the metronome; all music so performed would become of freezing stiffness, and I even doubt whether it would be possible to observe so flat a uniformity during a certain number of bars. But the metronome is none the less excellent to consult in order to know the original time, and its chief alterations.

If the conductor possesses neither the author's instructions, tradition, nor metronome indications—which frequently happens in the ancient masterpieces, written at a period when the metronome was not invented—he has no other guide than the vague terms employed to designate the time to be taken, and his own instinct, his feeling—more or less distinguishing, more or less just—of the author's style. We are compelled to admit that these guides are too often insufficient and delusive. Of this we have proof in seeing how old operas are given in towns where the traditional mode of performance no longer exists. In ten different kinds of time, there will always be at least four taken wrongly. I once heard a chorus of *Iphigenia in Tauride* performed in a German theatre *allegro assai, two in the bar,* instead of *allegro non troppo, four in the bar;* that is to say exactly twice too fast. Examples might be multiplied of such disasters, occasioned either by the ignorance or the carelessness of conductors of orchestras; or else by the real difficulty which exists for even the best-gifted and most careful men to discover the precise meaning of the Italian terms used as indications of the time to be taken. Of course no one can be at a loss to distinguish a largo from a presto. If the presto be two in a bar, a tolerably sagacious conductor, from inspection of the passages and melodic designs contained in the piece, will be able to discern the degree of quickness intended by the author. But if the largo be four in a bar, of simple melodic structure, and containing but few notes in each bar, what means has the hapless conductor of discovering the true time? And in how many ways might he not be deceived? The different degrees of slowness that might be assigned to the performance of such a largo are very numerous; the individual feeling of the orchestral conductor must then become the sole authority; and, after all, it is the author's feeling, not his, which is in question. Composers therefore ought not to neglect placing metronome indications in their works; and orchestral conductors are bound to study them closely. The neglect of this study on the part of the latter, is an act of dishonesty.

I will now suppose the conductor to be perfectly well acquainted with the times of the different movements in the work of which he is about to conduct the performance or rehearsals; he wishes to impart to the musicians acting under his orders the rhythmical feeling within him, to decide the duration of each bar, and to cause the uniform observance of this duration by all the performers. Now, this precision and this uniformity can only be established in the more or less numerous assemblage of band and chorus by means of certain signs made by their conductor.

These signs indicate the principal divisions, the accents of the bar, and, in many cases, the subdivisions, and the half-accents. I need hardly here explain what is meant by the 'accents' (accented and unaccented parts of a bar); I am pre-supposing that I address musicians.

The orchestral conductor generally uses a small light stick, of about a foot in length, and rather whitish than of a dark colour (it is seen better), which he holds in his right hand, to make clearly distinct his mode of marking the commencement, the interior division, and the close of each bar. The bow, employed by some violinist-conductors (leaders), is less suitable than the stick. It is somewhat flexible, and this want of rigidity, together with the slight resistance it offers to the air, on account of its appendage of hair, renders its indications less precise.

The simplest of all times—two in a bar—is beaten simply.

The arm and the stick of the conductor being raised, so that his hand is on a level with his head, he marks the first beat, by dropping the point of his stick perpendicularly (*bending his wrist* as much as possible; and not lowering the whole arm), and the second beat by raising the stick by a contrary gesture.

The time one in a bar being in reality, and particularly for the conductor, but the time of an extremely rapid two in a bar, should be beaten like the preceding. As the conductor is obliged to raise the point of his stick, after having lowered it, he necessarily divides this into two portions.

In the time four in a bar, the first gesture, or down beat, is universally adopted for marking the first accented part, the commencement of the bar.

The second movement made by the conducting-stick, from right to left, rising, indicates the second beat (first unaccented part). A third, transversely, from left to right, indicates the third beat (second accented part); and a fourth, obliquely, from down to up, indicates the fourth beat (second unaccented part).

It is of importance that the conductor, in thus delivering his different directions, should not move his arm much; and consequently, not allow his stick to pass over much space; for each of these gestures should operate nearly instantaneously; or at least take but so slight a movement as to be imperceptible. If the movement become perceptible, on the contrary, and multiplied by the number of times that the gesture is repeated, it ends by throwing the conductor behind in the time he is beating, and by giving to his conducting a tardiness that proves injurious. This defect, moreover, has the result of needlessly fatiguing the conductor, and of producing exaggerated evolutions, verging on the ridiculous, which attract the spectators' attention and become very disagreeable to witness.

In the time three in a bar, the first gesture made, from up to down, is likewise universally adopted for marking the first beat; but there are two ways of marking the second. The majority of orchestral conductors indicate it by a gesture from left to right. Some German Kapellmeisters do the contrary; and carry the stick from right to left.

This way has the disadvantage—when the conductor turns his back to the orchestra, as in theatres—of permitting only a small number of musicians to perceive the very important indication of the second beat; the body of the conductor then hiding the movement of his arm. The other method of proceeding is preferable; since the conductor stretches his arm *outwards*, withdrawing it from his chest; and his stick, which he takes care to raise slightly above the level of his shoulder, remains perfectly visible to all eyes. When the conductor faces the players, it is immaterial whether he mark the second beat to the right, or to the left.

However that may be, the third beat of the time, three in a bar, is always marked like the last of the time, four in a bar; by an oblique movement upwards.

The times five and seven in a bar would be more comprehensible for the performers, if, instead of indicating them by a particular series of gestures, they were treated as though the one were composed of three and two in a bar, and the other composed of four and three.

These different times, in order to be divided in this way, are assumed to belong to movements of moderate measure. The advice would not hold good, if their measure were either very quick or very slow.

The time two in a bar, I have already signified, cannot be beaten otherwise than as we have before seen—whatever its degree of rapidity. But if, as an exception, it should be very slow, the conductor ought to subdivide it.

A very rapid four in a bar, on the contrary, should be beaten two in a bar; the four accustomed gestures of a moderate movement becoming then so hurried as to present nothing decided to the eye, and serving only to confuse the performer instead of giving him confidence. Moreover—and this is of much more consequence—the conductor, by uselessly making these four gestures in a quick movement, renders the pace of the rhythm awkward, and loses the freedom of gesture, which a simple division of the time into its half, would leave him.

Generally speaking, composers are wrong to write, in such a case, the indication of the time as four in a bar. When the movement is very brisk, they should never write any other than the sign for 2/2, and not that for 4/4, which might lead the conductor into error.

It is exactly the same for the time three in a bar, fast 3/4, or 3/8. Then the conductor must omit the gesture of the second beat, and, by remaining the period of a beat longer on the first, only raise the stick at the third.

It would be absurd to attempt to beat the three in a bar of one of Beethoven's scherzos.

In slow movements the rule for these two times is like that for two in a bar. If the movement be very slow, each time must be divided; and consequently eight gestures must be made for the time four in a bar, and six for the time three in a bar, repeating (and shortening) each of the principal gestures we have before instanced.

The arm should take no part in the little supplementary gesture indicating the subdivision of the bar; merely the wrist causing the stick to move.

This division of the different times is intended to prevent the rhythmical divergences which might easily take place among the performers during the interval which separates one beat from the other. The conductor not indicating anything during this period (rendered somewhat considerable by the extreme slowness of the movement), the players are then entirely left to themselves, *without conductor;* and as the rhythmical feeling is not the same with all, it follows that some hurry, while others slacken, and unity is soon destroyed. The only exception possible to this rule is that of a first-rate orchestra, composed of performers who are well acquainted with each other, are accustomed to play together, and know almost by heart the work they are executing. Even then, the inattention of a single player may occasion an accident. Why incur its possibility? I know that certain artists feel their self-love hurt when thus kept in leading-strings (like children, they say); but with a conductor who has no other view than the excellence of the ultimate result, this consideration can have no weight. Even in a quartet, it is seldom that the individual feeling of the players can be left entirely free to follow its own dictates. In a symphony, that of the conductor must rule. The art of comprehending it, and fulfilling it with unanimity, constitutes the perfection of execution; and individual wills —which can never agree one with another—should never be permitted to manifest themselves. . . .

We will now speak of the conductor's method of beating in recitatives. Here, as the singer or the instrumentalist is reciting, and no longer subject to the regular division of the bar, it is requisite, while following him attentively, to make the orchestra strike, simultaneously and with precision, the chords or instrumental passages with which the recitative is intermingled; and to make the harmony change at the proper instant, when the recitative is accompanied either by holding-notes or by a tremolo in several parts, of which the least apparent, occasionally, is that which the conductor must most regard, since upon its motion depends the change of chord.

Many conductors have the habit, when directing the orchestra in recitatives, of paying no heed to the written division of the bar, and of marking an up beat before that whereon a brief orchestral chord occurs, even when this chord comes on an unaccented part of the bar.

In a passage such as this, they raise the arm at the rest which commences the bar, and lower it at the time of the chord.

I cannot approve such a method, which nothing justifies, and which may frequently occasion accidents in the execution. Neither do I see why, in recitatives, the bar should not be divided regularly, and the real beats be marked in their place, as in music beaten in time. I therefore advise that the first beat should be made down, as usual, and the stick carried to the left for striking the chord upon the second beat; and so on for analogous cases; always dividing the bar regularly. It is very important, moreover, to divide it according to the time previously indicated by the author, and not to forget, if this time be *allegro* or *maestoso,* and if the reciting part have been some time reciting unaccompanied, to give to all the beats, when the orchestra comes in again, the value of those of an allegro or of a maestoso. For when the orchestra plays alone, it does so generally in time; it plays without measured time only when it accompanies a voice or instrument in recitative.

In the exceptional case where the recitative is written for the orchestra itself, or for the chorus, or for a portion of either orchestra or chorus, it being then requisite to keep together, whether in unison or in harmony, but without regular time, a certain number of performers, *the conductor himself becomes the real reciter,* and gives to each beat of the bar the duration he judges fit. According to the form of the phrase, he divides and subdivides the beats, now marks the accents, now the semiquavers, if there be any, and, in short, indicates with his stick the melodic form of the recitative.

It is an understood thing that the performers, knowing their parts almost by heart, keep their eye constantly upon him, otherwise, neither security nor unity can be obtained.

In general, even for timed music, the conductor should require the players he directs to look towards him as often as possible.

An orchestra which does not watch the conducting-stick has no conductor. Often, after a pedal-point for instance, the conductor is obliged to refrain from marking the decisive gesture which is to determine the coming in of the orchestra until he sees the eyes of all the performers fixed upon him. It is the duty of the conductor, during rehearsal, to accustom them to look towards him simultaneously at the important moment.

If the rule just indicated were not observed, the passage could not be uttered with firmness and unity; the players, not watching the conductor's stick, could not know when he decides the second beat and resumes the movement suspended by the pedal-point.

The obligation upon the performers to look at their conductor necessarily implies an equal obligation on his part to let himself be well seen by them. He should, whatever may be the disposal of the orchestra, whether on rows of steps, or on a horizontal plane, place himself so as to form the centre of all surrounding eyes.

To place him well in sight, a conductor requires an especial platform, elevated in proportion as the number of performers is large and occupies much space. His desk should not be so high as that the portion sustaining the score shall hide his face. For the expression of his countenance has much to do with the influence he exercises, and if there be no conductor for an orchestra that does not and will not watch him, neither is there any if he cannot be well seen.

As to the employment of noises of any kind whatever, produced by the stick of the conductor upon his desk, or by his foot upon the platform, they call for no other than unreserved reprehension. It is worse than a bad method; it is a barbarism. In a theatre, however, when the stage evolutions prevent the chorus-singers from seeing the conducting-stick, the conductor is compelled—to ensure, after a pause, the taking up a point by the chorus—to indicate this point by marking the beat which precedes it by a slight tap of his stick upon the desk. This exceptional circumstance is the only one which can warrant the employment of an *indicating noise,* and even then it is to be regretted that recourse must be had to it.

While speaking of chorus-singers, and of their operations in theatres, it may here be observed that chorus-masters often allow themselves to beat time at the side-scenes, without seeing the conductor's stick, frequently even without hearing the orchestra. The result is that this time, beaten more or less ill, and not corresponding with that of the conductor, inevitably induces a rhythmical discordance between the choral and instrumental bodies, and subverts all unity instead of tending to maintain it.

Another traditional barbarism lies within the province of an intelligent and active conductor to abolish. If a choral or instrumental piece be performed behind the scenes, without accompaniment from the principal orchestra, another conductor is absolutely essential. If the orchestra accompany this portion, the first conductor, who hears the distant music, is then strictly bound to *let himself be guided* by the second, and to follow his time *by ear*. But if—as frequently happens in modern music—the sound of the chief orchestra hinders the conductor from hearing that which is being performed at a distance from him, the intervention of a special conducting mechanism becomes indispensable, in order to establish instantaneous communication between him and the distant performers. Many attempts, more or less ingenious, have been made of this kind, the result of which has not everywhere answered expectations. That of Covent Garden Theatre, in London, moved by the conductor's foot, acts tolerably well. But the *electric metronome,* set up by Mr. Van Bruge in the Brussels Theatre, leaves nothing to be desired. It consists of an apparatus of copper ribbons, leading from a Voltaic battery placed beneath the stage, attached to the conductor's desk, and terminating in a movable stick fastened at one end on a pivot before a board at a certain distance from the orchestral conductor. To this latter's desk is affixed a key of copper, something like the ivory key of a pianoforte; it is elastic, and provided on the interior side with a protuberance of about a quarter of an inch long. Immediately beneath this protuberance is a little cup, also of copper, filled with quicksilver. At the instant when the orchestral conductor, desiring to mark any particular beat of a bar, presses the copper key with the forefinger of his left hand (his right being occupied in holding, as usual, the conducting-stick) this key is lowered, the protuberance passes into the cup filled with quicksilver, a slight electric spark is emitted, and the stick placed at the other extremity of the copper ribbon makes an oscillation before its board. The communication of the fluid and the movement are quite simultaneous, whatever be the distance traversed.

The performers being grouped behind the scenes, their eyes fixed upon the stick of the electric metronome, are thus directly subject to the conductor, who could, were it needful, conduct, from the middle of the Opera orchestra in Paris, a piece of music performed at Versailles.

It is merely requisite to agree beforehand with the chorus-singers, or with their conductor (if, as an additional precaution, they have one), the way in which the orchestral conductor beats the time—whether he mark all the principal beats, or only the first of the bar—since the oscillations of the stick, moved by electricity, being always from right to left, indicate nothing precise in this respect.

When I first used, at Brussels, the valuable instrument I have just endeavoured to describe, its action presented one objection. Each time that the copper key of my desk underwent the pressure of my left forefinger, it struck, underneath, another plate of copper, and, notwithstanding the delicacy of the contact, produced a little sharp noise, which, during the pauses of the orchestra, attracted the attention of the audience, to the detriment of the musical effect.

I pointed out the fault to Mr. Van Bruge, who substituted for the lower plate of copper the little cup filled with quicksilver, previously mentioned. Into this the protuberance so entered as to establish the electric current without causing the slightest noise.

Nothing remains now, as regards the use of this mechanism, but the crackling of the spark at the moment of its emission. This, however, is too slight to be heard by the public.

The metronome is not expensive to put up; it costs £16 at the most. Large lyric theatres, churches, and concert-rooms should long ago have been provided with one. Yet, save at the Brussels Theatre, it is nowhere to be found. This would appear incredible, were it not that the carelessness of the majority of directors of institutions where music forms a feature is well known; as are their instinctive aversion from whatever disturbs old-established customs, their indifference to the interests of art, their parsimony wherever an outlay for music is needed, and the utter ignorance of the principles of our art among those in whose hands rests the ordering of its destiny.

I have not yet said all on the subject of those dangerous auxiliaries named chorus-masters. Very few of them are sufficiently versed in the art to conduct a musical performance, or so that the orchestral conductor can depend upon them. He cannot therefore watch them too closely when compelled to submit to their coadjutorship.

The most to be dreaded are those whom age has deprived of activity and energy. The maintenance of vivacious times is an impossibility to them. Whatever may be the degree of quickness indicated at the head of a piece confided to their conducting, little by little they slacken its pace, until the rhythm is reduced to a certain medium slowness, that seems to harmonize with the speed at which their blood flows, and the general feebleness of their organization.

It must in truth be added, that old men are not the only ones with whom composers run this risk. There are men in the prime of life, of a lymphatic temperament, whose blood seems to circulate *moderato*. If they have to conduct an allegro assai, they gradually slacken it to *moderato;* if, on the contrary, it be a largo or an andante sostenuto, provided the piece be prolonged, they will, by dint of progressive animation, attain a *moderato* long before the end. The *moderato* is their natural pace, and they recur to it as infallibly as would a pendulum after having been a moment hurried or slackened in its oscillations.

These people are the born enemies of all characteristic music, and the greatest destroyers of style. May Fate preserve the orchestral conductor at any cost from their co-operation.

Once, in a large town (which I will not name), there was to be performed behind the scenes a very simple chorus, written in 6/8, allegretto. The aid of the chorus-master became necessary. He was an old man.

The time in which this chorus was to be taken having been first agreed upon by the orchestra, our Nestor followed it pretty decently during the first few bars; but, soon after, the slackening became such that there was no continuing without rendering the piece perfectly ridiculous. It was recommenced twice, thrice, four times; a full half-hour was occupied in ever-increasingly vexatious efforts, but always with the same result. The preservation of allegretto time was absolutely impossible to the worthy man. At last the orchestral conductor, out of all patience, came and begged him not to conduct at all; he had hit upon an expedient: He caused the chorus-singers to simulate a march-movement, raising each foot alternately, without moving on. This movement, being in exactly the same time as the dual rhythm of the 6/8 bar, allegretto, the chorus-singers, who were no longer hindered by their director, at once performed the piece as though they had sung marching; with no less unity than regularity, and without slackening the time.

I acknowledge, however, that many chorus-masters, or sub-conductors of orchestras, are sometimes of real utility, and even indispensable for the maintenance of unity among very large masses of performers. When these masses are obliged to be so disposed as that one portion of the players or chorus-singers turn their back on the conductor, he needs a certain number of sub-beaters of the time, placed before those of the performers who cannot see him and charged with repeating all his signals. In order that this repetition shall be precise, the sub-conductors must be careful never to take their eyes off the chief conductor's stick for a single instant. If, in order to look at their score, they cease to watch him for only three bars, a discrepancy arises immediately between their time and his, and all is lost.

In a festival where 1200 performers were assembled under my direction, at Paris, I had to employ four chorus-masters, stationed at the four corners of the vocal mass, and two sub-conductors, one of whom directed the wind-instruments, and the other the instruments of percussion. I had earnestly besought them to look towards me incessantly; they did not omit to do so, and our eight sticks, rising and falling without the slightest discrepancy of rhythm, established amidst our 1200 performers the most perfect unity ever witnessed.

With one or more electric metronomes, it seems no longer necessary to have recourse to this means. One might, in fact, thus easily conduct chorus-singers who turn their back towards the chief conductor; but attentive and intelligent sub-conductors are always preferable to a machine. They have not only to beat the time, like the metronomic staff, but they have also to speak to the groups around them, to call their attention to nice shades of execution, and, after bar-rests, to remind them when the moment of their re-entry comes.

In a space arranged as a semicircular amphitheatre, the orchestral conductor may conduct a considerable number of performers alone, all eyes then being able to look towards him. Nevertheless, the employment of a certain number of sub-conductors appears to me preferable to individual direction, on account of the great distance between the chief conductor and the extreme points of the vocal and instrumental body.

The more distant the orchestral conductor is from the performers he directs, the more his influence over them is diminished.

The best way would be to have several sub-conductors, with several electric metronomes beating before their eyes the principal beats of the bar.

And now, should the orchestral conductor give the time standing or sitting down?

If, in theatres where they perform scores of immense length, it be very difficult to endure the fatigue of remaining on foot the whole evening, it is none the less true that the orchestral conductor, when seated, loses a portion of his power and cannot give free course to his animation, if he possess any.

Then, should he conduct reading from a full score or from a first violin part (leader's copy), as is customary in some theatres? It is evident that he should have before him a full score. Conducting by means of a part containing only the principal instrumental cues, the bass, and the melody, demands a needless effort of memory from a conductor; and moreover, if he happen to tell one of the performers, whose part he cannot examine, that he is wrong, exposes him to the chance of the reply: "How do you know?"

The disposal and grouping of the players and chorus-singers come also within the province of the orchestral conductor; particularly for concerts. It is impossible to indicate arbitrarily the best method of grouping the performers in a theatre or concert-room; the shape and arrangement of the interior of these places necessarily influence the course to be taken in such a case. Let us add that it depends, moreover, upon the number of performers requiring to be grouped; and, on some occasions, upon the style of composition adopted by the author whose work is to be performed.

In general, for concerts, the following disposal of the orchestra seems best: An amphitheatre of eight, or at least, five rows is indispensable. The semicircular form is the best for the amphitheatre. If it be large enough to contain the whole orchestra, the entire mass of instrumentalists will be disposed of along these rows; the first violins in front on the right, facing the public; the second violins in front on the left; the violas, in the middle, between the two groups of violins; the flutes, hautboys, clarinets, horns, and bassoons behind the first violins; a double rank of violoncellos and double-basses behind the second violins; the trumpets, cornets, trombones, and tubas behind the violas; the rest of the violoncellos and double-basses behind the wooden wind instruments; the harps in the foreground, close to the orchestral conductor; the kettle-drums, and other instruments of percussion behind or in the centre of the brass instruments; the orchestral conductor, turning his back to the public, at the base of the orchestra, and near to the foremost desks of the first and second violins.

There should be a horizontal flooring, or stage, more or less wide, extending in front of the first rows of the amphitheatre. On this flooring the chorus-singers should be placed, in form of a fan turned three-quarters towards the public, so that all shall be able easily to see the motions of the orchestral conductor. The grouping of the chorus-singers, in consonance with their respective order of voice, will differ according as the author has written in three, four, or six parts. At any rate, the women—sopranos and contraltos—should be in front, seated; the tenors standing behind the contraltos; and the basses standing behind the sopranos.

The solo-singers should occupy the centre, and foremost, part of the front stage, and should always place themselves in such a way as to be able, by slightly turning the head, to see the conducting-stick.

For the rest, I repeat, these indications can be but approximate; they may be, for many reasons, modified in various ways.

At the Conservatoire, in Paris, where the amphitheatre is composed of only four or five rows, not circular, and cannot therefore contain the whole orchestra, the violins and violas are on the stage; while the basses and wind instruments alone occupy the rows; the chorus is seated on the front of the stage, facing the public, and the women, sopranos and contraltos, turning their backs directly upon the orchestral conductor, are utterly unable to see his motions. The arrangement is very inconvenient for this portion of the chorus.

It is everywhere of the greatest consequence that the chorus-singers placed on the front of the stage shall occupy a plane somewhat lower than that of the violins; otherwise they would considerably deaden the sound of these instruments.

For the same reason, if there are not other rows for the choir in front of the orchestra, it is absolutely needful that the women should be seated, and the men remain standing up; in order that the voices of the tenors and basses, proceeding from a more elevated point than those of the sopranos and contraltos, may come forth freely and be neither stifled nor intercepted.

When the presence of the chorus-singers in front of the orchestra is not necessary, the conductor will take care to send them away; since this large number of human bodies injures the sonority of the instruments. A symphony, performed by an orchestra thus more or less stifled, loses much of its effect.

There are yet other precautions, relative especially to the orchestra, which the conductor may also take, to avoid certain defects in performance. The instruments of percussion, placed, as I have indicated, upon one of the last rows of the orchestra, have a tendency to modify the rhythm, and slacken the time. A series of strokes on the long drum struck at regular intervals in a quick movement will sometimes lead to the complete destruction of a fine rhythmical progression, by checking the onward bound of the rest of the orchestra, and destroying the unity. Almost always, the long drum player, through not observing the original time given by the conductor, is somewhat behindhand in striking his first stroke. This retardment, multiplied by the number of strokes which follow the first one, soon produces—as may be imagined—a rhythmical discrepancy of the most fatal effect. The conductor, all whose efforts to re-establish unanimity are then in vain, has only one thing left to do; which is, to insist that the long drum player shall count beforehand the number of strokes to be given in the passage in question, and that, knowing his part, he shall no longer look at his copy, but keep his eyes constantly fixed upon the conducting-stick; by which means he will follow the time without the slightest want of precision.

When a long *accelerando, little by little,* is indicated by the composer, for passing from an allegro moderato to a presto, the majority of orchestral conductors hurry the time *by jerks,* instead of quickening it equally throughout, by an insensible onward rate. This should be carefully avoided.

The same remark applies to the converse proposition. It is even more difficult to slacken a quick time smoothly, and without checks, so as to transform it little by little into a slow time. Often, from a desire to testify zeal, or from defect of delivery in his musical feeling, a conductor demands from his players *an exaggeration of nice gradations.* He comprehends neither the character nor the style of the piece. The gradations then become so many blemishes; the accents, yells; the intentions of the poor composer are totally disfigured and perverted; while those of the orchestral conductor—however politely meant they may be—are none the less injurious: like the caresses of the Ass in the fable, who crushed his master while fondling him.

And now let us instance many deplorable abuses that have obtained in almost all the orchestras of Europe—abuses which reduce composers to despair, and which it is the duty of conductors to abolish as soon as possible.

Performers playing stringed instruments will rarely give themselves the trouble to play a tremolo; they substitute for this very characteristic effect, a tame repetition of the note, half, and sometimes three-quarters slower than the one whence results the tremolo: instead of demisemiquavers, they make triple or double ones; and in lieu of producing sixty-four notes in a bar in four-time (adagio), they produce only thirty-two, or even sixteen. The action of the arm necessary for producing a true tremolo demands from them too great an effort. This idleness is intolerable.

Many double-bass players permit themselves—from idleness, also, or from a dread of being unable to achieve certain difficulties—to simplify their part. This race of simplifiers, be it said, has existed for forty years; but it cannot endure any longer. In ancient works, the double-bass parts were extremely simple; therefore there can be no reason to impoverish them still more: those in modern scores are rather more difficult, it is true; but, with very few exceptions, there is nothing in them impossible of execution; composers, masters of their art, write them with care, and as they ought to be executed. If it be from idleness that the simplifiers pervert them, the energetic orchestral conductor is armed with the necessary authority to compel the fulfilment of their duty. If it be from incapacity, let him dismiss them. It is his best interest to rid himself of instrumentalists who cannot play their instrument.

Flute players, accustomed to be above the other wind instruments, and not admitting that their part can be written below that of clarinets or hautboys, frequently transpose entire passages an octave higher. The conductor, if he do not carefully peruse his score, if he be not thoroughly acquainted with the work he is conducting, or if his ear lack keenness. will not perceive the strange liberty thus taken. Nevertheless, multitudes of such instances occur, and care should be taken to banish them entirely.

It happens everywhere (I do not say in some orchestras only)—it happens everywhere, I repeat, that violinists, who have, as is well known, to play—ten, fifteen, twenty of them—the same part in unison, do not count their bars' rest; each, always from idleness, relying on the others doing it. Whence it follows that scarcely the half of them come in again at the right moment; while the rest still hold their instrument under their left arm, and look about them. Thus the point is greatly weakened, if not entirely missed. I invoke the attention and rigour of orchestral conductors to this insufferable habit. It is, however, so rooted that they will only ensure its extirpation by making a large number of violinists amenable for the fault of a single player; by inflicting a fine, for example, upon a whole row, if one of them misses coming in. Even were this fine no more than half-a-crown, I will answer for it that each of the violinists would count his rests, and keep watch that his neighbours did the same, since it might be inflicted five or six times upon the same individuals in the course of one performance.

An orchestra, the instruments of which are not in tune individually, and with each other, is a monstrosity; the conductor, therefore, should take the greatest care that the musicians tune accurately. But this operation should not be performed in presence of the public; and, moreover, every instrumental noise—every kind of preluding between the acts—constitutes a real offence to all civilized auditors. The bad training of an orchestra, and its musical mediocrity is to be inferred from the impertinent noise it makes during the periods of quiet at an Opera or Concert.

It is also imperative for a conductor not to allow clarinet-players to use always the same instrument (the clarinet in B♭), without regard to the author's indications; just as if the different clarinets—those in D and in A, particularly—had not a special character of their own, of which the intelligent composer knows the exact value.

A habit as vicious, and still more baneful, has crept into many orchestras since the introduction of horns with cylinders and pistons: it is that of playing *in open sounds,* by means of the new mechanism adapted to the instrument, those notes intended by the composer to be produced *in closed sounds,* by means of the right hand within the bell. Moreover, the horn players nowadays, on account of the facility afforded by the pistons or cylinders for putting their instrument into different keys, use only the *horn in F,* whatever may be the key indicated by the author. This custom gives rise to a host of inconveniences, from which the conductor should use all his efforts to preserve the works of composers *who know how to write.* As to those of others, it must be confessed, the disaster is of much less consequence.

He should also set his face against the economical fashion adopted by certain theatres—called lyric—of causing the cymbals and the long drum to be played by the same performer. The sound of the cymbals when attached to the long drum—as they must be to render this economy feasible—is an ignoble noise, fit only for bands at tea-gardens. This custom, moreover, leads mediocre composers into the habit of never employing one of these instruments without the other, and of considering their use as solely confined to forcibly marking the accented parts of the bar. This is an idea fruitful in noisy platitudes; and one that has brought upon us the ridiculous excesses beneath which, if a stop be not put to them, dramatic music will sooner or later sink.

I conclude by expressing sincere regret at beholding choral and orchestral studies still so badly organized. Everywhere, for grand choral and instrumental compositions, the system of rehearsals in the mass is maintained. They make all the chorus-singers study at once, on the one hand; and all the instrumentalists at once, on the other. Deplorable errors, innumerable mistakes, are thus committed—particularly in the intermediate parts—errors which the chorus-master and the conductor do not perceive. Once established, these errors degenerate into habits, and become part and parcel of the execution.

The hapless chorus-singers, moreover, are by far the worst treated of all the performers during their studies, such as they are. Instead of giving them *a good conductor,* knowing the times of the different movements accurately, and proficient in the art of singing, to beat the time and make critical observations: *a good pianist,* playing *from a well-arranged pianoforte score,* upon *a good piano;* and *a violinist,* to play in unison or in octave with the voices as each part is learned alone—instead of these three *indispensable artists,* they commit them (in two-thirds of the lyric theatres of Europe) to the superintendence of a single man, who has no more idea of the art of conducting than of that of singing, who is generally a poor musician, selected from among the worst pianists to be found, or who cannot play the pianoforte at all—some old superannuated individual, who, seated before a battered out-of-tune instrument, tries to decipher a dislocated score which he does not know, strikes false chords, major when they are minor, or vice-versa, and, under the pretext of conducting and of accompanying by himself, employs his right hand in setting the chorus-singers wrong in their time, and his left hand in setting them wrong in their tune.

One might believe oneself in the Dark Ages, on witnessing such an exhibition of barbarism for the sake of economy.

A faithful, well-coloured, clever interpretation of a modern work, even when confided to artists of a higher order, can only be obtained, I firmly believe, by partial rehearsals. Each part of a chorus should be studied singly until it be thoroughly known, before combining it with the others. The same step should be taken with regard to the orchestra, for a symphony at all complicated. The violins should first be practised alone; the violas and basses by themselves; the wooden wind instruments (with a small band of stringed instruments, to fill in the rests, and accustom the wind instruments to the points of re-entrance) and the brass instruments the same; and very often it is necessary to practise the instruments of percussion alone; and lastly, the harps, if they be numerous. The studies in combination are then far more profitable, and more rapid; and there is then good hope of attaining fidelity of interpretation, now, alas, but too rare.

The performances obtained by the old method of study are merely *approaches* to achievement; beneath which so very many masterpieces have succumbed. The superintending conductor, after the butchering of a master, none the less serenely lays down his stick with a satisfied smile; and if some few misgivings remain with him as to the mode in which he has fulfilled his task, should no one venture at the close to dispute its accomplishment, he murmurs aside: *"Bah! vae victis!"* (So what! Losers weepers!)

QUESTIONS

1. In a music dictionary look up *hautboy* and *ophicleide*. What sort of instruments are these? How have they been replaced in the modern orchestra?
2. Why do you suppose orchestras have so many stringed instruments in

comparison to wind instruments? Show the proportion of stringed instruments, woodwinds, brass, and percussion, according to Berlioz's idea of the ideal orchestra. How does his orchestra compare with the modern orchestra?

3. Discuss Berlioz's "points of procedure of the sound," and his disposition of percussion instruments in the orchestra. Do you think this foreshadows the principles of stereophonic sound? How?
4. Berlioz indicates that, in his time, people with money "are ready to give 50,000 francs and more" for a great painting; yet would not give 50 francs to help produce, once a year, an important musical work. What do you think accounts for this? Has this practice changed any in our time?
5. How does one study to become a conductor? Does studying any particular instrument help? Look up some famous conductors and list the instruments they studied. Have they anything in common? What did Toscanini play? Berlioz? Bernstein? Koussevitsky? Ormandy? Stokowski?

PROGRAM MUSIC / 1 *Richard Strauss (1864-1949), unlike Johann Strauss, Sr. (The Father of the Waltz) or Johann Strauss, Jr. (The Waltz King), is a controversial figure. Half a dozen of his works have achieved wide popularity, while others have fallen into a musical limbo, from which they, from time to time, are temporarily freed. Music critics are still at considerable odds concerning the value of Strauss's music; no one, however, denies his mastery of orchestration. Frederick Niecks, late Reid Professor of Music at the University of Edinburgh, knew Strauss and wrote the following essay in 1906, at the height of Strauss's popularity.*

PROGRAM MUSIC AND **Richard Strauss**

FREDERICK NIECKS

THE HISTORY OF PROGRAMME MUSIC MAY BE SAID to be the history of the development of musical expression; at any rate, it presents itself as such if programme music is not understood in too narrow a sense. But what is programme music? The current notions concerning it are so vague and varied that it will be advisable to consider, before commencing our story, the term and the things signified by it. Some think that programme music is music which imitates sounds—the song of birds, the purling of the brook, the bustle and noises of war, &c. Others, allowing it somewhat larger scope, think that it is music which, besides the audible, imitates by analogy also the visible—effects of light, darkness, and colour, and all kinds and degrees of movement. Others again, with a more adequate conception, go much farther than this, and think that programme music is music which imitates not only the outward, but also the inward; which not only describes, but also expresses; which has to do with emotions and thoughts as well as with sense-impressions, with soul-painting as well as with body-painting. To not a few the last view seems absurd. They hold that nothing of the kind is within the capacity of music. But the pretension is by no means unreasonable. On the contrary, it is obviously and strikingly reasonable. Why should not music be able to express and excite emotions by imitating the sounds and movements by which they demonstrate themselves? . . . Here it will suffice to enumerate the means of expression at the disposal of the composer:

(1) Imitation of the human cries and the accents of speech as regards pitch, rhythm, loudness, and quality of tone.
(2) Imitation of the movements of the internal and external bodily organs that accompany the emotions—action of the heart, breathing, gestures, &c.
(3) Imitation of the sounds in nature, which are expressive directly and indirectly, indirectly by association.
(4) Imitation of rest and motion, strain and relaxation, pleasure and pain, by certain musical means—namely, consonance and dissonance, and the tendencies of tonality.

The prejudices as to programmes are many. That absolute music—by which we are to understand pure music, music with none but aesthetical qualities, music unconnected with anything definite in thought or nature, according to some a mere formal play with tones—is the

---

PROGRAM MUSIC AND RICHARD STRAUSS from *Programme Music in the Last Four Centuries* by Frederick Niecks; Novello and Co. Ltd.; 1906.

only legitimate instrumental music, was long the orthodox and all but universal doctrine, and even now has not become wholly extinct belief. Then, we find people who approve of a title, but object to a poem or a prose narrative prefixed to a piece of music. And yet, a title may imply a great deal more than a poem or a prose narrative. What vast subjects, for instance, are indicated by single words such as Faust, Hamlet, Manfred, Hebrides, Eroica, Hungaria, &c.! It is a mistake, although in accordance with a time-honoured definition, to say that programme music is music with an explicit verbal programme prefixed to it. Many of the compositions of Berlioz, Liszt, and Richard Strauss, the most famous masters in this *genre* of music, have nothing but simple titles. In fact, you may have programme music without even as much as a title. If the composer had a programme in his mind while composing, the composition is programme music, whether he reveals his programme or not. It used to be very common with composers to conceal their programmes. They were either afraid of the prejudiced critics, and kept their secret, like Weber in the *Koncertstück;* or were themselves affected by the prevailing prejudice, and tried, like Schumann, to excuse their practice by explanations intended to allay their own doubts as well as the wrath of others.

The prejudice, however, which has led to the largest amount of misconception and to an infinitude of preposterous criticism is the assumption that the composer gives in his music all that is set forth in the programme, whereas in reality the music is intended only as a commentary and illustration, not as a duplicate or translation of it. Indeed, the programme would be a superfluity if it did not contain something that music is unable to express at all or equally well. We cannot reason, give orders, and tell stories in music. It cannot name persons, times, and places connected with what it communicates, although it may characterize them and hint at them. On the other hand, we can express the infinite shades and degrees of moods and emotions better by tones than by any other medium. Of course, composers have often, from ignorance or presumption, attempted the impossible. But misuse does not justify the condemnation of use.

There are several other considerations worth pointing out. Usage reserves the term programme music for instrumental music with a prefixed verbal programme. But this should not prevent us from seeing facts as they are. A programme may be recited or sung before or with the music as well as printed. This difference in the enunciation of the programme does not make an essential difference in the character of the music. In fact, all good, that is, all expressive vocal music is programme music. Further, the programme need not be verbal at all, it may also be pantomimic or pictorial. Next, let us note the various characters of programmes. Three main divisions are easily distinguishable—the predominatingly descriptive, the predominatingly emotional, and the predominatingly symbolical. The descriptive (the materially descriptive) is the lowest kind of programme music, and is best used in combination with and subordination to one of the others. To make up for the absence of the emotional element is a difficult and rarely successful task. It is the musical element *par excellence*. Lastly, although a programme invites and admits deviation from the structural methods of absolute music, it neither necessarily demands abandonment of the classical forms, nor in any conceivable case excuses formlessness.

What shall be the starting point of our history? We may pass over the beginnings of the art, which are matters of conjecture, the antique and early medieval music, of which our practical knowledge is extremely scanty, and the polyphonic art-music of the 14th and 15th centuries, in which emotional and descriptive expression does not seem to have been, indeed, could not have been, a chief aim. Where expression was not altogether excluded from the old polyphonic compositions by the love of ingenuity of combination, it did not often go beyond the general, unspecialized states of feeling, such as calm, dignity, liveliness, agitation, vigour, langour, &c. A different state of matters began to develop in the 16th century. A striving after greater freedom, ease, lucidity, and suppleness became more and more noticeable, and consciously aimed at greater expressiveness or unconsciously contributed to the attainment of that aim. The cultivation of the madrigal and the more popular villanella and villota, the endeavour so to set the words to music as to remain intelligible, the experiments in chromaticism, tonality, solo song, instrumental music, and theatrical performances—all these had one origin, arose from one impulse, and tended one and all to the great revolution brought about towards the end of the century by the evolution of the instrumentally accompanied solo song (monody) and the musical drama. The 16th century, then, must be our starting point.

To escape the danger of losing ourselves in a multitude of isolated facts, we will endeavour to group them in periods corresponding to stages of evolution. Do not look, however, for perfect continuity and progression in one straight line; instead of it you will often see leaps, sporadic phenomena, zigzag movements, and retrogression as well as progression. Childish programme music, such as we find in the earliest stages, we still find in the last stage beside the highest developments. Observe that my periods overlap. Observe also that the early periods are to the last two what steps, porch, and vestibule are to a house or a temple.

First Period, 16th century: *Vocal programme music.*

Second Period, from the latter part of the 16th to the beginning of the 18th century, opening with the Englishmen Byrd and Mundy and ending with the German Kuhnau: *Isolated and tentative cases,* at first without exception crude and childish, and even later on mostly so, at least partially if not wholly.

Third Period, from the 17th to the middle of the 18th century, that of the French masters (lutenists and clavecinists) of musical miniature *genre* and portrait painting, which culminated in François Couperin: *First artistically satisfactory achievements in programme music.*

Fourth Period, the 18th century: Spreading of the cultivation of programme music and *more general striving after expressiveness in instrumental music,* as seen (*a*) in Overtures, *Entr'actes,* and incidental music to plays and operas, and the instrumental *ritornelli* and accompaniments of vocal compositions; (*b*) in Melodrama (instrumental accompaniment to the spoken word); and (*c*) in Symphony and Sonata.

Fifth Period, from the close of the 18th century: *Programme music in the larger classical forms and vitalization of the lesser forms.* First appears Beethoven, who, at least as regards the larger classical forms, is the principal inspirer of those who come after him.

Sixth Period, from about the fourth decade of the 19th century: *Departure from the classical forms and wider scope of subjects.* The inspiring geniuses of this period are Berlioz, Liszt, and Wagner.

To Richard Strauss (1864-1949), the much discussed, the problematic, we must now turn our attention. On certain points all the world is at one—on his virtuosic craftsmanship, his supreme mastery over all the resources of the art, his diabolical cleverness, and even his genius. But agreement ceases when we come to the consideration of the application of the craftsmanship, mastery, cleverness, and genius. Then opinions may be found as far apart as the poles, and even as heaven and earth. Then we may see ecstatic delight on the one hand and downright disgust on the other, and hear praise and blessings on the one hand and condemnation and curses on the other.

In Strauss's career as a composer there are clearly distinguishable two periods, the second of which was brought about not by evolution, but by revolution, and not by an inner, but by an outer impulse. . . . Strauss's musical training, which ran parallel with his secondary school and university education, was on classical lines, and during the short first period of his creative career he adhered to these lines. As belonging to this time and style we may indicate Op. 1-15, and add to them Op. 18, the most notable works of which are the Sonata for violoncello and pianoforte, Op. 6; the Serenade for thirteen wind instruments, Op.

7; the Symphony, Op. 12; the Quartet for pianoforte and strings, Op. 13; and the Sonata for violin and pianoforte, Op. 18.

In 1885 Strauss went to Meiningen, and there he made the acquaintance of Alexander Ritter, by whom he was converted and imbued with the principles responsible, indirectly if not directly, for the sensational works that have made the world stare and stand agape. From Dr. Arthur Seidl, the friend to whom Strauss dedicated his *Till Eulenspiegel,* we learn some interesting particulars about the composer's mental development and tendencies. He tells us of their hearing at the Munich University courses of lectures on aesthetics (Carrière), Schopenhauer (Fr. Jodl), and the history of culture (Riehl); and how in 1889, at the time of his friendship with Ritter—in the Wagner-Liszt period of his artistic development, and the Schopenhauer period of his intellectual development—Strauss suddenly struck up as it were a new tune, Dostoievski's *Raskolnikov* raising his enthusiasm and inciting him to psychological analysis and dissection, and Gerhart Hauptmann (still in the ante-"Weber" days) keenly interesting him on account of the progressive-naturalistic technique in the painting of the *milieu,* the presentation of human character, and the refinement of dialogue.

Some years later, at the turning-point of his life, there occurred a veering round from Schopenhauer to Nietzsche, in whom he became absorbed and found deliverance and recovery, or—shall we say?—freedom and health (*Loslösung und Genesung*). Strauss's attention was further arrested by John Henry Mackay and his novel *The Anarchists,* by Karl Henckell and his social lament "the times are forceful, they bring distress to heart and brain," and by the poet R. Dehmel, the poet, dramatist, and prose-writer Detlev von Liliencron, and the prose-writers Julius Hart and Otto Julius Bierbaum.

In short, Strauss bathed in the troubled waters of modernity and came out an ultramodern. A circumstance alluded to above deserves more than an allusion, and authoritative information enables me to speak of it more fully. When in 1885 Strauss came to Meiningen, Hans von Bülow introduced him to his old friend Alexander Ritter, whose opinions we know already. The latter was not slow to perceive the extraordinary talent of his new acquaintance, but also his conservatism and youthfulness in more respects than years. That Strauss was not as yet favourably impressed by Wagner's music may be easily accounted for by his father's violent anti-Wagnerism. Ritter set himself the task of showing the young man the way to clear and develop his views; of stirring up, not merely the musician, but the whole intellectual man, to artistic activity; and of awaking in him the notion that in order to attain an object it is necessary to have a mental grasp of it.

By means of Wagner's literary works Ritter revealed to Strauss the ideas which inspired that master's art-work. Nor was Ritter's influence confined to matters musical. It extended, for instance, to Schopenhauer's philosophy. The strength of Ritter's conviction and the ardour of his propagandism were irresistible; indeed, they were so great as on one occasion to draw from Strauss the remark that they were "directly suggestive," in the hypnotic sense. The acquaintanceship of the two men soon grew into intimate friendship. At Meiningen and at Munich, they were in close and almost daily intercourse; and when Strauss took up his abode at Weimar a lively, long-continued correspondence followed.

Later on, unfortunately, an estrangement arose, which, however, had nothing to do with Strauss's artistic development, as some supposed. Strauss told the writer of the interesting article on him in *The Musical Times of January,* 1903: "Ritter was exceptionally well read in all the philosophers ancient and modern, and a man of the highest culture. His influence was in the nature of a stormwind. He urged me on to the development of the poetic, the expressive in music, as exemplified in the works of Liszt, Wagner, and Berlioz." In short, Ritter stamped him, as Strauss himself declares, as a progressive musician.

Passing over the songs and operas, and even over his melodrama *Enoch Arden,* Op. 38 (recitation and pianoforte accompaniment), let us proceed to the symphonic works for orchestra of the second, the programmatic period; and be it noted at once that the nine compositions in question are not uniform in style, but progressive in regard to complexity, intensity, and expressiveness. In speaking here of progressiveness I leave it an open question whether the progress leads to greater or less perfection, to a desirable or undesirable end.

(I.) *From Italy,* symphonic fantasia, Op. 16 (1886; 1887). [Where two years are given, the first is that of composition, and the second that of the first performance. Where only one year is given, it is that of the first performance.] This work need not detain us; it is really a suite of four characteristic pieces, respectively entitled *In the Campagna, Amid the Ruins of Rome, By Sorrento's Strand,* and *Scenes of Popular Life in Naples.* We have here characteristic pieces of mood and scene with which conservative composers have made us familiar; in fact, the programmes indicated by the titles go but little beyond those of the composer's Op. 9, called by him *Mood Pictures:* (1) *On the still wood path;* (2) *At the lonely spring;* (3) *Intermezzo;* (4) *Dreaming;* and (5) *Heath Picture.* Of course, the means of expression and the force, sweep, and realism of the expressiveness are very much greater in the later work. As the composer himself says: "My symphonic fantasia *Aus Italien* is the connecting link between the old and the new method." In the composition next to be considered quite a different state of matters obtains.

(II.) *Don Juan,* tone-poem (after Nicolaus Lenau), Op. 20 (1888; 1889). Prefixed are three passages, altogether thirty-two lines, from Lenau's dramatic poem of the same name. The gist of the three passages may be briefly given as follows: (1) Don Juan's desire to rove through the immeasurable charmed circle of variously attractive womanhood, and die in a kiss on the lips of the last; (2) Mortifying individuals he worships the species; a woman's breath that to-day seems to have the fragrance of spring, may tomorrow be to him like the air of a dungeon; pressing forward to new and ever new victories as long as youth's fiery pulses fly; (3) The beautiful storm is stilled, the combustible material consumed, and the hearth has become cold and dark. —The printed programme gives only a few slight indications of the programme in the mind of the composer. In the latter were many particulars not in the former. Besides the generalities of infinite amorous desire, ceaseless alternation of passionateness and satiety, and final exhaustion, there are in the music three adventures with women of unlike character, and a duel with the father of one of them, by whose weapon Don Juan falls. The fatal sword-thrust, represented by a piercing dissonant high trumpet note, is famous.

(III.) *Macbeth,* tone-poem (after Shakespeare's drama), Op. 23 (1887; 1891). This work was composed four years before its publication, and before the composition of *Don Juan,* and consequently is the first of the master's symphonic poems, and properly dedicated to Alexander Ritter. Beyond the title, that is beyond the wide reference to the drama, there is little to indicate the particularities. This little consists of the word "Macbeth" above the sixth bar; and further on these words of Lady Macbeth: "Hie thee hither, that I may pour my spirits in thy ear, and chastise with the valour of my tongue all that impedes thee from the golden round, which fate and metaphysical aid doth seem to have thee crown'd withal." If a brief account of the work as a whole is wanted, we may call it an illustration of Macbeth's character and soul-struggles.

(IV.) *Tod und Verklärung* (Death and Transfiguration), tone-poem, Op. 24 (1889; 1890). This work, like *Don Juan,* has a programme prefixed—thirty lines in four divisions, forming a complete poem. (1) In a poor little room, dimly lighted, and awfully and ominously silent, except for the ticking of a clock, there lies on his bed, fallen asleep after an exhausting desperate struggle with death, a sick man, with a smile on his face as if he were dreaming of childhood's golden time. (2) Before long the battle begins anew between the desire for life and the power of death, but without victory on either side; and again there is silence. (3) Sleepless, as in a fever delirium, the sufferer sees passing before his inner eye the rosy dawn of innocent childhood, the more daring sport of youth, and the ardent striving of manhood that turns obstacles into stepping-stones to higher things, the storm and stress continuing until the hour of death that now strikes. (4) From heaven descends towards him, resounding grandly, what he had longingly sought here below: World-redemption and world-transfiguration. The programme of *Tod und Verklärung* is not only a more sufficient guide than that of *Don Juan,* but also the most musical of all Strauss's programmes.

(V.) *Till Eulenspiegels lustige Streiche* (Tyll Owlglass's merry pranks). *Nach alter Schelmenweise*—in Rondeau-form. (After the old rogue-manner—in rondo form); Op. 28 (1895; 1895). The 14th century hero of tricks and drolleries, whose fame still flourishes, and whose immortality is secured by words coined after him not only in the German, but also in the French language (*espiègle* and *espièglerie*), is supposed to have been a rustic born at Kneitlingen in Brunswick, who, after a vagabond life in many countries and cursory trials at many trades, died of the plague at Mölln in Lauenburg (four leagues from Lübeck), in 1350. His tombstone may still be seen. It is, however, of the 17th century, but may be the renewal of an older one. The history of his achievements was not written by himself, and when it was written many achievements of others were added to his own. It appeared first in Low German (1483), afterwards in High German (Strasburg, 1515). The latter may be the work of Thomas Murner. Now what has Strauss done with this rude but vigorous and vivacious *Volksbuch?* When Dr. Franz Wüllner gave the first performance of *Till Eulenspiegel's merry pranks* at Cologne, he asked the composer for an explanatory programme. Strauss replied: "It is impossible for me to furnish a programme to Eulenspiegel. Were I to put into words the thoughts which its several incidents suggested to me, they would seldom suffice, and might even give rise to offence. Let me leave it, therefore, to my hearers to 'crack the hard nut' which the Rogue has provided for them. By way of helping them to a better understanding, it seems sufficient to point out the two Eulenspiegel motives [they appear at the beginning of the work], which in the most manifold disguises, moods, and situations pervade the whole up to the catastrophe, when, after he had been condemned to death (a descending major seventh—F to G♭), Till is strung up to the gibbet. For the rest, let them guess at the musical joke which a rogue has offered them." The reason given for his reticence does not carry conviction with it. This the composer seems to have felt himself, and he may also have felt the unwisdom of a policy of concealment. At any rate he subsequently changed his mind, and gave to his commentator Wilhelm Mauke a score in which the names of most of the motives were entered with pencil. Here they are.

(1) Prologue. "Once upon a time there was a rogue. (2) Of the name of Till Eulenspiegel. (3) That was a mischievous sprite. (4) Away for new pranks. (5) Wait! you hypocrite! (6) Hop! on horseback through the midst of the market women! (7) With seven-league boots he makes off. (8) Hidden in a mousehole. (9) Disguised as a pastor he overflows with unction and morality. (10) But the rogue peeps out from the great toe. (11) Before the end, however, a secret horror takes hold of him on account of the mockery of religion. (12) Till as cavalier exchanging tender civilities with pretty girls. (13) With one of them he has really fallen in love. (14) He proposes to her. (15) A polite refusal is also a refusal. (16) [Turns away in a rage.] (17) Swears to take vengeance on the whole human race. (18) Philistine motive. (19) After proposing to the Philistines a couple of monstrous theses, he abandons the dumbfounded ones to their fate. (20) Great grimace from afar. (21) Till's *Grassenhauer* (vulgar street song). (22) [Watched by catch-poles, and collared by the bailiff.] (23) The judgment. (24) He whistles to himself with indifference. (25) Up the ladder! There he is swinging, his breath has gone out, a last quiver. All that is mortal of Till is ended. (26) [Epilogue. What is immortal, his humour, remains.]"

To this has to be added only one remark, namely, that the Straussite commentators hold that the composer had more in his mind than he confessed in the above, that he aimed at something higher than the mere illustration of a rogue's pranks.

(VI.) *Also sprach Zarathustra* (Thus spake Zarathustra), tone-poem (treated freely after Friedrich Nietzsche), Op. 30 (1896; 1896). It seems strange that a musician should go for a subject to a philosopher's book. But going to Nietzsche is not the same as going to Aristotle, Descartes, or Kant. Nevertheless the venture was strange. Zarathustra cannot be numbered with those literary works that yearn for musical treatment. For, although the poetical element in it may be predominant, it is impossible to eliminate the unmusical philosophical element without obscuring and denaturalizing the former. An explanation by the composer hardly improves the situation, as it fails to reduce the amount of philosophy implied. Strauss wrote in 1896: "I did not intend to write philosophical music or portray Nietzsche's great work musically. I meant to convey musically an idea of the development of the human race from its origin, through the various phases of development, religious as well as scientific, up to Nietzsche's idea of the *Uebermensch* [superman]."

Nietzsche's Zarathustra, who has nothing whatever to do with the Persian Zarathustra (Zoroaster), is a superman and a preacher of the gospel of the superman. "Man is a something that must be overcome.

What have ye done to overcome him. . . . What is the ape for man? A laughing-stock or a sore shame. Man must be the same for the superman, a laughing-stock or a sore shame. . . . I conjure you, my brethren, remain faithful to the earth, and do not believe those who speak unto you of super-terrestrial hopes! Poisoners they are whether they know it or not." Apart from what Strauss left untouched, there is this difference between the book and the symphony: Nietzsche brings before us a complete superman; Strauss, one in course of development. As to the contents of the composer's work his expounders are by no means at one. According to Arthur Hahn, Strauss begins with depicting a man who inquires into the solution of the world problem and the riddle of existence, and seeks in vain salvation in religion, in the whirlpool of life, and in science, all of which shows as much Faustian as specific Nietzschian spirit. The symphonist, we are told, depicts for us the development of the higher man to the Zarathustra personality; and his work is an artistic deposit from his subjective meditations and thoughts on Nietzsche and his book. Dr. Arthur Seidl will hear nothing of the "Faustian longing for knowledge," nothing of the stupid wearisome "solution of the world riddle"; but he, too, dwells on the preliminary degrees, the stages of feeling in the process of purification by which the tone-poet leads the growing Zarathustra to the perfection of the superman. But what indications does the composer give us of the programme in his mind? On the one hand, there is a preface, a quotation of the opening of Nietzsche's book, but this is in no way a programme. On the other hand, however, the composer supplies something like a programme by superscriptions that occur in the course of the work. Here they are with a few elucidations in square brackets: (1) Of the Back-worlds Men [the believers in a beyond of the worlds]. (2) Of the great Longing. (3) Of Joys and Passions. (4) The Grave-Song [over his earlier self]. (5) Of Science. (6) The Convalescent. (7) [The Dance Song. The superman has thrown off the burdens of the common man]. (8) The Night Song, or Drunken Song. ["Eternity of all things is sought by all delight . . . So rich is delight that it thirsteth for me, for hell, for hatred, for shame, for the cripple, for *world,* for this world! Oh, ye know it."]

(VII.) *Don Quixote* [Introduction, theme with variations, and Finale]. Fantastic variations on a theme of chivalrous character. Op. 35 (1897; 1898). There is no programme prefixed to this work; and, apart from the title, the composer vouchsafes only two programmatic indications—namely, two superscriptions in connection with the theme: "Don Quixote, the Knight of the Rueful Countenance," above the first half, and "Sancho Panza" above the second. The Introduction may be regarded as a picture of Don Quixote before the days of his knight-errantry, a picture of the state of his mind, full of the ideas imbibed from his beloved romances of chivalry. In the variations are described some of the achievements of the Ingenious Gentleman, Don Quixote of la Mancha. The following programme has been devised for them. How far the composer is responsible for it, I do not know. (1) First Sally, Dulcinea del Toboso, and adventure of the Windmills. (2) Don Quixote charges a flock of sheep, believing them to be the army of the mighty Emperor Alifanfaron. (3) Colloquies between the knight and his squire. (4) Don Quixote's assault of the pilgrims bearing a covered image, which he took for a great lady carried away by force. (5) The knight's watch of his arms. (6) Sancho Panza's assertion that a certain vulgar peasant woman was Dulcinea, and Don Quixote's indignation. (7) Ride through the air, while, with bandaged eyes, they were in reality remaining stationary on a wooden horse. (8) The enchanted bark. (9) Encounter with the two sorcerers, who, however, are only harmless priests. (10) Combat with the Knight of the shining Moon. Finale: Don Quixote's end. These variations are fantasias on a theme, not variations in the original acceptation of the word. This might be concluded, without looking at the contents, from the great differences in the length. But, of course, no one would expect from Strauss Haydn-Mozart variations, which indeed lie a long way behind us, as even Beethoven and Brahms make obvious. It has been said that Strauss's *Don Quixote* was a reaction from the high idealism of *Zarathustra;* but it has also been said that it is something more than a mere series of comic scenes. Here, then, in connection with Strauss's fantastic variations, repeats itself the old discussion about the deeper meaning of Cervantes's book, the fundamental idea of which, according to some, is the eternal contrast between the spirit of poetry and prose, between ideality and reality.

(VIII.) *Ein Heldenleben* (A hero's life), a tone-poem. Op. 40 (1898; 1899). This work has no printed programme nor any other programmatic indications. The ideas in the composer's mind, however, are not difficult to divine or even to understand; and moreover have been indicated by authorized commentaries. The general outline is as follows: (1) The Hero. (2) The Hero's Opponents. (3) The Hero's female companion. (4) The Hero's battlefield. (5) The Hero's works of peace. (6) The Hero's renouncement of the world and perfection. *Ein Heldenleben* has given rise not only to prose commentaries, but also to a descriptive, or rather transcriptive poem, the author of which is Eberhard König. Notwithstanding the realistic battle-picture contained in the composition, and the idealizing and generalizing features in the conception, we cannot be far off the truth in saying that Strauss himself is the hero of *Ein Heldenleben.*

(IX.) *Sinfonia Domestica,* Op. 53 (1904). The dedication is significant: "To my dear wife and our boy." The title and the dedication are the only hints we get as to the composer's programme. This 20th century symphony, which in form and content has nothing of the 18th and 19th century symphony, is a family idyll in which husband, wife, and child are the sole *dramatis personae*. It is a picture-book of domestic portraiture and incidents, conceived and executed with a happy, admiring, and proud husband and father's sympathy and enthusiasm. We might also call it: Family joys, woes, contrarieties, and humours. An interviewer of Strauss relates that it illustrates a day in the family life of Madame, Monsieur, and Bébé. The authorized synopsis of the work (which consists of a continuity of movements) runs as follows:

Introduction and development of the three principal groups of themes: Themes of the husband; themes of the wife; themes of the child.

Scherzo: Parental happiness; the child at play; lullaby (the clock strikes 7 p.m.).

Adagio: Doing and thinking; Love-scene; Dreams and cares (the clock strikes 7 a.m.).

Finale: Waking and merry dispute (double fugue); joyful conclusion.

The time has not yet come for a final judgment on Richard Strauss. In twenty years, perhaps in ten, we shall be able to speak with the calm, if not with the absolute impartiality, which a fair judgment presupposes. As yet the object is too new, too strange, too near, to justify the hope of attaining such a desideratum. A few critical remarks, without any pretension to finality, may, however, not be out of place and unwelcome to the reader.

There are two of Strauss's symphonic poems that have found wider acceptance than any of the others. These two are *Death and Transfiguration* and *Till Eulenspiegel.* As both works are decidedly modern in feeling, form, and means employed, it cannot be said that the people who prefer them are old-fashioned. We have therefore to look for another explanation, and I think we shall find it, in the case of the former work, in the thoroughly musical nature of the subject and in the sincerity of the treatment. *Till Eulenspiegel,* on the other hand, is a *jeu d'esprit,* one of the cleverest and most delightful imaginable, and eccentricities and extravagances would there be readily forgiven if they required forgiveness. The objections made to Strauss's music arise from the increasing admixture of unmusicalness and insincerity in his compositions, which undoubtedly contain so much that is truly beautiful and truly expressive in the best sense.

As every one knows, it is widely believed that the master himself looks upon his tone-poems as huge jokes played upon the public. I have heard many musicians—by no means of the pedantic, reactionary, and milk-and-water kind—express this view with conviction. Strauss denies the insinuation; and, of course, we must accept his word. But it is his own fault that the belief has sprung up and spread. He seems to have an irresistible itch to provoke the amazement and the horror of the multitude. He seems to have retained in him something of the *burschikos* character, something of the young university student, who, revelling, in the belief of his superiority, looks down upon those he calls Philistines and never tires of laughing and tilting at them.

But, alas! the superiority of these young men has mostly no better foundation than self-deception, and the so-called Philistines comprise in reality not only dullards but also wise men, men that know the measure of things and have learned to winnow chaff from grain. Indeed, this feeling of superiority is a rest of childishness that is generally thrown off when the youth becomes a man, or at least when the man reaches years of discretion. The spirit that dictated the extravagances of tone-painting, material and metaphysical—for instance, the cacophonies of the battle in *Ein Heldenleben* and the bleating sheep variation in *Don Quixote,* and the conundrums of *Zarathustra*—may also be seen in an unpublished title and a published note. Strauss originally intended to give *Till Eulenspiegel* this sub-title: "Symphonic Optimism in *fin de siècle* form; dedicated to the 20th century." And a note to a song, which ends a semitone higher than it begins, runs thus: "Singers who wish to perform this little composition before the termination of the 19th century are at liberty simply to ignore the new signature and remain comfortably in the opening key, so as to soothe their artistic conscience in regard to the formal correctness of the conclusion."

The out and out admirers of Strauss, the *enragés,* call this sort of thing *genial,* that is, look upon it as a mark of genius; whereas in reality it is, as has already been said, something very different, which might be euphemistically described as too excessively youthful. However, of the *Kraftgenies,* the storm and stress geniuses, for a while gaped at by the many and exalted by easily inflammable brains, time and history have the habit of making short shrift. But we should not leave un-noted what I am now going to mention. Strauss may say, as many a one has said before him, "Heaven preserve me from my friends." The claims they make for him make him ridiculous. Thus Paul Riesenfeld, who had written a "soul-analysis" of Richard Strauss, writes that the composer expostulated with him, and told him that he had interpreted into him (Strauss) too much philosophy, and thereby had led many a one into the temptation of seeking still more and more philosophy in his works. Indeed, Strauss maintains on the contrary that he is "altogether and always a musician for whom all programmes are only suggestions for new forms and nothing more."

Of course, Strauss, to escape from Scylla, falls here into Charybdis. He exaggerates, I am glad to say. If he spoke quite truly, he might be a musician, but could not be a tone-poet, and the use of the word tone-poem would be a sham. Strauss, however, expressed the same view to a London interviewer who signs himself "C.K." He said: "The poetical programme serves but to give an impulse to the discovery of new forms. The programme is a poetical help in creating new shapes. To use an extreme illustration, one might draw inspiration from this pianoforte stool. You have to find the musical equivalent for the poetical programme." On being asked whether he sketched a definite programme, Strauss replied: "Yes, with a view to giving it musical shape. You must not forget, however, that it is a musician who casts the programme. After all, poetry and music work hand in hand; music may represent any feature of life."

Of course, we cannot hold Strauss responsible for every word of this report; nor is an informal conversation in the course of a crowded day the best mode of setting forth one's aesthetic principles, which setting forth is, even under the most favourable conditions, a most difficult and risky proceeding. But taking the above quotations to be in the main correct, we cannot but be struck by the stress laid on forms and shapes, and the lack of differentiation in the subjects of the programmes. The pianoforte stool, even as an extreme illustration, is an unfortunate example. Perhaps the meaning of the obscure saying is that the composer chooses and constructs his programmes with a view to a musically effective collocation of parts. The following remarks of Strauss's, coming from a tone-poet, are somewhat puzzling, although of course the first statement is supremely true, and should be taken to heart by admirers of the chaotic: "The musical poem must have hands and feet, so to speak; must be ship-shape musically considered. Let him who likes look on it merely as a musical work of art. In *Don Quixote,* for instance, I show how a man goes mad over vain imaginings. But I do not wish to compel any listener to think of Don Quixote when he hears it. He may conceive it as absolute music if it suits him." Strange, a *tone-poet* who does not care whether his ideas are understood or not!

Strauss says truly that a composer must be a master of his craft, must not only have something to say, but also know how to say it. He, however, enunciates doubtful, nay pernicious doctrines when he continues thus: "For me absolute beauty or ugliness does not exist in music. What is truly and sincerely felt, and then faithfully and properly reproduced, is beautiful. Ideas of beauty are constantly changing. I may now directly aim at expressing the ugly in music; the achievement may be considered beautiful ten or fifty years hence. The question is, Does the composer succeed in musically representing what he aims at, even that which is ugly? Therein lies aesthetic justification. Amateurishness is ugly." The concluding part of this statement will be readily accepted. But is masterliness always beautiful? I should say, it may be always admirable, but certainly is not always beautiful. The use of the ugly in art is limited and must be qualified. Not every ugliness is admissible, and every ugliness admitted has to be aestheticized. This calls up a remark of Strauss's on dissonance. He is reported to have said: "What we consider a dissonance to-day, may seem smooth beauty to some of those who will come after us, or appear tame and pallid to others. The taste of the ear varies and changes in development." This is, on the whole, true enough, but the statement does not present the problem fully.

Dissonance is endurable in so far as it is intelligible, that is, in so far as its relationship to consonance is understood (felt) by the hearer. The power of this intelligence is increased by experience. We learn to dispense with the preparation of dissonances, and to put up with delayed resolutions. What is unintelligible to one generation may be perfectly intelligible to another. From this, however, it does not follow that it is impossible to make too great a demand on the endurance and the intelligence of the ear. And, then, dissonance by itself, unrelated dissonance, will always be unintelligible and unendurable. Neither genius nor time can raise dissonance to the independence of consonance. The rules of the schoolmaster can be overthrown, not the laws of nature.

Now, in the notorious battle of *Ein Heldenleben*—to take one of many examples—the composer treats dissonance as independent, self-sufficient, and the unavoidable result is noise not tone, a charivari not music, indeed nothing that even by the greatest stretch of the imagination can be called music. The effect produced is certainly realistic, and Strauss's battle may be more like a real battle than any musical battle picture ever conceived. But *cui bono?* What art-lover is the richer or the better for it? Where is its aesthetic justification? Who wants a realistic reproduction of discord unrelieved by harmony, ugliness unrelieved by beauty? Not the sane and healthy. Besides this specially glaring and especially outrageous case of misapplication of genius and maltreatment of a noble art, we meet with innumerable objectionable cases of a milder and more passing nature—with things that cannot or ought not to be expressed, with ways of expression that are not in accordance with the nature of music, which must obey the law of dissonance and cannot very well do without tonality. As to what cannot be expressed, take, for instance, the conclusion of *Zarathustra*. The contradictory tonalities B major and C major are intended, we are told by the commentators, to signify a purely intellectual concept, the world problem still facing man at the height of his knowledge and wisdom. But the music is not the expression of the thought at all, for thought and expression have here only one subsidiary quality in common, that of opposition and exclusiveness.

In short, Strauss has made use of an arbitrary non-conventional symbolism, which leaves the hearer unlimited freedom of interpretation. Regarded as absolute music, the passage in question cannot be defended; it is justifiable only by a poetic idea—but this idea should be at least guessable, and if it is not, ought to be verbally indicated by the composer. Strauss, ignoring the laws of dissonance and tonality, has, however, not only written series of dissonant intervals and chords, and any consecution of keys, he has also done what goes far beyond these ventures, he has even combined different keys simultaneously (like D and E♭), has combined what of necessity is mutually exclusive. If in this way a *valuable* effect is produced without the hearer becoming conscious of the device, its legitimacy might *perhaps* be admitted for discussion; but if the hearer becomes conscious of the device, discussion is out of the question and no words of condemnation can be strong enough. Strauss has furnished cases of both kinds.

Related to the abuse of dissonance is the mania for increasing the orchestra, chiefly for the purpose of making it more uproarious and ear-splitting. In a *Heroic* Symphony we may perhaps find excuse for 4 flutes, 3 oboes, *cor anglais,* 3 clarinets, 1 bass clarinet, 3 bassoons, 1 double bassoon, 8 horns, 5 trumpets, 3 trombones, 1 tenor tuba and 1 bass tuba, a strong force of percussion instruments, and the usual strings; but we cannot help wondering at the employment in a *Domestic* Symphony of even a greater number of instruments—including, besides the strings, 2 harps, 4 flutes, 2 oboes, 1 oboe d'amore, 4 clarinets, 1 bass clarinet, 4 bassoons, 1 double bassoon, 4 saxophones, 8 horns, 4 trumpets, 3 trombones, 1 bass tuba, 4 kettle-drums, triangle, tambourine, glockenspiel, cymbals, and big drum. There must be something wrong here. The suspicion of mania arises quite naturally. The disproportion between means and subject is ridiculously extraordinary. Not long ago I read a letter of a composer who clamoured for more instruments in the orchestra, in order to obtain a greater variety of colour. The public, which is getting tired of colour and nothing but colour, begins to clamour for design, above all for ideas. Moreover, variety and beauty of colour depend more on treatment than on number. Study the great masters of the brush, oh ye ambitious musical colourists! You will see that their greatness is not calculable by the number of colours on their palettes.

The root of the mischief with Strauss and other composers of to-day is in the false ideal they worship, in that boasted modernity, of which there is a particular German species. The fundamental fault of it—in music perhaps more than in literature and the other arts—is extravagance in thought, sentiment, and imagination, in line, mass, colour, sonority, and form. The worshippers of modernity regard as commonplace and unworthy of the attention of any but Philistines, the normal, natural, healthy, simple, temperate, graceful, harmonious, and well-balanced; and take delight in the abnormal, eccentric, morbid, complicated, violent, delirious, grotesque, swaggering, strutting, flamboyant, noisy, colossal, wildly jagged, and even monstrous. Modernity, not Nietzsche, is the parent of the superman, and the music that boasts of its modernity is his music. As to that magnificent superman—with the abolished God, the transvaluation of all values leading to a beyond of good and evil, and the ultra-individualism of the strong and its *Herrenmoral* that is a law unto itself—he is but a poor, pitiable creature, a weakling with a swelled head. These moderns would say something never said before and say it in an altogether new manner. This, no doubt, is the highest an artist can achieve. But it cannot be done by will, it must come spontaneously. No excess, no extravagance can make up for the want of spontaneous originality, nay, it will even kill or spoil the originality that exists. Force and freedom are noble qualities, but the former should not be brute force brutally exercised, and the latter should be freedom to do good, not to do evil. Notwithstanding the truths and half-truths of Nietzsche's work, notwithstanding the beauties and half-beauties of Strauss's, the former as philosophy and the latter as music are as a whole indigestible. At best each is, historically considered, but yeast for leavening or lymph for inoculation. In itself it is corruption, disease. Nietzsche ended his life in a lunatic asylum. For Strauss may be predicted a better fate—a phase of full maturity and perfect sanity.

There have been and there are composers who speak disdainfully of an existing style, simply because they are without the talent and training that would enable them to succeed in it. They are in the position of the fox in the fable who called the grapes sour that hung too high for him. Strauss is not one of these. He has proved by his early works that he can write effectively in the old style, and he has proved by his newer works that he has the stuff in him to develop that style. This we see from the heightened expressiveness of his music, emotionally and descriptively, and from the virtuosic and truly masterly handling of all the resources of the art. Consequently we look upon him with hope and great expectations, and implore him not to throw away his pen, not to return to earlier methods, but to proceed onward in a soberer spirit and a more single-hearted manner, in short, to commence his third period, where will be manifested the natural Strauss, purified from the dross that still clung to the gold in the second period.

QUESTIONS

1. Name a number of literary sources used as a basis for program music. How many titles of Shakespeare's plays can you find in the titles of musical compositions?
2. If you were a composer, how would you express musically the idea of love? hate? laughter? birds in the trees? Are these ideas expressible? Do you think you could be trained to express these ideas? If so, how?
3. Niecks tells us there are three main types of program music: those essentially descriptive, emotional, and symbolical. Can you give illustrations of any of these types?
4. What distinguishes Richard Strauss's first dozen or so compositions from his later ones? The answer may be had simply by studying the titles of his work. What can you tell from these titles?
5. Of the Strauss works Niecks described, which "program" seems to you to have the greatest appeal? List the nine works in order of their interest for you. Give reasons for your choices.

PROGRAM MUSIC / 2 *Nationalist music has been called the people's popular serious music. Practically every composer has tried his hand at nationalist music, some devoting most of their compositional efforts toward this end. Nationalist music (as a type of serious music) makes a special appeal to those who have difficulty in grasping the spirit and nature of music that is essentially abstract. Music with a "national" program is strongly akin to program music in general and may, in fact, be considered as program music. Homer Ulrich, musicologist and head of the music department at the University of Maryland, is the author of five books on music. He is not only a scholar but also a practicing musician, having played bassoon with the Chicago and San Antonio symphony orchestras.*

The National Schools

HOMER ULRICH

THE ART OF MUSIC IS IN A CERTAIN SENSE analogous to a language; indeed, it has often been called a "universal language." Two closely related possibilities of furthering the analogy may be noted: a language may be spoken with personal or regional accents, or even with different dialects; and out of its dialects new languages may be formed—somewhat in the way that the several Romance languages developed out of Latin. A glance at music history reveals how the first of these possibilities was realized. Composers from Haydn to Schumann "spoke" with a German accent, so to say, but remained within the language through the universal appeal of their utterances. At the same time such diverse composers as Rameau, Rossini, and Chopin "spoke" respectively with French, Italian, and even Polish idioms and inflections, yet remained universal. The music of these composers recaptured in an intangible way something of the national characteristics, spiritual sense, and personal aspirations of their respective people.

In the second half of the nineteenth century other groups of composers went some distance on the path of the second possibility, namely that of creating regional languages out of the universal tongue. Their method was to make overt use of their own folk songs, idioms, dances, and legends and to transform the universal aspects of the language to fit the new expressive material. These composers, unlike those of the first group, were active in geographical areas where political oppression or personal subjection were the order of the day—notably Russia and Bohemia. This tendency to employ indigenous materials is called "nationalistic" in music. Nationalism represents in a sense the pugnacious, self-assertive denial of a cultural inferiority; it is a form of artistic self-consciousness.

Certain necessary preliminaries to the formation of musical nationalism took place in earlier decades. The urge, in the late eighteenth and early nineteenth centuries, to preserve folk songs on a national basis had resulted in many collections of source material. The composers of that time had shown how the material might be used. Haydn and Schubert had turned in a few works, for example, to Hungarian Gypsy idioms; Beethoven had on occasion quoted Russian tunes; and both Haydn and Beethoven had interested themselves in folk songs

---

THE NATIONAL SCHOOLS from *Symphonic Music* by Homer Ulrich; copyright 1952 by the Columbia University Press. Reprinted by permission.

of the British Isles. And now the nationally minded composers in the period after about 1860 found it necessary to consider the musical worth of their own material in order to utilize and exploit their respective folk heritages. This was doubly desirable; for many composers of the time, faced with the tremendous accomplishments of Haydn, Mozart, and especially Beethoven, and unable to meet those giants on their own terms, were thus forced to express themselves on a smaller, more intimate scale.

A national music does not come into being as soon as folk materials are employed, however; for an essential part of national self-expression consists of unveiling the nation's soul in the music. This requires a composer of genius who, if he is to write music that will hold its own upon the universal scene, must present a universally significant content even though it is couched in national idioms and, perhaps, in national forms and color. The earliest of such composers were Michael Ivanovich Glinka (1804-1857) among the Russians and Bedřich Smetana (1824-1884) among the Czechs. Glinka in his operas, *A Life for the Tsar* (1836) and *Russlan and Ludmilla* (1842), introduced Russian, Polish, and oriental colors, painted a succession of brilliant nationalistic pictures, and made liberal use of Russian melodic and rhythmic idioms. The overture to *Russlan and Ludmilla* has survived on the concert stage. It is, however, not typical of the opera itself; its Italian brightness and energy as well as its universal humor and melodiousness are scarcely representative of Glinka's essential nationalism. Truly Russian orchestral music did not emerge until later in the century; it will be discussed in due course.

Smetana, on the other hand, was active in the orchestral field and was the creator of a Czech national music. His earliest works in the field, however, gave only faint promise of that accomplishment: the three symphonic poems written between 1858 and 1861 were inspired by western European literature and reflected the composer's admiration for the music and methods of Liszt. Theme transformation and a quantity of sequence repetition characterize these forgotten works. From 1863, after several years spent in Gothenburg, Smetana lived in Prague and was active in supplying the Czech National Theater with repertoire material. In eight operas, among them the well-known *Bartered Bride* (1866), he disclosed his fondness for Czech legend and literature and placed a great variety of folk songs and dances upon the operatic stage. More importantly, however, he revealed the Czech temperament in all its rhythm, color, and emotional vitality. These operas are nationalistic even when they do not embody folk songs. Yet at the same time the universal appeal of *The Bartered Bride,* for instance, is felt keenly; its characters are human beings, and a close relationship exists between Smetana's style and the lyric style of the Viennese masters, particularly Schubert.

His great contribution to symphonic literature is the cycle of six symphonic poems with the collective title *Má vlast* ("My Country"), written between 1874 and 1879 in spite of his complete loss of hearing. Here Smetana strove to recapture the spirit of Bohemia itself. The cycle is compounded of legend (*Vyšehrad* and *Šárka*), history (*Tábor* and *Blaník*), and description of landscape (*The Moldau* and *From Bohemia's Fields and Groves*). The Vyšehrad motive, quoted at the beginning of the cycle, is employed throughout the first poem and is mentioned in the second as well as the sixth; it plays little part in the thematic materials of the others, for one may do no more than trace a faint resemblance (based upon a sequence of falling intervals) between the motive and subsequent themes.

All six poems of the cycle are devoted to revealing the glories of the Czech heritage; it is this poetic idea rather than the Vyšehrad motive which unifies the cycle. Within each of the six symphonic poems, faint echoes of Liszt's practices are heard; a considerable amount of theme transformation is undeniable, and each work is divided into several sections which are often marked by contrasting tempos. Yet the sections of each work constitute in effect a four-movement connected symphony; and the harmony, the melodic and rhythmic elements, and the general color of the cycle are Smetana's own and hence stand for the Czech national style. Polkas and other dances appear on occasion—but also, notably in the love scene of *Šárka,* a breadth of melody that is closely akin to Wagner and has little in common with Czech idioms.

Smetana, like many others who adhered to the ideals of the neo-German party, depended upon poetic stimulus for his musical inspiration. Without relying upon realistic description or departing from clear, well-organized forms, he yet remained faithful to his programmatic ideas. Never obscure, always melodious or rhythmically alive, Smetana was content to remain on a somewhat local, intimate level. He showed little interest in posing problems of universal emotional significance and solving them musically. Thus he cannot be reckoned among the Promethean composers whose music benefits a larger group. It is perhaps inevitable that outside his own country *The Moldau* is the only work of the *Má vlast* cycle to have survived in the standard repertoire.

Antonín Dvořák (1841-1904) was far more prolific in the orchestral field and composed in a greater variety of forms and styles than Smetana. Influenced in turn by virtually all the great composers of the nineteenth century, he consistently returned to a fresh, problem-free expression and a love for his Czech homeland after each digression. In nine symphonies, five symphonic poems, several concertos, and almost two dozen miscellaneous works for orchestra, Dvořák disclosed a gift for pure melody and a grasp of the relationships between form and content unequaled by his nationalistically minded contemporaries.

Dvořák's nationalism is not outwardly as perceptible as that of Smetana—at least not in the orchestral works; nor was his interest in literary stimulus and programmatic content as consistent. The majority of his symphonies are in the sphere of abstract music. They are dedicated to presenting attractive, forceful, and contrasting melodies in forms which are basically those of the early nineteenth century. Occasionally a symphonic movement suggests dance rhythms or is an outspoken dance form—notably the *furiant* which serves in place of a scherzo in the so-called "first" symphony. But actual quotation of folk songs is held to a minimum. It is rather the Czech spirit, with all its impulsive alternation between gaiety and gloom, with its rhythmic vitality and physical energy, that comes to expression.

The first four of Dvořák's symphonies were not published during his lifetime; the remaining five, along with many works in other categories, were arbitrarily treated as to chronological order and opus number by his publishers. Thus one ordinarily gains a distorted view of Dvořák's development as a composer. The great maturity and considerable technical mastery revealed by the first symphony, for example, are truly astonishing—unless one realizes that it is actually his sixth work in the form.

Early works—insofar as they are available, and including categories other than the symphonic—reveal a Dvořák who was greatly attracted to the style of Wagner. Free, expansive forms and long, flowing melodies set in a rhapsodic manner are typical. A period in the late 1870's saw him greatly concerned with Czech folk materials; this phase is seen in the four *Slavonic Rhapsodies* and in the first set of *Slavonic Dances* (originally for piano four-hands, but later orchestrated), all of which were written between 1874 and 1878. The F-major symphony of 1875 makes lesser use of national elements, it is true; yet its slow movement is closely allied to the Slavonic and melancholy *dumka*.

About 1877 Dvořák was befriended by Brahms and became, in a sense, the latter's *protégé*. Thereupon he tended to shake off the earlier influences, develop his own style, and follow a musical ideal which in many ways resembles that of his great contemporary. The D-major symphony gives evidence of the program-free, eloquent, and logical manner of Dvořák in the 1880s; it is a joyous, sparkling work. And yet the A-minor violin concerto of about the same years reveals a free, rhapsodic expression combined with unmistakably nationalistic elements in a form which owes much to Liszt. Conversely, the *Scherzo capriccioso* of 1883 represents Dvořák at his imaginative and formal best. Cast in the form of a scherzo with trio, but containing long developments and brilliant transitions, it is a breathless, effective—and difficult—movement for large orchestra. The work deserves to be restored to the high place in the repertoire it once enjoyed.

With the D-minor symphony of 1884-1885 Dvořák reached new heights. Here is a "universal" work, as opposed to a national or purely personal one; the emotional scale of this symphony is far above any other of his orchestral compositions. From a technical point of view, he revealed himself here to be a master of thematic manipulation devoted to intense emotional expression; only Brahms among his contemporaries could write more concisely and logically. It is unfortunate that the D-minor symphony is not as well known as the ever-popular "New World."

The G-Major symphony of 1889 marks a complete contrast to the foregoing. For here is an easygoing collection of unrelated material, developed without any great emotional compulsion. Enjoyable in the manner of virtually all of Dvořák's music and containing a few enchanting passages, it cannot compare with the symphonies which precede and follow it. A cycle of three related pieces from 1891-1892 may be mentioned here. At first united under the title, "Nature, Life, and Love," the pieces were later issued as overtures with separate titles: *In Nature's Realm, Carnival,* and *Othello.* Bound together by a pastoral motive which appears at appropriate moments in the works, they mark a return of the programmatic element to Dvořák's music. The *Carnival,* especially, has retained its place in the repertoire; it brings to expression the composer's exuberant spirit and mastery of orchestration.

The E-minor symphony, the ninth of his works in this form, was written in 1893 during the first year of Dvořák's stay in the United States; its subtitle, "From the New World," is thus justified. As he had done elsewhere, he expressed the spirit of a people—this time the American people instead of the Czech, of course, but American as reflected in the life of the Czech community of Spillville, Iowa—without quoting folk melodies. A deliberately naïve air pervades the themes of this work; its melodies are not so much developed as repeated, and sequence repetitions and routine climaxes play a larger part here than in any other of his major works. This type of treatment is perhaps made necessary by the shape and content of the themes; the latter are in the main scarcely adapted to true symphonic treatment, and one may be sure that Dvořák was aware of this. For, almost as if to compensate for this type of theme elaboration, he makes a bow to sophisticated cyclical form: themes from the first movement appear in the second and in the third, and the coda of the fourth quotes liberally from all three preceding movements. The symphony as a whole is a brilliant, effective, and satisfying work; but it is not the most significant of Dvořák's compositions.

The B-minor cello concerto of 1894-1895 also belongs to the American stay; but his third year in the United States found Dvořák homesick. One may surmise a loss of interest in the American scene, and this is reflected in the romantic, somewhat melancholy tone which predominates in the concerto. A colorful, rhapsodic work resulted, one which exploits the solo instrument's technical possibilities without exceeding the bounds of good taste. It remains one of the most attractive works in the cello repertoire.

Dvořák's interest in program music was revived after his return to Prague. In 1896 and 1897 he wrote no fewer than five symphonic poems. The immediate stimulus was a collection of folk ballads. Terror, death, and fantasy are characteristic of the ballads he selected, yet he exercised great restraint and thematic economy in setting them to music. These works have not held their place in the repertoire; they are mentioned here only to give evidence of Dvořák's uncertainty as to his true mission as a composer.

An eloquent melodic quality shines through all of his works; in a sense, his lyric gifts were akin to Schubert's. His instinct for form and proportion was as highly developed as his melodic sense, and he possessed a technical ability and an imagination which allowed him at all times to balance these opposites. Extreme contrasts, embracing abrupt changes from dark melancholy to wild joy, are typical of his music; yet such contrasts are usually justified by the contexts in which they appear. Seldom did he allow mediocre passages to remain in his works; his self-critical sense was almost as keen as Brahms's. It is only by comparison with the very greatest—with a Beethoven or a Mozart, say—that the personal, subjective nature of his emotional palette is revealed. In all respects save those of profundity and eternal significance, Dvořák must be ranked among the finest of nineteenth-century composers.

To express Russian life and feeling, following the work of Glinka and Alexander Dargomijsky (1813-1869), became the underlying purpose of a group of enthusiastic musical amateurs who came under the influence of Mili Balakirev (1837-1910). The latter, together with Alexander Borodin (1833-1887), César Cui (1835-1918), Modest Moussorgsky (1839-1881), and Nicholas Rimsky-Korsakov (1844-1908), formed the nucleus (called "The Five") of a nationalistic school which exercised a great influence upon later generations of Russian composers.

The technical training and musical abilities of this loosely knit group were so varied, however, and their central purpose was so vaguely stated, that little solid, systematic work came from their respective pens.

Balakirev, largely self-taught, became interested in teaching and conducting; his compositions are few, and his function was principally that of acting as a gadfly to the others. Only Rimsky-Korsakov felt it necessary to pursue organized musical study later in life. The main preoccupation of the others seems to have been the composition of operas; and it is in the operatic field that their true worth as nationalists and musicians is to be measured. In every case, the quantity and quality of their purely orchestral works falls below their operas. Since none of Cui's works have survived in the repertoire, the following discussion will concern itself only with Borodin, Moussorgsky, and Rimsky-Korsakov.

In Borodin one encounters an element which runs through much Russian music: economy of thematic material, and with it, deliberate, monotonous repetition of melodic fragments. We have seen this in Tchaikovsky. This trait is not to be looked upon as a weakness in Borodin, but as the expression of an aesthetic creed different from that of German composers since Haydn. Borodin had demonstrated his ability to write along Classical lines and to develop themes in the German manner in his first symphony, in E-flat major, composed in 1862-1867. In the second, however, the repetitive method is fully revealed. The symphony is in B minor, was written between 1872 and 1876, and is his most important orchestral work.

A striking motive heard at the very outset impresses itself upon virtually the entire first movement. The few bits of contrasting melody that are introduced play little part in the structure of the whole; rather is there a constant dwelling upon or reflecting upon the first motive. Outwardly in sonata-form, in that the principal divisions of that form are well marked, the movement develops little thematic conflict. The scherzo is an orchestral tour de force in which themes are of minor importance; a few melodic fragments do appear, but they become lost in the rich, kaleidoscopic orchestral color. The slow movement is more orthodox and expresses something of a melancholy, quasi-oriental character that has, since Borodin, been taken to reflect the Russian temperament. The finale is a series of vivid, exciting episodes, based in part on contrasting themes but unified by the unfailing brilliance of the orchestral sound. Harmonies are free throughout the symphony, and a typical alternation of barbaric and intimate moods gives the work much of its national character. A third symphony was left incomplete at Borodin's death.

It is remarkable that the second symphony should be so closely knit both in structure and intention; for it was written across a four-year interval, was interrupted by work on other compositions and by Borodin's scientific studies and medical-administrative duties. There is a certain similarity in all of his works, it is true, in that his melodies are generally of folk-song type and tinged with oriental color, and that constant repetition with changed orchestration is the chief organizing principle. This basic similarity may be seen when two other orchestral works are compared to the symphony: the ever-popular set of "Polovtzian Dances" from the unfinished opera, *Prince Igor,* and a small symphonic poem, *On the Steppes of Central Asia,* the latter written in 1880.

Moussorgsky is even more sparsely represented in the orchestral literature than Borodin. A single composition, *A Night on the Bare Mountain,* is his principal representative. It was designed originally (1860) as incidental music for a lurid drama called *The Witches;* it suffered many modifications at the composer's hands (including one version for piano and orchestra, and a place in two operas) and, about 1882, at Rimsky-Korsakov's. Its present form as a symphonic poem is largely the work of the latter. The thematic material of the work is unified by a harsh, macabre quality which goes far toward carrying out the implied program—an orgy of witches and grisly apparitions, finally dispersed by the chimes of the village bells. The material and framework are Moussorgsky's, the sequence and arrangement Rimsky-Korsakov's. But the fantastic nature of the composition, its dramatic transitions, and its sheer excitement are undeniable, regardless of the author. *A Night on the Bare Mountain* is not, strictly speaking, within the body of nationalistic music. It does, however, testify to Moussorgsky's interest in Russian legendary subjects, an interest which animates the greater part of his operas.

Pictures from an Exhibition was originally a set of piano pieces composed in 1874; it was orchestrated about 1922 by Maurice Ravel, and in its new dress has added considerable luster to Moussorgsky's name. The ten pieces are descriptive sketches, and several of them are connected by a "promenade," a short interlude which represents the composer moving from one picture to the next. Quite apart from Ravel's masterly orchestration, the set reveals the depth of Moussorgsky's insight, his vivid imagination, and his forward-looking harmonic sense.

Rimsky-Korsakov, the youngest of "The Five," served a double function. As musical executor of Moussorgsky's fragments and unfinished works he prepared a number of compositions for practical performance; and as the most industrious and best-trained musician in the group he wrote more systematically and in greater quantity than his colleagues. About a dozen Russian historical and legendary subjects were made into operas and performed during his lifetime. But more than a dozen orchestral works were written also; several hold respected places in today's symphonic repertoire. One of them, *Antar,* began its career as Rimsky-Korsakov's second symphony in 1868, was revised and reorchestrated several times, and emerged finally in 1903 as a symphonic suite of four movements. It is constructed somewhat on the Berlioz model: it is a programmatic work, it contains a basic motive or *idée fixe* which appears in each movement, and it brings to expression four episodes in the adventures of the legendary Antar, an Arabian poet and desert hero. The movements describe Antar's encounter with the queen of the fairies, and his moods of revenge, power, and love, respectively.

Three compositions of 1887-1888, however, are the works upon which Rimsky-Korsakov's orchestral fame is most largely founded. A *Capriccio espagnol* was at first planned as a fantasy on Spanish themes for violin and orchestra—perhaps to serve as a companion piece to the *Fantasy on Russian Themes* for the same instrumental combination, completed in 1886. That plan was discarded, and the *Capriccio* was composed as a virtuosic set of five movements for orchestra. The composer was careful to point out that the brilliance of the work lay in the structure of the themes and in the piece itself: "It is the very essence of the composition, not its garb or orchestration." His considerable knowledge of instrumental idioms and technical possibilities, gained in part as an inspector of naval bands, stood him in good stead; he knew the difficulties and inmost nature of the instruments as perhaps no composer before him. As a result, the many gay, wild, or sentimental tunes in the *Capriccio* are well adapted to form an orchestral work of the greatest effectiveness.

The symphonic suite, *Scheherazade,* followed directly upon the *Capriccio.* For its literary subject-matter Rimsky-Korsakov turned again, as he had done for *Antar,* to the *Arabian Nights.* The suite is based upon the story of the sultan Schahriar, who is diverted from his habit of murdering one of his wives each night by the charm and narrative ability of Scheherazade. The movements are entitled "The Sea and Sinbad's Ship," "The Tale of the Kalendar Prince," "The Young Prince and Princess," and "Festival at Bagdad." Two themes run through the suite: a hard, brutal one, carried by full orchestra and symbolizing the sultan; and a suave, florid cadenza for violin and harp, representing Scheherazade. The themes appear in the manner of Berlioz's *idée fixe,* either to introduce the various movements or at significant moments within. It may be pointed out that the transformation of the sultan's theme in the course of the work represents the gradual weakening of his murderous resolve; the composer has written character sketches of the two protagonists rather than drawn simply a series of brilliant, fanciful oriental pictures.

The richness of color and orchestral mastery which characterize all of Rimsky-Korsakov's larger works are nowhere so clearly revealed as in

Scheherazade. An orchestra of standard, pre-Wagnerian dimensions sufficed him; yet he achieved a great variety of sonorous, delicate, massive, and even overwhelming effects. Like his contemporaries, he was much given to thematic reiteration and showed little interest in developing themes to provide closely knit forms; but the monotony dangerously inherent in this practice is avoided by the flexibility of his orchestration. Indeed, the virtuosity he revealed in this respect became something of a weakness. One becomes surfeited with the constant change of color and sound, one realizes that in Rimsky-Korsakov such elements are ends in themselves. Of all the Russian nationalists, he was perhaps the most effective in a superficial sense, yet his dramatic ability did not compare with Moussorgsky's, for example, or his perception of form and proportion with Borodin's. He possessed a full measure of sentimental and lyric qualities; yet these are often overlooked because of the exciting, forceful expression which is seldom absent from his music.

The remaining composition of 1888, called *Easter Overture* and *Russian Easter* among other variants, is essentially a fantasy on Russian liturgical themes and is designed to contrast the gloom of the days preceding Easter with the joy and merriment of Easter Sunday itself. A slow and somber introduction, in which a chantlike theme is presented in company with florid cadenzas for a solo violin, leads directly into an allegro that is brilliant, dark, and majestic in turn. Several themes, all suggestive of liturgical moments, are treated in Rimsky-Korsakov's usual manner: fragmentary repetition with changed orchestration. A large percussion section in which bells are featured adds to the festive mood of the final portion, and the composer's purpose of depicting the rejoicing on Easter is well achieved. The *Russian Easter* is a satisfying composition.

The type of symphonic suite introduced by Rimsky-Korsakov is found in the works of many Russian composers of a later generation. One of these is by Michael Ippolitov-Ivanov (1859-1935), a pupil of the former and for some years a conductor in Tiflis, the chief city of Transcaucasia. His familiarity with the music and topography of the region came to expression in the *Caucasian Sketches,* a suite of four descriptive movements. An array of Georgian (hence, partly oriental) melodies gives pictures of the mountains, villages, and mosques of the area, and a pleasant but scarcely significant work results.

The movement toward musical nationalism in the Scandinavian countries was neither as vigorous nor as productive of lasting results as in Russia and Bohemia. Further, leading Scandinavian composers were usually sent to Germany for their education; there they came under the influence of the German Romantic tradition and remained largely in its thrall. Niels Gade (1817-1890), the foremost Danish composer of his time, was typical in this respect. He became essentially a transplanted Mendelssohn "speaking" with a mild Danish accent. Sweet sentiment, a graceful style, and a narrow emotional range characterize many of his works—eight symphonies and several overtures among them. But an essential lack of virility and an avoidance of dramatic conflicts in those works have doomed them to virtual oblivion.

Edvard Grieg (1843-1907) was alone successful among Norwegian composers in impressing his individual yet nationalistic style upon the international concert stage. Two orchestral suites, arranged from music composed for Ibsen's play, *Peer Gynt,* about 1874-1875, have become universally popular. They reveal Grieg's full mastery of smaller forms and disclose the lyricism which was his outstanding characteristic; the eight pieces which constitute the suites are filled with charming melodies set to colorful and piquant harmonies. Grieg was primarily a composer of mood pieces in which a faint air of melancholy predominates; such moods come to full expression in the *Peer Gynt* music as well as in the suite, *Aus Holbergs Zeit* (a set of piano pieces arranged for string orchestra), and in the incidental music to *Sigurd Jorsalfar.*

Grieg, like many other composers of his time, received his training at Leipzig; Schumann's poetic, short-breathed style remained of great influence upon him. The fresh, open-air, and rhapsodic aspects of that style left their mark principally upon the A-minor piano concerto, composed in 1868—the work which best represents Grieg in the repertoire of today and which is one of his very few compositions in large form.

The concerto is representative of nationalism in that it breathes the spirit of Norwegian folk music. Folk songs as such are not quoted; but the subtle, often modal harmonies, the melodic lines which have a contour all their own, plus the dark and melancholy moods which prevail—these are national in their color and effect. The restraint and economy typical of Grieg elsewhere are less evident in the concerto. Forceful, brilliant, and even exuberant passages abound, and the virtuosic solo part is in the best Romantic tradition. In common with nationalists of other lands, Grieg showed little interest in thematic development and structural logic. Sequence repetitions of the kind found in Czech and Russian music are found to an even greater degree here—the material so repeated being Norwegian rather than Slavic, of course.

The first and last movements of the concerto are vigorous and are compounded of many short melodic fragments; the middle movement is songful and is based largely upon a single melody. But regardless of tempo and type of treatment, warm lyric qualities are seldom absent. It was Grieg's great accomplishment to develop a unique, truly personal style; its basis is a type of melody that hovers about the fifth of the scale rather than the keynote, and a piquant harmonic system. These, together with his penchant for sequences and his fragmentary, episodic forms, give Grieg's music an individuality possessed by few other composers. It is that individuality of style plus the eloquent and attractive melodic material which raise the concerto to its high place as one of the best-liked concertos in the repertoire.

The Spanish folk-music heritage, perhaps the most colorful in western Europe, was even later in coming to the notice of significant orchestral composers than any of the foregoing. And it is ironic that three French composers were among the first to include Spanish idioms in their larger works. Bizet, in his opera, *Carmen* (1875), had recaptured the characteristic melodic patterns, the inexorable rhythms, and the intense expression of Spain. At about the same time, Edouard Lalo (1823-1892) introduced a synthetic Spanish quality in his *Symphonie espagnole,* a five-movement concerto for violin and orchestra. The vivid orchestral colors as well as the exotic themes and rhythms of this work provide it with a picturesque quality that justifies the title in part. In the finale of his D-minor cello concerto of 1876, Lalo quoted a Spanish folk song; and many passages in the two other movements are filled with a type of rhapsodic expression that suggests the same national temperament. And finally, Emmanuel Chabrier (1841-1894) composed *España,* a rhapsody for orchestra, in 1883; this work is overtly Spanish in all its rhythmic and melodic aspects.

To such composers, who appropriated a national idiom purely for its qualities as entertainment, one may scarcely attribute a desire to solidify or preserve Spanish folk culture. And the Spanish-flavored works of such composers are, with the exception of *Carmen,* purely occasional pieces. To this group we may add Rimsky-Korsakov's *Capriccio espagnol,* discussed above. Not until about 1885-1890, in the time of Isaac Albéniz (1860-1909), was the basis for a Spanish national school established. Albéniz was active primarily in the field of piano music, however; significant orchestral composition are not to be looked for before the end of the nineteenth century.

Nationally minded composers continued to appear in the years after 1900, both in the countries already spoken of in this chapter and in other regions even more remote from the larger cultural centers. Indeed, one of the striking facts about the early twentieth century is that national musical interests continued to be served no less strongly than they had been in the period after about 1860. The works of many such composers were purely of local interest; as such they cannot be discussed here. Other nationalistic compositions have won and held places in the standard repertoire. They give evidence that national and universal appeal are still as compatible as they were in the music of Dvořák, for example, and that national idioms and dialects had not, in the nineteenth century, reached the limits of their respective expressive possibilities.

QUESTIONS

1. What makes a "patriotic" piece of music patriotic, when the music has no words? Can you give several examples of such pieces?
2. Do you think there is any relation between folk music and the music discussed in the preceding essay? What do they have in common? What are the differences?
3. What does Ulrich mean when he says, "Nationalism represents in a sense the pugnacious, self-assertive denial of a cultural inferiority; it is a form of artistic self-consciousness." Paraphrase this sentence and discuss its implications.
4. Ulrich says that Dvořák's "New World" Symphony "is not the most significant of Dvořák's compositions." Yet in America it is undoubtedly one of his most performed, most popular work. Can you suggest any reasons for this seeming disparity?
5. Can you name any American nationalist composers? Do we have any works by Americans comparable to Smetana's *The Moldau,* or Moussorgsky's *A Night on Bare Mountain,* or Grieg's *Peer Gynt* suite?

FORM / 1 *Unlike the materials of science, the materials of music are essentially the same now as they were in the nineteenth century. This fact becomes evident when we know that Albert Lavignac (1846-1916) wrote this essay over sixty years ago. What he had to say about the structure of music is just as valid now as it was then. In 1871 Lavignac became a member of the faculty of the Paris Conservatory of Music, where he taught sight-singing, ear-training, music dictation, and harmony. A six-volume work completed in 1882 covered the various techniques of taking musical dictation and resulted in dictation becoming a part of the standard curriculum in all music schools. Later, Lavignac edited the famous, standard reference,* Encyclopédie de la musique et Dictionnaire du Conservatoire.

INTRODUCTION TO FORM

ALBERT LAVIGNAC

THOUGH TREATISES UPON MUSICAL COMPOSITION are not unknown in catalogues, no man has ever written a work which teaches how to compose good music. A work of that kind, if such there were, might be abridged into two words: *have genius.*

With genius alone, it is possible to create grand and beautiful works; instances of this are not unknown; but how long and painful is the labour! The true condition for the production of healthy, robust works is to be able to unite with genius the treasures of acquired talent, of technic, and of erudition.

If the reader will take the trouble to make some brief investigations, he will very soon become convinced that all the great masters who have done honour to the art of music are, above all, *great thinkers,* very learned in their own technic, but also very thoroughly versed in scientific or literary studies; philosophers of a high rank; in short, men who have something to say or to teach, new thoughts or grand emotions to communicate.

Genius is to art what the soul is to the body, the nonmaterial principle which gives it life and governs it.

This is genius, which study can sometimes contribute to develop, but can never create in the individual who is not endowed with it by nature; it is without doubt a natural gift, this faculty of conceiving and creating new forms which have the power of producing feeling in other minds. We shall never have classes in inspiration; and still, inspiration is contagious in a certain measure, and to frequent the society of men of genius, of great artists, is at least to favour its development if the germ exists latent in the soul.

On the other hand, talent is never inborn, but is acquired only by study, with the aid of time. The musician who has talent but lacks the spark of genius, may write well, may even attain a certain nobility of style, especially if he possesses the faculties of observation and assimilation; but he is evidently dependent upon his predecessors and employs only their procedures. If he attempt anything original, it appears at once that he is doing this by an effort, not spontaneously.

Talent is the necessary outfit for genius; the better the tools are, the more thoroughly genius can trust itself to them, and the more unhampered are its manifestations.

INTRODUCTION TO FORM from *Music and Musicians* by Albert Lavignac; Henry Holt and Co.; 1899.

The man of genius *is in advance of his time;* he breaks out the path in which later those will walk who have admired him or, perhaps unconsciously, have felt his influence. For this reason he is rarely understood at first; he speaks a new language, we may say unknown by the public, to whom are addressed finally the manifestations of art; but once this same public has learned through him—more or less willingly, more or less rapidly—the new speech, it readily understands the men who follow this master, gleaning in his fields, exploiting what he has discovered. Hence the great successes of estimable artists of second rank, while the true genius is most frequently misunderstood in his time. Nor is this true in music only.

Since, then, genius is not taught, and scarcely can be defined, it is useless to speak longer about it; on the other hand, we can study the means of acquiring talent; these means are chiefly observation and practice.

By *observation* is meant the intelligent study, by hearing, reading, and analysis, of the great works of different epochs and of all the schools. This analysis must occupy itself first and chiefly with the general form of the work, its plan and its proportions, then with the conduct of the modulations, finally with the minute details peculiar to each master.

The restricted scope of this work does not permit me to multiply examples. I will give, however, a few instances of this analysis, selecting them among the best-known works, which every student can easily procure.

By *form,* I mean the general plan of a work, the great outlines of its architecture, omitting the details of its working out, which belong to the domain of harmony or of counterpoint. The form thus regarded is the great framework, the musical skeleton; and if I insist upon this definition, it is because I believe it indispensable for the comprehension of what is to follow. Just as the form of a sonnet may be described thus: "Two quatrains, followed by two triplets," which in no way decides the length of the lines and leaves a good deal of freedom in the arrangment of the rhyme, so musical forms have their elasticity and no more determine the number of bars than the number of notes. We speak here only of the general and comparative dimensions of a musical discourse, whose scheme we are now examining.

The principal important typical form of instrumental music is the *Sonata.* This is generally a work written for one instrument; when composed for two instruments, it is called a *duo;* for three, a *trio;* for four, a *quartet;* for five, six, seven, eight, nine, a *quintet, sextet, septet, octet, nonet;* but the general form remains the same. The Sonata for an orchestra is a *Symphony,* and when one instrument has solos, accompanied by the orchestra, the composition is called a *Concerto.* Because of its importance we shall now describe the Sonata form in all its purity as it has been bequeathed to us by the classic composers.

The Sonata is a succession of movements of different characters, destined to be heard consecutively: the first and last must be in the same key, the other movements in related tones, or in those so selected that the change of key will not offend the ear.

Every Sonata regularly constructed contains a first movement called the *Allegro;* a slow movement, the *Andante* or *Adagio;* and an animated *Finale.*

Between the first and second movements, or between the second and third may be introduced a short piece—a *Minuet, Scherzo,* or *Intermezzo.* Such is the general scheme.

The first movement, the foundation of the Sonata, is required to have a certain construction which is its characteristic. It is made up out of two themes, two musical ideas: the *first subject,* and another phrase, generally of a graceful melodic nature, called the *second subject* or "character phrase." It is divided into two parts: the first must begin in the principal key, and end in the key of the dominant; (if the principal key is minor, the first part may end in the relative major); the second part brings about a return to the principal key.

We will now examine the first part. After the theme has been announced and the principal tonality well established, a short episode leads to a cadence upon the dominant; by the device of equivocal chords, this dominant is considered as a tonic, and in this new key (the key of the dominant), which will persist till the end of the part, is presented the second theme; a new episode and a short coda follow, and this part is ended. The classic usage is to repeat it, probably that the listener may thoroughly grasp the two principal themes and lodge them in his memory.

We now come to the *second part.* This may begin in many ways. Here the composer is at liberty to give the freest scope to his imagination, and venture into remote tonalities, but without forgetting that the subject must be brought in again and presented a second time, just as it was before, in the same key, and ending in the same cadence upon the dominant; here, however, there is no change of tonality, the dominant remains the dominant, and it is in the principal key, not again to be abandoned, that the second theme makes its second appearance. Then follow another episode, having only very brief modulations or not any at all, a coda strongly affirming the tonality, and the final conclusion, the peroration. . . .

The Andante has a less clearly defined form. It is perhaps a mere Romance with its setting; it may be a theme with variations, as Mozart and Haydn often made it; and then there are the great Andantes of Beethoven, great Romances with many varied strophes, when each repetition of the theme is more and more richly ornamented; of this we have a model in the Sonatas, op. 22, and op. 31 (in G), in the Septuor, and in many Symphonies; finally, it may be nothing more than a simple introduction, longer or shorter, preceding the *Finale* and connected with it.

For the *Finale,* the usual form is that of the *Rondo,* which may be thus conceived: a *principal theme* presented *three, four,* or even *five* times, more or less adorned or varied, each repetition being separated from the preceding one by an *episode,* the whole ending with a *coda,* making the conclusion.

The musical form, the *Rondo,* is derived from the poetical form, the *Rondeau,* in which a first verse forming a sort of refrain is repeated at regular intervals. The first Rondos were undoubtedly the musical setting of Rondeaux; then this plan became introduced and acclimated into the instrumental style. . . .

Haydn and Mozart have often given the example of finales not shaped as Rondos, but in the form of the first allegro, from which they then differ only by the gay and sportive character of the principal theme.

The little accessory pieces, the *Minuet* and *Scherzo,* have also their classic form, which is the same for both. They differ in character and movement, the Minuet being always in 3/4 time, and having the ceremonious grace of the dance which it represents; the Scherzo (from the Italian *scherzare,* to joke) is light and sportive. It may be in 2-time or 3-time, but always in lively movement.

Their plan is most simple. A first part, very brief, ending either in the principal key or in that of the dominant, or else in the relative, so as to be taken up again; and a second part, often rather longer and finishing invariably in the principal key, form the bulk of the Minuet or Scherzo. Then comes the Trio, built in the same way as the Minuet, with two repetitions also, the Trio being in the same key, or in a related key, or in some other which was well-suited; for after the Trio, the Minuet came again, but this time without repetitions. All this is a matter of tradition. Exceptionally, there are sometimes two Trios, separated by a return of the Minuet. In this case it is usual to write each in a different key. Also there may be a Coda.

The *Intermezzo* has no determinate form. These little pieces are *hors d'oeuvre* of the Sonata. They fill a part like that of the ballet in an opera; they are a moment's diversion, after which the action goes on. I believe that Haydn and Boccherini were the first to introduce the Minuet, and Beethoven produced the first Scherzo; the Intermezzo is of more recent date.

There are many irregular Sonatas, in which the author strays from the classic plan while still preserving its spirit. Examples of this are the Sonata in C♯ minor, op. 27, one of the grandest conceptions of Beethoven's genius, which begins by an Adagio, followed by a very short Scherzo, the Finale taking the form of a first Allegro; also by Beethoven, the Sonata in A♭, op. 26, of which the first movement is an Andante with variations; the Sonata, op. 7, of Mendelssohn, whose four parts are connected without a break, the Finale ending by a recall of the beginning of the Allegro, like a snake biting its tail; Schumann's famous Quintet, whose peroration is a fugue in which the principal theme of the Allegro has the part of the subject, and that of the Finale, of counter-subject. There are many others among the great compositions, but they must all be regarded as exceptional, or, properly speaking, as works of free fancy conceived in a style resembling the Sonata, only bearing its name, however, for lack of any more accurate designation.

I have already said that all the great works of *chamber music,* from the *Duo* to the *Nonetto,* disclose the same plan.

In the Symphony it remains unchanged, but in larger proportions. The episodes are developed at greater length, the modulations are sometimes bolder; but the general conduct of the musical discourse, and the grand divisions remain the same. Who has not observed, moreover, that the great Sonatas of Beethoven, his Trios, give the impression of real Symphonies without an orchestra, whose missing instrumentation can be conjectured as in a faithful transcription?

The only frequent addition to the Symphony is that of an *Introduction* in a slow tempo, serving as prelude to the first movement, then taken up at once, as in the Pathetic Sonata of Beethoven, which thenceforward follows its regular course.

The Andante, the Scherzo or the Minuet, and the Finale, conform to the plans we have already described.

We now come to the *Concerto.*

Here the identity of design is a little more difficult to recognise, without, however, being doubtful on that account. The *Allegro de Concerto,* instead of being divided like that of the Sonata into two parts, of which the first is repeated, is divided into three *soli,* each preceded by a *tutti,* necessary to give the solo-player rest, to allow him to see that his instrument is in tune, if it be a violin or a 'cello; or, if he plays a wind instrument, to give him time to shake out the moisture condensed in the tubes—a proceeding not elegant, but unavoidable.

The *first solo* is like the first part of the Sonata, announcing the theme in the principal key, then going on towards the dominant to give the second theme, and concluding in the same key.

The *second solo* corresponds to the beginning of the second part; it consists in modulated developments drawn from the two themes, in ingenious passages, unforeseen combinations often foreign to the subject, surprises, and the like.

The *third solo* corresponds to the remainder of the second part from the reappearance of the first theme to the *coda finale*. Towards the close of this last solo, or separated from it by a short *tutti,* is a pause on the dominant, indicated by a hold. At this place, the performer, if he be an improvisatore as well, is at liberty to introduce a *cadenza* of his own, which may vary from a few passages showing his skill as a player, to a developed paraphrase of the whole Concerto. (The *cadenza* is an undoubted vestige of the traditions of the Italian school, where all vocal solos terminate thus.) The *cadenza* ended, the orchestra resumes and concludes.

The proportional length of the *tutti* has never been settled. In certain Concertos, the first *tutti,* preceding the entrance of the solo-performer, has almost the importance and the form of the first part of a Symphony; in others, it is but a few measures, as if merely to call attention and impose silence; lastly, it is sometimes totally omitted, and the virtuoso attacks, alone and at once, the first solo.

Of the *Andante,* nothing need be said; it is the same as that of the Sonata.

(The Concerto does not include the Minuet; some modern attempts have been made to introduce the Scherzo.)

The *Finale* is generally conceived in the Rondo form, but always varied with *tutti,* whose utility is not merely to give the solo-performer a few minutes of rest, but also, by silencing for a short time the timbre of his instrument, to give interest to its return.

Like the *Allegro,* the *Finale* may contain a *cadenza,* intended to display the skill of the virtuoso. . . .

More frequently still than in the Symphony and the Sonata, it happens that the composer writing a Concerto makes sacrifices to virtuoso display, and adopts a free form, departing from the traditional plan in order to bring out the qualities of the solo instrument or of the player; this is a matter of course. The two Concertos of Mendelssohn for the piano, the same composer's Concerto for the violin, the *Koncertstück* of Weber, are remarkable examples of exceptional forms. When the rôle of the orchestra has such importance that the solo instrument is no longer preponderant, appellations like this appear: *Concerto-Symphonique* or, even, Symphony with Viola solo, like the *Harold* of Berlioz, etc. Also there have been written *Symphonies Concertantes* for two instruments with orchestral accompaniment; there is even by Beethoven a triple Concerto for piano, violin, and violoncello (op. 56), which is never played, I know not why, for it is a very remarkable work. These are hybrid styles, connecting links, so to speak, between the Concerto and the Symphony, which as such are very interesting to study.

I have gone into such detail in respect to the form of the Sonata and kindred compositions, because of its preponderance in all the instrumental domain, from the mere solo for the harpsichord, piano, or violin, up to the complete development of the symphonic forces; but this type, important though it is, is not the only one that the student should know.

Another orchestral form is that of the *Overture,* which also it will be useful to analyse, although it is now but seldom employed (it would not do to take as a type the Overture of the *Magic Flute* which is an admirable symphonic Allegro in fugal style).

The Overture is midway between pure symphonic art and musical dramatic art, and derived from both.

Its object, usually, is to prepare the spectator for the emotions of the drama which is about to be performed in his presence, by placing him in the mood most suited to receive the impression vividly. Hence it is very often constructed out of the material of the work itself, or filled with allusions to its principal themes; sometimes, indeed, it becomes a veritable *Fantasia* upon the opera or opera-comique to which it serves as instrumental prologue. Its form cannot be fixed in advance, since it especially is modelled in accordance with the *scenario* of which it is but the prelude and commentary.

It is also needful to study the form of the operatic *Aria* at different epochs, although it is in the modern current no longer to write in this particular form. The Aria may have one movement or more; and many examples may be found in the famous scores which are vastly simpler to analyse than Sonatas and Symphonies. Also one must examine the construction of grand *Finales* of acts, and *ensemble* pieces in the various schools; they are more complicated and the differences are greater, but really require only time and some degree of a spirit of observation. It is well to know the manner and characteristic rhythm of the old dance-music, that one may not make such absurd blunders about them as, for instance, a *valse* in four-four time would be, or a march *prestissimo.* The following are some of these dance forms:

In duple time there are:

The *Gavotte* (2/2), in a moderate *tempo;* it has two sections and a trio, like a minuet, and each phrase begins with the up beat; the trio is quite frequently treated like a musette, or piece for the bagpipe.

The *Tambourin* (2/2), a very lively movement; it is divided into sections of 4, 8, 12, or 16 bars each, as a rule commencing with the up beat; the rhythm of the bass imitates a tambourine.

The *Jig* (*Gigue*) (6/8), very lively; the strains are of eight bars.
The *Sicilienne* (6/8), moderate; each beat is generally in a rhythm of dotted eighth, sixteenth, eighth.
The Auvergnaise *Bourré,* the Rigadoon; its general plan is like that of the tambourin, but with different scansion; each member of the phrase begins on the weak part of the up beat.
The *Allemande* (2/2 or 2/4), a lively rhythm, but a little heavy.

In triple time:

The *Minuet,* described in the Sonata form.
The *Galliard* (*Gagliarda*), gay and spirited, though not rapid.
The *Polonaise,* stately and elegant, having this peculiarity, that each phrase and member of a phrase ends on one of the up beats.
The *Chaconne* (*Ciaccona*), very rhythmic and not very rapid; it is a long series of variations, forming as it were, couplets.
The *Saraband,* slower than the minuet.
The *Courante,* slower than the saraband, notwithstanding its name.
The *Paspy* (*Passepied, Passa-mezzo*), still more lively than the galliard; the sections beginning on the up beat.

Either double or triple measure:

The *Passacaille* (*Passacaglia*), much resembling the chaconne, but with slower tempo.
The *Pavan,* a stately dance of Italian origin.
The *Musette,* whose bass is a pedal point single or double, but constant, like the drone of the instrument whence its name; when it is introduced as a trio in a gavotte, it is necessarily in duple time; etc., etc.

Many I omit; indeed it would be impossible to mention all. I do not think there are any dance-forms in quadruple time, which seems reserved for *marches;* on the other hand, solemn or religious marches have often been written in triple measure, and it is worth noting that the slow movement gains a special dignity from the fact that the stress comes alternately on the right and the left foot, as in the *polonaise.*

It must not be inferred from what has now been said, that every composition should as a matter of course be run in a known and adopted mould. Far from this, the composer remains at liberty to create new forms, and, as a matter of fact, good or bad he does create, every day; this is one of his functions, one of his duties. When they are good, these forms make themselves a place and remain, as new types, a lasting addition to the domain of art.

QUESTIONS

1. Is it possible to understand traditional forms without understanding the terms "tonic" and "dominant?" Why?
2. Look up the terms "binary" and "ternary" in a music dictionary. How do they apply to musical forms? Can you give an example of a binary form? a ternary form?
3. When we see the title *Sonata in C♯ minor,* what does the *C♯ minor* mean? If the sonata is in three movements does the C♯ minor refer to all the movements? Does it refer to any of the movements? Which?
4. What is the essential difference between the traditional first-movement form as found in a symphony and in the first movement of a concerto?
5. Can you suggest why we count three when dancing a waltz and two, or four, when dancing a fox trot? Can you think of the names of some other dances and their meter? Which do you think came first, the dance or the music for the dance? Why?

FORM / 2 *The problem of form in music is perhaps the most difficult for non-music students to grasp. Definitions of various musical structures, like the structures themselves, are frequently cast in abstract terms. For this reason even the interested student often sees these terms only as labels—words which mean little to him except as the names of things. In the training of their musicians the U.S. Navy School of Music has recognized this difficulty and has tried to present to its musicians a digest of forms in simple, straightforward terms that would lead them to a better understanding of the music around them. The following survey is from the Navy Training Course text,* Basic Music.

A DIGEST OF FORM

U.S. NAVY SCHOOL OF MUSIC

BEYOND CONSIDERATIONS OF MELODY, RHYTHM, AND harmony in music is the concept of musical form or structure. Form is the way in which a composer organizes what he has to say in a manner which will make it possible for the listener to understand the music, especially if the composition is longer than a minute or so.

Musical form depends upon unity and variety: unity to impress the listener that the music is organized, meaningful sound rather than nonsense; and variety, to sustain interest, to relieve boredom, and to provide contrast.

Unity is achieved by repetition, either exact or modified, of a musical idea. Variety comes about by using new material, or by using the original musical idea in such a transformed manner that the transformation itself gives contrast.

Repetition is two-fold: (1) the repetition of a short motive used in such a way as to build phrases, and (2) repetition of the phrases themselves, or of larger parts of the composition.

THE MOTIVE. As used by most significant composers, the motive is a short, meaningful melodic fragment which contains, in essence, the musical idea of the whole composition.

QUALITIES OF A MOTIVE. The significant aspects or qualities of the motive, and the way in which these qualities may be varied include the following:

1. The notes themselves. They may be varied by changing the order (a-b-c-d becomes b-a-c-d, b-a-d-c, etc.); by extension (a-b-c-d becomes a-b-b-c-d, a-a-b-c-d-d, etc.); by contraction (a-b-c-d becomes a-b-c, b-c-d, a-b-d, etc.); by extension and contraction (a-b-c-d becomes a-b-b-c, etc.)

2. The intervals. These include the melodic intervals making up the motive, and in addition the interval from the lowest to the highest note and the interval from the first to the last note. These may be varied by changing the quality (c-g, a perfect fifth, becomes c-g flat, a diminished fifth); by changing the size (c-f, a fourth, becomes c-a, a sixth); or by inversion (c-e becomes e-c). If successive changes are used, systematically increasing or decreasing the interval, but always in the same direction, one can speak of "developing" the interval.

3. The melodic curve. In general, a motive may go up, down, or zig-zag. The direction of the melodic curve may be changed by contrary

---

A DIGEST OF FORM from the United States Navy School of Music Training Course, *Basic Music*. Reprinted by permission.

motion (c-e-g-a becomes g-e-c-b) or by the use of retrograde (reverse) motion (c-e-g-a becomes a-g-e-c).

4. The rhythm. This may be changed by augmentation (all notes in twice the original value, or in some other multiple of it); by diminution (all notes in half, or some other fraction, of the value); by shifting the rhythm pattern in such a way as to reverse the positions of accents; by introducing, or omitting, or extending, or shortening the upbeat.

5. Transposition. The motive, or any of its variations, may appear on any degree, or in any key, that is appropriate to the musical purpose.

Phrases may be built on a succession of variants of the motive. These may overlap, and can, of course, be adapted to any immediate necessity, such as the establishment of a cadence, the chord of the moment, or the requirements of imitation.

PHRASE. The phrase is a unit of musical structure, roughly corresponding to the length of the breath, or to that of a line of poetry. Normally, the phrase extends through four measures of moderate tempo, but three-measure phrases and five-measure phrases are not infrequent. The phrase ends in a cadence of greater or less finality, depending upon the function of the phrase in the composition as a whole.

PERIOD. The period is made up of two phrases, the antecedent (first) phrase and the consequent phrase. Frequently the first phrase ends in a half cadence and the second in a perfect cadence, but this feature depends on the musical purpose. If the two phrases begin alike, the period is in parallel construction. Structures of the same type, but larger, such as the double period and the period of three phrases, are met with occasionally.

CHAIN OF PHRASES. Frequently a larger part is built up, not in period structure, but in a more or less loosely organized chain of phrases, which may be separated by cadences, but which frequently show *elision* of the cadence (the last chord of one phrase is used as the first chord of the next) or *dissolution* of the cadence (the harmonic progression is characteristic of a cadence, but the rhythm is not interrupted; the cadential measure is broken up into notes of small value). Phrase chains are frequent in the expositions of sonatas by Haydn and Mozart.

Musical Forms

THE COMBINATION of the various elements of music into understandable and interesting structures constitutes musical form. Much music falls into types, or musical forms, which resemble each other sufficiently to have acquired names; and a knowledge of these names and of the structural patterns they represent is essential to well-rounded musicianship.

However, it must be understood that these are forms and not formulas. While from the standpoint of theoretical analysis it would be convenient if musical compositions were all in clearly defined categories, with no overlapping, composers have never cooperated. A genuine composer uses set forms only to the extent consistent with his own purposes and has no hesitation in modifying existing forms or creating new ones.

A convenient broad classification of forms separates them into two groups: homophonic (one-voiced) forms and polyphonic (many-voiced) forms. In homophonic forms, the music is set forth in divisions called parts, and the texture usually consists of one prominent voice, the melody, which is accompanied by other voices which are subordinate to the melody. The usual plan is melody, bass, and one or more voices as "filler." Polyphonic forms, on the other hand, have a degree of independence in the voices, no one of which is consistently more important than any other. The linear divisions, or sections, are less clearly defined, and the musical meaning is made apparent by the interplay of the various voices. The differences will become more apparent to the student if he analyzes various examples, and if he becomes familiar with the list of forms which concludes this chapter.

HOMOPHONIC FORMS. Homophonic forms are classified into small forms and large forms, on the basis of relative complexity of structure, rather than on absolute length.

Small forms are built up of parts, which are simple in structure (period, double-period, or phrase-chain). These are arranged in two ways: the two-part song form (A, B) and the three-part song form (A, B, A). The letters are applied to the parts for identification, so that a two-part form consists of one idea which ends away from the tonic and a second, different part which returns to the tonic and so achieves balance. In three-part form, the first part (A) is followed by a contrasting part (B) with a return to the original idea. The (A) part of a three-part form either ends in the tonic, or leads, in its restatement, to a coda which establishes the original key and brings the composition to a close.

In the large forms, the individual parts are themselves small forms. Accordingly, the large form represents two levels of organization. For example, a rondo may have the form A-B-A-C-A-D-A, in which A is three-part form, a-b-a, and the other parts may be similarly complex.

The most important small forms are these:

- Two-part song form, A-B
- Three-part song form, A-B-A
- Minuet or scherzo, A-B (or A-B-A); C-D (or C-D-C); A-B (or A-B-A)

The most important large forms are:

Variation forms (A, A_1, A_2, etc., where A is complex)
Rondos: small rondo A-B-A
old (or second) rondo A-B-A-C-A-D-A
new (or third) rondo A-B-A-C-A-B-A
Sonata-allegro: exposition-development-recapitulation.

The sonata and the suite are forms made up of two or more (typically four) movements, each of which may be a large form.

All forms mentioned above are discussed in greater detail in the list of terms to follow.

POLYPHONIC FORMS. Counterpoint is the art of composing music by combining melodies. The music which results is known as polyphonic (many-voiced) music. This technique of composition was used almost exclusively from the time of the earliest music for more than one voice (shortly before 1000 A.D.) to the middle of the 18th century. After a period of emphasis on harmonic technique in the late 18th and the entire 19th centuries, counterpoint is again in the 20th century characteristic of the work of many important composers.

Certain musical structures have emerged which are called polyphonic, or contrapuntal, forms. These include the canon, the motet, the madrigal, and the Mass, as vocal forms, and the chorale prelude, the fugue, and the suite (in the sense of the classical set of dances of Bach's time) for instruments. Canons are also written for instruments. Occasionally a fugue is used as a movement in a sonata or a symphony, for example the Finale of Mozart's C major (Jupiter) Symphony. Each of the forms listed in this paragraph is discussed in some detail in the list which follows.

List of Terms

THIS LIST contains a brief discussion or identification of many of the terms used in connection with musical form. For more complete information, standard reference works should be consulted.

ALLEMANDE. A classic dance in 4/4 measure, moderately fast, usually with an eighth-note upbeat. See *Suite* (1). The name means "German dance."

ANTHEM. A piece of sacred choral music used in the service of Protestant churches, sung by the choir, rather than by the congregation. It is usually accompanied by the organ and may contain solos by one or more voices, and concerted passages for solo voices (duets, trios, or quartets).

ARIA. A solo song, occurring in an opera, oratorio, or cantata, which develops a dramatic, lyric, or emotional high point in the work. Unlike the recitative, it does not usually advance the action of the plot. In the 18th century, the aria normally consisted of an orchestral introduction, a long section for the accompanied solo voice, a section in contrasting key and style, and a reprise of the entire first section. For this reason, it was frequently called the "da capo" aria. Some composers, including Gluck, Wagner, and Debussy, did not maintain the difference between the aria and the recitative, but used a mixed technique, partaking of both declamation and expressive song.

ARIOSO. A style of solo song in opera or oratorio, resembling both the recitative and the aria. It maintains the careful treatment of the text characteristic of the recitative, but it is likely to be melodious, and to preserve something of the symmetry and key unity characteristic of the aria. Wagner's music dramas make wide use of the arioso.

BAGATELLE. Literally, a trifle. The name was applied by Beethoven and others to short piano pieces, usually in song form.

BALLAD, BALLADE. (1) A simple song. (2) A narrative poem, set to music, such as Schubert's *Erl-King*. (3) A piano piece, orchestral work, or choral work, which is patterned after the above definition. Chopin's four ballades for the piano are examples.

BASSO OSTINATO. Literally, an obstinate bass. A variation form in which a bass-line of 1, 2, or 4 bars is repeated over and over, with changing harmonies and melodies above. There are a few entire pieces of this sort, but frequently the basso ostinato occurs as one section of a larger work, for example in measures 118 through 128 of the last movement of the first symphony of Brahms.

CADENCE. An interruption to the movement of music, usually at the end of a phrase. The interruption is put into effect by one or more of the following devices:

(1) *Duration:* The final chord of the cadence, or at least the melody note, is comparatively long.

(2) *Melodic movement:* The final melody note of the cadence is an inactive tone.

(3) *Metrical position:* The final note of the cadence is usually in a strong metrical position, frequently on the first beat of the measure. However, a reverse may be true, in which case the cadence is called a feminine ending.

(4) *Chord progression:* The chord progression of the cadence is such as to give the feeling of repose.

Types of cadences: The harmonic element of the cadential effect is so important that cadences are usually classified according to harmonic progression:

(1) *Perfect authentic cadence:* V-I or V_7-I, both chords in root position, with the root of I in the highest voice. This is the usual formula for ending a piece, and is often preceded by a $I_{6\text{-}4}$ chord.

(2) *Perfect plagal cadence:* IV-I, sometimes used independently, but most frequent as the "Amen" sung after the last verse of a hymn.

Perfect cadences are sometimes called "full closes."

(3) *Imperfect cadence:* A weak form of the perfect authentic cadence. The chord progression is V-I or V_7-I, but one or the other of the chords is inverted, or the soprano note of the last chord is not the root.

(4) *Half cadence:* A cadence ending on V or on III of minor keys. Half cadences may also end on other degrees, but not the tonic.

(5) *Deceptive (or interrupted) cadence:* A special kind of half-cadence, in which the listener's ear is prepared for a perfect authentic cadence, but the final chord turns out to be some chord other than the tonic. (Examples: V-VI; V-IV).

CANON. A composition for two or more voice-parts, in which each of the parts in turn presents the identical melody (called the subject) in a way dictated by the first voice, and by the conventions adopted for the canon. The canon is the strictest of the contrapuntal forms using imitation.

Canons are described by the number of voices and the number of subjects. A canon 3 in 1 is a canon for three voices using one subject. A canon 4 in 2 is for four voices, using two subjects.

Canons may also be described by the interval of imitation and by the distance (in time) between the entrance of the subject and the beginning of the imitation. A canon may be written at the octave (fifth, sixth, etc.) after two measures (one beat, four measures, etc.)

A canon which returns to its starting point is a perpetual or infinite canon. A canon which has a definite close is a finite canon.

Imitation may be direct, but may also be in inversion (or contrary motion), in augmentation, in diminution, or retrograde.

Canons are usually independent, but may be accompanied by one or more voices which do not participate in the imitation.

CANTATA. Originally, a piece of music for singing, as contrasted to a piece to be played on instruments (sonata). Now the term usually refers to a sacred or secular work for soloists, chorus, and orchestra, something like a short oratorio or an opera not intended for action. Bach wrote more than 200 cantatas for performance in the Lutheran service before the sermon.

CAPRICE, CAPRICCIO. A fanciful and irregular sort of composition written in free style, resembling the *fantasia.*

CASSATION. A name applied by Mozart and others to some serenades, or suites, for various instrumentations, probably intended for outdoor performance.

CHACONNE or PASSACAGLIA. A composition consisting of a set of variations derived from a ground bass 4 or 8 measures long, usually in triple meter. Originally dances of Spanish origin, the chaconne and passacaglia have become the framework of some of the finest music of some of the greatest composers, for example: the *Chaconne* from Bach's D minor partita for violin alone, the *Passacaglia in C minor* by the same composer, Beethoven's *Thirty-two Variations in C minor,* Chopin's *Berceuse,* and the Finale of Brahms' Fourth Symphony. Some theorists make various distinctions between the chaconne and passacaglia as forms, but analysis of the music fails to show any consistent difference.

CHORALE. The German hymn developed by Martin Luther. It is of great musical importance because it became the basis of much German music up to the middle of the 18th century, especially in the chorale prelude for organ, and in the cantata. Bach harmonized about 400 of these traditional melodies and based much of his church music on them.

CHORALE PRELUDE. An elaboration of a chorale melody for the organ, used in the Lutheran service as a prelude to the singing of the chorale by the congregation. Fine examples were composed by Bach and Brahms, among others. The form is also sometimes called chorale elaboration or chorale figuration.

CONCERTO. A large work for soloist with orchestra, in the form of a sonata or symphony. It ordinarily consists of three movements, the first being in sonata-allegro form with a double exposition (a *ritornello* for orchestra and a second statement of the themes by the solo instrument), a slow second movement, and a rapid and brilliant third movement, usually a rondo. Nearly always the first movement has at the end of the recapitulation a six-four chord with a fermata, at which point the orchestra stops and the soloist plays an extended brilliant passage called a *cadenza* elaborating on the themes of the movement. Cadenzas may also be introduced at appropriate points in the other movements. Originally, cadenzas were improvised by the soloist, but Beethoven began the practice of writing them out exactly as he wanted them played. Today, the practice of improvising cadenzas has almost died out.

CONCERTO GROSSO. A form originating in the late 17th century, in which a small group of solo instruments (the concertino) is set against a larger body of accompanying instruments (the concerto grosso, sometimes called the ripieno). Handel, Torelli, Bach (particularly in the

Brandenburg Concertos), and Locatelli were great masters of this form. There has been a revival of interest in the concerto grosso in the 20th century in the work of Bloch and others.

COURANTE. A classic dance in rapid tempo, usually with 3/4 or 6/4 measure, with an upbeat of one quarter-note or three eighth-notes. The name means "running dance." See *Suite* (1).

DESCANT. (1) A term used after the 12th century to denote any kind of polyphony. (2) In modern usage, a countermelody, usually florid, superimposed above the principal melody of a chorale.

DEVELOPMENT. In the sonata-allegro, the section between the exposition and the recapitulation, consisting of a working out of fragments of the themes presented in the exposition, frequently using modulation. The development ordinarily ends with a retransition to the principal key, introducing the main theme.

In the fugue, the section after the exposition. It elaborates the subject by one or more of the following means: modulation, stretto, augmentation, diminution, fragmentary treatment, invertible counterpoint (with one or more counter-subjects).

DIVERTIMENTO. A type of suite typical of the late 18th century, written for various small instrumental combinations and intended for outdoor performance. There is no real difference between serenade, cassation, and divertimento in this sense. All were for much the same purpose; all have typically more than four movements; and none has the high degree of organization characteristic of the quartet and trio of the period.

DOUBLE FUGUE. A fugue with two subjects. These may be presented in various ways: (1) Subject A and subject B may be introduced together in two voices; (2) Subject B may appear as the first contrapuntal associate of subject A; and (3) The fugue may have a complete exposition of subject A, followed by another exposition displaying the association of the two subjects. Triple fugues are also possible.

DUO, TRIO, QUARTET, SEXTET, etc. Specific names, depending upon the number of participating musicians, for classical sonatas for instrumental ensembles. Duos or duo sonatas are usually for two string or wind instruments, or for one string and one wind. A duo sonata for piano and another instrument is ordinarily called by such names as a sonata for violin and piano, or for clarinet and piano, or even a sonata for piano with violin accompaniment (this was the title used by Mozart and Beethoven). In such works all parts are coordinate and of substantially equal importance.

EPISODE. In a fugal work, an interlude between statements of the subject. An episode may be for the purpose of bringing a section of the work to a close, in which case it is sometimes called a codetta (coda for the final cadence); or it may serve to modulate to a new statement of the subject in a different key; or it may have no other purpose than to provide for formal balance.

ETUDE. Basically, a piece written for the practice of some particular technical difficulty. As such, the etude is likely to have a repeated figure which contains the technical difficulty occurring throughout the composition. Some etudes are of sufficient musical value to have attained the stature of concert pieces, for example the *Etudes* of Chopin and Liszt and the *Symphonic Etudes* for piano of Schumann.

EXPOSITION. (1) In fugal works, the first section of the work, in which the subject is stated by each of the voices in turn, each statement after the first combined with the counter-subject or other appropriate counterpoint, and ending in an episode which leads to a cadence introducing the development. The cadence is frequently weakened by elision or may be dissolved. (See *Cadence*.)

(2) The first large section of a sonata-allegro, in which the main theme and subordinate theme are presented in contrast with each other, ending in a cadence in a related key, which ushers in the development.

FANTASIA (FANTASIE, FANCY). A name given to various kinds of composition which agree in being free in style, not restricted to any definite form.

THE FIGURE. The figure resembles the motive to the extent that it is a short group of notes. It differs from the motive, however, in that it serves only a subsidiary purpose, as an accompaniment.

FOX TROT. A term applied to a piece of music usually written in 4/4 or 2/2 meter played by a modern dance band for ballroom dancing.

FUGATO. A passage in fugal style appearing in a non-fugal composition. For example, a single variation in a set of variations may be a fugato; a concerted piece or a chorus in an opera or oratorio may be a fugato.

FUGHETTA. A short fugue.

FUGUE. Probably the most important of the techniques of contrapuntal writing. A fugue is a composition, usually for a fixed number of voices, either vocal or instrumental, in which a melodic idea, or subject, is treated by imitation in all the voices, and in which the imitative sections are separated by episodes.

Properly speaking, the fugue is not a form, because no two fugues are alike in structure. The formal aspect of any fugue depends on two factors: (1) the characteristics of the subject itself, whether it is suitable for stretto, or for statement in contrary motion, or can imitate itself in augmentation or diminution, and other similar considerations, and (2) the skill and imagination of the composer. However, some generalizations can be made, which should be verified by the analysis of a number of fugues.

The first section of a fugue, or *exposition,* states the subject by each of the voices in turn, alternating between statements in the tonic and in the dominant. The statements in the dominant are called *answers.* This procedure sets up a basic conflict which does much to produce the tension necessary to give drive and impetus to the work. As the second and other following voices state the subject or answer, the voices which have already entered proceed in counterpoint. If the counterpoint (or contrapuntal associate) is used consistently, it is called a counter-subject; if it is used invariably it is a second subject, and the fugue is a double fugue (see *Double Fugue*).

When all the voices are in, an episode, usually derived from the subject, leads to a cadence in a related key. This cadence closes the exposition, and introduces the development, which exploits the capabilities of the subject and its combination with itself and with other material of the exposition in whatever ways the composer thinks appropriate. There may be more than one development section, each exploiting a particular technique.

The final section of the fugue is the recapitulation, which may restate the subject in only one outside voice in the tonic, but which may introduce the subject in each of the voices in turn, in stretto, if feasible, to heighten the excitement, but usually in *repercussion* (that is, the statement of the subject by all voices in a different order of appearance from that of the exposition).

GALOP. A lively dance in 2/4 measure. Example: Galop from *Orpheus in the Underworld,* by Offenbach.

GAVOTTE. A dance consisting of two lively strains in 4/4 time, usually with an upbeat of two quarter-notes. It sometimes alternates with a musette, which is a gavotte over a drone bass, an imitation of bagpipes.

GIGUE (GIGA). A classic dance in 6/8 or 12/8 measure, in rapid tempo. The second part usually begins with the inversion of the main theme. See *Suite* (1).

IMPROMPTU. A piece in free style, as though improvised. Actually, an impromptu is likely to be a song form or a small rondo in spite of its name.

INTERMEZZO. An interlude; a piece of instrumental music between the acts of an opera.

INVENTION. A name used by Bach to describe a set of fifteen keyboard pieces in two parts, written for the training of his sons in composition as well as in performance. They resemble fugues in that they are imitative, but differ in the comparative freedom of their style, in the fact that imitation is normally in the octave in the inventions, and in their smaller size. Many other contrapuntal works by Bach and others, called preludes, duets, and other names, can be considered to be inventions. The three-part "inventions" frequently published together with the two-part inventions were called "symphonies" (*sinfonien*) by Bach.

LATIN AMERICAN DANCE FORMS. Latin American dance music is characterized by the use of a host of unusual percussion instruments, each of which has its particular assigned part. Rhythm is therefore the outstanding feature with harmony and melody in the background.

Rhumba: The rhumba originated in Cuba. The fundamental rhythmic pattern is played by the piano, bass, and bass drum.

Another variety of rhumba is the *Guaracha* in which the fourth beat of the bar receives two eighth-note accents.

Bolero: The Cuban or 4/4 bolero is entirely different from the original Spanish or 3/4 bolero. The bolero of today as danced in the modern ballroom is the Cuban variety.

Samba: A characteristic Brazilian dance form with rolling rhythm and a strong feeling of two to the bar.

Tango: A widely popular dance from Argentina. Main characteristic is the heavy accent on the fourth beat, or after-beat of four.

Mambo: A recent addition to the Latin American dance group. An outstanding characteristic is the strong accent on two and four in a two-bar pattern.

Additional Latin American dance forms in common use are the *Conga, Son, Calypso,* and numerous variants of the principal forms.

LIED. In the narrow sense, a German art-song, as written by Schubert, Schumann, Brahms, Wolf, and others. It is characterized by effective union of the music with the words, not only with respect to the natural accents and speech tone of the language, but also with the mood of the poem. A distinction is made between the strophic lied, which used the same music for each stanza of the poem, and the "through-composed" (*durchkomponiert*) lied, in which each verse is set differently, a device particularly suited to a poem in which the mood develops or changes from stanza to stanza.

MADRIGAL. Although the word appears as early as the late 13th century applied to vocal compositions in two or three parts, it refers chiefly to a type of secular polyphonic vocal composition which flourished in Italy and England during the last part of the 16th century and well into the 17th century. Although designed as a sort of vocal chamber music in the home, with one singer to a part, madrigals are commonly sung by choruses today. The fact that instruments were used to supply missing parts or to reinforce weak singers stimulated the use of instrumental music and the eventual development of music for instruments only.

MARCH. A musical composition designed to produce orderliness and spirit in the movement of troops, or to provide music for the accompaniment of processions.

Broadly, marches can be classed as processional or grand marches (with the funeral march as a special variety) and fast marches or quicksteps. Grand marches are in 4/4 or 12/8 meter, and in moderate tempo. Fast marches are two beats in the measure, either 2/2, 2/4, or 6/8. American marches, of the kind made famous by Sousa, Goldman, King, Panella, Chambers, Farrar, and others, consist of two repeated strains in the main key, followed by a trio in the key of the subdominant. The trio may consist of a repeated strain, followed by a contrasting break strain, after which the main theme of the trio is repeated, usually with reinforced or brilliant instrumentation. English marches often repeat the first two strains after the trio is played, making the form quite similar to that of a minuet.

Concert marches are written for the sole purpose of being played at concerts. Such marches usually contain features which make them unsuitable for marching.

MASS. The observance of the Eucharist in certain churches. Musically, it consists of the proper, intoned by the priest, and varying in content from day to day throughout the church calendar, and the ordinary, or invariable portion, which may be sung by the choir. When a "Mass" by a composer is spoken of, the ordinary is meant. This consists of six parts:

(1) *Kyrie eleison* (Lord, have mercy upon us)
(2) *Gloria* (Glory to God in the Highest)
(3) *Credo* (I believe)
(4) *Sanctus* (Holy, holy art Thou, Lord God)
(5) *Benedictus* (Blessed is He that cometh)
(6) *Agnus Dei* (Lamb of God, who takest away the sins of the world)

MAZURKA. A lively Polish dance in 3/4 or 3/8 meter, with emphasis on the second or third beat of the measure.

MINUET. A dance popular in Europe from about 1650 to the beginning of the 19th century, particularly valued as it was considered to be the best training in genteel deportment. It was in 3/4 meter, in moderate tempo. Serious composers used it as an optional dance in the suite (see *Suite* 1) and later in the symphony, in which use it was displaced eventually by the scherzo. It is normally written as a three-part song form, but may be in two parts. Frequently it has a trio, with da capo to the first minuet.

MOTET. A polyphonic choral composition setting Latin religious words other than those of the Mass. The great development of the motet was in the 16th century, notably in the work of Palestrina, Lassus, and

Victoria, who produced some of the finest music of all time in this form.

OPERA. One of the most important of musical forms, uniting at the same time the efforts of the poet (librettist), the actor, the stage-crafter, and the costumer with that of the composer. The musical requirements for performance are for soloists, orchestra, and chorus. Historically, and simultaneously in almost every era, opera has meant a great variety of styles and purposes, from light and even farcical operetta and musical comedy on the one hand to the most profound and moving drama on the other. National schools and individual composers have varied from one extreme to the other in balancing the relative weight of drama and music. Verdi, Wagner, and Mozart are among the most significant composers of opera.

ORATORIO. A dramatic work for soloists, chorus, and orchestra, the libretto of which concerns a sacred subject. It differs from opera in the fact that it is not written to be acted on the stage. There is generally more emphasis on the part of the chorus. The best known oratorio is *The Messiah* of Handel, only one of many fine works by that composer. Others are by Mendelssohn, Haydn, Beethoven, and among moderns, Walton and Honegger.

OVERTURE. (1) The orchestral introduction to an opera, oratorio, or cantata.

(2) A piece of keyboard or orchestral music patterned after the overture in the first sense, but intended for independent performance.

The overture originated as a device to get the attention of the crowd assembled to hear the opera. In the 17th century, two forms, each in three movements, arose: the Italian (fast, slow, fast) and the French (slow, fast, slow).

In Bach's time overture often meant a suite which began with a slow movement full of dotted rhythms, like that of the French overture, but which had additional movements in the form of dances.

The form of the modern overture is likely to be that of the sonata-allegro, but there are many overtures which are only medleys or potpourris of tunes. Some of these are associated with light operas.

PARTITA. Another name for suite (1), but usually referring to a rather elaborate suite, introduced by a movement not in dance rhythm, such as a prelude, overture, sinfonia, toccata, fantasie, or preambulum, introducing extra movements, such as gavottes, minuets, bourrées, airs, or polonaises, and frequently having doubles for one or more of the movements. The best-known partitas are a set of six by J. S. Bach.

PASSACAGLIA. See *Chaconne*.

PASSAGE. When a motive is used sequentially in a florid manner, or dissolves into a scale or arpeggio figure for the sake of brilliance, it is known as a passage.

PASSEPIED. A rapid dance, three beats to the measure, with an upbeat of one beat. It was occasionally used as an optional movement in a suite.

PASSION. A piece of sacred music, resembling an oratorio, based on the last events in the life of Christ, and derived from the custom in some churches of devoting four days of Holy Week to the reading of the story of Christ's life from the various gospels. Traditionally, in a musical passion, the story is carried forward by a tenor, "the Evangelist," who acts as narrator and who sings mostly in recitative. The part of Christ is given to a bass, accompanied by strings. Other parts sometimes appear for Peter, Pilate, Judas, and various other characters. The chorus is used for heightened moments of feeling, and for reflective passages. The greatest passions were written by Bach and Schütz.

POLKA. A lively Bohemian or Polish dance in 2/4 meter, with the first three eighth-notes accented, and the fourth unaccented. Another form similar to the Polka is the *Schottische.*

POLONAISE. A stately Polish dance in 3/4 meter, with each of the beats normally divided into two eighth-notes, but with the last half of the first beat divided into two sixteenth-notes. There is an important secondary stress on the second beat.

PRELUDE. (1) A piece played as an introduction to another, as a prelude and fugue.

(2) Any short piece in rather free style is likely to be called a prelude by its composer, for example the preludes of Chopin and Rachmaninoff.

RECAPITULATION. (1) In fugues, the section which prepares for the close of the work. The recapitulation may be elaborate enough to contain a statement of the fugue subject in the main key by each of the voices; or it may be limited to a single statement, in the bass or soprano. In any case, the recapitulation is usually followed by an extension, which is called a coda, leading to the final cadence.

(2) In the sonata-allegro, the section which follows the development and brings the movement to a close. It stands in the main key and presents both the main theme and the subordinate theme. It differs from the exposition, in that the two themes are almost always in the same key. Aesthetically, this procedure serves the purpose of reconciling the two themes, after building most of the movement on the conflict between them. The recapitulation is preceded by a retransition, and usually followed by a coda.

RECITATIVE. In the opera, oratorio, and other extended dramatic works a style of writing which imitates the effects of spoken language without much regard to melody or to rhythmic regularity. It is used for narrative, dialogue, or for situations unsuited to lyric expression. (See *Aria.*) In light opera, recitative is supplanted, for the most part, by spoken dialogue.

RETRANSITION. A transition, bridge passage, or extension which occurs as the final event in a development section. Its purpose is to prepare for the reentry of the main theme in the principal key. In classic works, this is frequently accomplished by dwelling on the dominant of the key.

RIGAUDON. An old dance in duple meter originating in southern France and occasionally used in the suite or as an independent number.

RONDO. A large form made by the contrast of a main theme with one or more contrasting subordinate themes. The theme (A) is likely to be a small song-form, or at least a chain of phrases or double period. Three types are distinguished:

(1) The small rondo (first rondo) in which there is only one digression. The digression may be a lyric theme, but is more likely to be a shifting, passage-like development of some fragment of the main theme. This is followed by a return to the original theme, this time, however, in more elaborate treatment and followed by a coda. The tempo of the small rondo is nearly always slow: andante or adagio. The slow movement of many sonatas and symphonies are in this form.

(2) The old (or second) rondo, which is a rapid piece, in which there are two or more different digressions, last of which is likely to be in a somewhat remote key.

(3) The new (or third) rondo, also rapid in tempo. It differs from the second rondo in having a return to the first digression. (A-B-A-C-A-B-A). This practice makes for greater unity.

Second and third rondos are often found as independent pieces, and are also quite frequent as the final movements of sonatas, symphonies, and similar works.

SARABANDE. A classic dance of Spanish origin in slow 3/4 or 3/2 measure, with the second beat accented or lengthened. See *Suite* (1).

SCHERZO. The word is the Italian word for joke, and this is typical of many specimens of the musical scherzo. Ordinarily, a scherzo is a movement in sonatas, symphonies, quartets, and the like, which replaces the minuet. Like the minuet, it is in triple meter, but it is faster. Haydn appears to be the first to have made the substitution, but Beethoven was the first to use it rather consistently. The name is also applied to separate works similar in form (which is identical with that of the minuet) but having tragic or dramatic implications, such as the scherzi of Chopin and Brahms for piano.

SERENADE. See *Cassation, Divertimento.*

SONATA-ALLEGRO. A large form used as the first movement of sonatas, symphonies, quartets, and the like, and separately as the overture.

The form depends for its interest on the use of two themes which are first stated in contrast, then developed, then finally reconciled. The main theme and subordinate theme are likely to be different in style, one heroic, the other lyric or elegiac; they are in contrasting keys or regions (tonic–dominant, or minor tonic–relative major). Structurally, they may be extended periods, or phrase-chains. There is usually a bridge passage leading from the main theme to the subordinate theme, and another from the subordinate theme to the cadence which ends the exposition.

The development section uses all sorts of techniques to explore or work out the two themes or fragments of them, separately and in relation to each other. (See *Development.*)

The recapitulation finally restates the themes but now in the same key. The movement, at least in the larger examples, is likely to have an extension at the end called a coda.

SONATA. A large form in several movements, each of which is also likely to be a large form. The same form is used for duos, trios, quartets, and other chamber music works; for symphonies, which are essentially sonatas for orchestra; and for concerti, which are sonatas for solo instrument with orchestra.

The typical large sonata is in four movements, the first a sonata-allegro, the second a small rondo or other slow movement in a related key, the third a minuet or scherzo in still another related key, and the final movement a rondo or another sonata-allegro in the main key. Works in three movements usually omit the minuet. A theme with variations may be substituted for any of the four movements.

SONATINA. A small sonata, with less elaborate treatment of thematic material than in the sonata.

SONG. In its broadest sense, vocal music, uniting words with melody. A distinction is made between folk-song, which is the work of unschooled composers, handed down and modified by tradition, and art-song, which is music composed essentially for performance by skilled singers. (See *Lied.*)

STRETTO. A type of imitation, frequent in fugues, in which the follower begins the imitation while the first statement is in progress. Stretto serves to produce increased tension or excitement.

SUITE. (1) A set of dances, basically consisting of Allemande, Courante, Sarabande, and Gigue, but frequently having an introductory movement, and interpolating other dances, such as Gavotte, Minuet, or

Passepied, and even pieces called "Air." This was the suite as written by Bach, Handel, and their predecessors and contemporaries.

(2) A set of pieces for open-air performance. (See *Serenade, Divertimento, Cassation.*)

(3) A set of pieces made up of theatrical music, such as Bizet's *Arlésienne* Suites, or of music around a central theme, such as Grieg's *From Holberg's Time,* or of assorted pieces, more or less related by occasion, key, or theme.

SYMPHONIC POEM (TONE POEM, *Tondichtung*). A romantic variant of the symphony, breaking down the separation into movements, and incorporating elements of descriptive music (imitating actual extra-musical sounds) or program music (music which seeks to tell a story). Good examples, besides those of Liszt, are symphonic poems by Richard Strauss and Smetana.

SYMPHONY. As used today, the name refers to an extended sonata for full orchestra. It originated in the middle of the 18th century with Sammartini, Stamitz, and Monn; was developed and more or less crystallized into classic form by Haydn, Mozart, and Beethoven and has been the subject of experimentation and development by almost every significant romantic and modern composer. A great part of the programs of symphony orchestras is made up of symphonies, symphonic poems, concerti, and overtures, all of which are closely related, and all of which are discussed separately in the present list.

TARANTELLE, TARANTELLA. A rapid Italian dance in 6/8 meter, so called either because it originated in the region of Taranto, or because the dance was long regarded as a specific remedy for the bite of the tarantula.

TOCCATA. Usually, a piece written to display rapidity of execution on a keyboard instrument. It is written in rhapsodic style, and resembles the fantasia. The harpsichord toccatas of Bach, however, are extended pieces alternating sections of brilliant passage-work with slow lyrical sections and with elaborate fugues.

TONE POEM. See *Symphonic Poem.*

TRIO. (1) A sonata for three instruments, such as a string trio for violin, viola, and cello; a piano trio, for piano, violin, and cello; or a woodwind trio, for oboe, clarinet, and bassoon. The possibilities of combination are almost limitless.

(2) The second large division of a minuet, scherzo, or march, after which the first part is repeated. It is called a trio because, as introduced by Lulli in the 17th century this part was set for three instruments, two oboes and a bassoon, by way of contrast to the full orchestra used in the first part.

VARIATION FORMS. Variation forms (sets of variations, theme and variations, etc.) are pieces of music constructed by presenting the same musical idea in several successive treatments, preserving the outlines of the original idea. Two main types may be observed:

(1) The ground-bass variations, in which the unifying element is a repeated bass line. This type is exemplified by the basso ostinato, the chaconne, and the passacaglia.

(2) The theme with variations, in which a melody is presented in many transformations. Some of these may be cast in other forms, such as a minuet, a canon, a waltz, or a march. A common device is the "division variations" in which the theme is broken up first into eighth-notes, then into triplets, then into sixteenths, and so on. There may be variations in the minor, slow variations, and so on, limited only by the inventiveness of the composer.

Variation forms have been the vehicle of some of the noblest musical communication, as witnessed by the *Goldberg Variations* of Bach, the *Eroica* and *Diabelli* variations of Beethoven, and the variations of Schumann and Brahms. Also, variations have produced some inferior music.

WALTZ. A dance in triple meter which developed from a German peasant dance, the Ländler. It arose in the last years of the 18th century, and in the first half of the 19th century a specialized type, the "Viennese" waltz, in the hands of Josef Lanner and the Strauss family, reached a tremendous vogue. It is characterized by one chord (and one real pulse) in the bar, which appears as a bass note with chord groups on the second and third quarter-notes. The second quarter-note of the accompaniment is anticipated a trifle in performance.

The waltz is still popular as a dance, although the steps have changed, and for modern dancing the waltz is played in more moderate tempo.

The form of the Viennese waltz consists of a slow introduction, perhaps anticipating the dance tunes to follow, then a series of four or five separate waltzes, each of two strains, with trio, and a da capo, and finally concluding in an extended coda which recapitulates the set of waltzes and ends with a whirlwind finish of some sort.

QUESTIONS

1. Find some musical compositions that are basically homophonic, and some that are polyphonic. Discuss the meaning of "independence of parts."
2. Listen to a rondo. Can you grasp the structure of this work? Are you aware of some musical idea that keeps coming back? Look up the word "ritornello" and discuss its relation to the rondo.

3. Why is it necessary to know that certain dances are in, say, 4/4 meter while others are in 2/4 or 6/8 meter?
4. Describe the basic structure of such popular songs as *Sweet Sue, Tenderly, I Got Rhythm,* etc. Can you think of any popular songs that have a two-part form?
5. Listen to your instructor play various cadences at the piano. Which do you feel have a greater degree of finality? Compare this experience with what is written in the section on cadences. Does your experience correspond to the technical definitions?

ABSOLUTE MUSIC / 1 *Sir Donald Francis Tovey (1875-1940), composer and teacher, is best known for his excellent essays in musical analysis. In 1914 he became Reid Professor of Music at the University of Edinburgh, succeeding Frederick Niecks, author of the earlier essay on Program Music. Tovey's musicianship and scholarship are impeccable. In addition to the ten books he completed between 1931 and 1939, he contributed most of the articles on music to the* Encyclopaedia Britannica. *In the following essay Tovey, in his characteristically warm style, discusses the principal chamber music ensembles and the music written for them.*

CHAMBER MUSIC

DONALD F. TOVEY

EVERY PECULIARITY OF THE PIANO IS IN KEEPING with the new and dramatic spirit which entered into all kinds of music from the operas of Gluck to the symphonies and string quartets of Haydn. To those who have in modern times been thrilled by the rediscovery of the organ-like richness of plain two-part writing on a harpsichord with 4-foot and 16-foot registers in play, nothing in the history of the sonata style is more surprising than the cheerfulness with which Mozart and Haydn accepted the renunciation of all attempts to apply such registers to the piano. Henceforth no written note was to represent more sounds than that of its own name and octave. The enrichment of harmony by doubling in octaves must be achieved by individual human fingers or players, and not by mechanical couplers. On the other hand, the sustaining of harmony was no longer exclusively the work of individual fingers; a pedal could prevent the dampers from stopping the sound when the fingers left the key, and so an arpeggio of single notes might leave behind a chord vibrating throughout four or five octaves with a rich and slowly evanescent sound transparent to all other instrumental tones. Thus the sonata ideals of chamber music and the style of the piano stimulated each other, and speedily determined the criteria which are valid from the time of Haydn to the present day. These classical criteria may be formulated under two headings, as follows:

I. Chamber music is music in large forms for a group of solo instruments on equivalent planes of tone and of equivalent musical capacity. The planes of tone need not be the same; on the contrary, the value of the piano in chamber music depends largely on its being inevitably on a different plane from all other instruments, but it has no difficulty in refraining from shattering the ensemble like a trumpet or a trombone, and the ear takes pleasure in low notes on a 'cello as a bass to full chords on the piano, the difference of plane being essential to the special effect. The introduction of the singing voice into the scheme, as in Schönberg's second string quartet and sextet, introduces a non-equivalent plane of tone, and accordingly goes beyond the classical criteria. A further step, both as to planes of tone and non-equivalence of musical resource, is shown in Schönberg's *Pierrot Lunaire,* where the singer is required to follow a prescribed rise and fall of pitch in a

---

CHAMBER MUSIC by Donald Francis Tovey from *Cobbett's Cyclopedic Survey of Chamber Music,* Volume 1; copyright 1929-30 by the Oxford University Press, Inc. Reprinted by permission.

speaking voice, carefully avoiding definite musical notes. In the opposite direction, Cyril Scott and Arthur Bliss use the singing voice without words in an instrumental ensemble.

The question of equivalent musical capacity was frequently raised in classical masterpieces by the use of the double-bass. In a mature style of chamber music this instrument, which, with the best of playing, cannot compete effectively with other stringed instruments in cantabile passages, justifies its existence as a support to large groups, especially such as contain wind instruments, as in Beethoven's septet and Schubert's octet. Even so, it associates itself naturally with the lighter and looser style of art typified by the serenades and divertimenti of Mozart. Early in the nineteenth century, Onslow, a prolific writer of chamber music, having occasion to use a double-bass as a makeshift for a 'cello, found the effect so satisfactory that he wrote numerous quintets for two violins, viola, 'cello, and double-bass. It is not clear from his notation in what octave he means the double-bass to play. Even in Dvořák's far more highly organized quintet in G, the double-bass does not seem quite at ease in the drawing-room, and its one shy cantabile remark in the minuet of Goetz's piano quintet is a pathetic triumph of unconscious humour.

Stravinsky's introduction of drums, trombones, and similar artillery into chamber music marks another new epoch with new criteria. What these criteria may be, we shall know when a propagandist arises who can convince us that a totally unprepared extemporization by a dozen players will not pass muster with him as a masterpiece of modern music. Stravinsky knows what he is doing; and experimental art is more important than experimental propaganda.

II. Chamber music requires no more than the number of players for whom individual parts are written; and every note written is intended to be heard. We have seen that chamber music before 1760 did not aim at this criterion; it was created with infinite labour by Haydn. The masters who may be taken as realizing it instinctively and imaginatively from first to last are Mozart, Beethoven, and Brahms. All who have attempted to write chamber music approximate to it at their best moments. But we may here profitably glance at some typical cases where music, otherwise beautiful and important, shows a defective sense of this criterion. It is interesting to note, by the way, that the criterion is never more severely maintained than in the most experimental works of the present day. Indeed, the desire to experiment with non-equivalent planes of tone and non-equivalent musical capacities goes naturally with the utmost sensitiveness to the individuality of each instrument. It is rather to the immediate successors of Beethoven that we must turn for examples of the confusion of thought natural to men who feel secure in a classical tradition not of their own making.

Certain tremolo passages in the string quartets of Mendelssohn are often, and not unfairly, quoted as bad examples of orchestral writing in chamber music. But here we must beware of a worse confusion of thought than Mendelssohn's. There is no harm whatever in one kind of good music sounding like another kind, if it has the virtues of both kinds.

If any good orchestral sounds can be realized by a string quartet, so much the better for the quartet. What is wrong with Mendelssohn's tremolos is that they are conceived mechanically on the analogy of orchestral passages, and carried to lengths which only an orchestra could make acceptable. On paper the storm in the development of the first movement of Beethoven's quartet, op. 74, looks quite as coarse, but it would at the outset be far too thick for orchestral writing, and its wonderful diminuendo is all drawn exactly to scale in a quartet which, as a whole, is one of the most ethereal compositions ever written. The same praise is due to such apparently crude simplicities as the stiff minims with which the violins and 'cello accompany the viola solo in the second variation of the finale. Dante or Milton never surpassed that calm—

"They also serve who only stand and wait."

We are on less slippery ground in dealing with the integrity of the parts in classical chamber music. An honest violinist will be compelled to say that the second violin part of a Mendelssohn quartet is more interesting than that of one by Mozart. But this does not make Mendelssohn a better quartet-writer than Mozart. His work is on such a much larger scale that it often droops and fails, like the full-sized machine of an inventor who does not realize that its powers do not increase in the ratio of its bulk to that of the working model. The sympathetic but critical study of Schumann's chamber music will show more clearly where the criterion applies. With a full and sonorous piano style, he has even more than Haydn's curious inability to refrain from putting into the piano part all that the other parts have to say. Indeed, he has altogether lost the power of sorting out his material into its proper planes, and the exquisite first trio of the scherzo of the piano quartet is in such a tangle of useless and arbitrary doublings that it is impossible to discover the persons of the dialogue. Mozart, Beethoven, and Brahms would have delighted in making it stand out as a beautiful dialogue between five singing parts, the three strings and the pianist's right and left hand, with no confusion between these parts and the supporting chords to which each instrument would contribute between its own distinct entries with the themes. It is impossible to argue that there is aesthetic value in Schumann's unclarified scoring of this passage. The piano quartet is more highly organized than its delightful and popular brother the quintet. But the perversity of inattention to the integrity of parts can hardly be more clearly demonstrated than by the fact that, while the string parts of the quintet are such a primitive mass of harmony that there is no reason why they should not be arranged for quartet, sextet, or string orchestra, the opening of the piano quartet shows serious practical reasons why it should have been a quintet!

We must not confuse the criteria of mere part-writing with those of the treatment of an instrument as a whole. There is no reason why a string quartet should not, by means of double stops, produce a passage that effectively imitates an octet. But there is no excuse for making a string quartet play for pages together in such masses of double stops that there is no more evidence of four individual players than in a piano four-hand duet. It is no defence that such writing (as in Grieg's G minor quartet) is "effective"; to prolong it is to do a ridiculously easy thing at the expense of all higher possibilities. César Franck's string quartet is in this way a disappointment to every one who can appreciate the essential, if sometimes harmlessly orchestral, quintuplicity of his great piano quintet. The string quartet is full of excellent organ music, and it imitates the organ very skilfully. But, except for the scherzo, which is full of anybody's brilliance, there is strangely little evidence that it is a quartet at all.

These criteria are unquestionably correct, whatever disputes may arise as to their application. In conclusion, it may be as well to enumerate, and occasionally comment on, some of the principal combinations used in chamber music, beginning with Haydn.

I. *Duets*

(a) Two violins: magnificently exploited by Spohr, whom the severe discipline of this problem stimulated to his best work.

(b) Violin and viola, represented by two masterpieces of Mozart written to help Michael Haydn to complete the execution of a commission for six. The extra low fifth of the viola greatly eases the pressure on an imagination confined by the violin to a bass no lower than its open G.

(c) Two 'cellos: a magnificent medium, very sonorous in spite of its severe restrictions, and very little explored.

(d) Piano and violin. The most frequently attempted form of chamber music, and by far the most treacherous. The progress, from the use of the violin as a hardly necessary accompaniment to its perfect partnership in the ensemble, is beautifully shown in the works of Mozart's childhood, from his seventh year to his twelfth. There is a gap between these and his adult sonatas. With occasional lapses, his later sonatas, like Beethoven's, make severe but legitimate demands on the players' and listeners' capacity to focus the two planes of tone into one picture. For this reason duets for

(e) Piano and 'cello are much easier to write when it occurs to a composer to attempt them. There are far fewer 'cello sonatas of all kinds than violin sonatas in existence; but a much larger proportion of the former is good.

(f) Piano and a wind instrument. Here, as with other combinations, the horn and the clarinet have had the best chances, the flute being inconveniently weak for the piano, the oboe being apt to pall when not frequently relieved by other tones, and the bassoon being insufficiently appreciated except as a comedian, though Mozart wrote a sonata for 'cello and bassoon. Technical limitations, even when so severe as those of the natural horn, do not hamper the composer's imagination once it has been stirred, but he is absolutely inhibited by the suspicion of an incompatibility of tone.

II. *Trios*

(a) String trios for violin, viola, and 'cello are a rare tour de force not necessarily less valuable than string quartets. Mozart's divertimento—trio in E flat—is a marvel of euphony, and proceeds for pages together without a double stop. Beethoven's string trios are among the very greatest works of his first period.

(b) Trios for two violins and 'cello are mostly the aftermath of the continuo period.

(c) Trios for piano, violin, and 'cello. Of all combinations with piano this is the one that has stimulated composers to the finest results. Haydn's trios, imperfect as they are in point of integrity of parts, are full of his grandest forms and most pregnant ideas. Mozart sets the standard with his inevitable schematic accuracy. The autographs of his trios are written in a way that shows to the eye one of the important normal criteria of the style. He writes the violin above and the 'cello below the piano. And with all their rich subsequent developments of piano style, both Beethoven and Brahms retained the idea of the 'cello as an independent bass below the piano, but, like Mozart, giving it freedom to mount to its highest regions, and neglecting none of its possibilities.

The ordinary notation which puts the violin and 'cello together above the piano expresses another fact about the combination: viz. that when the piano is combined with two or more instruments, these tend to form a single antiphonal body of tone. This is equally the case when a wind instrument enters the combination; the three distinct planes of tone separate easily and naturally into two groups; namely, the piano and the other two instruments. Some of the combinations represented by important works are:

(d) Piano, clarinet, and violin (Mozart);

(e) Piano, clarinet, and violoncello (Brahms, Beethoven);

(f) Piano, violin, and horn (Brahms).

The piano and two wind instruments have also been successfully combined, the softest combination being with clarinet and horn. Publishers are reluctant to undertake the sale of such works unless alternative arrangements for more usual instruments are provided. When the composer executes these with freedom, the results are extremely instructive, both where they succeed and where they fail to give an adequate translation of the original.

(g) Among curious trio combinations mention should be made of Beethoven's tour de force for two oboes and cor anglais, a full-sized four-movement work within the compass of less than three octaves and with no possibility of a chord in more than three parts. His jocular serenade for flute, violin, and viola has inspired Reger to two essays in this slender combination.

III. *Quartets*

(a) In the string quartet for two violins, viola, and 'cello we have the purest and highest revelation of chamber music and perhaps of all music. Its criteria need no further discussion here.

(b) The flute and the oboe have each been deliciously combined with strings in short works by Mozart.

(c) Quartets for piano and strings are surprisingly rare considering the popularity of the existing classical examples. Mozart's two masterpieces should have belonged to a set of six. They show with the utmost clearness the principle of setting the strings in antiphonal mass against the piano, and are at the same time exquisitely polyphonic. Later publishers tried to atone for former errors by arranging Mozart's clarinet quintet, D major string quintet, and quintet for piano and wind, as piano quartets. Nothing can be learnt from these.

Apart from three juvenile essays, Beethoven's only piano quartet is an arrangement of his quintet for piano and wind, op. 16. The piano part is unchanged, but the string parts are full of excellent new detail inserted during the long rests of the wind instruments, these rests being unnecessary for string players.

Mendelssohn's three juvenile quartets are wonderful for a boy of thirteen, and the third, in B minor, has many intrinsic merits. After this there is nothing important, except the beautiful Schumann quartet, before the masterpieces of Brahms.

IV. *Quintets*

(a) String quintets differ little from quartets. The favourite extra instrument is a second viola, but, apart from the merely decorative works of the 'cellist Boccherini, the combination with a second 'cello is revealed as a majestic art form by Schubert in his great C major quintet.

(b) The clarinet makes a glorious combination with a string quartet, as has been shown by Mozart and Brahms. Mozart also wrote a charming little quintet for the curious combination of one violin, two violas, 'cello, and horn. His most unclassifiable quintet is the adagio and rondo for flute, oboe, viola, 'cello, and glass harmonica, evidently a most skilfully planned combination.

(c) Quintets for wind instruments present a peculiar problem, especially centred in the group of the five different members, flute, oboe, clarinet, horn, and bassoon. Even under the stimulus of a prize competition, nothing great has been achieved, though an extraordinary amount has been written for this combination. Towards the middle of the nineteenth century that ingenious calculating machine, Reicha, turned out an incredible number of such quintets. He was too sure of his ground either to fail in securing euphony or to show why he took all this trouble. The great composers have not been attracted by the problem of making coherent chords out of five utterly different timbres, and the only time Mozart combined the flute with another wind instrument in chamber music was when he also employed the glass harmonica. The term "wind quintet" suggests to lovers of classical music a work of very different calibre, namely, Mozart's glorious quintet for piano, oboe, clarinet, horn, and bassoon. Beethoven's early and easy-going imitation of this is also well known, especially in his above-mentioned arrangement as a quartet for piano and strings. With Mozart the oboe leads, and with Beethoven the clarinet.

(d) Piano quintets, i.e. quintets for piano and string quartet, differ in no important aesthetic point from piano quartets. It is surprising how few have been written, and how abnormal is the position of those that are known as classics. Schubert's comparatively early *Forellen* quintet is a voluminous and loose-knit serenade in five movements. Schumann's, the most popular of all, has, as already noted, no inner necessity to be written for a quintet rather than for a quartet or sextet or any larger combination. The masterpiece of Brahms, which sets a pure standard for the style, attained its final form only after a chequered existence, first as a quintet for strings with two 'cellos, and then as a sonata for two pianos.

V. *Sextets, &c.*

(a) The two glorious masterpieces of Brahms for two violins, two violas, and two 'cellos are unmistakably inspired by the example of Schubert's great string quintet.

(b) Octets for strings, i.e. four violins, two violas, and two 'cellos have tendencies to top-heaviness and internal congestion. Spohr accordingly hit upon the device of double quartets, for two string quartet groups treated antiphonally. The genius of the boy Mendelssohn had, however, already discovered at the age of fifteen that two hundred and fifty odd antiphonal combinations are more interesting than Spohr's pair, and so he enjoyed himself without scruple in his octet, and communicated his enjoyment to others.

(c) Most of the larger combinations of chamber music result from the grouping of strings with more than one wind instrument. The effect is often said to be semi-orchestral, but this is a mere illusion arising from the fact that wind instruments are seldom heard outside the orchestra, which they therefore suggest to the hearer. As a criterion, it is on a level with that of the backwoods critic who regretted that so superior a composition as Beethoven's op. 59, no. 1, had not been played by a larger band. The character of works like Beethoven's septet and Schubert's glorification of the same scheme and combination as an octet (with the addition of a second violin) is neither orchestral nor hybrid, and in the one point where they differ from the purest chamber music, the introduction of the double-bass, the effect is essentially different from that of an orchestral bass. The style was perfectly understood by Mozart and Haydn, the serenades and divertimenti of Mozart being on every sort of scale, and sometimes for the queerest combinations. Such works are often voluminous, Beethoven's and Schubert's schemes of six movements with grand introductions to first movement and finale being typical, but the style is festive and the texture loose. In fact, the brilliant fixed contrasts of tone between the various instruments of these combinations go best with as light a style as the grand sonata forms will allow. The very terms serenade and divertimento suggest as much, and if the notion of chamber music is widened to tolerate the heavy-footed double bass, it may as well also allow the first violin to behave more like the solo instrument in a concerto than would be seemly in a string quartet.

(d) Compositions for wind instruments alone are most successful when pairs of each kind are taken; otherwise the balance of every chord is a tour de force. The greatest works in this line are Mozart's two octets for two oboes, two clarinets, two horns, and two bassoons. Both are entitled serenades (like all Mozart's works for wind instruments alone), but the one in C minor is a grand and pathetic work, full of wonderful counterpoint and a most un-serenade-like seriousness. It is led throughout by the oboes, the tone of which becomes very fatiguing to the ear even with the finest playing. Perhaps this is why Mozart afterwards arranged it as a string quintet, in which form it is well known. The other octet is led by the clarinets, and, though far slighter, can thus be far more easily produced. But the fact that Mozart is said to have first expanded it from a sextet by adding the oboes, and afterwards to have added two cors anglais, shows that we are leaving the region of a chamber music that tolerates no vagueness as to the number of players. The limit is reached in the same composer's glorious serenade for two oboes, two clarinets, two basset horns (alto clarinets), four horns, two bassoons, and contra-fagotto or double-bass.

Beethoven's works for wind instruments tell us only what he could learn from Mozart, and to pursue the subject into later times would be to lose our thread in a mass of detail.

QUESTIONS

1. What are the essential differences between the chamber music ensemble and the symphony orchestra? Does the size of the group affect the kind of music the group can play? How is it affected?
2. Is there such a thing as vocal chamber music? Can you name any vocal chamber works? What determines whether or not you have such a work?
3. Can you name any instruments that have not been used in chamber music ensembles? What accounts for an instrument being used, or not being used?
4. What does Tovey mean when he says that certain piano quartets should have been quintets? Why does he think there ought to be an additional player? What does he mean by "the integrity of the parts?"
5. Check up on the seating arrangements of various chamber groups: string trio, string quartet, piano trio, piano quartet. Can you suggest why the players sit in these positions? Would other seating arrangements do as well? Why?

ABSOLUTE MUSIC / 2 *Chamber music is often considered the most "highbrow" of all music. In this essay Philip Hart probes the personalities of the men in the Budapest Quartet—perhaps the best-known of all the string quartets—with the purpose of showing that chamber music performers may have many of the same qualities as non-musicians. Hart's association with musicians has been a long one. Starting in the early 1930s, when he bought his first Budapest recording, he then went on to buy a record shop and, later, to become a concert manager. At present Hart is associated with the management of the Chicago Symphony Orchestra, where, no doubt, he will continue to make the kind of delightful observations we find here.*

Four Russians Called
БУДАПЕ́ЩТ

PHILIP HART

AMONG MUSICIANS THERE HAS LONG BEEN A SAYING, usually attributed to Jascha Heifetz, which runs as follows:

ONE Russian is an anarchist;
TWO Russians are a chess game;
THREE Russians are a revolution;
FOUR Russians are the Budapest String Quartet.

For more than a quarter of a century, four exuberant Russians masquerading as Hungarians have been the most widely traveled, the most highly paid, the most enthusiastically acclaimed of professional string quartets. Violinists Joseph Roisman and Alexander Schneider, violist Boris Kroyt, and 'cellist Mischa Schneider—plus others who have been at one time or another members of the Quartet—are the creators of a unique musical institution with a Hungarian name, a Russian brilliance of technique, a predominantly German repertory and tradition, and a sense of style strongly influenced by a great French quartet. And unlike most quartets, which end up as one leader and three followers, the Budapest Quartet is a musical democracy which has fused four extroverted individualists into a profitable and musically rewarding ensemble.

While a good many other groups have disintegrated because of irreconcilable temperaments or expired from sheer starvation, the Budapest—in spite of personnel changes and its uncompromising standards—has prospered for nearly three decades. It has sold over two million long-playing records (a figure regarded with considerable awe throughout the record industry) and it is, by common consent, the Number One chamber music attraction in the concert hall. Moreover, in its concerts as in its recorded repertory, the Budapest has won and held this preëminence without diluting its musical integrity. It presents the same image to Topeka as it does to New York City.

The Budapest String Quartet was at the midpoint of recording its stereo version of the complete Beethoven quartets when its members gathered at 9:30 one morning in the East 30th Street studio of Columbia Records in New York City. Joseph Roisman was the first to arrive, wearing a short-sleeved white shirt and his usual businesslike expression, as he warmed up on tricky passages from Beethoven's *Harp* Quartet. Mischa Schneider was breaking in a new G string on his Gofriller cello,

---

FOUR RUSSIANS CALLED BUDAPEST by Philip Hart from *High Fidelity* Magazine, May 1961. Reprinted by permission.

playing alternate *arco* and *pizzicato* passages from the same piece. On his music stand was a dog-eared cello part in the margin of which he had carefully noted the city and date of every performance in which he had played this particular work. Mischa's cello parts are a veritable historical atlas of the Quartet's travels since 1930, ranging from Indonesia to Israel to Idaho.

In the control room, second violinist Alexander Schneider—invariably known as Sascha—was gradually waking himself up by reading the *New York Times*. A few minutes later, violist Boris Kroyt arrived with his wife, Sonia, who soon departed uptown on a shopping tour. Kroyt's warming up was interrupted by the arrival of Recording Director Howard Scott and Engineer Fred Plaut. While Plaut set up the microphones in front of the Quartet's chairs, the three players in the studio gathered about Scott to determine, in a typically animated argument, the time they were to meet that evening at Scott's apartment for dinner. All decisions—from a questionable reading in late Beethoven to the choice of a lunch time restaurant—are reached by the Quartet in an atmosphere resembling a debate in the French Chamber of Deputies.

While the dinner appointment was being settled, Sascha emerged casually from the control room, cast a bemused eye at his three colleagues in argument, and removed his sports jacket, revealing an elegant red and gray plaid waistcoat. He was about to unpack his Strad when he noticed that Scott had retreated from the argument, and forthwith he descended upon Scott himself.

"What kind of a . . . do you think you are?" he railed in mock rage at Scott. "Because I'm just a lousy second violinist, you ignore me! If I were a conductor, I know what you would say. 'Yes, Maestro! No, Maestro! Certainly, Maestro! Just as you say, Maestro!' " He rubbed his hands in exaggerated obsequiousness and walked away from Scott, grinning with satisfaction.

In a few minutes the four players took their places in front of the microphones, not in their normal concert positions, but in a wide curving arc, each sitting on his own idea of the most comfortable chair: Roisman at the extreme left on a low-backed wooden chair; then Sascha on an old-fashioned wooden piano bench, the lid tilted forward by stuffing the *New York Times* under one edge; Kroyt, on a chair identical with Roisman's; and Mischa, at the extreme right, on a cushioned adjustable piano stool.

Both Scott and Plaut have worked for many years on the Quartet's recordings and are well versed in its special brand of humor. Despite their many years before the microphones in Europe and this country, the Budapest still approaches each recording session as an ordeal, in which everything conspires to frustrate a good performance.

"Just wait," remarked Plaut, who first recorded the Quartet in 1941. "They will talk again about how wonderful it was in London." (The Quartet last recorded there in 1936.)

"In the early days they complained about having to stop every 4½ minutes," continued Plaut, as he adjusted the balance controls on the console. "Then, when tape came, they stopped every time they made a mistake or thought they could play a passage better. Now they usually go through a whole movement, or even two, without stopping."

By this time, everyone was ready for the first take, and, after one false start, the Quartet played straight through the opening movement of Opus 74, while Scott made occasional notations in his miniature score.

The end of the movement marked the beginning of another argument. There were three alternatives: to listen at once to the tape; to repeat the movement just played; or to go on to the next movement. In this case, under Scott's quiet persuasion, the decision was quickly made: they went on to the slow movement. At its conclusion, another noisy argument ensued as the four moved to the control room.

"We should play the whole quartet all the way through, and then do it movement by movement."

"It is absolutely impossible to play so early in the morning."

"I think we should meet at Howard's at 7 o'clock."

"We must hear how it sounds now, before we waste time."

"I whistled an E flat two bars before G."

"How will Joe get his nap if we meet at 6 o'clock?"

"It is best to get one movement at a time right."

"Now, in London, it was better. . . ."

While his three colleagues took their places in the crowded booth, Sascha drew up a chair outside the open door, and settled down with his newspaper. Mischa sat next to Scott, following the score intently, now and then requesting Plaut to replay a passage. Once, when there was an obviously wrong note, the offending player took an exaggerated bow. Sascha periodically abandoned the *Times*, either to listen to a crucial second-violin passage or to engage in animated conversations on Scott's outside telephone.

By this process of intense dedication, relieved by outbursts of nimble humor—a process repeated for eight to twelve days every year for nearly three decades—the Budapest Quartet made another contribution to the recorded repertoire for which it has become world-famed.

There was a time when the Quartet could create a first-class musical scandal by lunching at four separate tables in New York's Russian Tea Room; now it is generally agreed that the secret of its durability is the very individuality of the personal forces that have been so successfully channeled into great performance, without shattering the Quartet by centrifugal force. Not that the brink of crisis has not on occasion been reached. Sascha Schneider, certainly the most extraordinary second violinist before the public, was absent from the group for ten years because it was impossible for him, at the time, to realize his own artistic aims within the Quartet.

Another reason for the Budapest String Quartet's continued success as an entity is that it was formed, not by a single agreement among four men or by one player's choice of three colleagues, but rather by the gradual acquisition of new members discriminatingly chosen to fit into the ensemble. Though founded in 1917 by four Hungarians, the Quartet did not attain its present distinction until it was invaded by Russians between 1927, when Roisman joined as second violinist, and 1936, when Kroyt replaced the last Hungarian. Although all four members of the Quartet were born in Russia, each completed his studies in Germany or Austria—Roisman and Kroyt in Berlin, Sascha in Vienna, and Mischa in Leipzig. Stylistically, they balance Russian volatility with a solid German tradition. As Russians they avoid the typically dry German tone, but they have an individual and collective respect for the composer's text which seems more German than Russian. On a number of occasions members of the Quartet have spoken highly of the old Capet Quartet, a French group active in the 1920s and 1930s, whose records, never issued in this country, reveal qualities of balance, texture, and intensity similar to the Budapest. Residents of the United States since 1938, and all naturalized citizens, the members of the Quartet are an extraordinarily cosmopolitan group.

In operation, the Budapest is a "democracy" in which both musical decisions and business matters are settled by a majority vote, though if a one-man minority has sufficiently strong convictions his colleagues will find a mutually acceptable compromise.

"What do you do," the Quartet is often asked, "when you have a two-to-two tie?"

"We ask the composer."

If the composer is alive, he is consulted directly; if not, the score and other relevant musicological data are studied. This is not as fatuous as it may sound: when three or four of the Quartet agree upon an interpretative liberty, it is accepted with the authority of collective insight. When there is no such preponderance of agreement, the conservative course of a more literal reading is preferred.

Contrary to legend, the Quartet does not avoid joint social engagements whenever possible, and some of my own most delightful times with them have been occasions, often after concerts, when I thoroughly enjoyed the interplay of these four varied personalities in a relaxed setting.

At any gathering, one is aware of the presence of the Quartet—not just their physical presence, but a special magnetism in the atmosphere—as they enter a room. Sascha will probably embrace his hostess—and any other pretty woman—with exaggerated but nonetheless genuine affection. Roisman will politely but intently inquire about his host's pipes and tobacco. Kroyt will turn on the television to learn the latest baseball scores, information eagerly discussed by all four. Mischa will survey the walls and bookshelves to locate new or interesting paintings and books. Before the evening is out, Sascha may give a "Lieder recital," in exaggerated German and with Kroyt at the piano.

A critical moment in the history of the Budapest Quartet is now recalled by its members as "The Night We Lost Joe." Walking back to their hotel in the pitch dark after a concert in Nagoya, Japan, in 1953, his colleagues suddenly discovered that Roisman had fallen into a deep ditch, breaking his left wrist. An Army doctor set the fracture, and the Quartet returned to the States.

Back in Washington, X rays showed that Roisman's bones had not been set properly in view of the delicate control required of a violinist's left hand. After the fracture was broken again and reset, Roisman faced a difficult recovery not knowing whether he would ever play again. At first he could not even place his Guarneri del Gesù under his chin—his wife had to hold it for him—but through special exercise and remarkable perseverance, he not only recovered full use of his left hand but, within five months, was playing again in the Quartet.

This episode reveals an intensity of purpose which is not apparent from the urbane and reserved appearance of Roisman on the concert stage. The least extroverted member of the Quartet, his calm sense of purpose is a stabilizing force among his more volatile colleagues. Having been "graduated" from second violin to first, he seems never to have forgotten his resolve not to dominate the Quartet. I once heard a long and vitriolic diatribe by the "leader" of another quartet to the effect that Roisman played too much "inside" the Budapest. Yet, it is this very role of "first among equals" that so distinguishes Roisman's contribution.

Roisman was born in Odessa in 1900 into a musical family; as a young girl, his sister played duets with David Oistrakh, another native of Odessa. Through the generosity of the wife of a wealthy importer, Roisman and Kroyt both, though not together, were sent to study in Berlin. Roisman returned to Russia during World War I, but emigrated in 1923 via Czechoslovakia. There he met his wife, herself a Hungarian and the only authentic touch of Budapest in the present Quartet. Eventually he settled in Germany, where he joined the Budapest Quartet in 1927.

Roisman's attitude towards his colleagues is often one of tolerant amusement: the last to join in rehearsal clowning, he is the first to remind the others, "Gentlemen, we have work to do." When the Quartet goes to a party, he is more inclined to sit on the sidelines, smoking one of his vast collections of pipes, watching the amusing antics of Kroyt and the cavorting Schneiders with a quiet smile. Traveling, he knows the best Chinese restaurants—a taste he shares with the Schneiders—and is the first to arrive at the airport for the next stage of the tour. He plans his itinerary carefully to assure an afternoon nap when possible, and he takes the first available plane rather than wait for the last possible flight.

Boris Kroyt, Roisman's fellow-townsman from Odessa, often appears to be the clown of the Quartet, and his battle with the English language is the source of much of the Budapest's well-deserved reputation for humor. (Though all four speak Russian, French, and German, they generally use English, even in the privacy of rehearsal.) Kroyt is known for his passion for gadgets, ranging from electric shavers and cameras to a Lincoln Continental. His colleagues allege that his collection has reached such proportions that the Kroyts have had to move into the closets, leaving the rooms for the loot. The Schneider brothers also take an avid interest in motor cars, but Kroyt, by common consent, is granted a special *expertise* in matters automotive.

Behind this mania for gadgets one finds a serious musician with a knowledgeable feeling for all the arts. Unlike Roisman, Kroyt remained in Berlin after his student days and took part in its stimulating musical life during the Twenties. He recalls that the Expressionist artist Käthe Kollwitz lived for a time in the same apartment building, and he played both violin and viola in avant-garde concerts featuring music by Schönberg and his group. In fact, until he joined the Budapest in 1936, Kroyt played both instruments regularly; once he appeared with the Berlin Philharmonic performing the violin solo in the Brahms Concerto and the viola solo in Berlioz's *Harold in Italy* on the same program.

The Budapest Quartet is blessed by the tremendous vitality of its inner voices—Kroyt's Deconet viola and Alexander Schneider's Strad. Sascha has been first violinist in his own quartet and a concert soloist in his own right. He delights in holding forth on the sins of conductors and of managers, whom he considers to be no better than parasites at their best and prostitutes at their worst. In this, Sascha qualifies as an expert, as he is a part-time conductor and an impresario himself.

The years between 1945 and 1954, when Sascha was "on his own," gave him a chance to prove himself away from the Quartet—as soloist in concertos and unaccompanied Bach; in recital with pianist Eugene Istomin and harpsichordist Ralph Kirkpatrick; as a chamber musician in the Albeneri Trio and New York Piano Quartet; as conductor in New York, Prades, Puerto Rico, and Dumbarton Oaks. Record collectors will particularly remember the nearly complete Haydn cycle he made with his own quartet for the Haydn Society.

Sascha also functioned as arranger for many of the activities in which he participated. Employing no regular manager, he made business arrangements himself, through a secretary listed on his letterhead as "Patricia Taylor." It was not long before his friends discovered that the nonexistent secretary was one of Sascha's typical inventions: her first name was a feminization of Ralph Kirkpatrick's surname; the second was a translation of his own name (German "*Schneider*" equals English "tailor").

Sascha is an ardent supporter of causes. Both he and Mischa suffered in their youth from Russian and Polish persecution of the Jews in their native Vilna, and one of their sisters died at Dachau in World War II. When, in 1949, Mercury Records was recording as much as it could of Frankie Laine in anticipation of one of Petrillo's recording bans, Sascha worked long hours in the studio band to earn quick money for a Spanish orphanage in France supported by Casals.

At about that time, I recall spending an evening in Sascha's New York apartment, while he talked of preliminary plans for the Casals festivals in France. On this same occasion, Alexander Calder dropped in to adjust a mobile hanging over Schneider's piano. The mobile was rattling sympathetically with certain notes on the piano, and Calder was fascinated with this new artistic challenge. While Sascha struck the offending notes on the piano, Calder mounted a stepladder, with pliers and tinsnippers in hand, to "tune" the mobile.

Though Sascha had to give up a number of his projects when he rejoined the Quartet in 1954, he still does a formidable amount of extra work. He organizes the Casals festival in Puerto Rico, conducts chamber orchestra concerts at New York's New School, and spends much of his summer vacation at Rudolf Serkin's school at Marlboro, Vermont. In the fall of 1959, at one of Schneider's New School concerts, Peter Serkin, Rudolf's young son, made his New York concert debut as piano soloist under Sascha's direction.

Now fifty-seven years old, four years senior to Sascha, Mischa Schneider is a smaller, less flamboyant version of his brother. On stage he is grave, his thinning hair almost white. When he travels he is most likely to spend his spare time in museums and in bookshops, or shopping for presents for his wife and his two young sons, at home near Washington. He has been married three times and has grandchildren by both his daughters—one in Florida, and the other in Copenhagen. He is a devoted paterfamilias, speaking with affectionate enthusiasm of his children and grandchildren.

Mischa is perhaps the most complex and worldly-wise personality among the Quartet, in which he plays the part of a delicately adjusted balance wheel. He has strong bonds of affection with each of his colleagues, and they in turn are deeply devoted to him. Though Roisman is senior in terms of service, and Kroyt at sixty-five is oldest of the Quartet, Mischa is the elder statesman of the group. The Budapest has been managed by the Friedberg office for thirty years, but Mischa has the responsibility for most of its business details. He is also the Quartet's chronicler, keeping detailed records of all performances, recordings, and financial matters.

One evening when Mischa was in New York for recording sessions, he joined me for dinner at his favorite restaurant in Chinatown. Like that of countless other evenings in the past two decades, this evening's conversation was memorable for the range of Mischa's interests and his compassionate understanding. He ordered the meal—itself a work of art, for Mischa is a connoisseur of food—and we savored it leisurely while we talked of a variety of things: our respective children; the Beethoven quartets and the hazards of recording; national and international politics; the inevitable personal and musical gossip that are the small talk of musicians and managers. We had an early dinner because Mischa had still to call on the widow of a close friend who had recently died.

"No compromises"—accent, of course, on the second syllable—is the watchword by which these four men have for nearly thirty years guarded their remarkable career. During these decades the Budapest has met with extraordinary perception and catholicity of taste the challenge of that most demanding of music, the literature of the string quartet—a distillation of some of the profoundest ideas of the greatest composers from Haydn to Bartók. The Budapest's Beethoven has long been one of the prime experiences of our time; its Haydn and Mozart combine elegance of phrase and tone with a robust spirit, and its Romantics are approached with vitality and clarity of texture.

The Quartet's repertory is well represented on records, with one notable exception. Though not specializing in modern music as do the Kolisch or Juilliard Quartets, the Budapest's concert repertory includes practically all the major scores of this century, among them many American works. Unfortunately, the only contemporary scores it has recorded—the Hindemith E flat Quartet, the Bartók Second, and the Milhaud Octet—are no longer available.

To hear the Budapest's extraordinary precision of attack *and* release, its uncanny unanimity of vibrato and rubato, is to know technique far beyond the limits of mere virtuosity. The texture is warm and rich, vital without sacrificing clarity or taste; the musicianship is impeccable, yet individual and probing; there is power and sweep without violating either the composer's intent or the traditions of style. But these are merely external manifestations, and end results, of an intense and intent combination of four vibrant individuals dedicated to their art in a manner which fulfills Arthur Schnabel's dictum that greatness is achieved only by following "the line of most resistance."

QUESTIONS

1. Were you aware that long-playing records of the Budapest Quartet have sold over two million copies? Are you surprised by this figure? Why?
2. Can you think of any other endeavors that require the combination of independence and teamwork that it takes to play in a string quartet? How are these endeavors the same? How are they different?
3. How do the personalities of the four men in the Budapest Quartet measure up to the popular stereotype of the serious musician? What is the popular stereotype? Why do you think so?
4. Can you reconcile the quartet's strong interest in baseball with their strong interest in Beethoven? Are these interests compatible? Or do these interests contradict each other? Why?
5. Listen to a string quartet. What would you say is the function of each of the players? Can you hear all four parts? Do some parts seem more important than others? Why do you think they are able to keep together so well without a conductor? Who starts them? Who stops them?

THE SYMPHONY / 1 *Between 1900 and 1921 Philip H. Goepp, a Philadelphia lawyer, organist, teacher, and writer, wrote the program notes for the Philadelphia Orchestra concerts. One result of this employment was a series of books by Goepp entitled* Symphonies and their Meanings. *In this essay Goepp tried to show that the symphony (characterized as music to be played rather than sung) grew out of man's desire to express himself in tones as well as in words. Though many writers on music may not agree with Goepp's thesis, his essay is nonetheless stimulating, strongly presenting one provocative view.*

INTRODUCTION TO THE SYMPHONY

PHILIP H. GOEPP

ART, IT WOULD SEEM, BEGINS ITS CAREER, LIKE MAN, by leaning on another. Thus, sculpture was first subordinate to architecture. Painting, in turn, was the foster-child of sculpture, in the beginning merely tracing outlines and features, much like an infant writing with guided hand.

Music in Greece followed slavishly the metre of the poetry. In the early church, before Gregory, the words of the liturgy were intoned with complete subservience to the rhythm of the verse, so that agreement of singing was possible only when the chorus followed the arbitrary leader.

It is most valuable to see clearly the final evolution of the independent art of absolute instrumental music as the latest link in this chain. Leaning on the words and story of the drama, music developed, on the stage of the opera, melody, and its accompaniment in tones colored by various blending and contrasting instruments. She was preparing her pallet. In the church, following the lead of the service, music was exploring all the possibilities of polyphonic combination and of architectural complexity by algebraic computation. But in neither church service nor in opera was she progressing unaided. Of course, walking with a cane is different from depending on a guiding parent. So differs the music of Palestrina from that of Ambrose. But even in the great Bach's works music had not thrown away all her supports. She first learned to tread her independent course, speaking her message purely in her own language of tones unaided by words, when she lisped the first sonata, which, in orchestral dress, is the symphony.

It must be remembered that the entire growth of the art of music, and what was really the slow manufacture of its elements and forms, was wrought within the Church. This development began when to the unison chant was added the servile accompaniment of a second voice, keeping always its unaltered respectful distance. It ended when all the changes of fugal counterpoint had been rung with mathematical ingenuity. But until modern centuries there had not been a thought of music without words, of unsung music. When the absurdly artificial forms were abandoned by mutinous singers, the organ took the place of the unwilling voice and invited further composition for its special performance.

But this had nothing in common with secular instrumental music

---

INTRODUCTION TO THE SYMPHONY from *Symphonies and Their Meanings* by Philip H. Goepp; J. B. Lippincott Co.; 1897.

and its origin. For the elements, we must go back to the strange attempts at opera by Italian amateurs. The very convenient date of the first opera—1600—is an excellent landmark in gauging the growth of unsung secular music—the year when Peri's *Eurydice* was produced in Florence. It is in the formless preludes and interludes of the players that the germ of the symphony lies. The first conception of flowing *cantabile* melody, which is the very fibre and tissue of every movement, came in the early opera. (There is absolutely no kinship between this *melody* and the fugal *theme* of the church school.) With these the dance, of obscure origin, completes the foundation on which sonatas and symphonies were reared.

If we enter the forge in which these materials were being welded into the great forms of the symphony—in other words, if we study the precursors of the masters—we find, indeed, little promise of intellectual significance, or, for that matter, of pleasurable amusement. But, in art, periods of exclusively formal growth always lack imaginative power. It is like latent heat, when ice changes to water. Great men, it would seem, are content with the form they find, hiding the lines with their fulness of thought. Shallower minds, sensitive to popular demand, tinker at new devices of outward novelty. Thus, Sebastian Bach did not find the sonata sufficiently perfected. Haydn was the first master to approve. Therefore, in a review of the history of musical thought rather than of musical structure, it may fairly be said that the sonata and the whole school of secular instrumental music did not begin before Haydn.

The analogy between Bach and the secular masters is striking. In his earlier generation he found nothing but the strict forms of the church school. He gave them their essential artistic purpose; he crowned their development by endowing them with the highest expression of religious feeling. When a master thus reaches the greatest height, a lower level must be started in another direction, leading to a second master.

If we take a survey of this new stream of worldly composition—melodies with artificial accompaniment, digressions of rippling scales or tripping arpeggios and suddenly intruding crashes of full chords—and contrast it with what is found in the church school with its precise, dignified, and elaborate structure of voices, independent in melody, yet interdependent in harmony, the question comes, What new spirit moves here? How can there be, almost at the same time, two opposite phases of the same art, both honored by the greatest masters?

Clearly, here is the latest, though not the weakest, wave of the Renaissance pulse. The same rebellion against the all-absorbing intellectual domination of the Church, the same resistless wave of earthly feeling and its expression, apparent in painting and in the literatures of England, France, and Italy, is here manifest in the youngest of the arts.

Why the movement is so late in music need not be discussed beyond saying that the art was jealously and exclusively fostered by the Church. All its forms, its whole framework had been devised solely for worship. An entirely new garb must be created before it could venture from the cloister into the gay world without great awkwardness and stiffness. Much depth of feeling or intellectual emphasis must not be expected of the first century of this new phase. The early works show their reactionary origin by utter frivolity and shallowness. Until an actual fitting form was obtained, there was a constant striving after a satisfaction of this very need, a self-conscious kind of emphasis of mere sound; the composer sought to fill in as many black notes as possible.

The beginning of Haydn's career marks the final attainment of this form, and at the same time a sudden spring of true poetic feeling. The result was what is commonly called the sonata, which is really what we are considering; for a symphony is nothing else than a sonata written for the orchestra. In the light of the absolute newness of unsung music is seen the fitness of the name "sonata," that which is merely sounded, in contrast with that which is sung, the "cantata." Nowhere, I venture to say, in any phase of art, is the shock greater than of this burst from the sombre, confined, careful, intellectual process of the cloister to the free, irresponsible fancy dancing first over the meadows and in the forests, then into the life of men, the turmoil and the triumph of war, the romance and ecstasy of human affection.

It is clear, then, why the expected order—first of the less defined, second of the more clearly significant phase of the art—should be reversed. Within the cloister music had reached a high and complex power of expression of those feelings which were there sanctioned. Without, all was new and vague; there were no words or forms of expression for the new life. It must begin with the ABC of a new language. To condemn the first fruits of this stage for lack of definiteness of meaning would be to misunderstand the very purpose of all art. While definite language is not impossible to art, this is not its chief function; no more is mere beauty of outline. If a sentiment be expressed and transmitted, the medium of its transmission will be entitled to its place as an art of form. The language of prose has not the power thus to express and transmit all sentiment, though it may entitle its field in a rough sort of way. What prose cannot, the other arts must do, each in its peculiar region, not, perhaps, without encroaching mutually. Each art, beginning with primordial feelings, will translate more and more delicate shades in a constantly refining process, the form always reacting on the sentiment and suggesting an advance.

This must account for the vagueness of the earlier great works for instruments. But even in Haydn the pastoral element, the poetry of nature, discovered anew, is unmistakable, as is the peculiar playfulness of his humor. In fact, the appearance of humor of any kind in music in the eighteenth century is as absolutely new as anything can be under the sun. Imagine how utterly inconceivable it would have been to the long line, stretching through many centuries, of the worthy fosterers of music in the Church.

The sonata was said by a German critic to be intended by the earliest writers to show in the first movement what they could do, in the second what they could feel, in the last how glad they were to have finished. The simplicity of this interpretation—and no doubt it is accurate—emphasizes the vagueness of the real sentiment. In the hands of great men the form very soon attained a much more dignified plan.

In technicalities the essence is often lost. There is no value in analysis in itself. Yet a clear view of the general purpose is not dimmed by a glance at those elements which have in them more than mere technical value. The question is not merely what is the general purpose of the symphony, but what is the special value of the accepted model in carrying out this purpose. And, as has been said above, the first requisite in the listener is an intelligent grasp of the work.

In short, what is the essential of the much-mentioned sonata form; of the outline of the other movements; indeed, of the structure of the whole? A few relentless *wherefores* will bring us to the right point of attack. Nor can the answer lie in a technical statement of theme, of development, of tonality, and so on. But the one clear and grateful approach is by an historic view, where we see the need—the real *raison d'être*—of each cardinal element.

In the first place, the main stress of the symphony—indeed, of most absolute music—is centered on what is called the sonata form. It is the mould in which is cast the first movement: the serious burst of aspiring thought. The second, to be sure, is of no less dignity. But it is in complete contrast with the stress and strife, the stirring progress of the first. It is a calm lyric utterance from the high level to which the first mood has ascended. It does not need the discussion of the other. Simplicity of statement in the verses of a song is its natural utterance. Nowhere is the depth of genius of the highest master better shown than in the Andante—that profound, broad sympathy of Beethoven, distinct from the statuesque pathos of Haydn, or the stately grace of Mozart. Here was reflected Beethoven's highest trait, that which bound men to him most strongly. In the third phase the feeling of relaxation is undoubted, and, fittingly, the form, even in the highest flights, is based on the dance. The mood has passed from the spirit's stir and spring through pathos to humor. In its original conception this effect of relief, of restraint from the tension of the early movements, was continued in the last. A form peculiarly fitting for careless joy existed in the Rondo, where the melody appeared and vanished with graceful interludes, which later developed into lesser tunes. Discussion was supplanted by a constant, playful alternation of the various melodies. As the symphony grew a more serious utterance of poetic feeling, the last movement often rose to a second climax; and—here appears the meaning of form and of detail—the rondo yielded then to the Sonata type.

What, then, was this sonata form? What are the elements of its power for this new poetic expression?

Again, in the historic view, it is at once amusing, pathetic, and enlightening to see the struggles which preceded the great discovery. In Bach's time the approved form was the suite of dances, transplanted from the itinerant street-players to the new clavichord or newer pianoforte. At best this was a mere series of unrelated dances, idealized, to be sure, with expansion and polyphonic treatment. It was the holiday music of the learned musician, his only secular vent; and it afforded the special form for a kind of public tournament between rival players and composers. But, with the best intention to be worldly, there was over it the stern, ascetic, intellectual stamp of the Church spirit. What was the reaction of treatment which must answer the reaction of secular feeling?

The peculiar quality, as in the strict Church forms, was an unrelieved *monothemism*. Impressed with the traditional simple theme of counterpoint, men could not escape it; they lacked the artistic conception of the dual element, of balance, of contrast. The mystery, the strangeness, is that, not to speak of the eventual solution, the need itself was not clear. And unless we can see the very need, we cannot grasp the full meaning of the sonata and symphony.

In a general way, it was felt, there must be rebellion against the Church process—no more learned counterpoint; no textual theme frugally sounded without harmonic surroundings, like the verse of a sermon; no eternal ringing of its relentless burden, like the doom of dogma without a hint of repose, of cadence—on and on, the voices ever multiplying the warning phrase to a final massive climax of solemn architecture. Away with it all! There must be no taint of fugue in the new spirit. . . .

Now see the features of this new expression as they carry out this new feeling. There must be a better and simpler meaning for our technical big words. What seems the first, the most significant, the most potent, is a clear sense of harmonic residence, what the musicians call tonality, as against the gray color, in the fugue, of a key vague until the end. Again, it seems, there is the impulse to utter a sense of worldly repose, in defiance of the constant strife in the fugue, which knew no rest until the final end.

Nowhere is this constrast clearer than in the piano works of Sebastian Bach and of Domenico Scarlatti. They were contemporaries, almost to the year. But Scarlatti had caught the earthly spirit in sunny Italy, under the inspiration of his father Alessandro, the founder of the new *aria*. Bach, somehow, could never get clear of the shadow of the cloister. With the German his dance-moods are still o'ercast with the pale hue of meditation. He was glancing out of doors through the windows of his study. The Italian was roving with a firm foot in the fields; he was ringing out his tintinnabulations with clearest note of tonal serenity and certainty—still always the same one tune. He could have but a single idea at a time; no broad sense of balance, of contrast, of perspective. On such a basis there could never rise a structure of much serious dignity. But this is not all.

We must see, too, the strange alternative of the qualities of *Bach* and of *Scarlatti:* of vague reflections and of clear tonal simplicity. It seems that tonality must be at the expense of depth. The voices were borrowed for harmonic subservience, and must cease to discuss the theme. In a sense they were degraded from counsellors to train-bearers. So, in an ideal sense, there was a temporary loss of dignity. But this simplicity was after all a gain.

So far the elements are the same of the other secular moulds, of the song, the dance, and the rondo. We have not yet come to the final typical trait of the strict sonata. It was a reconciliation of the various needs: first, of this tonality, the sense of certain harmonic location; second, of relief from monotony of single melody, a sense of duality; finally, of a quality which had been too completely lost with the fugue.

And this very stirring search has shown what a peculiar place the fugue filled. Let us return, for a thought, before the days of unsung music. Our art is still walking hand in hand with her older sister Poetry, but unmanageable, restless. One day a master dreams his melody for the instrument alone. Now it is clear that music must somehow atone for the new want of words. A song deprived of words is and remains incomplete. The clear meaning is gone, there is mere vacant beauty. Here begins the stir for a definite language of pure tones. And this is significant, too: none of the older forms were the achievement of music itself, its self-found utterance. They are foreign; they belonged to poetry, like the song, or to the dance, like the minuet. See, therefore, how this new *sonata* form is actually the first proper mode of expression of the pure art of music. *It says something in mere tones.*

From another point of view, the half-conscious want of the early masters in their search was this: they were dissatisfied with mere lyric burst, mere singing of the tune; *they must talk about it; they must get somewhere.* They quickly felt that melody was, after all, mere theme or text; there was no progress until you discussed it.

This element of discussion, of progress, which, in a sense, had been lost in the fugue, now achieved in a novel way, was the crowning virtue of the new form for sonata and symphony. So here is the problem: to express the definiteness which had been lost with the words; to go beyond mere striking of the melody; to start the pace for a genuine art, which, beyond creating pretty phrases, will find a language for ever deepening and ever differentiating shades of feeling, approaching the clearness of verbal thought. Finally, in the structure of the whole work will lie the art-form, which will build and co-ordinate in supplementary moods one homogeneous expression of a great emotional idea.

How this special purpose of discussion was carried out, the need being clear, will be easily seen; further, too, how each element—of tonality, of duality, of discussion—reinforced the other.

The final achievement was this:

A melody begins with clear intonation of the key, by harmonic sounding of the main chord. It is succeeded presently by a second, which is contrasted in every way—in character, in movement, and in key. Now see how duality helps tonality. Black is black, after all, only in contrast with white. So the original tonic key is not really clear, until a departure into the complementary dominant, with the second melody. Thus the contrast, with well-marked cadence, sharpens the effect of each.

When the two melodies have been stated, there is, of course, a sojourn, a cadence, in the complementary key, the dominant. This in itself invites a return homeward to the original, or tonic. At the same time, the clearness of stated melodies is assured by a repetition from the beginning. And now the story really begins: the characters are described; now they act and talk; the several musical ideas are discussed, singly or together, to new surprises of climax and beauty; they take on the guise often of new melodies, or melodies of kindred beauty are suggested. Thus (not to bind ourselves beyond the hint of analogy) the themes pass from the mere phase of lyric utterance to that of epic narrative, not without strong dramatic power. Now must come the close; and see once more the interrelation of key and theme, of tonality and duality. The melodies reappear in the original order, but with change in key; for the second must close in the tonic. And, again, the balance is maintained; for, while the earlier melody had the advantage of first appearance, the second has the last word in this, the principal tonal territory.

And thus a symphony (which, etymologically, means a sounding together, using, as it did, all the resources of instrumental sound, and in Beethoven's Ninth even pressing voices into service) had, from the time of Mozart, the ambitious purpose of expressing a sort of modulation through three or four moods of one dominant feeling. I use the word "feeling" for lack of a better. In its highest phase, this purpose sometimes is a kind of poetic view of life, colored by what is at the time the individuality of the composer.

QUESTIONS

1. Do you believe that music played by instruments can express more, or less than can be expressed by voices? Why?
2. Listen to the first and second themes of an opening symphonic movement. How do these themes contrast? Do they have the same tempo? texture? melodic flow? rhythmic vitality?
3. Check the number of movements in various symphonies. Why do you suppose some symphonies have three movements, while others have four movements? If you knew there were symphonies that had only one movement, or five movements, how would you justify the number of movements?
4. In the preceding essay, what is meant by "humor" in music? Can music actually make one laugh, be "funny?" Look up the word "scherzo" and discuss its meaning.
5. Listen to a piece by Scarlatti, and another by J. S. Bach. How do they compare? Can you mistake one for the other? Why?

THE SYMPHONY / 2 *Frederic Louis Ritter (1834-1891), music historian and conductor, came to Cincinnati in 1856 from Strasbourg and organized the Cincinnati Philharmonic Orchestra. Later, he became professor and director of the school of music at Vassar College. His teaching interests then led him to write a series of music books aimed at college music students. Among his works are included a two-volume history of music, a book on English music, and another on American music. In the following essay Ritter discusses the important position of Haydn in the early development of the symphony, together with a commentary on the influence of K.P.E. Bach on Haydn's contribution to the symphony.*

The Invention of the Symphony

FREDERIC LOUIS RITTER

THE INSTRUMENTAL FUGUE, THE CANON, AND THE suite, each one based upon the intricate arts of counterpoint, and as such the representative musical art-forms of the seventeenth and the first part of the eighteenth centuries, received at the hands of Handel, and especially of J. S. Bach, the highest degree of development and perfection. These forms may thus be regarded as the culminating point of a great epoch of musical art.

Though much cultivated by succeeding composers, the above-mentioned masters' rich contrapuntal resources and deep spirit, that gave these art-forms life and meaning, have been found almost entirely wanting in the latter. The earnestness and elevated art-practice of J. S. Bach and Handel did not suit the majority of composers, who were rather anxious for success, and that very often at the cost of pure art itself. Apart from this, the dawn of a new epoch, in a political and social sense, was already felt; and art, so closely connected with man's life, participated in the great transformation that gradually prepared the advent of the nineteenth century.

The radical and in many instances sudden and extremely harsh and violent changes that affected the social order of things at the end of the eighteenth century also changed the taste, the views, the intellectual requirements and aspirations of European nations, all more or less under the impetuous influence of the great French Revolution. New and far-reaching events now gave new food to the mind, and at the same time pointed to a new direction in the realm of thought; and art-life, running side by side with intellectual life, moulded new contents into new and adequate forms.

. . . At the end of the eighteenth century instrumental music began to dispute the field with its older sister, vocal music, and reached, through the wonderful works of Haydn, Mozart, and Beethoven, a high point of beauty and poetical meaning, often surpassing, in richness of harmony, boldness of conception, brilliancy of effect, the best efforts of vocal music. From the subordinate position of a mere harmonic accompaniment to vocal forms, instrumental music now built up its own forms, independent of vocal music. On the other hand, the form of the sonata, the string quartet, the symphony, superseding the old forms mentioned above, revealed such a wealth of exquisite musical ideas, that

---

THE INVENTION OF THE SYMPHONY from *The History of Music* by Frederic Louis Ritter; The Oliver Ditson Co.; 1883.

the works of the old masters were for a time entirely set aside as antiquated.

Joseph Haydn is generally considered as the father of modern instrumental music; and, in their chief points, his works mark the beginning of a new epoch. The artist, however, who through his writings and his style influenced Haydn in no small degree, and whose instrumental compositions served him and even young Mozart as models, and who may be thus regarded as the real precursor of modern instrumental music, was Karl Philip Emanuel Bach, son of the celebrated J. S. Bach, born at Weimar, in the year 1714. His father taught him music, not with the intention of allowing him to choose it as a profession, but rather as a fine accomplishment. The artist's nature was, however, too strong in Philip Emanuel; and, having finished his university education, he devoted himself entirely to the practice of music.

He went afterwards to Berlin, where he eventually became pianist and accompanist of King Frederick the Great. In Berlin he remained till the year 1767, when, after the death of Telemann, he accepted the situation of musical director in the city of Hamburg, where he died in the year 1788. In Philip Emanuel Bach the instrumental composer is already predominant over the vocal one. Although his vocal compositions are not without merit, yet his instrumental ones, and, above all, his sonatas for the piano, are of more than merely historical importance, and at this time exercised a great influence on all the principal musicians of Germany. . . .

The composer, however, whose instrumental works mark a new epoch in the history of music was Joseph Haydn, born March 31, 1732, at Rohrau, a small village in Austria. Through a happy accident, the Vienna chapel-master Reuter, on a tour through the country, happened to visit the school where Haydn was placed under the direction of his cousin Frankh, the schoolmaster of Hainburg. Reuter heard the eight-year-old boy sing, was charmed with his voice, and accepted him as one of the choir-boys for St. Stephen's Cathedral at Vienna. While there Haydn studied as much as chance would allow; he also tried his young powers at divers compositions. He felt, however, the want of a guide to initiate him into the rules of harmony and counterpoint; but, not being able to afford to engage a competent teacher under whose direction he might learn those rules, he bought, with some money his father had sent him, Fux's *Gradus ad Parnassum,* and Mattheson's *Vollkommener Kapellmeister*. The money was sent him to buy clothes with.

He was sixteen years old, when, in consequence of the change of his voice, he was dismissed from the choir and reduced to the greatest poverty. Though experiencing all sorts of privations and trials, his profound and disinterested love for his art never once deserted him: all his endeavor was to render himself master of the means that would enable him to become a fine artist. After many vicissitudes and material wants of all kinds, he succeeded, at the age of twenty-seven, in obtaining an engagement in the private orchestra of Count Morzin, as second chapel-master, with a salary of two hundred florins. In 1760 he entered the service of Prince Esterhazy. In 1790 he received an invitation from London to produce some of his compositions, which were much admired by the English. It was by means of the liberal profits he obtained in England that he was afterwards able to live independently and free from pecuniary troubles—a benefit he never could have acquired while in the service of the Esterhazys, in spite of the greatest industry and very modest living. Haydn died May 31, 1809, much respected and loved.

Among the vast number of compositions which mark his long and laborious life, we find a hundred and eighteen symphonies, eighty-three stringed quartets, twenty-four trios, forty-four pianoforte sonatas, five oratorios, fifteen masses, nineteen operas, a hundred and sixty-three pieces for the baryton (a kind of viola di gamba), German and Italian songs for one and three voices, and many other pieces.

Haydn may be considered, with justice, as the creator of the modern symphony and the stringed quartet—at all events, as the composer who gave the forms of modern instrumental music greater significance and beauty of formal construction, by means of his great originality, rich inventiveness, and ingenious treatment of orchestral resources. He breathes, so to say, his own sympathetic soul into all his tone-forms, makes his instruments sing like the inspired organs of an ideal sphere. A healthy humor, in all its lights and shades, touching pathos, and unreserved joy, in fact, all the more tender and *naïve* feelings (seldom darkened by deep passion) that fill the human heart lie unfolded in his charming tone-pictures.

The contours of the form of the sonata, the symphony, the quartet, the trio, etc., were already in a great measure developed when Haydn began to compose. Ph. E. Bach, as we have seen, cultivated the pianoforte sonata with great success; and his works served as models to other composers. Haydn studied Bach's compositions constantly and with great benefit. He used to say, "Those who know my works thoroughly will find that I owe a great deal to E. Bach—that I understood and studied him diligently. Once he even paid me a compliment to this effect."

The form of the sonata is the type of modern German instrumental music. The overture, the symphony, the stringed quartet, etc., are all based on the form of the sonata. Ph. E. Bach's and others' sonatas are composed, as a rule, of three different movements; the whole construction is, however, in an aesthetical sense, more calculated to present agreeable contrasts than to form an organic whole based upon one fundamental idea, determining the emotional character of the composition. Though Haydn received from his predecessors the idea of the successive movements, the manner in which he developed and enriched each one of these movements makes him appear as the real creator of this special art-form of instrumental music.

Mozart and Beethoven accepted it in principle, and, according to their artistic individuality, enlarged upon it without changing its fundamental arrangement. The first movement, generally an *allegro,* received at the hands of Haydn greater significance and meaning, and, by means of more logical thematic development and construction, greater formal compactness and unity also.

Three distinct parts compose, almost invariably, the allegro movement of Haydn's sonatas: first we find the principal idea or theme, giving the entire movement its character; the material of the second part is composed of motivos taken from the first part, richly varied and changed according to the laws of modulation and contrapuntal imitation; the third part is, on the whole, a repetition of the first. By means of the peculiar thematic construction of the second part and the close repetition of the first part as a third—forming in this way a satisfactory close—the unity of the form of the whole movement is advantageously preserved, while the intensity and effectiveness of the mother thought are in every way heightened.

It is Haydn's merit that he elevated what appears in the works of his predecessors as mere momentary fancy, or improvisation, to a principle of formation. The second movement, *largo, adagio,* or *andante,* which Ph. E. Bach, in his sonatas, constructed with much taste, plays in some of Haydn's a more conspicuous *rôle,* being in itself a complete *morceau,* rather broad in harmonic treatment, but full of tender and noble sentiment, contrasting most happily with the vigorous and fiery expression of the first movement. This generally leads to a finale full of sprightliness, charming humor, and delicate *naïveté*. The form of the finale is that of the rondo, a style of composition in which one principal melody or theme is conspicuous by means of frequent periodical repetition. Haydn's pianoforte sonatas are a source of much exquisite, healthy, fresh music. Much that the student finds in Mozart's and especially in Beethoven's sonatas will be better understood when he is well acquainted with Haydn's similar works.

Haydn is very often regarded as the creator of the *stringed quartet.* It will in no way lessen the great share of merit due to his ingenuity in having been able to give to the form of the stringed quartet such prominence in modern musical art, if we point out compositions for two violins, viola, and violoncello written long before he was born. The older composers, however, were not particular in naming such instrumental pieces canzones, sonatas, symphonies; these different forms were yet in the process of organic development; the characteristic lines of demarcation in a formal as well as in an aesthetic sense were not yet clearly drawn. . . .

The form of the stringed quartet was a favorite one with Haydn, who cultivated it with decided predilection during his long career as a composer. The form he gave it is that of the sonata, already explained here; adding, however, the *menuetto,* which generally finds its place between the second, slow movement, and the finale. The development of modern orchestral music was advantageously influenced by the successful cultivation of the stringed quartet, as it forms the basis of all orchestral works of any importance. Being the touch-stone of a good composer, every artist with earnest aims strove to master its form, though a very small number only succeeded in writing such quartets as present more than a passing interest. . . .

The orchestral symphony, to a very great extent also the creation of Haydn, is likewise based upon the form of the sonata. Similar to the stringed quartet, it admits the *menuetto* as an additional movement, which generally finds its place between the second, slow movement and the finale. Owing to a greater variety of instrumental means, every movement gains in ampleness and richness of formal development: every thought, every melody is filled with deeper and broader emotional contents.

The word "symphony" (*sinfonia*) was used long before Haydn, to designate generally pieces of music composed for different instruments. These pieces at first had no distinct formal character; they were principally played in the way of introduction to cantatas, operas, or church music. In the course of time the short introductions gained larger dimensions; pieces consisting of different movements, contrasting in time and rhythm, took the place of the insignificant preludes, ricercare, fantasias, and all kinds of dance tunes. . . .

Lully, in France, invented the overture to serve as a fit introduction to his operas. Scarlatti, in Italy, placed before his operas a suite of pieces, which he called symphony, consisting of three movements, *allegro, adagio, allegro;* leading into each other without interruption. This latter form of orchestral pieces is very probably the beginning of the modern symphony. The establishment of orchestral bands at the principal courts throughout Europe—the result of the growing fancy for instrumental music—created at the same time a desire for suitable orchestral pieces. Intelligent leaders of such bands were not always satisfied with playing Lully's overtures or Scarlatti's symphonies only; they tried their hands at these forms independent of the opera or oratorio. Thus every movement of these pieces gradually received a more ample development. Among the many musicians who then composed such orchestral symphonies, Ph. E. Bach may be regarded as the one whose works exercised a marked influence on the endeavors of Haydn himself.

However, when one compares Haydn's symphonies with those of his predecessors, the difference is in every way so great that but for the historical facts, one would be induced to regard Haydn as the original creator of this form of instrumental music. Haydn composed his first symphony in the year 1754. He composed one hundred and eighteen during his lifetime; of these only a few are occasionally performed now. Haydn was always a very industrious man and had but little help from others in the study of the fundamental rules and principles of his art. It is astonishing how great an influence Haydn alone has exercised on the development of modern instrumental music; and how successful his own endeavors were when one considers how little the field of the stringed quartet and that of the orchestral symphony were cultivated at the time he began to write. It must, however, be borne in mind that, but for the timely opportunity that offered itself to him of leading an excellent, though small, band of orchestral performers, who entered willingly into all his intentions, with whom he could venture to try all his new experiments, his talent might have taken quite another direction, or vanished unperceived; for it is of no small consequence to inventive talent to find a soil advantageous to the cultivation of new ideas, and to be fortunate enough to live to gather the ripe fruit.

Haydn, by means of his industry and original stamp of talent, was well fitted for impressing on the material with which he had to work his own individuality and aim; and once embarked in the new direction, with every step he went forward he had to invent, to improve, to build up, to enlarge. He taught the orchestral instruments a new language. Though the art of instrumentation brought to such a height in our days had not yet revealed to him all its great mysteries, yet his orchestral combinations are nevertheless as characteristic, and in their way as effective as they are original and ingenious, especially in the great symphonies composed for London.

Haydn's symphonies reveal his whole emotional world, child-like *naïveté,* unrestrained joy, good-natured humor. Though the greater part of his numerous instrumental compositions are now forgotten, yet enough of them remains to bear witness to his great genius, his extensive musical knowledge, and the unremitting devotion he entertained for his beloved art. To the very last of his artistic career he grasped every opportunity of improving and enriching his talent; and the works of his great contemporary, Mozart, whose exceptional genius he gladly recognized and admired, in many ways influenced the style and the form of his later compositions.

Of Haydn's contemporaries—and he had quite a number of distinguished ones—Mozart was the greatest. Though many years younger than Haydn, and also, in some respects, a disciple of this latter, Mozart, by means of his great inventive powers, created while yet a youth such important works that as a composer he soon took rank next to Haydn. Mozart . . . commenced his musical career as a virtuoso on the pianoforte. He early became acquainted with the works of the best masters who composed for the pianoforte; and, above all, with Haydn's sonatas, then justly admired by every connoisseur. Besides his great talent, he had the good fortune to be under the personal direction of an exceptional artist, his father, Leopold Mozart, in whom he found a faithful and conscientious counsellor and critic, and under whose watchful eyes his first efforts in composition were made.

The sonata, then the favorite form of the musician as well as of the amateur, received his especial attention; he composed quite a number for different instruments. Although he followed the sonata as constructed by Haydn, on the whole, he differed, notwithstanding, in many points from his models, enriching, enlarging here and there, according to his own imaginative powers. For instance, Haydn often bases his first movement on one principal idea or theme; Mozart, for the sake of greater contrasts, generally associates with the first distinctive theme a second—the first rather spirited; the second of a predominantly singing character and rather quiet in sentiment. Not in this respect alone do we feel the composer's forming hand; but the fact of his having been a fine executant renders each period of his tone-poem richer in brilliancy of passages, effective variations, and exquisite, tasteful ornaments. Everywhere his own amiable individuality is felt. . . .

. . . The form of the symphony, as developed by Haydn, was in its main features adhered to by Mozart. The step he took beyond Haydn is to be found in a more richly colored instrumentation. In Mozart's symphonies there exists more freedom in the use of instrumental means: the motivos, the groundwork for thematic progression and contrapuntal combinations, are more frequently intrusted to wind instruments. Groups of certain instruments are opposed to other instruments, alternately taking part in the discussion of a principal thought, thus forming euphonious and characteristic contrasts, giving at the same time more variety of tone-color to the whole composition.

The melodic element, the cantilena, like all Mozart's melody, is imbued with more warmth of feeling, and deeper and nobler expression.

The whole contents, though still the emanation of pure joy and ideal happiness, already present a strong undercurrent of melancholy, bordering here and there on sadness. The struggles and many great disappointments which the noble-hearted artist had so rudely experienced during the latter part of his life left their gloomy stamp upon his soul (G minor symphony). Some of Mozart's symphonies already reveal moments of that deeply melancholy emotion which fills Beethoven's finest instrumental works.

Haydn and Mozart, the great representatives of a higher order of instrumental music, called forth a number of followers and imitators. I may mention Gyrowetz, Pleyel, Pichl, Kozeluch, Wranitzky, Dittersdorf, Vogler, Romberg, A. Hoffmeister, Fesca. Though some of these composers' works once enjoyed universal popularity with musical amateurs, often disputing the palm even with those of Haydn and Mozart, they have, with few exceptions, sunk into oblivion, the giant Beethoven having unmercifully put out their little borrowed lights.

QUESTIONS

1. What do the sonata, string quartet, concerto, and symphony have in common? What are their differences?
2. What do we mean when we say that Haydn "invented" the symphony? Does this kind of inventing follow the same thought-process as the invention of, say, the telephone, or the automobile? In what ways, if any?
3. Beethoven completed his Ninth Symphony at the age of 53. By the time Haydn was 53 he had already completed about 80 symphonies. Can you suggest reasons for this? Did Haydn have more time to compose? Was Haydn a "better" composer? Was Beethoven a "lazy" composer?
4. Why did Haydn feel he owed a debt to K. P. E. Bach? What did K. P. E. Bach do for Haydn?
5. Look up *Esterhazy* in a music dictionary or encyclopedia. Are there any jobs today that are similar to the job Haydn held with the Esterhazys? Is such employment a help to a composer, or a hindrance? Discuss both sides of the question.

THE CONCERT SOLOIST / 1

Jascha Heifetz (1901-   ) is considered by many a violin virtuoso ranking only below Paganini—and some believe that he would have been able to show Paganini a fingering trick or two. In any case, the position of Heifetz as the master violin technician of our century is firmly established. Paganini presented his fireworks in an atmosphere of hocus-pocus and deviltry; Heifetz presents the same works calmly, almost impassively. Charles O'Connell wrote the following essay in 1947 while he was musical director of the R.C.A.-Victor Company. Between 1930 and 1944 he was, as he put it, "solely responsible for virtually every Red Seal record made in America." As a business associate and as a friend, O'Connell was able to report with authority on Heifetz at work and Heifetz at play.

Jascha Heifetz

CHARLES O'CONNELL

"AND WHO, MR. O'CONNELL, WILL PAY THE HOTEL and traveling expenses of myself and my representative, from New York to Philadelphia, Camden and return?"

"*You* will, sir."

The question was asked with the iciest hauteur, which is perhaps why my answer to Jascha was rather "curt, clear, concise." The occasion was the first recording I had undertaken with Heifetz, more than ten years ago [in 1937]; it was also one of the first I had ever been responsible for, and I felt a certain strain. I had been warned that Heifetz was aloof, difficult, and overbearing; and that if he felt he could successfully impose this attitude once, I'd never thereafter be able to cope with him. All this was untrue, and though Jascha accepted my statement calmly and without question, I have to this day regretted its uncompromising and abrupt quality. I have come to understand him rather well, and from that understanding has developed a warm and durable friendship, highly prized indeed. One of the things I began to understand on that very first occasion of our working together was that Jascha not only likes, but insists upon having, everything strictly *en règle,* and strictly in accordance with his understanding of the *règles*. In the instance I cite, Jascha wasn't interested in the few dollars involved in a two-day sojourn in Philadelphia or Camden, where our studios were located at the time. He was very much interested in seeing to it, personally, that the company would fulfill all its obligations, and pay his expenses, if it were "so nominated in the bond." For my part, I was very much interested in seeing to it that expenses were kept at the minimum, because at that stage of the renaissance of recorded music, any disbursement for which I was responsible would be gone over with a rather jaundiced eye, and I had obtained authority to proceed with recording under our contracts only on my representation that it would cost nothing except our materials and labor. I was happy, therefore, that Jascha so meekly accepted my verdict, and I began at once to regard him with a much more friendly eye. The truth was that his contract required him to present himself, at a mutually convenient time, at our studios in Camden or elsewhere, to complete the requirements of our recording agreement. There was no stipulation respecting the expenses of his traveling, and I was determined that we would not be responsible for them. The records we made—the Richard Strauss sonata, a lovely little

---

JASCHA HEIFETZ from *The Other Side of the Record* by Charles O'Connell;

piece called *An Einsamer Quelle,* and one or two other *morçeaux*—wouldn't have justified much financial investment anyway. Wonderful they were, but the Strauss sonata, difficult, ungrateful, and appealing mostly to the connoisseur, never sold very well. Anyone who ever thought Heifetz "cold," however, should listen to his tone in *An Einsamer Quelle*! Not many did.

At this same recording session I had a rather startling experience of the fiendish accuracy of Jascha's sense of pitch. Naturally, I had had our piano, a fine Steinway concert grand that had been used for a season by Rachmaninoff and then bought by Victor, tuned for the occasion, and the tuner had finished not five minutes before Jascha arrived. I asked him to stay around a few minutes until we could get started, and it was rather fortunate that I did so. Jascha came in, laid down his violin case, walked over to the piano, touched a note and said, "This piano is out of tune." I indignantly disagreed, and Jascha just as vigorously insisted he was right. He touched another note and I said, "If that 'A' isn't absolute 440 I'd give a ten-dollar bill to anybody who would prove it." Jascha said, "You are right, it is a 440 'A,' but I tune to 444." Whereupon I recalled the tuner, Jascha gave the tuner his "A," and we sat there and waited while the piano was pulled up to 444 "A" from top to bottom. I may be wrong about the exact frequency of Jascha's "A," but at least it was not more than three or four cycles different from the standard 440.

Curiously, Heifetz and I had another disagreement over expenses, and this time in connection with one of the last of his recordings, the Walton concerto, which he recorded with the Cincinnati Symphony under Eugene Goossens' direction. I had been at some difficulty and very substantial expense in arranging this recording. Jascha and Gene were quite leisurely in making the records—which is as it should be, but Victor, footing the bills, doesn't see it that way—and when after considerable unexpected cost and other irritations I was confronted with a bill for about sixty dollars for traveling expenses, from Jascha, it was too much; not too much money, but too much irritation. Sixty dollars isn't a great sum in comparison with the several thousands I had spent for the orchestra musicians' services, but out of sheer mulishness I wouldn't pay it. There was considerable acidulous correspondence between J. H. and myself, both of us being pretty stubborn. I had a feeling that I'd have to capitulate eventually, so I cast about for some kind of face-saving device and thought I had found one. I agreed to pay Jascha not his traveling expenses, but rather the recording fee of a union musician, which in fact we were required, by our arrangement with the American Federation of Musicians, to pay any player who recorded for us, be he Heifetz, Rachmaninoff, or some obscure fiddler. This would have amounted to eighty-four dollars, as against the sixty-odd dollars Jascha demanded for expenses. Jascha very calmly, firmly and good-naturedly refused the eighty-four dollars and reiterated his demand for sixty. He got it. Ever since we have regarded each other as poor businessmen. He says I am because he thinks I wanted to pay more than he asked; I think he is because he took less than he should have been paid.

Once convinced he is right, Heifetz is the most stonily stubborn individual I have ever met. He has a set of principles devised by himself, and as far as I know wholly admirable. No power this side of paradise can force or persuade him to deviate from them by one-tenth of one degree. In the instance I have just cited, he felt that, regardless of what his contract might say, the company had asked him to change his plans and the course of his tour in order to make a record, and therefore should in equity be responsible for the personal expenses he incurred. That the making of the record was to his advantage, that the company spent some thousands of dollars in making it, had no bearing on the case. His expenses should be paid—by the company. Why didn't he take the larger sum offered him and call it expenses? For three reasons: his very sensitive conscience would be troubled, his meticulous accounts would have to include something equivocal, and he would be tacitly accepting working conditions imposed by the musicians' union, which at the time he was vigorously opposing. This last seemed especially entertaining to me later when I found that for many years Jascha has been an honorary member of the union—the Los Angeles local, I think. In return for his services, gratis, at a benefit sponsored by the local years ago, the privileges of a union worker—but not the responsibilities —were bestowed on him. I wonder if Mr. Petrillo knew this when Jascha was so vigorously having at him.

Certain aspects of his playing really represent corresponding qualities of the man himself. Of his personal and artistic integrity, almost unique in the whole world of musicians, I need not speak. But he is also careful, meticulous, precise, scrupulous, and ethical in everything he does. He is reluctant to make a promise, or any kind of commitment whatever; but once made, agreements and promises are kept to the letter. This has been embarrassing to him at times, I am sure. I could almost see his mental distress on one occasion when, I suppose, he must have come as close as ever he could to breaking his word. Some very nasty reports about me had been brought to him, very likely in confidence, and he actually writhed in indecision as to whether he should tell me of them to protect me against those who were circulating them, and in doing so violate his *parole* to people much closer to him than

I was—or, knowing these stories to be untrue, let me go on in ignorance of them until the inevitable damage resulted. Jascha never explicitly quoted these stories to me or mentioned anyone's name as author of them (I got the facts from other and less scrupulous sources), but in retrospect I can see that he gave me more than one subtle warning, and many an oblique suggestion, which I was too naïve at the time to appreciate.

Heifetz is so direct and honest himself that he often doesn't see, or at least doesn't want to see, dissimilar qualities in others. We had been for some time agreed on the validity of a project that had become a "pet" of mine and of which J. H. was to be an important part. I have long believed that all the truly great masterpieces of music should be recorded by *all* the ablest interpreters. There are conductors other than Beecham who have something to say in Mozart, others than Koussevitzky can set forth the music of Tchaikovsky. Stokowski is not the only exciting conductor of Wagner. Every great interpreter projects every great work with authority and intelligence, if not necessarily definitively; and each first-rank interpreter has an audience that thinks *he* is number one man, and that is entitled to satisfaction on records. It was part of my plan that *each* of the most distinguished violinists under contract to us should, as circumstances made it practicable, record *all* the unequivocal masterpieces of violin literature. I wanted first of all Heifetz, whom I consider absolutely *hors de concours* of living instrumentalists, to undertake all the five or six really master concertos. The project had progressed. He had recorded the Sibelius with Stokowski (and discarded it, I thought unreasonably); he made it again in England, satisfactorily; he had done the Brahms with Koussevitzky; his Tchaikovsky was in our catalog; the Walton, which he considers as ranking with the others I have mentioned, was in prospect; so were the Mendelssohn, the Chausson *Poème,* and the Elgar. The presence of Toscanini, and the excellence of the NBC Symphony, suggested the possibility of a glorious Beethoven concerto, and I agreed with Jascha that if arrangements with Mr. Toscanini could be made, we would undertake the work at the first opportunity.

I was unable, for more than a year I think, to penetrate to Toscanini with this idea. It was necessary at the time, for reasons I don't recall, to approach the maestro through Samuel Chotzinoff. I didn't anticipate any difficulty here, since Chotzinoff is Jascha's brother-in-law, and might be presumed favorable to Jascha's project. Month after month went by; Jascha needled me, I needled Chotzinoff, and nothing happened. Finally I decided that a violation of NBC-Toscanini protocol was less important than a rift between Jascha and myself: I went directly to Toscanini (who possibly had been prepared by J. H.). I found him instantly responsive, and we recorded the concerto in one of the most strenuous and rewarding working days I can recall.

This recording brought about one of those occasions when Toscanini must have thought I was insane. I had, after some prolonged and serious efforts, convinced him that NBC's Studio 8H was not a satisfactory place for making records, and we had definitely decided to do them elsewhere. Now, however, I insisted on making the Beethoven concerto in that studio. I had good reasons, I think. Toscanini and Heifetz are both precisionists. With them, a sixteenth note is exactly so long and no longer. If, upon the note that is played, you superimpose the resonant period of a concert hall, you either to some extent soften and blur the musical line, or if the effect is exaggerated, actually distort time values, and in any case rob the music of a certain intimacy and clarity of detail. Carnegie Hall, where if my own taste were to decide, we would have made this recording, has a resonant period (when no audience is present) of approximately one second. You may call it "echo," if you wish. NBC's Studio 8H, to which Toscanini had accommodated the balance of his orchestra, has a resonant period of about six-tenths of a second. If you don't believe four-tenths of a second make a world of difference, listen to two records made respectively in these halls; or recall, if you can, the quality of the broadcasts of the Philharmonic-Symphony and those of the NBC Orchestra when Toscanini first came. Records show a proportionate difference.

It is difficult to record with enough clarity and detail and precision to please Toscanini; when at the same time Heifetz is involved, the difficulties are multiplied not by two but ten times over. Heifetz may not be more the perfectionist, but he has better natural equipment for being one. It is pleasant to report that my judgment was accepted by both artists, that the recording session was without untoward incident though it exhausted, through its length and tension, everyone concerned, that the records were approved by Heifetz and Toscanini, and indeed are of jewellike perfection. It was rather entertaining to observe these two men, so alike in some ways, yet so disparate in age, disposition, and musical outlook, working together during this recording. Outwardly they observed the most rigid punctilio; actually they were as wary as two strange cats, each determined to give the other no opening for criticism, each fiercely resolved upon perfection in every mood and tempo. I must say in candor that this did result, I think, in rushing of tempo here and there, but perhaps this is merely my perverted and malicious imagination. At any rate, the records were issued. Not inappropriately, the album in which they were presented to the public bore on its cover a huge multicolored jewel—an attempt on my part at flattering

Heifetz, which he completely ignored. "Heifetz" (and Jascha didn't know it) means "jewel."

Heifetz cold?

IF YOU mean, "Is he cold in human relationships?" I answer with an emphatic negative. If you mean "cold" musically, my answer is precisely the same. If you mean that his playing is preternaturally perfect technically, if you mean that every move of bow and arm and wrist and finger is absolutely controlled, exquisitely calculated, if you mean that he never abandons himself to emotion or tears a passion to tatters, if you mean that his approach to music is objective, that he scrutinizes it as a lapidary examines a gem stone, weighing, assaying, evaluating the spiritual and intellectual qualities, if you mean that he brings to bear upon music intelligence and intuition of singular power and penetration—if by "coldness" you can mean these things, I'll agree that Heifetz in his music is cold. I have never been convinced of the soundness of the Horatian advice *"Si vis me flere dolendum est primum ipsi tibe"*—"If you wish me to weep, you must first weep yourself." I know no artist, musician or other, who can afford to abandon himself to emotion; I know no musician who ever does. Such abandon is a luxury the audience pays to enjoy; the performer has other things on his mind, and must have. Emotion is certainly the motive power of art, but emotion *isn't* art, it's nature; music and painting and acting are devices, essentially *un*natural, for sublimating, transmitting, and regenerating emotion, and are not designed, primarily at least, for the emotional debauchery of the interpreter.

When Heifetz appears on the stage there is no posturing. "What went ye out to see? A reed shaken by the wind?" You often do—but not at a Heifetz recital. You do perhaps observe a face of Oriental impassiveness, but I think that this expression, or absence of it, comes about because Heifetz pours into his playing every last iota of concentration, of nervous and muscular strength, of a co-ordination of mind, heart, and hand so exquisitely adjusted and so precise that even a smile or a frown would disturb it. If you consider, too, that despite a certain arrogance of manner Heifetz is actually diffident and really modest you will understand, I think, how it happens that he can give an impression of remoteness and frigidity.

I will not forget an incident, one not without certain humorous aspects, that came about in connection with Jascha's recording of the Brahms concerto. It illustrates not only his artistic integrity, but at the same time a degree of human warmth I found quite touching. We had as usual spent a great deal of recording time and money on this work, as indeed the importance of the music and of the artists would dictate. Ten days later I took the records to Koussevitzky, who had conducted, and to my secret surprise, he approved them without reservation. I was surprised because I had noticed certain details that I thought the fastidious conductor of the Boston Symphony would not overlook. Frankly, I was gratified too, because authority—and money—to make this recording had not been easy to get; having obtained them, I was eager and anxious about making the investment a profitable one.

A few days later, in the backwash of a February snowstorm, I drove from Camden, New Jersey, to Heifetz's place in Connecticut, and my troubles began. I skidded from ditch to ditch on those country roads, fearing not so much for my pretty Zephyr, or even for my own bones, as for those precious records. I became lost, and to be late for an appointment with Jascha is unforgivable. In attempting to make up lost time I was arrested and further delayed. Finally, when embarrassed, panting, but triumphant I produced the records in Heifetz's house, the final appalling blow fell. They wouldn't fit his phonograph.

Let me explain that at the time—I assure you not since this experience!—test records, that is, the "proofs" submitted to the artist for his approval, were rather roughly made. Their playing surface was good enough, but they varied in diameter quite considerably, and were always more than twelve inches in this dimension. Heifetz had a Capehart automatic instrument, so designed that a record even a little in excess of twelve inches in diameter would not fit on the turntable. If you think Jascha's face is cold you should have seen it when this situation developed! I had to think fast, and I did get an idea. "You call this a farm, don't you, Jascha?" A tight-lipped affirmative. "Well then, a farm must have tools; tools must be sharpened; you must have a grindstone; where is it?" It was Jascha's turn to think fast, and he did. Grinning like a little boy, he led me to the tool house where we found a grindstone, one that was operated by pedals like a bicycle. For more than two hours we slaved there, alternating in pumping the wheel and pressing the records edgewise against it. I dare say you have often noticed that records break or chip easily around the edge—but don't ever think the material isn't hard!

Finally we had the records roughed down so that they would fit on the turntable. Really they were marvelous. The same little troubles I had noted at the audition with Koussevitzky were there; no matter how tightly I'd close my ears they wouldn't go away, and at the appearance of each one Jascha would look at me with the eye of a basilisk. I knew I was lost before we had finished, but determined to bluff it out to the bitter end. Jascha knew perfectly well how much the company had at stake; he knew Koussevitzky had already approved the records; and he know how desperately I wanted the records approved, how much this approval would mean to me personally and professionally. We discussed them rather vaguely, Jascha knowing that he couldn't approve them, and knowing that I knew he couldn't, knowing too that I hoped he would.

Canny Jascha! Kindly Jascha! Somewhat cruel Jascha! He couldn't honestly approve those records; he had reason to believe that his non-approval would not encourage the possibility of doing them over again in Boston; he knew that I knew every musical reason why he couldn't give his approval. So he didn't give it. He said, in effect, that he would neither approve nor disapprove the records; that I might take them back to Camden without his veto, and he implied that we might issue them. "But," he said (and he was taking a hell of a gamble), "you are a musician, Charlie. I know exactly how you feel, and you know exactly how I feel about these records. You are also a friend. Consider everything involved, and use your own judgment." It is impossible for me to convey to you the importance of this remark by Heifetz. He wasn't trying to evade responsibility; that would be impossible for him. He didn't and doesn't care about the opinion of anyone but himself in musical matters. He was, however, giving me a bolt-hole, to use or not use as seemed wiser to me. At the same time he knew, the fox, which side would win when my musical and personal feelings came into conflict with more material considerations. The records went back to Camden as "not approved"; the sky did not collapse, Koussevitzky was easily persuaded to do them again, and the result is a truly beautiful recording of the Brahms.

I did not have so much luck with Jascha in the case of another and more recent recording. Arthur Benjamin has written a quite fascinating work for violin, viola, and orchestra, and Heifetz wanted to record it as his annual concerto. Circumstances made it necessary to do the recording in California. The only orchestra and conductor available were the Janssen Symphony of Los Angeles and its founder-conductor, Werner Janssen. William Primrose played the solo viola part. After a bitter struggle, we finished the recording, but I fear you will never hear it. It was a trying experience for Werner, unaccustomed to our kind of recording, with a new orchestra, and everyone ill at ease and somewhat in awe of the great Heifetz. The whole atmosphere was charged with animosities. The record is a good one, a satisfying one, as perfect technically as records ever are. Perhaps Werner should have made some places a little smoother; perhaps if he had exhibited more poise and less fever, Jascha would not have been so antagonized. At any rate, approval of the records has been long withheld by Heifetz—Primrose and Janssen dissenting; and I think, and I have told Jascha that I think, his approval is petulantly, capriciously, and unfairly withheld.

That amazing series of chamber-music works issued by Victor during the last several years represents the beginning of another long-range project in which Heifetz was a most interested, helpful, and enthusiastic collaborator—indeed, the mainspring. I think it is extraordinary that a group of virtuosos, men of such extraordinary individuality, force, and diverse temperaments could come together, even in music, and so completely submit themselves to ensemble. This is the final proof not only of great musicianship but of greatness of spirit—and these qualities I would never deny to Heifetz, to Rubinstein, to Primrose, and certainly not to my beloved friend, the late Emanuel Feuermann. Making these records, though it represented extremely taxing labors on the part of the artists, was really a joy. There were difficulties, to be sure, but somehow the spirit of this ensemble made itself felt so strongly that all difficulties, personal and other, were resolved quickly and amicably. There was no haste, there was no compulsion, there was no thought of anything but making music, making it beautiful, and making it permanent. I think everyone sensed that an extraordinary achievement was being accomplished, though, like big-league ball players when a pitcher is trying for a no-hit game, we kept our mouths shut and our fingers crossed until it was all over. The issue of these records put Victor definitely, if perhaps only temporarily, in the leading position so far as recorded chamber music is concerned, which is exactly what I wanted to accomplish. However, I have no means of knowing whether the success of these works will be followed up by others of equal worth. I do know that the same ensemble cannot be gathered together again, for the untimely death of Feuermann completely destroyed the enthusiasm and the spirit that had made these records possible, and therefore Jascha has flatly refused, despite any and all inducements, to undertake further recordings of this kind.

The preparation for the chamber-music records had put everyone under considerable strain. The players had slaved for months to perfect themselves in interpretation and ensemble. The actual recording took its toll of everyone's nervous energy. When the last record had been made satisfactorily, an impromptu party was arranged, and I understand it was quite a party. I did not join it because my own nerves had been rubbed raw from morning to night for too many days in the studio, and I honestly feared that the reaction which might come about at a gay party could lead me to indiscretions of speech that I might later regret. I have celebrated more than once with Jascha, however, and he himself has been host at some notable *fiestas*. When I first knew him he occupied an enormous apartment at 247 Park Avenue—an apartment so big that two full concert Steinways standing at one end of it looked, from the other end, like miniature grands. I am sure that room was a hundred feet long, and it was a marvelous place for entertaining. I have seen well over a hundred people seated in it, and nobody was crowded. I remember this particular occasion because I had the pleasure of seeing a copy of the first edition of my book, *The Victor Book of the Symphony,* auctioned off by Albert Spaulding for $18.50.

The room was filled with magnificent pictures, French furniture, rugs, and tapestries. Behind one of the rarest of these tapestries was a little door, and if you pushed the tapestry aside and went in through this little door you were in an old-fashioned barroom, complete to the soap painting on the mirror, the sixteen-inch bass spittoon on the floor, and a bartender's license, issued to Jascha Heifetz, framed on the wall. There was also a working cash register, and I mean to say it worked, for Jascha demanded some contribution, whether it was a penny or a twenty-dollar goldpiece, for each and every drink he served. He would ring up your money with a flourish, and I know a certain charity that profited very handsomely.

Jascha likes a party as well as anyone else. When he has work to do, however, nothing will tempt him to gaiety, and he lives the life of an anchorite. I do not believe he has ever been intemperate in anything. He loves good food and drink, indulges in them moderately, and loves good company the while. He is fond of the theater and likes music well enough to go to concerts other than his own. His house in Connecticut was an old one, remodeled and enlarged, and this had been done in such taste that the exquisite simplicity of the original house had not in any way been compromised. His home in Balboa, California was somewhat more to my taste. It was designed in accordance with the Frank Lloyd Wright school of modern architecture, largely of native materials. It was beautiful, practical, and *gemütlich,* which is enough for any house to be. But I think Harbor Island at Balboa is little better than a mud-flat. Jascha's interest in boats, of course, led him there, and doubtless for him it was an eminently satisfying location, since his yacht was anchored practically in the living-room.

Heifetz preserves his youth of body and spirit very remarkably, I think. He is about my age, and that is our affair; and he has been before the public since he was a child. His face is yet unlined, his bow arm strong and firm, his left hand knows no error, and his nerves, though acutely sensitive, are under rigid and utterly perfect control. I remember when Jascha used to get himself pinched for speeding once in a while, and there are those who know of gay escapades in Paris and elsewhere. But these are a tale that is told.

QUESTIONS

1. Do you think a concert artist should be above such considerations as fees, travel expenses, and similar items that deal with money? Have such considerations anything to do with his personality? his sensitivity? his concern for his art? Give your reasons.
2. Do you think it would make any difference to you whether a recording of, say, the Beethoven violin concerto was played by Heifetz, or by Isaac Stern? What is the point, if any, in having the same work recorded by different performers? Discuss this question.
3. When watching a musician perform, do you want him to show visible emotion, or do you prefer a calm, "cool" approach? Give the reasons for your answer.
4. Can you suggest reasons why instrumental concert artists are usually either pianists or string instrument players? What about woodwind and brass instrument players? Why are they so rare on the concert stage?
5. Why should anyone attend "live" concerts when one can listen to the same selections on a high-fidelity set at home? List all the reasons for and against going to concerts. Discuss your choices.

THE CONCERT SOLOIST / 2

Abram Chasins is an American concert pianist, composer, and music director of New York City's famous "classical" music radio station WQXR. He made his debut in 1929 with the Philadelphia Orchestra, playing his own piano concerto. In the course of his brilliant career Chasins has had special opportunities for knowing and for understanding the great pianists of our time, many of whom he has described in his book, Speaking of Pianists. *Chasins' relationship to Vladimir Horowitz is especially engaging, because each owes a considerable debt to Arturo Toscanini. The first American music conducted by the Maestro was Chasins'; and Horowitz married Toscanini's daughter, Wanda.*

VLADIMIR HOROWITZ

ABRAM CHASINS

JANUARY 1928 WAS A MEMORABLE MONTH IN THE life of Vladimir Horowitz. When he singled it out, I immediately assumed that its significance derived from his sensational New York debut. But I was mistaken. Horowitz had already tasted success; he had already vanquished audiences in great cities. I am not saying that he was casual about his American triumph, but that something else happened. It happened a few days after his arrival in the city that was to become his home, and one day before he was to conquer it in a flaming performance of Tchaikovsky's First Piano Concerto with Sir Thomas Beecham, who also took his first American bow that night. The memorable event was the realization of an even greater dream: Horowitz met his musical idol, Sergei Rachmaninoff.

At that first meeting in Rachmaninoff's apartment, there was no music, just music talk. In one hour they were fast friends. The following evening Rachmaninoff attended Horowitz's debut, as did Hofmann, Lhevinne, Moiseiwitsch, Levitzki, and every other pianist in town. The audience went wild, and the critics groped for fresh superlatives to describe the triumph. But it was a letter from Rachmaninoff containing warm praise and sober advice which proved most deeply satisfying to Horowitz.

"If he had written me that I played miserably, I would still have been happy," Horowitz said.

Some weeks later he was scheduled to play Rachmaninoff's Third Concerto with Walter Damrosch, who had fathered its *première* almost two decades earlier, with Rachmaninoff as his soloist. When Rachmaninoff learned of the concert, he offered to accompany Horowitz in a rehearsal, playing the orchestral part on a second piano. They met in the famed basement of Steinway's piano salon. Horowitz modestly reported that Rachmaninoff said very little, that he merely made a few suggestions. But Rachmaninoff told me that he was completely overwhelmed, that he listened open-mouthed as Horowitz pounced upon the fiendish work with the fury and voraciousness of a tiger.

"He swallowed it whole," said Rachmaninoff. "He had the courage, the intensity, and daring that make for greatness."

These capacities were not always recognized, and Horowitz's career had not been a series of unqualified successes. Following a modest and

---

uneventful debut at the age of seventeen in his native city, Kiev, Horowitz played in Moscow, Tiflis, Odessa, Kharkov, and other Russian cities for two years without setting fire to any of them. Recognition of his superior gifts came in Leningrad when he played twenty-three concerts during the 1923-4 season. Recognition, but no money. He left Russia in the fall of 1925 for Germany, accompanied by his manager and friend, Alexander Merovitch. In Berlin, three recitals were booked on borrowed money, to take place early in 1926 within a two-week period.

"At the first concert, I was very nervous," Horowitz said. "I didn't play well, but I was fortunate. No critics came."

Three days later he played again.

"It was better." One critic attended—an important one. He wrote: "With Horowitz, our pianistic culture is again awakened."

Horowitz was gratified, but startled because he had been hearing Schnabel, Backhaus, and Edwin Fischer during the months before his own appearances. He was given an extra date and the chance to play the Tchaikovsky Concerto with a small orchestra. The third recital finally covered expenses, but nothing much happened.

Hamburg was next on the itinerary. Two recitals were booked in the ballroom of the Atlantic Hotel. Few people came to the first one, but the critics were there.

"A good artistic success," admitted Horowitz. "But, as usual, no money."

Several days later, anticipating nothing more than an idle afternoon, Horowitz and Merovitch went to Hamburg's famed zoo. They spent the afternoon walking around. When it began to snow, they turned back to their hotel. They were dead tired and chilled from the outing. Near the entrance of their hotel they caught sight of the local concert manager. He began gesturing wildly and shouting in a stream of German, not a word of which Horowitz understood. Merovitch translated excitedly that the manager had been searching for them all day because a woman pianist who had been scheduled to play a concerto that night at an orchestral concert had fainted during the rehearsal. Would Horowitz substitute?

The concert in question, Horowitz told me, was comparable to a Saturday night at Carnegie Hall with the New York Philharmonic.

"It's the chance of your life!" exclaimed Merovitch. "What do you say?"

Horowitz hesitated. Exhausted and cold, with no practice, no food, and no shave that day!

"What time is the concert?"

"It's going to start any minute with the symphony."

"All right. Tchaikovsky Concerto. Has the orchestra got the score and the parts? Get me a glass of milk," Horowitz said all in one breath.

A phone call brought assurances that the music was in the orchestra's library. Horowitz ran up the stairs to shave and dress. Mentally, he practiced the score while shaving, for he had not touched a note of the concerto since he had played it at that little concert in Berlin ("With result, zero," he said).

The trio arrived at the hall just as the conductor, Eugen Pabst, was finishing the symphony—not knowing whether he had a soloist or, if he had, what music was to be played. When he walked into the artists' room during the intermission, he was quickly informed of the situation. He nodded and, without a word of greeting, gave Horowitz a cold stare, opened the score, and started right off in French:

"Look, you. I conduct like this. This is *my* opening tempo. Here, I take it this way. There, I take it that way."

"Oui, monsieur, oui, monsieur," Horowitz repeated, bowing from the waist, thoroughly intimidated.

"Just watch my stick," said Pabst, "and nothing too terrible should happen."

After the orchestral opening, Horowitz started. Upon hearing his first crashing chord, Pabst spun around in amazement. At the second, he jumped off the podium and sprinted to the piano, staring incredulously at Horowitz's hands. He stayed right there until the conclusion of the first cadenza, his face a study in disbelief while his arms beat time—Horowitz's time. When it was all over, the piano lay on the platform like a slain dragon and the whole house rose as one, screaming hysterically. Pabst grabbed his soloist and hugged him repeatedly, while the audience tore the place apart. The leading critic reported that "not since Hamburg discovered Caruso has there been anything like this."

"That was my big break," said Horowitz. "Who knows? If not for this concert, maybe my career would never have amounted to much. Today, if one plays well, it is not enough. My Russian success meant nothing at all to Europe or America."

The second Hamburg concert was hastily rescheduled, moved from the Atlantic Hotel Ballroom to a concert hall seating three thousand. Within two hours of the announcement, the hall was sold out. Horowitz was on his way. Paris was next: two recitals booked in small halls. His artistic success was such that he had to play five, culminating in a last recital at the Paris Opéra, an event duly recorded in the annals of Parisian triumphs.

I heard the glamorous story of that recital from friends who were there in 1926 and witnessed the wild excitement that night. They recalled the arrival of vanloads of gendarmes summoned to control an inflamed audience that refused to leave the hall and was breaking up everything not nailed down.

Thirty years later Horowitz told me a sequel to the event which would have shocked any member of that bewitched mob. It seems that their hero left Paris later that evening for his debut in Rome, sitting up all night in a third-class coach, meditating wryly on the exuberance of their ovation—and munching on a tired cheese sandwich that had taken his last sou.

I was reminded of a similar story told by Paderewski, who said that it always amused him to be typed as the Admirable Crichton of the keyboard, pocketing fortunes from houses packed with worshippers. "They forgot," he said, "but I never have, the long climb, the years of slavery which yielded only a lot of experience, but small audiences, little response, and no money."

"My early successes followed a similar pattern," Horowitz agreed when I told him this story, "Prestige galore, but only enough money to pay off some of my debts, to cover the expenses of halls, hotels, transportation, and food. But in Paris I had an unexpected 'break' that had a long-term result. Arthur Judson was there." A contract was signed for twenty-five concerts in America—a tour to be launched in 1928 as only Judson could launch it, including a debut with the New York Philharmonic and appearances as soloist with Koussevitzky in Boston and Stock in Chicago.

"New York was all right," Horowitz said, "but Chicago was a second Hamburg. Isn't it curious that in three countries my success came in other than the first cities? In Russia it was Leningrad, not Moscow; in Germany, Hamburg instead of Berlin; in America, it was Chicago, not New York. The major cities came later."

The pattern was broken in Italy and England. London became a "Horowitz town," though not at once. A Wigmore Hall recital in 1926 "brought nobody and nothing." On Horowitz's return in 1930, he took the city by storm, playing Rachmaninoff's Third Concerto at Queen's Hall with Mengelberg conducting. Ernest Newman grappled for adjectives. The Londoners had found a new idol. Earlier, Horowitz had added Rome to his conquests. First came the usual artistic success with small financial returns; then came the invitation to reappear the next season, starting with a command performance for the Queen of Italy.

Ten years after his career had been launched, Horowitz's fame had spread throughout France, England, Italy, Germany, Belgium, Holland, Switzerland, Scandinavia, and the United States. Then in 1936, following an appendix operation, Horowitz withdrew from the platform for two years. "I had a lot of things to think about," he said. "One cannot go through life playing octaves."

It was a modest comment. Horowitz's octaves are not just octaves. Nor are his scales and double notes just scales and double notes. They always dramatize the music he plays. They have a controlled intensity unmatched by any other pianist. They are played with flawless honesty and accuracy, with speed and volume that make his rivals sound tame and timid by comparison. The subtle restraint of his pedaling, the variety of his touch and accentuation, his relentless rhythm in bravura, and the sheer excitement he generates have been worth anyone's price of admission. A Horowitz recital was always an experience, but it was rarely a deep experience. His playing of the intellectually and emotionally profound literature revealed his limitations. He was unhappily aware of it. It was one of the things he decided to think about.

Horowitz's "comeback" was staged at a charity affair in Zurich, at which he shared a program with the Busch Quartet, playing a group of Chopin solos. He returned to the United States in 1939 under the immigration quota before the outbreak of the Second World War. Since then he has left our shores but once for a two-month European tour in 1946. Through the years, audiences continued to react to his devastating mastery, but were able to note an ever growing human and musical sensitivity. His climactic power never lost its terrifying quality, but he was now able to play meditative passages without restlessness, lyrical passages without tampering with their simplicity. He was even able to smile occasionally. The full expressivity and charm of maturity which began to accrue to Horowitz were most noticeable during what to date have proved to be his last public performances—in 1953, marking the silver anniversary of his American debut.

Will Horowitz play publicly again? I do not think he knows any more than we do. I went to see him, and during the evening I asked him this question.

"I still love music. I practice. I am making some records. I read. I love to talk with friends, to look at my pictures, to listen to recordings, to study a great deal of vocal and symphonic music I never previously had a chance to know. I don't know, but I don't think I will play again in public."

Retiring at the height of one's popularity and powers is unusual. The thing I find even more unusual about Horowitz is the way he is now working, the intensity with which he is seeking greater fulfillment within himself. He has not "let down" at all. He is more dedicated than ever. He played for me that evening. Along with the intellectual and emotional enhancement of his personality has come a richer, more serious, more communicative artistry. The fabulous virtuoso has unexpectedly become an introspective musician.

Absence from the concert platform could well account for his greater philosophic serenity, for the virtuoso who captured the public imagination never gloried in that part of his musical life. Concerts terrify him. People *en masse* frighten him. He always found it easier to learn five new compositions than to attend one social gathering. Today he seldom goes out except to take a walk. Exercise has always been important to him.

"Rachmaninoff once told me," he said, " 'if I don't walk, my fingers won't run.' "

Not only do Horowitz's fingers run with miraculous speed and accuracy, but also the man himself moves at a very brisk, decisive pace. Even in moments when he seems completely relaxed—and they are rare—he is half-coiled and ready to spring. When you visit him, he is full of vitality and cordiality, fueled by an enormous energy. Withal, there are shyness, simplicity, and genuine modesty.

Superficially one could conclude, from Horowitz's quiet charm and diffidence, his wide-eyed wonder about everything, that he is unworldly and naïve. He is anything but. He is aware and astute about the world and people. He has a distinguished collection of French impressionist paintings that he himself has selected with unerring taste and at minimum cost through shrewd evaluation and negotiation.

When he plays canasta and is certain that he has no safe discard and is bound to hand over a fat frozen pack, he will turn toward his opponent looking like a pathetic child, hold out his cards helplessly, and whimper: "Take it. Take any card. I cannot bear to put it down myself." Many an unlucky pick has saved him from the disaster of a bad decision.

He is not always so ingratiating. Socially, Horowitz can be a difficult guest . . . when he shows up. But professionally he is among the most generous of colleagues. If a musician for whom he has little regard is being discussed, you can hardly drag a word out of Horowitz. If an artist he respects is under discussion, even one he may dislike personally, Horowitz will always find something highly complimentary or kind to say, and will mean it. Once we were talking about recorded versions of the Rachmaninoff Second Concerto. There is one that has always aroused me to strong language. "Yes," said Horowitz, "it is not at all good, and it is not right for any artist to allow himself to be so misrepresented. But, you know, I am sure that he left immediately for Europe and never heard the play-backs, and that some stupid engineer finished the job."

Horowitz now lives in a spacious private house in midtown Manhattan, surrounded by his pictures, two Steinway concert grands, and a fine library of music, books, and recordings. His solo discs are made in his living room. He also teaches a little, his interest confined to promising young artists.

Mrs. Horowitz, the former Wanda Toscanini, is a remarkably understanding and devoted companion. Their daughter, Sonia, has become expert at record-editing and tape-splicing, and she works on her father's and grandfather's discs and tapes of their concert performances.

Should Horowitz announce a public concert tomorrow, it would cause a riot at the box-office. Never before has he had so much to give and to get. He can command any fee and any appearance he wants. At the moment, and it may not be true of the next moment, he does not seem to want. Let us hope he changes his mind. Unblemished perfection brought to meaningful maturity is uncommon to any generation, especially to ours.

QUESTIONS

1. Can you suggest reasons why a concert performer can present a concert in one city that is met rather indifferently, and then go on to play the same concert in a second city where he receives wide acclamation?
2. Is it possible in our society for a great pianist to go on for years earning a small amount of money? What accounts for this? Do you think the situation is the same now as it was thirty or forty years ago?
3. Do you think a pianist's playing could be affected by his nationality? Do you think Russians, for example, perform works in a manner different from, say, the English? If there are differences, what would they be?
4. Why would a man at the peak of his musical career decide to stop playing publicly? Is this common in other fields of endeavor? Can you name any people who have reacted to success in this way?
5. Look up some material on Arthur Judson. How did he earn his living? What is his function in music? How has he affected the course of music?

MUSIC FOR PIANO / 1 *Ernest Hutcheson (1871-1951) was a concert pianist before he became President of the Juilliard School of Music in New York City. After an early career as a child prodigy, Hutcheson continued to amaze the concert-going public with various virtuoso feats. On one occasion he performed three concertos in one evening (Liszt, MacDowell, and Tchaikovsky); another time he played three Beethoven concertos in one evening. Despite this tremendous virtuosity, Hutcheson's position as a music educator provided him with a strong interest in the piano playing of amateurs; that is, the playing of the piano for enjoyment and without concern for the profit motive. In this essay, Hutcheson explores the advantages of being an amateur pianist.*

THE AMATEUR PIANIST

ERNEST HUTCHESON

SINCE THE BEGINNING OF THE EIGHTEENTH CENtury the piano has been the friend and confidant of the great composers. Scarlatti, Handel, Bach, Haydn, Mozart, Beethoven, Schubert, Mendelssohn, Schumann, Chopin, Brahms, Liszt, Debussy, to mention only the most eminent of a long lineage, wrote voluminously for it or its predecessors the spinet, harpsichord, and clavichord, and lavished on it much of their finest thought and inspiration. A majority of them not only were great composers for the instrument but also rank among its most famous performers.

Some interesting exceptions to this general statement may be noted. Many composers of opera have kept exclusively to their own special field, contributing practically nothing in the purely instrumental forms. One may spend a lifetime in the enjoyment of music without encountering a single original piano piece by Gluck, Rossini, Bizet, Gounod, Verdi, Wagner, or Puccini. Almost all the Italian and most of the French opera-writers might be added to this group. The talented English contemporaries Elgar, Delius, Holst, and Vaughan Williams and a few of the leading exponents of ultra-modern music, notably Schönberg and Stravinsky, have also written comparatively little for the piano.

It remains true that the piano is the favored daily companion of the musician, and it is scarcely surprising that its literature is one of amazing wealth, surpassed in music only by that of the orchestra. Most complete of instruments with the exception of the grand, unwieldy organ, the piano may justly be accounted a miniature orchestra within itself. The most intricate scores are susceptible of adaption to its keyboard for use in the rehearsal and illustration, sometimes in the actual performance of operas and other large works when the full orchestra is not available. Commanding an immense range of pitch, dynamics, and polyphony, the ten fingers of the pianist can execute almost anything that is capable of expression in tone.

The piano is the friendliest of all musical instruments. Though entirely independent of others, it by no means wraps itself in haughty isolation. It willingly and effectively co-operates with strings or wind instruments in any conceivable combination for the performance of chamber music, and it obligingly offers its services to the soloist who may need a harmonic background to his melody. It thus becomes the

---

most universal and indispensable medium of music. It is a familiar sight and sound in every cultured home, and in these days of transmission by air no radio station could operate without it for twenty-four hours.

As an essential feature of its friendliness the piano is the most merciful of instruments to the beginner. If you take up the violin, assiduous effort is required before you can play even a simple piece in tune and with attractive tone, whereas on the piano a very novice can produce agreeable sounds, and though you may hit wrong notes, you cannot play too flat or too sharp. With a tone and a pitch ready-made, so to speak, and with the advantage of sitting in a natural and comfortable position, the player with but a moderate facility can almost from the start make real music, creating beauty for himself and others.

It would be as foolish as it is unnecessary to make extravagant claims where so many are valid. Admittedly the piano cannot sing like the violin or the human voice, for the simple reason that it cannot sustain an undiminishing tone, let alone swell on a note. But it has its own idiom, and within that idiom it attains a melos perfectly satisfactory to the ear. In fact, the singing quality of the piano is constantly emphasized by musicians, teachers, and the public, doubtless partly because, being difficult of acquirement, it is held a special merit alike of a good instrument or a good player. Long ago, in his preface to the *Inventions,* Bach desired the student "above all to obtain a cantabile style of playing." When Mendelssohn wrote his *Songs without Words* for piano, the implicit assumption went uncontested by the world. Later we find Thalberg entitling a series of transcriptions *L'Art du chant appliqué au piano,* and still later Anton Rubinstein confesses that he modeled his noble tone in emulation of the rich voice of the famous tenor Rubini.

No one would wish to deny that the action of the piano is naturally percussive: the strings are struck by hammers of felt. Instead of being ashamed of the fact, it should be one of our aims to take the greatest possible advantage of it whenever proper occasion presents itself. It is precisely the extraordinary variety of effect possible between extremes of tone and quality that gives the piano its peculiar character and value.

From what has been said it should be clear that the piano is an ideal vehicle for the art of the amateur. The wonders of its literature are easily accessible to him; a very great proportion of the material is well within the reach of a moderate technique, and the most difficult masterpieces are at least readable for better acquaintance. I think of the amateur in a very wide sense, from the lover of music who slowly and painstakingly masters a few pieces, each one a small triumph of pleasurable labor, to the more accomplished player who reads with facility, associates himself with others, sometimes professionals, in chamber music, and acquires a fairly large repertory that he performs well and musically. I have known amateurs who had no reason to quail before the *Sonata Appassionata* of Beethoven or some of the standard concertos; nor would their performance excuse a merely indulgent nod of recognition from the listening artist.

In some respects the amateur is at a distinct advantage over the professional. His activity is devoted entirely to music of his own choice; he is under no obligation to a ticket-buying audience, and therefore need not hesitate to play although his program is not quite "up to concert pitch"; and he has the leisure to browse in the lush pastures of the literature often denied to the traveling artist busied with a limited yearly concert repertory. The concert player is made sadly aware that the best of everything is not good enough for the critical fraternity, but no one reproaches the sincere amateur for failure to achieve impossible perfection, maintain breakneck speeds, or fathom all the depths of Beethoven's soul. Finally, the amateur enjoys an enviable freedom in forming and expressing personal opinions without the responsibility to the public and the restraint of courtesy toward colleagues to which the expert is rightly subject.

QUESTIONS

1. Are there as many pianos in private homes now as there were, say, 25 or 30 years ago? Why do you think so?
2. Do you have a piano at home now? What is the function of the piano in your home at present? Is it the same now as it used to be? If you have no piano, do you wish you had one? Why?
3. Look in the "Yellow Pages" of your telephone book under "Musical Instruction" and count the number of piano teachers in your city. Are you surprised by the number listed? How many do you think are not listed? Would piano teaching be a lucrative profession? Why do you think so?

MUSIC FOR PIANO / 2 *Frédéric Chopin (1810-1849) is listed among the greatest composers of music for the piano. At the age of 19 he was already an important composer and a pianist of the highest eminence. He was in his time the pianists' pianist, numbering among his admirers such virtuoso performers as Liszt and Czerny. In 1839 Robert Schumann, on hearing several of Chopin's piano pieces, wrote, "He is and remains the boldest and proudest poetic spirit of the time." Chopin's last ten years were bound up with his relationship with the novelist George Sand (Mme. Dudevant)—a relationship that ended in mutual bitterness. Herbert Weinstock has written half a dozen books on music. The following essay from* Chopin, The Man and his Music *shows us Chopin a year before his death.*

Chopin at 38

HERBERT WEINSTOCK

ON FEBRUARY 16, 1848 CHOPIN GAVE A CONCERT AT the Salle Pleyel. For this, his last public appearance in Paris, the program read:

1. Trio—Mozart, played by Chopin (piano), Jean-Delphin Alard (violin), and Franchomme (cello)
2. Arias—Mlle Antonia Molina di Mondi
3. Nocturne and Barcarolle—Chopin, with the composer at the piano
4. Aria—Mlle Antonia Molina di Mondi
5. Étude and Berceuse—Chopin, with the composer at the piano

INTERMISSION

6. Scherzo, Adagio, and Finale from the Cello Sonata in G minor—Chopin, played by the composer and Franchomme
7. New aria from *Robert le diable*—Meyerbeer, Gustave-Hippolyte Roger
8. Préludes, Mazurkas, and Waltz in D♭ major, opus 64—Chopin, with the composer at the piano

In the rooms on the rue Rochechouart that Wednesday evening at half past eight an audience of three hundred—having purchased tickets to a total of six thousand francs (they could have had as many of the best seats at the Opéra for thirty-six hundred)—heard the visibly ailing sorcerer weave his unique spells. The political situation was darkening: the revolution that overthrew Louis-Philippe broke out the following Tuesday. But nothing of the glamour and glitter of Chopin's Paris was lacking therefor. His close friends, knowing how seriously sick he was, were amazed to see that when he took his place before the keyboard his wasted condition showed only in an exceeding pallor. He walked erect, his dress was that of the eternal dandy. There was no faltering. But there was also no volume beyond a *forte,* and the sorceries were woven among infinite gradations of *piano* and *pianissimo* built up with breathtaking sensitivity to climaxes at the volume where a Liszt climax would have begun. In the Barcarolle the dynamics were reversed by a man conscious of his lack of physical reserve: the piece's tremendous upheavals of sound were replaced by a shimmering *pianissimo* that shook the most musical among his listeners. Again and again in the flower-filled room they called Chopin back. He had to repeat the D-flat Waltz. By then he was holding himself to effort by a fierce expenditure of will. Retiring to the green room for the last time, he all but fainted.

He had bade farewell to the great city that was his adopted home. In twenty months he would be dead.

But Paris did not wish to let Chopin go. Subscriptions were begun for another concert, which was announced for March 10. The wind of rebellion, breaking through on Chopin's thirty-eighth birthday, swept away the possibility of that concert, among the least of its victims. Perhaps Chopin had somehow foreseen the Revolution, in fact, for there had been public announcement before it occurred that he would shortly be leaving the city. A Scottish lady six years his senior, Jane Wilhelmina Stirling, had been one of his devoted pupils. With her sister, Mrs. Erskine, she had long been pressing upon the ailing man an invitation to visit Scotland. Now, with the aristocratic society of Louis-Philippe's reign collapsing about him, he had no reason left for remaining in France. He decided to cross the Channel again for the first time in eleven years.

On March 4, while preparing his departure, Chopin called on Mme. Marliani and there accidentally encountered George Sand. Their conversation was brief. On February 28 Solange Clésinger had given birth to a daughter. On March 3 Chopin had written her: "The arrival of your little daughter has given me, as you may suppose, more joy than the arrival of the Republic." And on Sunday, March 5, he wrote to Solange again, this time to tell her of his encounter with her mother:

> Yesterday I went to Mme. Marliani, and as I left I met your mother at the vestibule doorway; she was coming in with Lambert. I said good-day to your mother, and my second phrase was: had she had any news of you lately. "A week ago," she replied. "You have not heard anything yesterday or the day before?" "No." "Then I can tell you that you are a grandmother; Solange has a daughter, and I am very happy that I am able to be the first to give you the news." I bowed and went downstairs. Combes the Abyssinian (who has fallen right into the Revolution on arriving from Morocco) was with me, and as I had forgotten to say that you are doing well, an important thing, especially for a mother (now you will understand that easily, Mother Solange), I asked Combes to go up again, as I could not manage the stairs, and tell her that you are getting on well, and the child too. I was awaiting the Abyssinian at the bottom of the stairs when your mother came down with him and put to me, with much interest, some questions about your condition. I answered that you had written me a few words yourself, in pencil, the day after the birth of your child, that you have suffered a great deal, but that the sight of your little daughter has made you forget it all. She inquired of me whether your husband was with you, and I answered that the address of your letter seemed to me to be in his handwriting. She asked me how I am; I replied that I am well, and requested the concierge to open the door. I bowed, and found myself in the Square d'Orléans on foot, escorted by the Abyssinian.

"I suppose that she is happy in the triumph of republican ideas," Chopin added. But though he received word in a few days that Solange's child had died, he did not see George Sand again. She had returned to

Nohant, and he went to England, arriving in London on the night of Holy Thursday, April 20. Mrs. Erskine and her husband had taken lodgings for him at 10 Bentinck Street, Cavendish Square, where he found all manner of details thoughtfully arranged, including chocolate to drink and note-paper with his monogram. He had made the Channel crossing "without much seasickness," he wrote Gzhimala, but he had been forced to rest briefly at Folkstone. He did not long remain in Bentinck Street, but moved to a spacious apartment at 48 Dover Street. By May 6 he was writing Adolf Gutmann that he had three pianos—an Érard, a Pleyel, and a Broadwood—in his rooms. "But what is the use," he complained, "when I have no time to play on them?" His days were being crowded with more social activities than were good for a man who was intermittently spitting blood and being forced to rest from wasting attacks.

On May 11 Chopin wrote to Gutmann:

I have just returned from the Italian theater. Jenny Lind sang for the first time this year, and the Queen showed herself for the first time since the Chartists. Both produced a great effect—and, on me, so did old Wellington, who sat beneath the Queen's box like an old monarchical dog in his kennel under his crowned Lady. I have met J. Lind, and she very graciously sent me a most excellent stall with her card. As I had a good place, I heard well. She is a typical Swede, not in an ordinary light, but in some sort of polar dawn. She is tremendously effective in *Sonnambula*. She sings with extreme purity and certainty, and her soft notes are steady and as even as a hair. A stall costs 2½ guineas.

In another letter he told of being invited to play with the Philharmonic, but said that he would much prefer to give a morning recital in a private house, "with admission limited to a certain number of persons." He noted that all the Parisian pianists came to London, but were not all successful: "They want classical things here." And so, to Gutmann and Gzhimala at least, Chopin poured out the small talk of his weary London life. He would not play at the Philharmonic because "there one must play Beethoven, Mozart, or Mendelssohn." Mme. Viardot sang her own arrangement of some of his Mazurkas at Covent Garden, and they were encored. On May 12 he dined with Lind, who then sang Swedish folksongs until midnight. By that date he had five pupils.

Chopin's depression was exaggerated by financial worries, particularly because his landlord was threatening to double his monthly rent of twenty-six guineas. Up to June 2 he had had "only two paid evenings at 20 guineas." He was continuing to give a few lessons at a guinea each, and had no plans for a public appearance. At an evening at the Duchess of Sutherland's, however, he played before Victoria, Albert, the Duke of Wellington, and many others of the highest rank. Tamburini, Lablache, and Mario also performed that evening, and Chopin had two short talks with Victoria and one with Albert. He still refused to play at the Philharmonic, which permitted only one rehearsal—and that public—paid nothing, and found success synonymous with Mendelssohn's music.

It would be possible for him to start life afresh, Chopin remarked to Gzhimala, if he had some days free from blood-spitting, if he were younger, and if his afflictions did not prostrate him. Finally, he succeeded in giving a matinee concert with Mario at the house of Mrs. Sartoris, 99 Eaton Place. This was on June 23. It left him with the wish to give another, and he believed that the two together might net him three hundred guineas, little enough in view of his expenses in rooms just off Piccadilly at the zenith of the London social season.

Finally, one day when spending some time in the company of Manuel Patricio García, Chopin was offered the drawing-room of Lord Falmouth's house at 2 St James's Square for another matinee. As García was Mme. Viardot's brother, Chopin then felt that he must invite her to assist him in the concert, though he did not wish to, apparently because he resented her reporting to George Sand about his welfare. She again sang some of his Mazurkas, and things generally went well. This was July 7; three days later the *Daily News* reported on the "numerous and fashionable assembly":

M. Chopin performed an Andante sostenuto and a Scherzo from his Opus 31, a selection from his celebrated studies, a Nocturne and a Berceuse and several of his own Preludes, Mazurkas, and Waltzes. . . . His music is as strongly marked with individual character as that of any master who has ever lived. It is highly finished, new in its harmonies, full of contrapuntal skill and ingenious contrivance; and yet we have never heard music which has so much the air of unpremeditated effusion. . . .

And yet five days later Chopin wrote to Gzhimala:

After deducting lodging and carriage, all I shall have been able to scrape together will perhaps not add up to more than 200 guineas (about 5,000 francs). In Italy you can live a year on that, but here not half a year. The *season* is almost over. I have not yet played at the Queen's palace, though I have played before the Queen (at the Sutherlands'). The Duchess of Suth[erland] has left London. So perhaps the Queen's director has dug a pit for me because I did not return his call or because I refused to play at the Philharmonic. If the season here lasted six months I could gradually get known after my fashion, but as it is, there is no time.

Chopin had met both Thomas and Jane Welsh Carlyle, who heard him play, probably on July 7. Writing from Chelsea on August 5 to his friend the Reverend Alexander Scott, Carlyle said:

If you see M. Chopin, pray offer him my hearty regards. I hope we shall get some language to speak in by and by, and then get into more plentiful communication. An excellent, gentle, much-suffering human soul, as I can at once see without language.

Mrs. Carlyle was deeply impressed both by Chopin himself and by his compositions. Lamenting, like her husband, that the barrier of language made it impossible for her to talk to Chopin, she communicated with him by letter through Jane Stirling, enclosing a mediocre poem by someone else with a request that it be translated and presented to Chopin. "I prefer his music to all others," was her judgment, to which she added that it pleased her particularly by its aristocratic reserve, the way it withheld its inner nature from all but the elect. It is lamentable that no comment by Chopin on either of the Carlyles survives.

Victoria and Albert soon went to Scotland for the summer, and most of society followed them. Chopin's few pupils deserted him. Jane Stirling and her relations were bombarding him with invitations to visit them in Scotland. To Gzhimala he wrote:

> My Scottish ladies are kind, and I gave them your letter; but they bore me so that I don't know what to do. They want to insist that I should go to their homes in Scotland; that's all right, but nowadays I have no heart for anything. Here whatever is not boring is not English.

Finally he had no choice. He accepted an invitation from Miss Stirling's brother-in-law, Lord Torphichen, to stay at Calder House, which was located in Midlothian, twelve miles from Edinburgh. He also agreed to play at Manchester in a concert to be shared with Mme. Marietta Alboni.

From Calder House, on August 19, Chopin sent to his family in Warsaw a very long report on his experiences in London. Having described his appearances at the Duchess of Sutherland's, Mrs. Sartoris's, and Lord Falmouth's, he added:

> After that evening at the Duchess of Suth[erland]'s, I was told that I was to play at the Queen's palace; but I did not play, why I do not know. Probably because I did not apply for it, and here you have to apply for everything, there is such a congestion of things. Not only did I not apply, but I did not call on the Kapellmeister of the court, or rather, the man who arranges concerts for the Queen and conducts the Philharmonic Society's orchestra (which gives the best concerts here, resembling the Conservatoire in Paris). The Philharmonic Society invited me to play for them: a great favor, or rather honor; everyone who comes here tries for it, and this year neither Kalk[brenner] nor Hallé played, despite much effort. But I refused, and this made a bad impression on musicians, and especially on conductors. I refused once because I was not well; that was the reason I gave; but the real one was that I should only have had to play one of my concertos with the orchestra, and these gentlemen give only one rehearsal, and that in public, with entrance by free ticket. How can you rehearse and repeat! So we should have played badly (though apparently they know my concertos, and Mrs. Dulcken, a famous—hm!—pianist here, played one last year there); so I sent regrets to the Philharmonic Society. One newspaper took offense at this, but that doesn't matter. After my matinees many newspapers had good criticisms,

excepting the *Times,* in which a certain Davison writes (a creature of poor Mendelssohn's); he doesn't know me, and imagines, I am told, that I am an antagonist of Mendelssohn. . . .

Saying that he had come to know many personages of the great world, Chopin mentioned Carlyle, Samuel Rogers, Dickens, George Hogarth, Lady Byron ("I understand why she bored Byron"), and her daughter, Lady Lovelace. Among his many royal and titled acquaintances he listed Lady Combermere—at whose home he had one evening met the Duke and Duchess of Cambridge—Count Montemolin (the Carlist pretender), Lady Norton (Richard Brinsley Sheridan's granddaughter, famous for her marital troubles and her opinions on divorce), Lady Blessington, and Count D'Orsay.

The letter continues at length with descriptions of Chopin's trip from London to Edinburgh, of Calder House, of what he calls the English *"vie de château."* He mentions having heard from Solange Clésinger, and at once darts off into a long tale about George Sand:

Her biography has been printed and sold in the streets; written and signed by Augustine's father, who complains that she demoralized his only daughter and made her into Maurice's mistress; that she gave her in marriage, against her parents' will, to the first comer after having promised to marry her to her own son. He quotes her own letters. In short, a hideous business that today is known to all the scum of Paris. It is vile of the father, but the thing is true.

He was still blindly and completely on Solange's side in the continuing family quarrel, and therefore opposed to Sand herself and to Maurice, who had more become the shining center of his mother's life.

In a letter to Voitsyekh Gzhimala, also written on August 19, Chopin remarked that the Scottish climate was not agreeing with him: for two days he had been spitting blood. Yet he was planning to go to Manchester, eight hours distant by railway, to appear in a concert on August 28. He had September invitations to houses near Stirling and Glasgow. Early in October "if it is not yet cold (they say that the weather is still good then, and it will bring in about one hundred pounds)," he planned to play in Edinburgh again. Then he glanced more than two months ahead: "What to do with myself next, I am afraid to think." It seemed to him that there was nothing for it but to return to republican Paris, and he therefore asked Gzhimala to speak to his concierge and the woman who aired and cleaned his rooms.

On the day when Chopin sat in Calder House writing to his family in Warsaw and his friend in Paris, the following notice was run in the *Manchester Guardian:*

Concert Hall—The Directors beg to announce to the Subscribers that a Dress Concert has been fixed for Monday, the 28th of August next, for which the following performers have already been engaged: Signora Alboni, Signora Corbari, Signor Salvi, and Mons. Chopin.

In the clean-aired outskirts of Manchester the ailing Chopin was the guest of an industrial potentate named Salis Schwabe. And on August 28 he duly appeared at the "Gentlemen's Concert," only to be outshone by the dazzling Alboni and diminished by the feebleness of his tone in a hall containing an audience of twelve hundred. The program would now be considered a gigantic pudding. An orchestra played Weber's *Rubezahl* and Beethoven's *Prometheus* overtures and that to Rossini's *Il Barbiere di Siviglia*. Chopin played an Andante and a Scherzo, Études, a Nocturne, and the Berceuse. What the singers performed is not recorded, but their accompanist was George Alexander Osborne, an accomplished pianist who had studied with Kalkbrenner in Paris, where in 1831 he had played at Chopin's first concert.

Because Osborne had heard him under more intimate conditions, had known him in happier days, Chopin begged him to leave the hall while he played. Osborne naturally did nothing of the sort. "Notwithstanding this appeal I was present," he wrote, "unknown to him, in a remote corner of the room, where I helped to cheer and applaud him. I heard him then for the last time, when his prediction was in part fulfilled, for his playing was too delicate to create enthusiasm, and I felt truly sorry for him." Chopin appeared thrice during the concert. During the last of these appearances he won the sort of applause that demanded an encore. To the surprise of his listeners, he did not repeat what he had just played, but instead performed something brief that was described as "a fragment of great beauty."

Lingering with the hospitable Schwabe for some days, Chopin rested. Then he went north to Edinburgh. There, after a short but uncomfortable stay in a hotel, he became the guest of a Dr. and Mrs. Lishchinski, with whom he was delighted to be able to speak Polish. By sending their children to stay with friends, the Lishchinskis were able to make room for Chopin and his manservant in two rooms, one of them normally the nursery. These were on an upper floor, and Chopin was by then so weak that the amiable doctor had to carry him up the stairs. Mrs. Lishchinski later told Frederick Niecks that her guest rose late and had soup in his room. His manservant, in addition to keeping his master's clothes in the pink of neatness, curled his master's hair each day. More importantly, Mrs. Lishchinski said that after dinner Chopin, frequently suffering from the cold, sat before the open fire. The Scottish climate was undoubtedly bad for a weakening man in the advanced stages of tuberculosis.

From Edinburgh, Chopin went, probably about September 1, to visit another of Jane Stirling's sisters, Mrs. Houston, a widow who lived in some grandeur at Johnstone Castle, eleven miles outside Glasgow. From there, beginning on September 4, he wrote a long letter to Gzhimala. After describing many events and individuals, he suddenly broke out:

> This letter was begun yesterday, to be finished today; but the weather has changed; it is bad outside, and I am cross and depressed, and people bore me with their excessive attentions. I can't breathe, I can't work, I feel alone, alone, alone, though I am surrounded [Here according to Hoesick, seven lines of the manuscript letter are so crossed through as to be illegible.]
>
> Why should I bore you with my jeremiads! You have troubles of your own, up to your ears. I should cheer you up with my letter. Were I in good humor, I should describe to you one Scottish lady, a thirteenth cousin of Mary Stuart (*sic*!! Her husband, who bears a name different from his wife's really told me that.) Here it's nothing but cousins of great families and great names that nobody on the Continent has ever heard of. Conversation is always entirely genealogical, like the Gospels; who begat whom, and he begat, and he begat, and he begat, and so on for two pages until you arrive at Jesus.

Near the end of the letter, Chopin wrote:

> Today is the 9th. I send you my old letter of Sept. 4. Forgive this scrawl; you know what an effort writing sometimes is for me; the pen burns under my fingers, my hair falls out, and I can't write what I want to say, only a thousand futile things.

While still at Johnstone Castle, Chopin received word that Prince and Princess Alexander Chartoriski (she his good friend Princess Marcelline) and their young son were visiting in Edinburgh. Ill and exhausted though he was, he quickly entrained for that city, and was shortly speaking Polish with the Chartoriskis in a glad reunion. After a brief visit with them, however, he had to travel back to Glasgow, where he had undertaken to give an afternoon concert in Merchant Hall. Because of the hour—two-thirty p.m.—and the price of the tickets—half a guinea each—his audience was limited to wealthy and unoccupied members of the local aristocracy and the near-by county families. The Chartoriskis also attended, and then dined with Mrs. Houston and Chopin at Johnstone Castle.

Chopin is said to have earned sixty pounds from his Glasgow concert, which took place on September 27. Repeating the pieces that he had played in Manchester, he was assisted by a singer, Mme. Adelasio de Margueritte. Among the friends who had visited Glasgow to hear him were Jane Stirling's aged brother-in-law, Lord Torphichen, and Lord and Lady Murray, she formerly his pupil in Paris. And from Glasgow he went to spend some days with the Murrays at their home in Strachur on Loch Fyne. Still expending his small remaining supply of energy on travel, he then went to Keir, in Perthshire, near Stirling Castle, seat of that distant cousin of Jane Stirling who was currently head of the Stirling clan. From Keir on October 1 he wrote Gzhimala the by then usual mixture of gossip and profound lamentation:

If I don't write you jeremiads, it's not because it would not console me, for you are the only person who knows all about me; but because if I once start there will be no end to it, and forever the same. I am wrong to say *the same,* because for me the future constantly grows worse. I am weaker. I can't compose anything, less from lack of desire than because of physical hindrances; every week I bump up against a new tree-branch. And what can I do? . . . The whole morning, until 2 o'clock, I am fit for nothing now; and then, when I dress, everything strains me, and I gasp that way until dinner-time. Afterward one has to sit two hours at the table with the men, look at them talking, and *listen* to them drinking. I am bored to death (I am thinking of one thing and they of another, despite all their courtesy and French remarks at table). Then I go to the drawing-room, where it takes all my strength to be somewhat animated—because then they usually want to hear me—; then my good Daniel [his manservant] carries me up to my bedroom (as you know, that is usually upstairs here), undressses me, gets me into bed, leaves the light; and I am at liberty to breathe and dream until morning and time to start all over again. And when I get a little used to it, then it is time to go somewhere else; for my Scottish ladies give me no peace; either they come to fetch me or they take me the round of their families (*nota bene,* they make their folk invite them constantly). They are stifling me out of *courtesy,* and out of the same *courtesy* I don't refuse them.

Three days after this despairing letter to Gzhimala, Chopin was again in Edinburgh. There, in the Hopetoun Rooms in Queen Street, he gave, not the conventional singer-assisted concert of the time, but a recital without assistance. The program read as follows:

1. Andante et Impromptu.
2. Études.
3. Nocturne et Berceuse.
4. Grande Valse Brillante.
5. Andante précédé d'un Largo.
6. Preludes, Ballade, Mazurkas et Valses.

To commence at half-past eight o'clock. Tickets, limited in number, half-a-guinea each.

The critic of the *Edinburgh Courant* reported on October 7:

Of his execution we need say nothing further than that it is the most finished we have ever heard. He has neither the ponderosity nor the digital power of a Mendelssohn, a Thalberg, or Liszt; consequently his execution would appear less effective in a large room; but as a chamber pianist he stands unrivalled.

This precisely summarizes the opinion of Chopin's playing held, and often expressed, by the best-equipped of his contemporaries.

The cold Scottish winter was drawing in. There was an increasing threat of cholera, which had already begun to spread northward from London. Chopin fell deeper and deeper into weakness, ennui, despair. His round of visits, however, went on—to Wishaw, Lady Belhaven's house, to the castle of the Duke of Hamilton. He was stricken with a severe cold, through which Dr. Lishchinski miraculously nursed him with homeopathic nostrums. Finally—perhaps as much to escape from his "Scottish ladies" embattled on their home ground as to begin his return to Paris—Chopin went south to London. There, a desperately sick man, he arrived on October 31. He stopped at 4 St. James's Place. His cold had returned upon him strengthened, and another homeopath, a Dr. Mallan who was a brother-in-law to Lady Gainsborough, treated him. For fifteen days Chopin could not stir from his room. Then, fortified by medicines, he went on November 16 to the Guildhall to take part in a great concert and ball being given for the benefit of Polish refugees. It was his last appearance in public anywhere.

QUESTIONS

1. Study the program at the start of the Weinstock essay. In what ways does this program differ from concert programs today? Is the program made up of old music? of new music?
2. Look up the value of a guinea in 1848. The essay tells us that the great Chopin gave piano lesses at a guinea each, with few takers. What could be bought in London in 1848 for a guinea? Was a guinea a good fee for the time?
3. What, exactly, was the reason Chopin refused to perform in London and in Scotland as frequently as he was asked? Would you say he was snobbish? high-handed? arrogant? conscientious? Give your reasons.
4. Check the titles of the Chopin pieces named in this essay. What do they have in common? Would you say Chopin wrote absolute music or program music? Why?
5. Certain writers have suggested that Chopin's music reflects the sickliness he felt much of his life. Listen to some Chopin pieces and discuss this question. Do you agree? Give your reasons.

MUSIC FOR VOICE / 1 *In ancient times music was not treated as a separate art. It was inextricably tied to other, more primitive, aspects of society. For this reason little is known with certainty about the special development of, say, singing, before the early Christian era (from about 200 A.D. to 1300). It was only with the organization of the Church that we find organization and method in the treatment of vocal music. W. J. Henderson (1855-1937), a prolific writer on music (ten books), was music critic for the* New York Times *and, for his last 35 years, music critic for the* New York Sun. *The following essay is from his* Early History of Singing.

THE DAWN OF THE ART

WILLIAM JAMES HENDERSON

THE MODERN ART OF SINGING BEGAN WITH THE establishment of schools for the study of the correct manner of delivering the liturgical chants of the Roman Catholic church. These chants were derived from still older music used in the ceremonials of Jewish congregations or in the worship of the gods of Egypt and of Greece. Secular song also had a measurable, but comparatively small, influence in the formative period of vocal art, for some of the early fathers found it necessary to warn their followers against the seductions of this style. St. Clement, the second successor of St. Peter, wrote: "It must not be possible to confound us with the singers and buffoons who for a piece of bread or a cup of wine come to divert people who are feasting."

Before the foundation of Christianity the ancients sang in the Temple, in the theatre, and in the home; but we do not know whether they possessed anything which we would call "method." Nor does this greatly signify to us. Our own art is the child of the Catholic church and its history must be traced from the moment when that church became a single organization, its functions centralized under the dominion of one monarch, and its musical style informed by a well defined purpose.

Until that time this music was uncertain in its progress, which was distracted by the operation of numerous agencies, not only musical, but also religious and political. It is not essential to our purpose that we should rehearse in detail the various steps in the march of church music from the hour when Christ and the apostles sang at the Last Supper the "Great Hallel" of the Jewish service.

To undertake such a study would involve us in endless difficulties without bringing sufficiently remunerative results. We should find ourselves confronted with a mass of fragmentary information, much of it leading to no conclusions. Basic facts of vital import would be too often missing. The most skilful scrutiny of scientific research has served only to demonstrate that they are lost beyond recovery. Our best course, therefore, will be to note some of the most significant facts bearing on the earliest history of modern vocal art, and to show briefly how the various influences which gathered about its cradle made their presence felt.

We must, then, recollect that Christianity was born in Judea, where the ceremonials of Moses reigned in the temples devoted to the worship

---

THE DAWN OF THE ART from *Early History of Singing* by William James Henderson; Longmans, Green and Co.; 1921.

of Jehovah. The country, however, was under the dominion of Rome, and its borders were incessantly crossed by the children of that indomitable empire. At the same time the wily and restless Greeks, both those of the motherland and those of the even more sophisticated blend of Alexandria, were not unknown in the land of Benjamin and Manasseh.

Furthermore we must not forget that the excursion of the religion into the world began early. It was at Antioch in Syria a little more than forty years after the birth of the Saviour that his disciples were first called Christians, and it was in this city that a brilliant and powerful branch of the Catholic church speedily grew up. We need hardly be reminded too, that in the middle of the first century St. Paul was writing epistles to churches in Greece itself, and we have what many historians regard as satisfying evidence that St. Peter visited the Christians in Rome.

It will be understood readily that the early influences brought to bear on Christian church music were chiefly Hebrew and Greek, and that out of the materials of these two kinds of song the first chants of the church were made. Of this formative period we can attempt hardly an outline. Its inner history is too obscure and complicated for our edification, even could we be certain that we are in possession of all the facts. We may with profit turn aside for a moment to glance at the moment of solidification of the elements. To do this we must look for an instant at the movement of the Roman world.

The story of music has habitually been told as if it had developed without relation to general history or influence by it. But no one can be blind to the tremendous significance of the events which culminated in A.D. 324 in the unification of the Roman empire under Constantine. That these events had a bearing on modern music cannot be gainsaid, but in a work such as this they cannot be recounted in detail. We have already intimated that no general system of liturgical chant could exist while the Roman empire, and consequently the Roman church, were divided into so many parts. Nor was the church itself an established institution until Constantine had crushed his great enemy Maxentius in the West and brought grovelling to his feet Licinius, his sole remaining foe in the East. The conquest of Byzantium was the last step toward the reunion of the Roman dominions, partitioned 37 years earlier by Diocletian. The authoritative establishment of the Catholic church was not long delayed, though the cautious Constantine eluded the ceremony of baptism till late in his life.

The music of the early Christians, as we have already noted, was largely Jewish. The gradual emancipation of Catholic music from Jewish influences went hand in hand with the swift spread of Christianity. The parent church of the Christian world was that of Jerusalem, and its first fifteen bishops were Jews. Its rigid adherence to Mosaic law and to the ancient ceremonials of its people aroused frequent, but not quickly successful, opposition. It was not till the religion of Jesus had spread into the adjacent lands that the supremacy of Hebrew law and custom was overthrown. To the century in which the identity of the Hebrew body called the Nazarenes was preserved we owe the characteristics of Jewish music found in the early Christian chants. To the rapid spread of Christianity through other parts of the bulky Roman empire we owe the introduction of characteristics entirely dissociated from the Hebrew. Those who wish to trace the entire history of this movement of Christianity in its absorbing details should refer to the celebrated fifteenth chapter of Gibbon's *Decline and Fall of the Roman Empire,* where the story is told with graphic brilliancy and the philosophy of the events discussed with penetrating insight.

We may now take a swift survey of the early church music with the purpose of determining its nature and the tendencies of its progress. From the very beginning vocal music was engaged in its life-long effort to reach a perfectly artistic equipoise of the two fundamental elements, the literary and the musical. The oldest form of modern art music is the chant, and in that form the rhythm, accent, and movement of the music are those of the text. This principle followed vocal music into the service of the Christian church, and the early liturgy included portions chanted in a style which possessed melodic sequences of tones, but which had no rhythm, nor measure, and naturally no harmonic basis.

But we shall see that even at the outset, when the fathers of the church had no thought of vocal or musical art, the art principle was present, unrecognized by them. The element of floridity, which passed into the service of the church even as early as St. Paul's time, was the agent of musical freedom. Through it independence of movement eventually found its way into the music of the church, for soon after the singing of several notes to a syllable became permissible the purely musical expressiveness and decorative quality of that style became patent to the fathers. From the time when they found that the beauty of the chant could be heightened in this way we may date all the experiments in real composition.

One feature of the Byzantine chant, adopted from the chants of Syria and Persia, and traced also to the religious song of the Hebrews, becomes significant here. In the intoning of certain texts to fixed chants it was the custom to retain carefully the accented parts of the melodies by joining them to single syllables. When it was impossible to sing the text to the melody without doubling notes the repetitions were always made on the unaccented portions.

Here we discern the elementary form of the syllabic chant, the form which endeavors to give one note—or not more than two—to each syllable. This form may be called the recitative of church music. It is the form in which the simple communications of the liturgy are set forth. In its earliest period, as in its latest, the music of the church reserved its most decorative style for the expression of the higher religious emotions; and in the infancy of the art we find the congregation singing florid phrases in the utterance of the responses which formed essential parts of the antiphonal service.

But the progress of congregational singing did not end here. About the end of the third century it assumed in the church of Persia an importance quite significant. Bardesanes, a leader of the heretic sect of gnostics, brought a new life into the services of his people by composing psalms and hymns in which the congregation had a much larger share than it formerly had when its singing was confined to the responses. The Catholics found it necessary to confront this movement and did so by adopting the new method, which thus spread from Persia into Antioch and thence to the entire Orient.

The plan was to divide the congregation into two demi-choruses, one of men, the other of women and children, each delivering a verse of the psalm. After these two deliveries, one by each choir, both united in singing the refrain. Sometimes this refrain was one of the ancient responses, always brief; sometimes new chants, somewhat longer, were composed. The new style was called *antiphonia,* and was introduced into Rome under Pope Damasius, who was pontiff from 366 to 384, into Milan by St. Ambrose in or about 386, and at Constantinople by St. John Chrysostom in 390. This antiphonal singing was certainly as old as the Psalms, and probably was known when Miriam sang her song of triumph. At any rate it belonged to the Jewish church and came thence into these early Christian ceremonials.

We have now before us the two basic elements of modern vocal art, the plain chant and the florid. In the earliest liturgies the latter is found only in the portions allotted to the people, while the syllabic style appears to have been used wholly for the utterances of the priests. In this fact there is a significance which in my opinion has not received sufficient consideration. The singing of responses more or less florid by the congregation, when taken in connection with the texts used for these responses, indicates a tendency, whether conscious or unconscious, to move toward a purely musical expression of emotion.

The early church had two principal liturgies. That of Alexandria and adjoining Egypt was arranged by St. Mark; that of Jerusalem by St. James, the second bishop of the Judean city. In both of these liturgies the Greek exclamation *Kyrie eleison* appears as a congregational response. We find also (at least in the liturgy of St. James) the Hebrew interjection, *Alleluia,* which St. John in his Revelation heard even the celestial choir singing. We find this triumphant praise of the Lord in these eastern liturgies at the close of the Cherubic hymn.

Naturally we have no record of the music which these oriental congregations employed in their alleluias and kyries. But from historical developments of a little later date we were justified in the inference that from the very beginning the restrictions of the rigidly syllablic chant did not apply to the jubilations or the supplications of the people, who were always accorded a wider latitude of musical utterance until the melodic elaborations became too difficult for them. Then the singing of the responses, as well as other parts of the service, was confided to the choir, but the extended manner of treating the syllables handed down from the earliest times was retained. The florid kyrie, amen, and alleluia began with the responses of the congregation.

M. Amedée Gastoué, professor of chant in the Schola Cantorum of Paris, has put forth the latest and most convincing examination of the early church music, and his conclusions embrace the important determination that some chants have come down to us in the forms known in Gregory's time. In his *L'Art Grégorien* he has ably discussed this matter. To set forth briefly his points, the books of the Roman chant which have come down to us show a distinct unity of character. We have not many manuscripts, but the fidelity with which they were reproduced from the second half of the eighth to the ninth century assures us that we possess the chants of the Gregorian antiphonary in the form which they had acquired at that period. Can we go back further—perhaps to Gregory himself? Most probably; for beside the unity of tradition, which is demonstrated, we have a criterion in the chants themselves.

Internal criticism reveals differences of style in certain chants. We have the knowledge that in the second half of the seventh century some chants were added to the primitive Gregorian repertory. Hence, when we find chants revealing a style of a period anterior to these, we are justified in believing that they were preserved in their authentic form, which the Schola Cantorum guarded and of which that school attributed the editorship to its founder Gregory.

In his masterly articles on the chant in the *Encyclopédie de la Musique et Dictionnaire du Conservatoire* the same author, writing at a later date, defines more clearly his conviction that we have in our possession not only chants of the so-called Gregorian, but even some of the earlier period, the Ambrosian, preserved with jealous care by the diocese of Milan. He says:

> The character of the Ambrosian melodies, approaching the Gallican and Roman styles, is nevertheless wholly individual. The matter can be summed up briefly thus: in comparison with the Gregorian chant the simple melodies are very simple and the ornate ones very ornate. The simple chants have in general much charm; the luxuriant vocalises, on the other hand, do not present the artistic distinction which the Roman melodies ordinarily show. The study of the Ambrosian repertory is of puissant interest when one compares it with the Roman. In effect the liturgy of Milan has preserved a sufficiently great number of pieces which one finds again in the Gregorian ritual, pieces going back to the formation of these repertoires. The Milanese chant gives us these pieces in their original state, often defaced, while the Roman presents them in an elaborate artistic form or in the shape of a different variation of the same theme.

The conclusions of M. Gastoué, though not identical with those of M. Gevaert in his masterly work on the ancient chant, lie in the same region in so far as one vital point is concerned, to wit, that we still possess certain chants in their early forms and that we therefore have some definite knowledge of the character and style of Christian church music of the period of its childhood, at least as far back as the final years of the fourth century. For the purposes of the present work the value of these researches lies in their demonstration of the early entrance of that flexible vocal style called florid, upon which modern vocal art reared itself.

The beginnings of this elastic song are to be found in the Catholic antiphonary. Gastoué invites our attention to his conclusion that the responses sung by the people in the eastern churches in the first century were much like those still used in the daily Mass and the minor festivals. He quotes these examples from the Vatican edition of Pope Pius X.

The first of these is in the form of the daily Mass; the others, which are variations of the first, are for minor festivals. These forms were already traditional throughout the Latin church in the tenth century, and M. Gastoué believes that they belonged originally to the antiphonary of Ambrose. At any rate it seems safe to say that they belong to the most ancient relics of Gregorian chant and that they preserve early formulae employed in congregational responses.

Men had groped after a vocal expression of emotion long before the birth of the Christian church and it is not astonishing that the influence of older manners of praise and jubilation affected the infant song of a new worship. Over two centuries before the Christian era Demetrius Phalerius had noted that the Egyptian priests sang on the vowels in honor of their gods. A little later Nichomachus is telling us that the seven planets produce each a certain sound and that the priests in glorifying their divinity invoked him with inarticulate tones and without consonants. One purpose of this was to propitiate the genii who inhabited the stars of our system. The singing of the proper vowel set in vibration the necessary sympathetic waves.

Engel in his *Music of the Most Ancient Nations* pictures an Assyrian sculpture representing vocal and instrumental musicians welcoming a returning conqueror. "One of the female singers," he notes,

> is holding her hand to her throat in the same manner as the women of Syria, Arabia, and Persia are in the habit of doing at the present day, when producing on festive occasions those peculiarly shrill sounds of rejoicing which have been repeatedly noticed by Oriental travellers. Dr. Clarke (*Travels in Various Countries,* E. D. Clarke, London, 1810) says, "They are caused by trilling the tongue against the roof of the mouth without the utterance of any distinct words. Yet this singular mode of expressing joy is all that constitutes the alleluia of the ancients. When Lord Hutchinson first entered Cairo after the capture of the city, he was met by a number of women who greeted him with alleluias; they accompanied him through the streets, clapping their hands and making this extraordinary noise in a loud and shrill tone. It seems to be a constant reiteration of the same syllable uttered with the utmost rapidity."

It is unnecessary to our purpose that we should trace the successive steps in the early expansion of the florid element in the musical ritual of the church. We shall see later that florid singing became of large importance and that the ancient practice of carolling on vowels reissued in the form of prolonged cadences on alleluias, amens, kyries, and other words, and furthermore that elaborate vocalizations of single vowels, such as the "A" in alleluia or amen, had assumed permanent positions in the service. The attitude of the church toward such song is formulated in some words of St. Augustine written in regard to the *jubili,* one of the types of wordless praise. He says:

"He who jubilates does not utter any words, but a joyous sound without words: for it is the spirit lost in joy, expressing it with all its power, but not arriving at a definition of its sense."

We may now make a brief enumeration of the steps which led to the clearer definition of the modern art of singing.

Early in the fourth century Pope Sylvester founded a school of chant in Rome. In 367 the Council of Laodicea forbade congregational singing and placed the musical service in the hands of the trained choir.

Naturally we know practically nothing about the method of Pope Sylvester's singing school, though we see one of its fruits in the transfer of the service to the choir. But it is safe to conclude that the school was instituted for the study of the chants themselves and not for that of vocal technic. . . . The business of committing the chants to memory was one of the most arduous and prolonged tasks of the church singer of these ancient days. But it is as certain as anything can be that, since unity in delivery had to be attained, the schools speedily discovered that they must impart the rudiments of a style. And as soon as this was recognized, the subject of uniform phrasing had to be taken up, and this inevitably led the instructors directly to the consideration of management of the breath. And so from the endeavor to form a style of delivery for the church chant must have come the discovery of the fundamental elements of vocal technic.

Chant is a smooth and flowing kind of melody. Hence its singing requires a perfect legato, and it is beyond question that the rule recently repeated with so much emphasis by the Solesmes fathers, that there must be no approach to staccato in the delivery, was formulated in the earliest days of vocal study. When the instructors in the school of Sylvester had recognized the vital necessity of a pure legato, they must have found themselves confronted with the difficulty of uniting this with a clear enunciation, without which a church service would become a piece of empty sound.

Thus then, the search after a correct style of chant singing carried the early singers directly to the fountains of vocal art. All that remained to be added was a moderate amount of facility in the florid passages, a facility which was destined to develop into unexpected and amazing brilliancy.

QUESTIONS

1. What are some of the distinctions between the art-song and the folk-song? Between the art-song singer and the folk-song singer? Can you make value judgments of these? Why?
2. Why does Henderson believe it is necessary to give us some general history of the Roman world? What is its relation to the beginnings of singing?
3. Discuss the relation of music to words in vocal music. Which do you think is more important? Why? If you were a songwriter would you start with words or with music? Give your reasons.
4. Look up "antiphonal." What are the advantages or disadvantages of antiphonal singing?
5. Look up some passages in songs where each syllable of the text has its own tone. Compare these to passages where a syllable is held over two or more tones. Can you suggest reasons for the differences?

MUSIC FOR VOICE / 2 *Although the names of famous composers of the past are generally well known to the public (even if their music is not), the same is not true of singers. There are singers whose names are familiar—Caruso, Jenny Lind, Nellie Melba—but famous singers are generally left without fame once they have stopped making public appearances. In the following essay Henry C. Lahee discusses a number of male singers who in their time were famous. Today few of the names are familiar. Yet these were men of music who helped create the vocal tradition. Lahee (1856-1953) wrote eight books on music and, as head of a musical agency, had first-hand experience with many famous singers.*

TENORS & Baritones

HENRY C. LAHEE

THE OPERATIC TENOR IS FREQUENTLY AS MUCH OF A trial to the impresario as the soprano. Brignoli would feel hurt unless he received what he considered the proper amount of applause, and then he would have a sore throat and be unable to sing. Ravelli had a mortal hatred of Minnie Hauk, because she once choked his high B♭ with a too comprehensive embrace, and his expression of rage, being understood by the audience as a tremendous burst of dramatic enthusiasm, was, in consequence, loudly applauded. Nicolini, in behalf of Patti, once went out and measured the letters on a poster. It had been agreed that Patti's name was to be in letters half as big again as those used for any other singer. It was discovered that the name of Nevada, who was also a member of the company, was a fraction over the stipulated size, and all the posters had to be cut in such a way that a strip was taken out of Nevada's name, and the middle dash of the E and of the A's was amputated.

Some tenors have travelled with numerous retainers, who always occupied seats at the theatre for the purpose of directing the applause, but nothing of the kind has ever been heard of with a contralto or basso.

Ernest Nicolini, who made his début in 1855, was for some time considered the best French tenor on the stage, but he is better known as Madame Patti's husband than as a singer. Nicolini died in January, 1898.

Fancelli and Masini were tenors of merit, with beautiful voices; also Brignoli, who for twenty years lived in America. Fancelli was a very ignorant man, scarcely able to read or write. According to Mapleson, he once attempted to write his name in the album of the Liverpool Philharmonic Society, with deplorable results. He wished to write "Fancelli, Primo Tenore Assoluto," but after great efforts, which resulted in overturning the ink-bottle, the signature appeared thus: "Faneli Primo Tenore Ass—"

Masini's voice was more sensuously beautiful than Fancelli's, and he was more full of conceit. He travelled with a retinue of ten people, including cook, barber, doctor, and lawyer. He also distinguished himself in London by sending word to Sir Michael Costa, the conductor of the orchestra, to come around to his apartments and run through the music of his part, as he did not care to attend the rehearsal. Costa did not go, and Masini returned to Italy in great wrath.

TENORS & BARITONES from *Famous Singers of Today and Yesterday* by Henry C. Lahee; L. C. Page and Co.; 1898

Joseph Victor Amédée Capoul, who made his début in 1861, was for many years considered one of the best tenors on the French stage. He was born in 1839, at Toulouse, and entered the Paris Conservatoire in 1859, gaining the first prize in comic opera in 1861. He was good-looking and had a pleasant voice, somewhat marred by vibrato, and he was an excellent actor in both light and serious parts. He visited America first in 1873, as a member of Strakosch's company, which included Nilsson, Miss Cary, Campanini, Maurel, Del Puente, and others not so well known, and to which were afterwards added Pauline Lucca and Ilma di Murska. He was also chief tenor of a French Opera Bouffe Company, which visited America in 1879-80. . . .

Theodore Wachtel was for a long time one of the leading German tenors. He was the son of a stable keeper in Hamburg, and began life by driving his father's cabs. He was born in 1823, and obtained his first operatic engagements in 1854, singing in several German cities. His first appearance in London was in 1862, when he sang the part of Edgardo in *Lucia* and made a complete failure. His later appearances brought better results, and yet his popularity was gained more on account of the fine quality and great power of his voice than from any artistic use of it. His high C was his chief attraction, and this note he produced from the chest with tremendous power.

Wachtel sang in America during several seasons. He died in Berlin in 1893.

The greatest German tenor, however, for many years was Albert Niemann, who was blessed with a magnificent voice and a fine appearance, suitable for the impersonation of Wagner's heroes, in which he excelled. He was born in 1831, at Erxleben, Magdeburg, and went on the stage in 1849. At first he sang only small parts, or else in the chorus, but, as he improved with study, he attracted the attention of Herr von Hülsen, General Intendant of the Royal German Theatres, who took him to Berlin. He enjoyed a great reputation for a quarter of a century in Germany and was selected by Wagner to sing Siegmund at Bayreuth, in 1876. Until he came to America in 1886, and 1887, when his voice had long since departed, his only appearances out of Germany were in the unsuccessful production of *Tannhäuser* at Paris, in 1861, and he sang in London in '82. In 1887 he formally retired from the stage.

Heinrich Vogl won distinction as an interpreter of Wagner rôles. He was born in 1845, at Au, near Munich, and was instructed in singing by Lachner, and in acting by Jenk, the stage manager of the Royal Theatre, Munich. At this theatre he made his début in 1865 as Max in *Der Freischütz*. He was engaged at the same theatre almost permanently after his début and was always immensely popular. In 1868 he married Theresa Thoma, also a singer of renown, and from that time they generally appeared together.

Vogl played Loge, in the *Rheingold,* and Siegmund, in *Walkyrie,* when they were produced in 1869 and 1870, and his greatest triumphs have been gained in Wagner's operas. When the Trilogy was produced at Bayreuth, in 1876, he played the part of Loge, and was highly praised for his admirable declamation and fine acting.

Theresa Vogl was the original Sieglinde, at Munich, and was very successful in Wagner opera. She was born in 1846, at Tutzing, Bavaria, and studied singing at the Munich conservatory, appearing first in opera at Carlsruhe in 1865.

As Mario's powers began to wane, people wondered who would succeed him, and many based their hopes on Antonio Guiglini, a native of Fano, Italy. Guiglini was born in 1827, but did not appear in England until 1857, when he sang at Her Majesty's Theatre. He possessed a sweet, high tenor voice and an elegance of style which some critics complained of as cold, languid, and drawn out. His singing was without variety and his acting colorless and tame. Notwithstanding all this, he was called by one eminent critic "the best that has been heard since the arrival of Tamberlik," seven years previously.

Guiglini's career was, however, of short duration, for he became insane in 1862, and died at Pesaro three years later.

In 1872 a tenor appeared who at first seemed to be a worthy successor to Mario—Italo Campanini, who was born at Parma in 1846. He first attracted public attention by singing the part of Lohengrin when that opera was produced at Bologna, in 1871, and beginning with 1872, he was engaged every season for ten years in London. His first engagement in America was in 1873, when he was a member of a company organized by Mapleson, which included Nilsson, Annie Louise Cary, Capoul, and Maurel. In America he became very popular, although he was considered in Europe to have disappointed the high expectations which his early career had justified. He had a pure tenor voice of richest quality, but owing to some fault in his method of production it decayed rapidly, and his declining days were a succession of unfortunate and unsuccessful attempts to regain his lost powers. As an actor he was melodramatic rather than powerful, and he was looked upon as a hard working and extremely zealous artist.

Campanini had a varied and highly interesting experience of the triumphs and vicissitudes of life. He was the son of a blacksmith and was brought up to his father's trade, which he first left to go soldiering with Garibaldi. He returned after the war, and his vocal powers were soon discovered by a musician who happened to hear him sing and secured for him a course of free tuition in the Parma conservatory. At the age of twenty-one he commenced his career as an opera singer. He met with some success, and was engaged to travel in Russia for twenty-four dollars a month. On his return to Italy, Campanini went to Milan and took lessons for a year with Lamperti, when he appeared at La Scala in *Faust*.

His repertoire was remarkable, consisting of over eighty operas. Beginning his career with a salary of eighty cents a night, he rose until he received, under Mapleson's management, $1,000 a night, and in one season with Henry E. Abbey he was paid $56,000, yet he died poor as well as voiceless. He was simple and unaffected in his manners, and, like many of his fraternity, careless and improvident, but he had many friends and with the public was very popular on ample grounds.

Mapleson relates that when he first engaged Campanini to appear in London, he was one day sitting in his office when a rough-looking individual in a colored flannel shirt, with no collar, a beard of three or four days' growth, and a small pot hat, entered and announced that Campanini had arrived in London. "Are you sure?" exclaimed the impresario, wondering how it could interest the individual before him. The strange-looking being burst out laughing and declared that he was quite sure, as he was himself Campanini. It was a terrible crusher for Mapleson to find that his great star was such a rough-looking customer, but Campanini more than justified the reports about his singing as soon as he made his first appearance on the stage.

An American who had the honor of being for three years first tenor at the Royal Opera House, Berlin, and nine years first tenor at the Vienna opera house, is Charles R. Adams. He was born in Charlestown, Mass., in 1834, and after some study with Boston teachers went abroad, where he became a pupil of Barbière in Vienna. After acquiring a high reputation in Europe, he came to America as a member of the Strakosch opera company in 1878, being associated with Miss Kellogg, Miss Cary, Miss Litta, and others. In the following years he decided to remain in Boston . . . [where he] devoted his time chiefly to teaching.

The latter half of the nineteenth century has witnessed the growth of the Wagner opera. In several ways has the doctrine of Wagner made itself felt in musical art. Operas no longer consist of a series of solos, duets, and concerted numbers, with an opening and closing chorus, all strung together in such a manner as to give the greatest opportunities to the soloist. An opera at the present day [1898] must be a drama set to music. The action of the play must not be interrupted by applause, encores, and the presentation of flowers. This continuity of action is noticeable in every opera of modern times, whether German, Italian, or French, and in itself marks a decided forward movement in the annals of lyric art.

There have been many complaints that the singing of Wagner opera ruins the voice, but to contradict this statement we have only to look at the careers of the greatest Wagnerian singers—Materna, Lehmann, Brandt, Niemann, Winkelmann, Vogl, the De Reszkes, Nordica, Brema, and others who have sung the music of Wagner for years without any unlooked-for deterioration. The fact is that they learned the art of vocalization, while many who have come before the public as Wagnerian singers have been practically ignorant of the first principles of voice production. To shout and declaim does not by any means constitute the Wagnerian idea. The music is as singable as the most mellifluous Italian opera of the old school, although it does not call for the flexibility and execution which were considered the great charm of singing in the time of Malibran, Jenny Lind, and Grisi. An eminent London critic writes: "We were tired to death of German coughing, barking, choking, and gargling, when suddenly Jean de Reszke sang Tristan beautifully."

Jean de Reszke is a native of Poland, having been born at Warsaw in 1852. His father was a councillor of state and his mother an excellent amateur musician. Their home was the center of attraction for many notable artists and musicians, so that the children were brought up in an atmosphere of art. Jean was taught singing by his mother, and at the age of twelve sang the solos in the cathedral at Warsaw. He was educated for the profession of the law, but his love of music was such that he decided to prepare himself for the operatic stage, and began to study with Ciaffei, and later on with Cotogni. He made his début in 1874 at Venice as a baritone, and for some years sang baritone parts, until he found the strain telling upon his health. He phrased artistically and possessed sensibility, and his voice was of excellent quality; but feeling that he was not fully prepared, he retired from the stage for a time and studied with Sbriglia in Paris. In 1879 he appeared again, but as a tenor, in *Roberto,* at Madrid, when he made a great success, and from that time he was regarded as one of the greatest tenors of the age. . . . his successes have been chiefly in Wagnerian rôles. . . .

Probably no tenor since the days of Mario has awakened such widespread public interest. His estates in Poland, which in 1896 were extensively improved for the reception of his bride, the Countess Mailly-Nesle, his love of horses and of sport in general, as well as the jealousies of the numerous ladies who vied with one another for his smiles, all in their turn formed themes for newspaper and magazine comment. The personal appearance, as well as the geniality of the great tenor, helped to make him an object of interest, for he is a man of great physical beauty and grace.

Jean de Reszke created a furore in America, and has visited the country several times under the management of Abbey and Grau. When that company failed in 1896, De Reszke attempted to form an opera company to finish the season and in so doing he incurred a great deal of popular indignation by his treatment of Madame Nordica, who felt obliged to leave the company, and by inducing Madame Melba to assume Wagnerian rôles, in which she proved to be a failure. He became the object of newspaper attack on account of the large price which he demanded for his services, but much of this indignation is unmerited for the simple reason that the remedy lies with the public rather than with the singer. An opera singer is justified in getting as much money as his services will bring, and as long as he finds people, whether managers or public, who are willing to pay that price, he will ask it. When the price is refused, it lies with him to determine whether he will sing for less money or withdraw, and it seldom happens that it is necessary for a thoroughly popular artist to withdraw, except at the end of his career. Patti received her highest prices when she was past her prime, and the same may be said of almost every great artist. The reason may be found in the fact that their greatness does not dawn upon the general public until years after their position is earned.

In 1896 Jean de Reszke married the Countess Mailly-Nesle, to whom he had been engaged for several years. She is an amateur musician of exceptional ability, and a lady of much personal beauty.

One of the more recent stars in the operatic firmament, and which is at its height, is Ernest Marie Hubert Van Dyck, born in Antwerp, 1861. He at first intended to become a lawyer and for a time studied jurisprudence at Louvain and Brussels. His musical gifts and love of art could not be repressed or hidden, and whenever he sang his voice created so great a sensation that, in spite of family opposition, he went to Paris to study. As a means of helping himself he was for a time assistant editor of a Parisian paper, *La Patrie*.

In 1883 Massenet heard him sing at a private party at which they were both guests and was so much struck by his voice and style of singing that he asked him then and there to act as substitute for a tenor who was ill and could not fill his engagement. The occasion was the performance, under Massenet's management, of a cantata, *Le Gladiateur,* by Paul Vidal, at the Institut de France.

Within two hours Van Dyck studied and sang the tenor solos with such an effect that he immediately became the topic of conversation among musical Parisians.

He was now engaged by Lamoureux, the champion of Wagner in Paris, for a term of four years, during which he sang the rôles of Tristan, Siegmund, etc. In 1887 he sang Lohengrin, but its production caused a great deal of excitement, owing to political causes. Nevertheless, the performance formed a golden epoch in the history of Wagnerian art.

Van Dyck was now induced by Levy and Goo, of Bayreuth, to take part in the production of *Parsifal* in 1888. For this he was drilled by Felix Mottl, and he made so great a success that he was at once engaged for the following year.

He has proved himself the finest representative of the character of Parsifal that has yet been heard, even Winkelmann not being excepted. Since 1888 Van Dyck has been engaged at Vienna.

Mr. Van Dyck married, in 1886, the daughter of Servais, the great violoncellist and composer. He is a knight of Baden of the order of the Lion of Zahringen and an officer of the Academy of France.

Of Wagnerian tenors, Anton Schott and Hermann Winkelmann gained a high reputation. The former made his début in 1870, but his career was interrupted by the outbreak of the Franco-German war, through which he served, as he had also served through the war of 1866 against Austria. Although his reputation was high in Germany, he made a comparatively small impression in England. Winkelmann took the part of Parsifal at Bayreuth, when, in 1882, sixteen performances of that work were given under Wagner's supervision. He also came to America with Materna and Scaria, making a good impression.

Max Alvary also was well known in the United States as a Wagnerian singer. He made his operatic début in 1881 and appeared in the Metropolitan Opera House, New York, in 1885, since which time he has been heard in America during several seasons. His best parts were Siegfried, Tristan, and Tannhäuser, and he was for many years leading tenor at the Opera in Hamburg. His death, in November, 1898, at the age of forty-one, was the result of an accident.

Of the Italian school, Francisco Tamagno holds a high position in the operatic world . . . as a robust tenor. He excells in dramatic rôles, such as Otello and Arnoldo, and he made a great success in *Cavalleria Rusticana*. In heroic rôles he sings and acts with a simplicity, power, and authority not surpassed by any other tenor of this generation. He was born at Turin, and began his musical education at the age of eighteen. His début was made in Palermo, at the age of twenty-three, his studies having meanwhile been interrupted by military duties. In Venice he sang with Josephine de Reszke, the sister of Jean and Edouard, who had a short but brilliant career. For many years he remained at La Scala, where he was immensely popular. He is tall, big-chested, and erect, always imposing, and, unlike most Italians, he has fair hair and blue eyes. An American critic wrote of him as "hurling forth his tones without reserve, and with a vocal exuberance not reached by any living tenor. He quells and moves by overwhelming strength and splendor."

Tamagno was once the defendant in a lawsuit brought against him by the manager of the opera in Buenos Aires. It appears that in 1890 the tenor was engaged for a season of forty performances, for which he was to receive $130,000. Of this sum $31,000 was paid in advance before he would leave Italy. When he arrived at Buenos Aires a revolution broke out, and only four performances of opera were given. The manager endeavored to recover his money. An interesting feature of the trial was that it brought out the fact that Tamagno always travels with a claque of eight, and that it is stipulated in all his contracts that he shall have eight tickets for their use. This, however, has been denied, and it is stated that Tamagno has not read a criticism of his singing for years, knows nothing about the critical opinion of him, cares less; also that the eight tickets are intended for his family. He is said to be the highest-priced tenor of the age.

Before leaving the tenors a word should be said concerning Edward Lloyd, who in England seems to have inherited the mantle of Sims Reeves. He was born in 1845, and was educated as a chorister in the choir of Westminster Abbey. He has devoted himself entirely to concert and oratorio singing, and possesses a voice of the purest quality, with a style noted for its excellence and finish.

Henry Guillaume Ibos, also, a French tenor formerly a cavalry officer, who made his début in 1885, is a singer whose voice possesses much beauty. He was born at Toulouse in 1862, and has appeared with much success in France, Russia, and England. He also made a tour in 1897-98 in America.

There are tenors coming to the surface continually. Some will sink into obscurity, while others will ascend the ladder of fame; but we must leave them to the future and pay a little attention to the baritones, of whom Van Rooy has recently made his mark as Wotan. He has a tremendous voice, sings with ease, and gets a pleasing softness into his tones. He is likely to be well known in the future.

Charles Santley, who is known in England as the greatest baritone of the Victorian era, was born in Liverpool in 1834. Having a voice of fine quality, extensive compass, and great power, he left England to study in Milan in 1855. Returning in 1857, he took lessons of Manuel Garcia. In the same year he appeared in oratorio, singing the part of Adam in the *Creation*. His first appearance in opera in England was in 1859, as Hoel in *Dinorah* at Covent Garden.

Although Mr. Santley sang almost all the baritone rôles in opera, he was not noted for histrionic powers, but rather for his vocal abilities, and his power of seizing on the exact sentiment and significance of his part.

In 1871 he visited the United States as a member of the Carl Rosa opera company, during which time he reaped substantial honors. In 1889 he made a concert tour in Australia.

In 1892 Joseph Bennett, the eminent critic, wrote: "The foremost baritone of the day is still with us, and though his physical means have suffered changes which no skill can avoid, he is a greater artist than ever and retains plenty of vitality for his work."

Mr. Santley married, in 1859, Miss Gertrude Kemble, the granddaughter of the celebrated actor, and his daughter, Miss Edith Santley, had a short but exceedingly brilliant career as a concert singer, previous to her marriage, in 1884, to the Hon. R. H. Lyttelton.

Jean Baptiste Faure, a French singer, will be remembered as the creator of the part of Mephistopheles in Gounod's *Faust.* He was a good musician and a fine actor, and he owed more to his genius as a comedian than to his voice, which was of great compass, though not of a brilliant quality. In the winter of 1861 he made his first appearance at the Grand Opera in Paris, though he had made his operatic début nine years before at the Opera Comique. For many years he remained at the Grand Opera, during which time he was a prominent figure in operatic history.

Faure was born in 1830 and was the son of a singer at the church of Moulins. His father died when he was but seven years old. At the age of thirteen he entered the solfeggio class at the Conservatoire in Paris, to which city his family had moved when he was three years old. At the breaking of his boy's voice he took up piano and double bass, and was for some time a member of the band at the Odéon theatre. After his voice was settled he joined the chorus at the Théâtre Italien, and in 1850 again entered the Conservatoire, where he gained, in 1852, the first prizes for singing and for opera comique.

He is a man of refined tastes and great culture and an enthusiastic collector of pictures. In 1859 he married Mlle. Lefebre, an actress at the Opera Comique. Of Faure's Mephistopheles, in *Faust,* a critic of 1876 writes, "No impersonation of this character at all approaching the general excellence of his could be named." What Faure respected most was the intention of the composer. It is impossible for any one to penetrate more deeply into a part, to adorn it with more delicate gradations of light and shade, to hit upon more felicitous contrasts and juster intonations, to identify himself more thoroughly with a character or an epoch. He proceeded by degrees, led his audience to sublimest heights of enthusiasm by cleverly calculated stages—he fascinated them.

Of French baritones, Victor Maurel is the one who has succeeded Faure. His creation of the part of Iago, in Verdi's *Otello,* was considered a masterpiece of lyric acting, and Iago is . . . his greatest rôle.

Maurel was born in 1848 at Marseilles, and, having a penchant for acting and singing, began to play in comedy and light opera in his native town. His ambition soon led him to Paris, where he entered the Conservatoire and studied singing with Vauthrot, and opera with Duvernoy. He gained the first prizes in both subjects in 1867.

In 1869 he made his début in *Les Huguenots,* but he was not considered sufficiently successful to secure a permanent engagement, so he went for a series of tours in Italy, Spain, and America. His first London appearance was made in 1873, when he took the part of Renato at the Royal Italian Opera, and was engaged there, as a result of his success, every year until 1879, playing the parts of Don Giovanni, Tell, Almaviva, Hoel, Peter the Great, Valentine, Hamlet, and the Cacique. He also played Wolfram and the Flying Dutchman, and in 1878 appeared as Domingo in Massé's *Paul and Virginia.*

In 1879 he once more appeared in Paris, taking the part of Hamlet. His name had become established since his previous appearance in that city, and he was now a most decided success.

About this time M. Maurel undertook the management of Italian opera at the Théâtre des Nations. His enterprise was hailed with joy by the Parisians, who were desirous of having Italian opera.

Maurel surrounded himself with a company of the finest artists, including Mesdames Marimon, Adler-Dévriès, Nevada, and Tremelli, and Gayarré, the brothers De Reszke, and Maurel himself.

Notwithstanding the attractions offered, the outlay exceeded the income, and M. Maurel relieved himself of a large amount of money in a remarkably short time. His financial disasters in no way interfered with his artistic successes, and his production of Massenet's *Hérodiade,* on February 1, 1884, was a great triumph.

Victor Maurel combines a good voice with a most attractive personality and a great love of his art. He is undoubtedly to be considered one of the greatest baritones of the present day. As an actor M. Maurel is magnificent, as a singer he has never had a marvellous organ, but he has used it with exquisite art. If he ceased to sing he would still be one of the greatest of Shakespearean actors. As Iago he is insidiously great, as Rigoletto overwhelming and thrilling.

He first visited the United States in 1874, and he was at once accepted as a great artist.

Amongst operatic baritones of the past twenty years Señor Guiseppe Del Puente, a Spaniard, descended from an old and noble family, must be mentioned. He was born in 1845, and studied at the conservatory at Naples. Being a true artist in his instincts, and having a fine voice, he speedily excelled. He became connected with the best operatic enterprises, and was always popular on account of his handsome stage presence, dramatic capability, and fine, rotund, musical baritone voice. He was equally valuable in the comedy parts of light opera, or the heavier ones of serious opera.

He was well known in America in the eighties, when he belonged to the Mapleson company, and sang with Gerster, Valleria, Scalchi, Ravelli, and Galassi.

The greatest English baritone of the present day is Ffrangçon Davies, whose voice was declared by Sims Reeves to be the purest baritone he had ever heard. Besides having this beautifully pure tone, he has perfect control of the breath, and remarkable breadth and intelligence.

His first appearance took place at Freetrade Hall, Manchester, at Mr. de Jong's concerts in January, 1890.

Mr. Davies was born at Bethesda, Carnarvonshire, North Wales, and, after receiving his early education at Friar's Grammar School, at Bangor, he obtained an exhibition at Jesus College, Oxford. He gained his B.A. and M.A. degrees, but was not devoted to studies only, for he stood well in the athletic world of his University, playing football in his college team and rowing in the Varsity trial eights.

After leaving Oxford, he began to study music seriously and entered the Guildhall School, taking lessons later with Shakespeare. He has a large repertoire of baritone operatic parts, in which he has sung with great success, and he is one of the best oratorio and concert baritones of the day. He visited America in 1896 and confirmed the good accounts which had preceded him.

In the list of famous baritones of the present day, America is admirably represented by David Bispham, who has gained his greatest reputation in the part of Falstaff in Verdi's opera of that name.

Mr. Bispham was born in Philadelphia, in 1857, his father being a Quaker. Like many of the singers of to-day, he was intended for a commercial career, but, being more interested in music, he eventually allowed his love for art to overcome his desire for business, or, as he has himself said, he went the way of least resistance. His father's musical proclivities manifested themselves on the flute, which instrument he played beautifully, and young Bispham solaced the leisure hours of his youth with the guitar and zither, but never learned much of any other instrument. On every possible occasion he sang. He was a member of several choral societies and church choirs and had the advantage of many musical friends. He took parts also in amateur dramatic performances, and thus made some progress in his art.

In 1885 he gave up business and went to London, where he has since resided. He studied with Vannucini, Shakespeare, and Lamperti, and in 1891 made his début in London in *La Basoche,* scoring an instantaneous success. He also made a provincial tour with Sims Reeves.

Mr. Bispham has a repertoire of nearly fifty rôles and can sing entire parts in German, Italian, French, and English. There are few artists who work as conscientiously for the general good of art, and there are few who have made so general a success in such a wide variety of rôles, among the best of which are Wotan, Wolfram, and Beckmesser. He is also without a peer on the concert platform as an interpreter of Wagner.

He was seen in opera in America in 1896, and his artistic efforts made a deep impression, for he is one of the few artists who combine with unusual vocal accomplishments great dramatic powers.

QUESTIONS

1. What is the true meaning of the words "Prima donna?" What is the connotation of these words? Can you suggest how this special meaning came about?
2. What is the meaning of "claque?" Discuss its present uses in music. Discuss the ethics of having a claque. Do other professions employ claques? Can you name any?
3. What is the particular value of reading through a catalog of names of famous singers? How many of the names in Lahee's essay are familiar to you? Why do you suppose they are familiar?—or not familiar? Make a list of names of persons famous in a field with which you are familiar. Are there students in the class to whom these names are not familiar? Why?
4. Can you suggest why so few American singers were included in Lahee's essay? Can you name any famous American singers? Which ones?
5. Compare the opera singer with the oratorio singer, and both with the concert stage singer. What special qualities do they have in common? In what ways do they differ?

OPERA AND BALLET / 1 *Nineteenth Century operas hold an unrivaled position in the repertory of present-day opera houses. Whereas most of the operas from the eighteenth century and before have been forgotten (those of Mozart and Gluck being the principal exceptions), the operas of von Weber, Rossini, Donizetti, Bellini, Verdi, and Wagner have kept their popularity down to the present time. In the following essay Lionel Salter presents, with felicity and good humor, a survey of the work of these and other composers. Salter is an English harpsichordist and a conductor for the British Broadcasting Company. He is also critic for the* Gramophone *and Director of Music Productions for the B.B.C.'s Television Service.*

The Heyday of Opera

LIONEL SALTER

BY THE TIME OF MOZART THE OVERTURE HAD come to be of some importance in the dramatic scheme. The earliest operatic overtures had been mere flourishes to engage the audience's attention and get it to stop talking: Lully set the fashion (followed for nearly a century) for a highly organised formal orchestral prelude consisting of a slow introduction leading to a fugal *allegro* (and then sometimes a minuet). But Gluck, in his reforms of the opera, felt that the overture should have a more direct reference to the drama which followed, and set the atmosphere for it. This theory he put into practice in his own works, where we find for almost the first time a consistent relationship of mood between the overture and the opera: in *Alceste* and *Iphigenia in Tauris* the music actually flows straight on between the two. This scheme was adopted by Mozart in *Idomeneo* (as well as in *The Abduction from the Harem* and, later, *Don Giovanni*), but an innovation of Mozart's was to introduce in the overture themes from the drama itself. In *Don Giovanni,* for example, the very first music we hear is the fateful theme of the stone guest who is to bring about the Don's downfall; and *The Magic Flute* overture is interrupted by the thrice-repeated call of the trumpets which the priests of Sarastro are later to blow in their solemn ceremonies.

An even closer alliance was forged by Beethoven in his sole opera, *Fidelio* (which was never really successful although the first version of 1805 was twice radically changed for later productions). Indeed, in a sense the overture and the opera were too closely identified in his case. For, seeking constantly for perfection, he wrote altogether four different overtures: the first three were called after the heroine, Leonora, but the third in particular (using themes from the opera) sums up the action so profoundly and with such dramatic force that to play the opera after it is like going over the ground twice over. Besides which, it proved impossible to step from the tension, dramatic climax and final rejoicing of the overture back to the simple atmosphere in which the action opens; so that eventually Beethoven was forced to write a shorter and less weighty fourth overture—which is thematically independent of the opera.

OPERA IN FRANCE. Fidelio was based on a true incident during the French Revolution, though in the story the scene is changed to Spain. The heroine has disguised herself as a boy and taken service as a jailer's

---

assistant in order to rescue her husband, who has been imprisoned (without any trial) by the governor, his political enemy: her attempts to save him from being secretly murdered look like failing, when a trumpet is heard off-stage announcing the arrival, in the nick of time, of a Minister of State on a visit of inspection. (The off-stage trumpet provides a thrilling moment during two of the *Leonora* overtures also.) The work is what has been termed a 'rescue opera,' such as had already been made familiar in France by Méhul and, above all, by Cherubini, who though of Italian birth contributed largely to musical life in Paris, and whom Beethoven greatly admired. Another foreign composer who did much to raise the prestige of French grand opera (as opposed to *opéra comique,* a lighter, more romantic style with spoken dialogue instead of recitative, successfully practised by composers like Boieldieu) was Spontini. His grandiose heroic operas, which to please French taste made good use of the ballet, were taken up enthusiastically in Germany and held the stage there until ousted by the new German opera style established by Weber's *Der Freischütz.* It is worth noting, incidentally, that at the start of the century the tenor finally replaced for good the earlier male-soprano hero; and this pattern of casting has remained to the present day. The emphasis, however, was at first entirely on vocal display, the tenor's position being hotly contested by the leading soprano, who expected the composer to provide her with plentiful oportunities for showing off her virtuosity.

THE ITALIAN SCENE. The singers in Italian opera still ruled the roost, and, like favoured film stars of today, had the power to approve or reject what was offered them. They often insisted on new solos being written for them, sometimes had very definite ideas about how they would 'make their entrance,' and even on occasion dictated the choice of words if they had some particular 'mascot' word they liked to have in their big solos. The composer had to stomach the facts that his music would be regarded as a basis which the star performers would embroider at their pleasure, and that he would probably have to re-write a good deal of it during rehearsals: after all, he was usually hired for the season by a theatre manager and had to write an agreed number of works specifically for that particular company. He would be lucky if any opera ran for more than a couple of dozen performances, and always had to have the next one ready up his sleeve in case of sudden failure. In any case, the public would pay little attention to much of the performance. Opera was very much an occasion for social intercourse, and besides holding constant polite conversations in each other's private boxes, it was quite common for the audience to eat or gamble while the music was going on: in fact, less important arias were sometimes known as *arie di sorbetto* (refreshment arias). The grand opera (*opera seria*) of the time consisted largely of solo arias and duets, with few larger ensembles, and the story was carried forward in long recitatives. In contrast, the comic opera (*opera buffa*) had more ensembles, and unlike the *opera seria* usually had a bass as one of the principal singers (often a 'heavy father' or crusty old bachelor).

ROSSINI AND HIS FOLLOWERS. A composer who raised *opera buffa* to new heights, and who became the idol of all Europe, was Rossini, whose rhythmic zest and gift for writing sparkling melodies, as well as his brilliant handling of the orchestra, conquered Italy, London, Vienna, and Paris alike. His particular specialty was to end his overtures (which, out of sheer laziness, he sometimes used over again for other operas) with a long exciting orchestral build-up which earned him the nickname of 'Signor Crescendo.' Yet only one of his works firmly holds the stage today, the sparkling *Barber of Seville* (to whose story *The Marriage of Figaro* is the sequel); though occasionally his *Cenerentola* (the Cinderella story without the magic) is performed. Rossini did not write comic operas: he did much for *opera seria* also, introducing bass soloists and ensemble work as a normal thing; and he made some attempt to control his singers' accustomed privileges. His most important serious opera was *William Tell,* written (in French) for Paris in 1829. When, after its triumphant first night and acclamation by all the music critics, Rossini found that a change of government meant the cancellation of the rest of his contract with the Paris Opéra, he suddenly gave way to the exhaustion which the composition of forty operas in less than twenty years had cost him, and thereafter, though he lived nearly forty years more, wrote next to nothing.

Two more Italian composers may be mentioned here who inherited Rossini's skill in writing for the voice. The refinement and grace of Bellini's music has frequently been likened to that of Chopin, who admired him greatly, and whose delicately ornamented melodic line owes much to the example of Bellini. His works are rarely heard today in England, though *La Sonnambula* (*The Sleepwalker*) is still played in Italy, and *Norma* (about a Druidic priestess in ancient Gaul) was revived not long ago at Covent Garden; but on the whole his melodic gifts have not compensated for the lack of dramatic power and the shallowness of his orchestration. Donizetti was a most prolific writer, with sixty-five works to his credit, and like Rossini excelled in both the serious and comic styles. Of the former, his chief work is *Lucy of Lammermoor,* based on Walter Scott (it set the fashion for florid 'mad scenes' for operatic heroines); of the latter *The Daughter of the Regiment* and the popular *Don Pasquale* are outstanding.

SUPERNATURAL AND HISTORICAL SUBJECTS. In Germany, as we have seen, the influence of Cherubini and Spontini had made itself felt, but in the ensuing years some native composers came to the fore and headed German opera in a new direction—that of what is known as Romanticism, with the emphasis on folk-lore, legends, and the supernatural. Spohr's *Faust* pointed the way, but the first work of genius in this field was Weber's *Der Freischütz,* a German forest legend about a hunter who, in order to win a competition, accepts a pact with the devil and is provided with magic bullets. This opera, produced in 1821, created a furore and has retained much of its popularity. It is a *Singspiel,* that is to say with the music interspersed with spoken dialogue (not until Spohr's *Jessonda* and Weber's own *Euryanthe* two years later were attempts made at continuous music in German opera); but the famous scene of the casting of the bullets in the Wolf's Glen utilised the speaking voice over music (known technically as *melodrama*) most effectively. *Der Freischütz* is also noteworthy as one of the earliest operas in which the overture is compounded of material from the opera itself. Hundreds of German romantic operas by lesser composers followed, but they have become of purely local interest, and we must now follow another German who worked mainly in Paris—Meyerbeer.

France at this time was the operatic hub of Europe, but apart from Boieldieu the only native French composer of reputation was Cherubini's pupil Auber, who wrote several *opéras-comiques,* including *Fra Diavolo,* sometimes heard today. He also wrote some serious operas, of which one, *Masaniello* (whose story dealt with a revolution against oppression), fired the Belgians to revolt against their Dutch rulers: it was also one of the first operas to have a tragic ending. Rossini's supremacy over the French operatic stage, stemming from his *William Tell* (1829), faded before the bright light of the newcomer Meyerbeer (who was fully aware of his debt to Auber, Rossini, and Weber). His works, planned on the vastest scale, demanded sumptuous stage settings and very large orchestras (for which he wrote elaborate parts), but despite the head-shaking of the management they made the fortunes of the Paris Opéra. The supernatural element which was so conspicuous a feature of *Der Freischütz* was exploited by Meyerbeer in *Robert the Devil* (1831), which was largely responsible for the fashion for 'church scenes.' Then, taking his cue from Auber, he produced two historical operas, *The Huguenots* and *The Prophet,* which by their sheer size and length, besides their tense subjects, made a deep impression. His manner was imitated by his contemporary Halévy, who scored a triumph with *The Jewess;* but none of these ambitious blood-and-thunder works are produced nowadays, and the likelihood is that we should find them intolerably dated.

THE BRIGHTEST STAR OF ITALIAN OPERA. At almost the same time as Donizetti was writing his last operas, a new star was rising and beginning a career which sums up by itself the whole development of Italian opera during the next forty-five years. Verdi's beginnings were humble: he came of a poor peasant family, and the music in his blood was the vigorous but often crude music of the people. Faced with his earliest works, it is only with an effort that one remembers that opera was originally an aristocratic entertainment: the vocal parts here are intended not for the elegant interpreters whom Bellini had in mind but for the lusty voices beloved by the uncultivated public, and the orchestration has more than a hint of the brass band style in which Verdi was brought up. But his melodic vitality and sense of stage effect are undeniable; and in addition to these virtues he showed an increasing interest in characterisation. His personages are not just stock figures but are real people, with all the complications of character one meets in real life. It was also Verdi's fortune to become associated, in the Italian public's mind, with the movement against Austrian rule; and his constant clashes with censorship served to endear him to his audiences.

His first operas made particularly effective use of the chorus. Then followed *Ernani* (based on Victor Hugo, the dramatist most in vogue with the Romantics) and *Macbeth* (which Verdi later revised—it is the latter version which we hear nowadays); but the earliest of his stage works to have remained firmly rooted in the repertoire of today's opera-houses is *Rigoletto* (1851). Some of its immediate success was due to the play (again by Hugo) having been banned; and even as an opera —a particularly sensational one—it was necessary to change a real-life King of France into a fictitious Duke of Mantua. What is of special interest is that Verdi had the daring to make the principal character not merely a baritone, but an ugly hunchback into the bargain. Two years later Verdi brought out two more operas—the involved, passionately romantic *Il Trovatore* (*The Troubadour*), which was a success, and the much more original *La Traviata* (based on Dumas's *The Lady with the Camellias*), which was the reverse. Its failure had been attributed to the absurdity of having a very stout actress take the part of the heroine (who is supposed to die of consumption) and to the generally low standard of singing; but the audience was also considerably taken aback at an opera having for its plot a middle-class, everyday subject of its own time.

VERDI'S LATER OPERAS. Invited to write an opera for Paris, Verdi followed Meyerbeer's lead (in *The Huguenots*) by choosing a massacre for the subject—*The Sicilian Vespers;* but as the Austrian censorship refused to allow the representation of any revolt against authority, the libretto had to be changed before it could be presented in Italy. Similarly *A Masked Ball,* which marked a new high level in ensemble writing and orchestral colour, and which mingled tragic and comic elements, had to suffer an absurd transplantation of its plot from Sweden (where its story of a royal assassination belonged) to Boston, U.S.A.! Yet Verdi's fame had by now made him the leading Italian composer of his time, and his work was in great demand throughout the world. Of his next three operas, *The Force of Destiny* was written for St. Petersburg, *Don Carlos* for Paris and *Aïda* (1871) for a new opera-house in Cairo (to celebrate the opening of the Suez Canal). This last work, designed as a spectacle on the grandest scale, represents one of the highest peaks in Verdi's output: it combines theatrical magnificence with a great warmth of human emotion, and technically, besides the grandeur of the writing for orchestra and chorus (which reaches its climax in the Triumph Scene of the second act) and the originality of the final scene, which shows two simultaneous lots of action, it is remarkable for its dramatic continuity. Verdi had come a long way from his early days, when it was enough to provide a series of immediately effective melodies for his singers: in *Aïda* the thought is far more distinguished, and the breaks between musical numbers are reduced to a minimum.

Some years previously Verdi had made the acquaintance of the poet and musician Boito (whose own *Mephistopheles* has, despite its great length, kept the stage in Italy, if not elsewhere). Together they worked on a Shakespearian opera, *Othello,* which was produced in 1887, when Verdi was 73 years old. It was a triumph, although some of the critics could not at first appreciate the great developments which had taken place in the composer's style. His music was now truly continuous, the dramatic recitative being fused with the lyric sections, and the orchestra being given a new importance (though it never steals the limelight from the singers). Then, to everyone's astonishment, Verdi proceeded to write with Boito yet another opera, and, for the first time in his career, a comic opera at that—and this at the age of nearly 80! *Falstaff* is an amazing achievement, for the brilliance and grace of its invention, its lightness of touch, and the warmth of its characterisation: musicians agree in thinking it his masterpiece, though with the general public it has never had the easy popularity of his early operas such as *Rigoletto* and *La Traviata.*

THE RISE OF THE NEW GERMAN STYLE. In the same way that Verdi monopolises Italian opera for so long, so, by one of those curious parallels, German opera in the second half of the nineteenth century is summed up in the work of Wagner, whose influence was without question the most far-reaching in the whole history of the art. He first came into prominence in 1842 (the same year as Verdi's early *Nabucco*) with *Rienzi,* a Meyerbeer-ish piece written to his own libretto—as was always his practice—with orchestration which audiences of the day found intolerably noisy. (The same fault had been found with Meyerbeer's operas.) The following year saw the production of *The Flying Dutchman,* in which among other styles Wagner carried on the romantic, supernatural tradition established by Weber, though giving the orchestra a more important role. His interest turning towards old German legends, he produced *Tannhäuser* (1845) and *Lohengrin* (1850), whose idiom was at first regarded as quite beyond understanding, though now they are regarded as the most easily approachable of all Wagner's operas. Of *Lohengrin,* whose orchestral writing revealed a most original imagination at work, Liszt said that 'with it the old operatic world came to an end'; but in fact it consisted in essence of the old series of set numbers—arias, ensembles, and choruses. One thing which was new was the orchestral prelude to each act, setting the mood for the following scene. There was no overture built on various themes from the opera or summarising the development of its action: indeed, only once more, in *The Mastersingers,* was Wagner to write a formal overture made up of elements from the work itself—and even that was to run straight on into the opening scene.

The unsettled circumstances of Wagner's life at this time—he was a political exile for twelve years—created serious obstacles to the production of his works; but they gave him time to clarify his mind about his operatic ideals. Thinking along the lines laid down by Gluck, he envisaged opera as something quite different from the forms then current: he was working towards an 'art of the future,' a *music-drama* to which each of the elements of the theatre—libretto, music, staging, scenery, costumes, lighting—would contribute its part. In such a fusion of the arts, all at the service of the drama, the personality of the singers could not be allowed to intrude. It would be impossible to continue breaking up each act into separate numbers and recitatives: the music would have to be continuous, flexible enough in character to be more declamatory or more lyrical as the situation demanded, but planned *as a whole.* To unify his music-drama Wagner evolved a system of developing 'leading motives' (themes attached to persons, ideas or emotions, which recur as the characters return or are mentioned or the ideas and emotions come to the fore). This was not entirely new, as is sometimes supposed: Spohr had used the device for structural purposes in his *Faust* (1816), and others had pointed the way before that. (Incidentally, it was Spohr, too, who had first cast scenes as continuous wholes without breaks.) The ebb and flow of these leading motives created a kind of running commentary on the action and thus gave a major role in the unfolding of the drama to the orchestra. The musical emphasis, in short, had moved from the stage to the orchestra pit, and in his later works Wagner's vocal parts actually grow out of the orchestral texture. The orchestral forces themselves had to be of unprecedented size to keep pace with his imaginative demands—whoever before would have dared to ask for eight horns or six harps, for example? Nor did Wagner allow himself to be restrained in any particular by the limitations of existing instruments: special instruments, such as a bass trumpet and a whole family of tubas, had to be built to satisfy his requirements. Even the musical language employed had to be expanded to express the depths of emotions which Wagner brought into play; and his greatest contribution to the art of music (as distinct from that of opera alone) lies precisely in the enormous development of chromatic harmony (and hence melody) for which he was responsible. Similarly with every facet of the theatre: he bubbled over with ideas about production, scenery, and costumes.

WAGNER'S MATURE MUSIC-DRAMAS. All these innovations—which were to set the musical world ablaze—were brought into play with his next creation, a drama on a vast scale based on the old German legend of *The Nibelung's Ring*. Wagner wrote this as a tetralogy, that is, a sequence of four operas, each occupying a whole evening; and the *Ring* cycle is now recognised as one of the greatest landmarks in the history of opera. Actually, his original intention had been to write one drama called *Siegfried's Death*, but the plot was so difficult to make clear that he found himself obliged to add a preliminary drama to introduce it, then another to explain *that*, and finally yet another to get back to the fundamentals of the story. That is why we get one of the tiresome features of *The Ring*—the way various characters enter and relate the whole plot (so far as it concerns themselves) up to the point at which they have arrived—a kind of 'new readers start here.' The resources required by *The Ring* were so enormous (they are still a strain on any opera-house) that, not surprisingly, Wagner had to wait a long time for its production, even in separate parts; but by a stroke of good fortune, the eccentric young King Ludwig II of Bavaria became a fervent admirer of the composer, and enabled him to build a theatre—to his own plans, of course—exclusively devoted to performances of his works. Bayreuth is still the centre of the Wagner cult: if it did nothing else it persuaded audiences that opera (or music-drama, rather) was something to be taken seriously.

Among the innumerable points of interest in *The Ring* are the orchestral preludes (not overtures) to the operas. *Rhinegold* begins, with breath-taking boldness, with 136 bars of nothing but the chord of E flat, rolling upwards from the orchestral depths, to represent the bed of the great river from which the action springs; and the music flows imperceptibly into the start of the opera. Similarly, before the curtain goes up on *The Valkyrie* there is a 120-bar representation of a storm, out of which Siegmund staggers on to the stage; while to start Act 3 the orchestra depicts the Valkyries flying through the air on their battle-steeds. In each case, in fact, the orchestral prelude serves a specifically dramatic purpose.

In *Tristan and Isolde* (which Wagner wrote during the long period spent on *The Ring* but which was produced first, in 1865) the prelude expresses the almost unbearable intensity of the classic love-story which is the basis of the opera, and Wagner pushed his chromatic harmony to new limits which many of his contemporaries found quite intolerable; but it served as a major stepping-stone to twentieth-century music. Three years later came another masterpiece, this time a romantic comedy called *The Mastersingers of Nuremberg*. In its mediaeval subject of a young knight-musician winning over the conservative Guild of Mastersingers by the beauty of his unorthodox songs can easily be seen Wagner's allegory of himself in his own musical world. His last opera, *Parsifal,* is a large-scale religious drama which, in this country at least, is more likely to be heard in concert performance than in the theatre, to which many people still think its subject is ill-suited.

QUESTIONS

1. Opera has been called the "silliest of the arts." Can you suggest why this is? How does an opera differ from a musical comedy? an oratorio? Are these forms "silly?"
2. For many people the taste for opera is controversial. List whatever appeals to you in opera, and whatever does not appeal to you. Compare and discuss these items.
3. In most operas the hero is usually a tenor, and the villain a bass or baritone. The heroine is usually a high soprano and the villainess (if there is one) is a low soprano or contralto. Discuss the choice of these voices for their special roles. What, for example, makes a tenor more "heroic" than a bass?
4. Look up *aria* and *recitative*. What are their functions in opera?
5. What, exactly, are the differences between *opera seria, opéra comique, opera buffa,* and *music-drama?* Can you give examples of each?

OPERA AND BALLET / 2 *There is little question that people were dancing shortly after there were people. There was dancing in ancient Egypt, in Greece, and in Rome. It was not until the Renaissance, however, that the ballet as we know it came into its own. Court dances with costumes and scenery became a commonplace, the whole reaching a climax in the court of Louis XIV in the Baroque era. Ballet eventually became connected with opera but in our own time has reverted to its early, separate form, under which it has attained wide popularity. In the following essay Humphrey Searle, composer and music historian, presents a survey of the best-known and most popular of the grand nineteenth century ballets.*

The Grand Romantic Ballets

HUMPHREY SEARLE

DURING THE EIGHTEENTH CENTURY BALLET HAD begun to spread outside its original homes in France and Italy, and by 1800 it was firmly established in several other countries, notably in Russia, where Empress Anne founded a State School of Dancing in 1735. The Royal Danish Ballet also dates from this period, and it is in fact one of the oldest companies with an uninterrupted history. This company was fortunate in having the gifted choreographer Bournonville at its disposal in the early part of the nineteenth century, and he created for it a number of ballets which are still performed by the company to-day. (The Royal Danish Ballet even have a ballet in their repertoire with eighteenth-century choreography, *The Whims of Cupid and the Dancing Master,* but this is little more than a curiosity). The ballets of Bournonville mark the beginning of the romantic ballet of the type we know in *Giselle,* for instance; that is to say, the dancing is not purely classical, but includes a good deal of mime, and the subject is usually based on some poetical idea, as for instance in Bournonville's version of *La Sylphide*—not to be confused with *Les Sylphides* of many years later. Other ballets in the Royal Danish Ballet's repertoire include *Napoli* and *A Folk Tale:* these are all full-length ballets lasting the whole evening, as indeed was the usual practice in nineteenth-century ballet, and they include a good deal of mime and are extremely realistically staged. Unfortunately the musical side of these ballets does not match the choreography or staging: the music is mostly a hotchpotch of tunes by various Danish composers, of whom Niels Gade, a contemporary and follower of Mendelssohn, and Lumbye, a composer of popular dance tunes, are the only ones to be known outside Denmark. Of course this kind of musical hotchpotch was quite common in the days of the purely classical ballet, when the dancing had complete primacy and the music was considered of little or no importance, provided it gave a reasonable background to the dancer's movements. But in the Romantic period mime was becoming more and more important, and it was essential that the music should be properly fitted to the stage action and, what is more, should be a unified conception. It is true that this ideal was not satisfactorily attained until the days of Delibes and Tchaikovsky, but at any rate the nineteenth century saw a gradual tendency towards a more serious conception of the ballet as a whole.

During this period France remained, as before, the chief home of

---

THE GRAND ROMANTIC BALLETS from *Ballet Music: An Introduction* by Humphrey Searle;

the ballet, and a very large number of ballets were produced in Paris which have since passed into oblivion. These were mostly full-length ballets in three or four acts, lasting a whole evening. Usually there was some kind of fairly simple story which was mimed, interspersed with a good deal of dancing—general dances for the corps de ballet, variations for solo dancers, pas de deux, pas de trois, pas de quatre, etc. The dénouement of the story normally came at the beginning of the last act, and the remainder of the ballet usually consisted of a divertissement containing a number of dances which had nothing to do with the story, but sometimes had a separate theme of their own. This pattern has, indeed, survived into the full-length ballets of to-day. We need waste no time in discussing those French ballets which have dropped out of the modern repertoire: but there are three, or perhaps three and a half, which should be discussed in some detail.

The earliest full-length ballet to remain in the present-day repertoire is *Giselle,* originally produced at the Académie Royale de Musique in Paris on 28 June 1841, with Grisi as Giselle and L. Petipa as Albrecht. The scenario was evolved by Theophile Gautier and Vernoy de St. Georges. Gautier got his original idea for it when reviewing Heine's book *De l'Allemagne,* and he wrote to Heine saying how charmed he was with 'all those delicious apparitions you have encountered in the Harz Mountains and on the banks of the Ilse, in a mist softened by German moonlight.' This quotation gives a very fair idea of the atmosphere of the ballet, even if the 'German moonlight' is seen here through French eyes. The choreography was by Coralli and Perrot, and the music by Adolphe Adam, a composer who lived from 1803 to 1856 and devoted his life to the theatre; but of all his numerous grand and comic operas and ballets only *Giselle* and some extracts from his comic opera *Le Postillon de Longjumeau* have survived into the present-day repertoire. He probably learnt his theatrical sense from Boieldieu, with whom he studied at the Paris Conservatoire, but he was not a composer of a very strong personality; in fact he is severely attacked in the first edition of Grove's Dictionary of Music, published in 1890, where it is stated that: 'His melodies are frequently trivial to absolute vulgarity: the structure of his concerted pieces of the flimsiest kind: all this, no less than the choice of *hasardé* subjects, seems to indicate the gradual decline from the serene heights of Boieldieu's humour to the miry slough which has swamped that sweetest growth of French national art, the comic opera, and the murky surface of which reflects the features of Beethoven's countryman, Jacques Offenbach. It is a fact of ominous significance that Adam regarded with interest, and gave his journalistic aid to the theatrical creation of that enterprising composer—the *Bouffes Parisiens.*' We do not feel so harshly about poor Adam these days, but there is no doubt that the continued success of *Giselle* depends far more on its dancing than on its music.

Nevertheless Adam's score for *Giselle* is, at least, extremely competent, and often very apt for the dramatic action. Indeed the music is very closely related to the dance, and there is no elaborate symphonic development; it is more in the style of the older dance suites. Though the melodies often seem commonplace and even perfunctory at times, nevertheless they do fulfil their function in providing danceable numbers. The score is written in a series of short, almost fragmentary sections, and the composer's skill is shown in the way in which he alters and varies the speed and character of each successive dance, so that the score does add up to a dramatic whole. One can say, in fact, that the whole is greater than the parts, and many a greater composer, or one who could have written more distinguished individual dances, may well envy Adam's dramatic skill in building up a large structure out of somewhat unpromising material. In a sense this is what ballet music should aim at, at any rate in a dramatic ballet: if one is too taken by individual numbers one tends to think of a ballet as consisting of a chain of separate dances rather than a dramatic whole. Such music is of course ineffective in the concert hall—but that is not its place. It is intended to be listened to as an adjunct to the dance, and it supports the dancing by adding its rhythmical, emotional, atmospheric, or dramatic qualities. I am not saying that all ballet music should be like *Giselle*—Heaven forbid—but I do feel that the simplicity of the music here does disguise a greater dramatic power than many people realize.

The first act of the ballet is concerned with the love of Count Albrecht, who is disguised as a peasant, for the peasant girl Giselle, her discovery of his deception and her death. The simplicity of Giselle's character is well expressed in the music, but the dramatic scenes tend to be somewhat naïve musically. However the unison passage associated with Hilarion is very effective despite its extreme simplicity. But, as we saw above, Adam never attempts to develop a musical theme, though as the act proceeds he does use some of the material that has already been heard, and his handling of these reminiscences of earlier themes is often very apt; for instance, the restatement of the pastorale theme from the first part of the act in the later mad scene. There is a certain similarity to Donizetti in the cast of melody and in the alternation between lyricism and drama. The chief aim of the music is to express the story clearly and make a direct appeal to the audience, and in this it succeeds very well.

The second act is concerned with the Wilis, brides who have died before their wedding day. Giselle rises from her grave and joins them. Then Albrecht returns, not realizing what has happened: the Wilis make him their victim, and the act ends with his prostration over Giselle's grave. Although this act, in contrast to the first, is chiefly concerned with supernatural beings, Adam makes no attempt to express this in the music, which continues much as in the first act; and many of the dramatic passages are underplayed, such as the storm at the beginning of the act, which is over almost before it has begun. However the lyrical passages are expressive and effective, and the music at least provides an adequate support for the dancing. *Giselle* was originally scored for a fairly small orchestra, consisting of double woodwind with the addition of cor anglais, two horns, two trumpets, one trombone, timpani, percussion, harp, and strings. Most modern companies arrange the score for whatever combination they have available, increasing it, as at Covent Garden, or reducing it where necessary. In the versions used by some companies considerable rescoring has taken place, but at any rate *Giselle* does remain in the repertoire of practically every important ballet company of to-day, and it has always remained a favourite with the public. It may be added that Adam also composed ballet scores for *Faust* for a London production in 1832, and for *La Jolie Fille de Gand* in 1839. Neither of these has remained in the repertoire; nor has his score for *Le Corsaire*.

The French nineteenth-century ballet composer who is best known to us to-day is Léo Delibes, who lived from 1836 to 1891. He was a pupil of Adolphe Adam at the Conservatiore and thus had an early apprenticeship in the French theatrical tradition. His first works were comic operas and operettas which achieved some success. In 1863 he became an accompanist at the Opéra itself, and three years later he was commissioned to write the music for the ballet *La Source,* in collaboration with the Russian ballet composer Minkus. Minkus was well known as a composer of ballet music of an extremely conventional type, and this direct comparison of the two composers gave Delibes the chance of really making his reputation. Of the four scenes of the ballet Minkus wrote the first and fourth and Delibes the second and third, and after the first performance on 12 November 1866 the following notice appeared in *La France Musicale:* 'The style of the two composers is essentially different and easily recognizable at a first hearing. Minkus's music has a vague, indolent, and melancholic character, full of grace and languor. That of Delibes, fresher and more rhythmic, is much more complicated in orchestration, and sometimes a little more ordinary. I should add that this difference in style is perfectly justified by the contrasting character of the two parts of the ballet.' The critic of *Le Ménéstral* went even further and wrote: 'The first act, despite several pretty details, seemed a little thin, but the music of the last scene contains some charming and often very expressive melodies. The second act is brilliant and does great credit to Delibes: it is certainly the most successful and noteworthy portion. The whole of the score could have been entrusted to the young composer, and this will doubtless be done on another occasion.'

The story of *La Source* is concerned with Naïla, the Spirit of Spring, who influences an intrigue at the court of the Khan of Ghendjib. The somewhat conventionally oriental plot contains magic flowers, evil mists, and other trappings of this kind. The concert suite from Delibes' music has become well known, and a favourite item from the ballet is the 'Naïla Waltz,' which has been effectively transcribed for piano as a concert piece by Dohnányi. At any rate, *La Source* made Delibes' reputation: he was immediately asked to write a divertissement, 'Le Pas de Fleurs,' for insertion in *Le Corsaire,* a ballet by his old master, Adolphe Adam, and shortly afterwards he was commissioned to write *Coppélia.*

Delibes' first full-length ballet, *Coppélia, ou La Fille aux Yeux d'Émail,* to give it its full title, was first produced at the Paris Opéra on 25 May 1870, with choreography by St. Léon. The book, by Nuitter and St. Léon, was suggested by E. T. A. Hoffmann's character of Dr. Coppelius, the inventor and controller of mechanical puppets who also appears in Offenbach's opera *The Tales of Hoffmann.* Delibes' music made an immediate impression. Writing three days after the première, the critic of *Le Figaro* said: 'M. Léo Delibes has composed for the three scenes of *Coppélia* a distinguished, piquant, and colourful score, excellently orchestrated. . . . It is very difficult to write for dancing with a little artistry, taste, and style. . . . M. Delibes has succeeded in avoiding the commonplace.' Accustomed as they were to an extremely mediocre standard of ballet music in French theatres—Adam's *Giselle,* though hardly a very original work, was a masterpiece compared with the average ballet score of the mid-nineteenth century—it is no wonder that the critics acclaimed Delibes' work, for it combines successfully the art of pure ballet music—music which is solely concerned with the dance and is incapable of standing alone without it—with that of attractive dramatic music of the lighter kind. Delibes' score contains both these kinds of music, and its tunefulness and effectiveness has kept it alive to this day.

The two main elements in the plot are Dr. Coppelius, the doll-maker, trying to impart life to his creations, and the simple love story of Swanilda and Franz. Apart from the set dances, Delibes' score simply but effectively portrays the course of the story. There is little music of symphonic stature but the ballet nevertheless makes a definite dramatic entity.

The ballet is in three acts (or tableaux, as they are called). Before the first act comes a Prelude, beginning slowly with a suave passage for four horns followed by a flowing string melody. A short 'working-up' passage leads to the brilliant Mazurka, which we are to hear again in the first act. Then follow short cadenza-like passages for woodwind which lead to the first act itself. This begins with a waltz, which, though attractive and tuneful in its own right, also serves as a suitable accompaniment to Swanilda's dance and her gestures of friendship to the doll seated in the window—it is this combination of tunefulness and choreographic suitability which has ensured the success of Delibes' ballet music. Next comes a scene in which Franz makes his bow to the doll: to his delight she responds, and her jerky movements are admirably expressed by the double-dotted woodwind rhythm. Next follows the scene of the Burgomaster's entry and the general interest expressed in the happenings in Coppelius's house, and then a Ballade, a simple violin solo containing the 'Hungarian cadence,' during which Swanilda tests Franz's fidelity with an ear of wheat. The next dance is a 'Slavonic theme' with four variations and a coda in quicker tempo. Then follows the well-known 'Csárdás,' beginning with a broad and well-marked melody in D which leads to a more lively 'allegretto' and finally an 'allegro' and 'presto'—but though the form of the traditional Hungarian csárdás is observed here, the music hardly has the authentic Hungarian flavour. Then there is a sortie for the dancers, and the finale of the act, a movement in C minor which is linked rhythmically with the doll music heard earlier, hints at the mystery of Dr. Coppelius' house, which we are to explore in the following act.

The entr'acte before this act begins in the same way as the finale of the previous act, as if to remind us that it is Dr. Coppelius who will shortly be our concern. Then it leads into a repeat of the waltz from the first act. The curtain rises on the entry of the girls into the room where the Doctor keeps his mechanical puppets. Their hesitation is delightfully expressed by a featherweight melody for muted violins staccato. Then comes another descriptive scene, while Swanilda explores the room: suddenly the dolls are awakened and set in motion, and we have the noisy 'Musique des Automates.' Next follow descriptive scenes for the successive entries of Coppelius and Franz. In a rather heavy, Germanic type of dance Coppelius invites Franz to drink with him. Swanilda, who has now taken the place of the doll Coppélia, is produced, and we have the 'Danse de la Poupée,' followed by her 'Bolero,' to which she does a Spanish dance, and her 'Gigue,' a Scottish dance. The act ends with a dramatic scene in which the plot is discovered and the girls are chased out of the house. Throughout this act, the most dramatic in the ballet, Delibes alternates sections of dramatic music with set dances, and the combination of the two is extremely effective.

The third act consists almost entirely of a divertissement, beginning with the 'Marche de la Cloche,' the scene of the Presentation of the Bell, which serves as a simple but well-proportioned overture. Then follows the 'Fête de La Cloche,' a series of dances of various characters. The first is the 'Valse des Heures' (Heures Matinales), the well-known 'Waltz in E♭,' which is familiar to concert audiences. Next comes 'Aurore,' a solo dance with a colourful and expressive 'moderato' introduction followed by a light but not very distinguished 'allegretto non troppo.' 'La Prière' is an expressive little piece, a 6/8 'andante' in E♭: in 'Le Travail,' representing the mid-day hours, a melody in thirds is accompanied by a ceaseless 'spinning-wheel' type of figure. There follows 'L'Hymen,' a betrothal dance. The next piece, 'La Paix,' is now performed as a pas de deux for Swanilda and Franz. Its viola melody, 'andante espressivo,' is as near to romantic nobility as Delibes ever attained. The next dance, originally the 'Marche des Guerrières,' is now performed as a variation for Franz: it is a brilliant, if slightly crude, piece of martial music. Then comes Swanilda's variation, originally the 'Danse de Fête,' an 'allegretto' in G. The ballet ends with a final 'Galop,' originally the 'Dance of the Evening Hours,' which is an effective piece with plenty of vivacity.

It will be seen that some changes from the original have been made in the latter part of the third act, and in fact most modern ballet companies make their own alterations to *Coppélia*. The version described above is that performed at present by the Royal Ballet. This derives, not from the original choreography of St. Léon, but from the version prepared for the Maryinsky Theatre by Ivanov, and reproduced in later years by Sergeyev and Cecchetti. In addition Dame Ninette de Valois revised the whole production in 1954, and this version is now used by both the Royal Ballet companies. The Royal Danish Ballet presents a rather different version in which there is very much more mime and less dancing. This is also used by the Festival Ballet in England. The score of *Coppélia* is for normal symphony orchestra, with double woodwind, four horns, two cornets, two trumpets, three trombones, tuba, percussion, harp, and strings. The scoring is in no way unusual, but is rather more symphonic in style than was usual in Paris then.

In spite of the success of *Coppélia* Delibes did not wish to write nothing but ballet music, and his next stage work was the opera *Le Roi l'a Dit,* which however was little more than a *succés d'estime* when produced at the Opéra-Comique in 1873. However he returned to the Opéra three years later with the mythological ballet *Sylvia,* which was first produced on 14 June 1876. The book was by Jules Barbier and de Reinach, and the choreography was by Mérante. Again the music was a great success, and *L'Opinion* wrote on the day after the first performance: 'M. Léo Delibes has written a score which reveals the hand of a master symphonist. The picturesque choice of themes, the highly-coloured orchestration make this ballet to my mind an exquisite work, perhaps too refined and delicate for the glare of the footlights.' To-day we find the music light and tuneful rather than symphonic, but it was clearly a cut above the other ballet scores of the time, and a good deal of the music is familiar from concert performance. The ballet itself has never been quite so successful as *Coppélia,* but a good many modern companies have performed it at one time or another. The present Royal Ballet production at Covent Garden dates from 1952 and has new and very effective choreography by Frederick Ashton. As in *Coppélia,* about half the music accompanies the dramatic story—the mime music is indeed more emotional in quality than that of *Coppélia,* and at times achieves an almost Wagnerian flavour—while the rest is dance music which is fully capable of standing on its own, with its considerable melodic appeal, even if it does not pretend to any great depth of expression, and it fits the stylized plot to perfection. The orchestra is the same as for *Coppélia,* plus an additional harp.

Like *Coppélia, Sylvia* is in three acts. Before the first act there is a Prelude; then the curtain rises on a scherzo-like dance in quick tempo for the fauns, dryads, and woodland folk. In the next dance, a pastorale called 'Le Berger,' Amynta dreams of the nymph he has seen in the forest: this is followed by 'Les Chasseresses,' hunting music of no particular distinction—Sylvia and her nymphs appear. After a short 'Intermezzo' comes the 'Valse lente,' with its unusual melody very much in the French style. It somehow combines aristocratic distinction with popular appeal. There follow a 'Scene' and a 'Cortège Rustique,' and the act ends with a dramatic scene portraying the capture of Sylvia by Orion. An entr'acte, which again makes use of the 'Valse lente,' prefaces the second act, in which we see Sylvia as Orion's captive. After the opening 'Scene' comes the 'Pas des Ethiopiens,' a violent dance in which piccolo and percussion play a prominent part. Then in the 'Chant Bacchique' Sylvia begins to make Orion drunk in order to effect her escape. This followed by the 'Scene' and 'Dance of the Bacchante,' during which two dancers play tambours de Basque on stage, and in the final 'Scene,' Sylvia escapes through the help of Eros.

The last act, as in *Coppélia,* is mainly a divertissement, and contains much of the music which is well known from the concert suite. It begins with the famous 'Marche et Cortège de Bacchus,' an extended and brilliant march in the best theatrical style, to which the villagers honour the god of wine. In the following 'Scene' Amynta returns, and in the ensuing 'Barcaroll' discovers Sylvia among the slaves of Eros. This barcarolle, as well as the later 'Pas des Esclaves,' contains an important part for alto saxophone—an early example of its use. Now follows the divertissement proper, beginning with the famous pizzicato movement which has made Delibes' name universally known. Next come a number of dances for the various principals: an 'andante' with a prominent part for violin solo; a variation for Amynta; a pas de cinq; a 'pas des Esclaves'; a dance for the Muses and Apollo; a valse-variation for Sylvia; and a final 'Stretto-Galop.' The ballet ends with an apotheosis at the temple of Diana and the appearance of Endymion. Some of the dances in the divertissement in the Royal Ballet production are taken from Delibes' earlier ballet *La Source:* these include Amynta's variation and the dance of the Muses. The 'andante' with violin solo is a pas de deux, the 'Pas des Esclaves' is used for a dance of two goats, and the valse-variation is omitted (at one time it was used in *Coppélia*): in addition several of these dances have been specially rescored for the Royal Ballet production. As a whole *Sylvia* is an extremely effective score, and it is perhaps surprising that the ballet has not had the wide appeal of *Coppélia,* especially as so much of its music has become well known. Probably the stronger dramatic story of *Coppélia* has been found more interesting than the somewhat stylized classical myth of *Sylvia.*

After *Sylvia* Delibes wrote no more full-length ballets, but turned his attention mainly in the direction of opera, producing *Jean de Nivelle* in 1880 and his best-known work, *Lakmé,* in 1883. Between these two operas he also wrote the incidental music for *Le Roi s'Amuse,* the Victor Hugo play on which the libretto of Verdi's *Rigoletto* is based. Delibes' music includes a set of dances 'in the olden style,' a kind of pastiche of seventeenth-century French dance music, but extremely well done in their way. This suite is also familiar to concert audiences. (The passepied, incidentally, makes use of the same theme from the sixteenth-century Arbeau's *Orchésographie* which Peter Warlock used as the second movement of his *Capriol Suite.*) It is a pity that Delibes did not concentrate more on ballet, for his other works, with the possible exception of *Lakmé,* have never been greatly successful, whereas his two full-length ballets justify his claim to be regarded as the father of modern ballet music. . . .

The first school of dancing in Russia was founded in 1735: the first director of it, however, was a Frenchman, and most of the dancers were foreigners to start with, though gradually Russian dancers began to take a larger and larger part in the ballet companies of Moscow and St. Petersburg. After a succession of French directors, there arrived in St. Petersburg in 1847 yet another Frenchman, Marius Petipa from Marseilles. He controlled the destinies of dancing in Russia for over fifty years and was responsible for raising the standard of Russian dancing to the level we know to-day. In fact by the end of the century the Russian dancers were the finest in the world; and Petipa also improved the standards of choreography. He was the real creator of the ballet d'action, and was also the first to insist that the leading dancers should be recruited from the corps de ballet, which of course meant that every member of the company had to be technically first-class. Petipa composed fifty-four new ballets besides reviving a number of old ones, and his work prepared the way for the modern ballet.

But even with Petipa's reforms a good deal of conventionality remained in the ballet. The choreographer, composer, designer, and librettist all tended to work in watertight compartments without any preliminary collaboration. Often the composer knew nothing about the subject of the ballet, but was simply ordered to turn out so many variations, entrées, marches, etc. As a result most of the ballets produced during this period have not survived in the repertoire, and it says much for Tchaikovsky's feeling for the medium that he was able to rise above the handicaps imposed on him and produce three masterpieces of ballet music.

Tchaikovsky may be justly described as the ballet composer *par excellence:* he had an extraordinary gift for catching the exact atmosphere needed in a particular dance, and his almost unfailing gift of melody and his feeling for orchestral colour ensured that he would be able to convey this feeling to the audience. Curiously enough his dramatic gifts, so evident in his later symphonies, failed to work so well when he applied them to opera, and though there are many fine and moving dramatic moments in *Eugene Onegin* and *The Queen of Spades,* for instance, the music somehow lacks the inevitable rightness of his ballet scores. Yet Tchaikovsky had comparatively little success as a ballet composer in his lifetime. The reasons for this are uncertain, but it would seem that his ballet music, immediately appealing as it is to us to-day, was thought complicated and obscure by those of his contemporaries who could not see beyond the conventionalities of composers like Minkus.

Le Lac des Cygnes, perhaps the most famous of Tchaikovsky's three full-length ballets, began life as a small ballet written for the children of his sister Alexandra Davidov. They performed it during a summer holiday at Kamenka in 1871 when their uncle was on a visit to them. Four years later, when Tchaikovsky was commissioned to write the music for the *Le Lac des Cygnes* ballet, he used some material from this score. The first production took place at the Bolshoi Theatre, Moscow, on 20 February / 4 March 1877, with choreography by Reisinger, an Austrian of mediocre talent. About a third of Tchaikovsky's score was omitted as being too complicated to dance to. This production was a failure, as one can well imagine. Tchaikovsky, always self-critical, attributed this failure to the poverty of the music, and resolved to re-write it. But in the end he never did. The ballet was revived in Moscow in 1880 and again in 1882, with new choreography by Hansen, but it was still not a success, and it was not until after Tchaikovsky's death that *Le Lac des Cygnes* came into its own.

This was due to the enterprise of the veteran choreographer Petipa, who sent for the score and became enthusiastic about the music. He determined to mount the ballet in a new production, in collaboration with Ivanov, who was responsible for the more romantic and legendary parts of the ballet while Petipa himself looked after the more brilliant and realistic sections—though exact details of the collaboration are not known. The second act was given in 1894 at the Maryinsky Theatre in St. Petersburg in a memorial programme of Tchaikovsky's works—he had died in the previous year—and the whole ballet was mounted at the same theatre on 15 / 27 January 1895. In spite of the contradictory elements caused by the collaboration of the two choreographers—which many modern ballet companies further complicate by altering the sequence of dances and making numerous cuts—*Swan Lake* has remained the epitome of the romantic ballet ever since that day and has increased in strength and popularity with the passage of time. The story has a powerful, romantic and lyrical atmosphere, and also allows of the introduction of both purely classical and character dances. The underlying unity of the ballet is strengthened by the music, which is not only effective throughout but also emphasizes the poetry and romance of the subject. It does, in fact, make one believe in fairy tales, and this is where Tchaikovsky's genius as a ballet composer lies.

The music consists mostly of self-contained numbers. Although Tchaikovsky does not follow the story dramatically in quite such a detailed way as the music of earlier ballets like *Giselle* or *Coppélia* does, he expresses its general mood much more closely, and this can be felt even in the indifferent performances of the ballet to which we are sometimes subjected. The ballet is in four acts and consists of some thirty-six separate numbers. As various different versions of the music can be found in productions by different companies to-day, it will be as well to describe these numbers in detail, in the order given in the piano score published in 1949 by the Tchaikovsky Foundation in New York. This conforms to the Petipa production of 1895.

The first act begins with an introduction in the mood of the poetical and romantic 'Swan music' which is to dominate the lake scene in the second act. The curtain rises on dance No. 1, a brilliant 'Scene' in quick tempo for the celebrations of Prince Siegfried's coming of age. Then, in the 1895 version, follows a pas de trois in which light and charming solos for the two girls in 2/4 time alternate with a vigorous 6/8 for the man. All three join in a brilliant, quick 'Coda' in 4/4 time. (In the 1877 version the waltz (No. 4) came at this point.) Number 3 is again a 'Scene,' for the entrance of the Princess-Mother, and No. 4 in this version is the well-known waltz, which rises to a great climax. Number 5 is a pas d'action, a comedy scene between Wolfgang and one of the girls. This replaces a pas de deux in the 1877 version which is now usually transferred to Act III, where it provides the material for Odile's famous solos. Number 6 is a short introduction leading to No. 7, the 'Danse des Coupes,' an excellent polacca of symphonic stature. In the 'Finale,' No. 8, the Swan theme itself is heard for the first time. This haunting oboe melody acts as a unifying element throughout the ballet.

The second act, the scene by the lake, has often been given as a separate ballet: indeed this is the only part of *Swan Lake* which most ballet companies have in their repertoire, and the Royal Ballet was the first company outside Russia to perform the ballet complete. It begins with the well-known introduction based on the Swan theme. Then No. 10, an 'allegro' 'Scene,' shows the arrival of the huntsmen and the discovery of the swan maidens and Odette. The music of the mime scene between Odette and the Prince is marvellously expressive, and the harsh brass chords which herald the arrival of the sinister Rothbart are extremely striking. As chords they are nothing out of the ordinary, being the diminished sevenths which were so dear to every romantic composer throughout the nineteenth century, but it is the way in which they are introduced which is novel and arresting. Then comes the entry of the swan maidens and their waltz. After this woodwind chords and harp cadenzas lead to the famous pas de deux, one of the best-known pieces in all ballet music. This begins with a violin solo accompanied by harp chords—what could be simpler and yet more effective?—and later the solo cello takes over the theme while the violin weaves a poignant countermelody. (Incidentally, this pas de deux and the preceding waltz came just before the end of the act in the 1877 version, but they are now invariably placed in the middle, as in Petipa's version.) Next comes the equally well-known 'Dance of the Cygnets,' with its chirpy four-square rhythm, followed by a new and more brilliant version of the waltz. Then comes a solo for Odette, and finally in this group of dances is the 'Coda,' a vigorous 6/8 dance, simple in style but brilliant both musically and choreographically. Then the mood changes back to that of the beginning of the act, and the swan music returns as Odette and the swan maidens disappear, leaving the Prince and his huntsmen gazing forlornly after them.

The third act, the brilliant ballroom scene, begins with the entry of the guests, followed by general dances. Then a fanfare heralds the appearance of Odile, followed by the mime of choosing the Prince's bride. None of the girls please the Prince, who believes Odile to be Odette. (In the Royal Ballet production Odile does not appear till after the mime of choosing the bride, at the second fanfare.) The next number was a pas de six, but this was never performed outside Russia, and the present Bolshoi ballet production does not include it either. Then comes a series of characteristic national dances—Spanish (which includes castanets and a good deal of national colour), Neapolitan, with an agile trumpet solo which strikes quite a 'modern' note, csárdás, and a mazurka. The order of these dances is sometimes varied. The 1877 version began with the 'Csárdás,' and this is followed by the present-day Royal Ballet production. After the characteristic dances comes a pas de deux for Odile and the Prince in the form of a waltz, with a lush string melody which leads to another of Tchaikovsky's superb solo violin passages. Next come two solos with music interpolated from other sources: first one for Odile, to an orchestrated version of Tchaikovsky's piano piece Op. 72, No. 12, and then a vigorous dance for the Prince to music composed by Drigo. Finally we reach the 'Coda,' which is brassy, noisy and brilliant: in this occur the famous thirty-two fouettés with which Odile dazzles both the Prince and the audience. The music of the 'allegro' which ends the act returns to that of the earlier mime of choosing the bride. The Prince chooses Odile, but then discovers that he has been deceived and that she is not Odette. The curtain falls on his disillusionment.

In the fourth act we are back by the lakeside. Both the 1877 and the Petipa versions begin the act with an entr'acte, and Petipa follows this with another interpolation, an orchestration of Tchaikovsky's Waltz in E♭, Op. 72, No. 11. Then comes a mournful dance for the swans who await the return of Odette, followed by a dance for the cygnets, a lovely and nostalgic little movement in B♭ minor which is almost reminiscent of Chopin. (The Royal Ballet version slightly alters the order of these numbers. It uses the music of the cygnets' dance as an entr'acte, and then leads from part of the original entr'acte and the final part of the swans' mournful dance to the interpolated waltz in E♭.) Then an agitated passage heralds the return of Odette, followed by storm music, which in the Royal Ballet version is somewhat cut. Next comes the music of the Prince's arrival, and after this Petipa interpolated another of Tchaikovsky's piano pieces, Op. 72, No. 15. The final section of the act, an 'allegro agitato,' is a short symphonic development of the Swan music, in syncopated rhythm and working up to a stirring climax.

Such is the sequence of the music in Petipa's 1895 production of *Le Lac des Cygnes*. The Royal Ballet company follow the 1877 version for Act I and Petipa for Act II. The general dances for the corps de ballet at the beginning of Act III are omitted, and the changes in Act IV have already been noted. But the choreography remains based on the Petipa-Ivanov version, as reproduced by Sergeyev. The version shown in London in 1956 by the Bolshoi Theatre Ballet was based on a new choreography by Gorsky which is different to Petipa's in many respects, but the musical changes were less fundamental. Acts I and II were similar to the versions used by the Royal Ballet: in Act III the general dances for the corps de ballet are retained, while the order of the characteristic dances were varied—Petipa's interpolations were also retained. in Act IV Petipa's interpolation of the 'Waltz in E♭' was omitted but other music was interpolated after the Prince's entry.

Tchaikovsky's second full-length ballet, *La Belle au Bois Dormant* (*The Sleeping Beauty*) was first produced at the Maryinsky Theatre, St. Petersburg, on 2/14 January 1890. The production was of unusual splendour, but the ballet was not a great success at first. However it soon established itself as a favourite and has remained so ever since, though productions of the whole ballet outside Russia have not been common—here again the Royal Ballet has shown unusual enterprise, having added the ballet to their repertoire as long ago as 1939.

The ballet is in three acts and contains some twenty-nine numbers: before the first act comes a 'Prologue.' This begins with a short introduction in which the music associated with the evil fairy Carabosse soon leads to the flowing 6/8 melody which is characteristic of the Lilac Fairy. This in turn leads into the first number, a lively and attractive march which accompanies the entrance of the lords and ladies and the mime of Catalabutte. The music here is bright, gay and theatrical in the best sense of the word. Then follows a 'Dance Scene,' a graceful slow waltz with divided strings. In the ensuing pas de six the fairies present their gifts. This is a set of six variations—in the ballet sense of a solo dance and not the musical one of variations on a theme—with an introduction and coda. The names given to these Fairy Dances in the present Royal Ballet production are: Fairy of the Crystal Fountain, a flowing 2/4 dance in B♭ major; Fairy of the Enchanted Garden, a staccato 6/8 dance in G minor; Fairy of the Woodland Glades—this dance is remarkable for the sustained brass chords accompanying the melody on pizzicato strings; Fairy of the Song Birds, an agitated fluttering for piccolo solo; Fairy of the Golden Vine, a brilliant, lively movement; and finally The Lilac Fairy, a waltz in C major.

The original version had different titles for these dances, as may be seen in the piano score published by the Tchaikovsky Foundation. These are: Candite, Coulante, Flour, Falling Crumbs, Singing Canary, Violente, and The Lilac Fairy. After the six variations comes a coda, a lively 'allegro' movement in 4/4 which is begun by the men and works up to a splendid climax. Then comes the 'Finale of the Prologue.' A suave clarinet melody accompanies the Lilac Fairy as she approaches the cradle of the Princess Aurora to bestow her gift. She is interrupted by the entrance of Carabosse, whose music is written in a vigorous 4/4 time. It is brilliantly scored and is developed symphonically as the dance progresses. Her derisive laughter and sneering are most effectively portrayed; again, as in Rothbart's music in *Le Lac des Cygnes,* Tchaikovsky uses only diminished seventh chords, but they are most ingeniously handled.

Act I begins with a 'Scene,' 'allegro vivo' in E major, which evokes an atmosphere of festivity: within this comes the incident of the spinners being discovered but pardoned by the King. Tchaikovsky takes this dramatic interlude in his stride, portraying it musically yet not destroying the symphonic shape of the music. Next comes the famous Waltz, well known in the concert hall, and one of Tchaikovsky's finest creations in this genre. The succeeding number consists of three short sections which act as an introduction to the 'Rose Adage,' again one of the most famous movements in all ballet. Its spacious melody is developed into a movement of magnificent theatrical colour. After the more sprightly dance of the Maids of Honour and the Pages there is an expressive solo for Aurora in the style of a slow waltz, with the melody on a solo violin and a delicate accompaniment in which short harp glissandi are prominent. The coda of this number, described by Petipa in his notes as 'general excitement and dancing' begins with a 2/4 'allegro giusto' in G major. Aurora returns with the recapitulation of the first theme, and an ingenious transition into the final number of the act is made by the superimposition on the music of the coda of the rhythm of the waltz which is to follow—as it were a presentiment of the tragedy to come. This waltz begins in E♭ major, at the point where Aurora seizes the needle, but her dance is abruptly broken off when she pricks herself, and there follows a striking dramatic passage based on Carabosse's music. Her tiny dance of death, based with Bach-like economy on a single semiquaver figure, is extremely effective, and her metamorphosis into sleep is accompanied by a symphonic development of the Lilac Fairy theme, which rises to a great climax and then dies away.

The second act begins with a kind of divertissement. First comes the music of the hunt and then of the game of blind man's buff: then follow a 'Scene' and four dances, those of the Duchesses, Baronesses, Countesses, and Marquises—the Baronesses' dance is often omitted. This little divertissement ends with a farandole, which curiously enough is in mazurka rhythm. Next comes the arrival of the huntsmen, with a repetition of the music heard at the beginning of the act, and leading into the Lilac Fairy music. Aurora enters with a strongly rhythmical 'allegro vivace,' and this is linked to the next number, a pas d'action. This is one of Tchaikovsky's large-scale dramatic creations: it begins with a cello solo theme with many subtle changes between 6/8 and 2/4 time. There is a short melodious 'allegro commodo' in B♭ (a variation for Aurora) before the 'presto' with its quick repeated notes, and rushing staccato scale passages effectively portray Aurora's disappearance.

Before the third act, as performed at Covent Garden, comes the 'Panorama' (andantino in G) which is well known from the concert suite. This is here played as an interlude, but originally accompanied a transformation scene on the stage. Next, in this version, comes the scene of the Prince's search for Aurora, which originally came in the second act. This leads to the real opening of the act, a lively 'allegro' movement in D. A brilliant polacca with a Chopinesque flavour accompanies the entry of the fairy-tale characters, who now appear in procession, led by Puss-in-Boots and the White Cat. Then follows a pas de trois for Florestan and his sisters in the form of an 'intrada,' four variations (in the ballet sense) and a coda. The intrada, a flowing 6/8 movement in B♭, is one of Tchaikovsky's loveliest melodic inspirations, the tune twisting and turning on itself while never losing the insistent rhythm nor becoming monotonous. The variations consist of the 'Silver Fairy Polka,' a variation in 5/4 time which is normally cut at Covent Garden, and the 'Diamond' variation. The 'Coda' uses some of the material of this last variation and develops it with rushing scale passages to an agitated ending.

Now comes a pas de caractère, 'Puss-in-Boots and the White Cat,' one of the most successful examples of cat music ever written: Tchaikovsky has caught not only the sounds that cats make but also their feline essence. This is followed by the well-known 'Blue Birds' pas de deux, which is in several sections. Its first number, 'adagio' in C, is chiefly an interchange between flute and clarinet. At first the clarinet echoes the flute phrases, but later the position is reversed. The two instrumental parts are similar and closely woven together throughout, to portray the unity between the Prince, changed by magic into a bird, and the Princess Florina. Next follows a virile waltz for the man, and then the girl's Andantino, with its delicate flute part adorned with grace notes. The 'Coda' does not return to any of the previously heard music and is based on new material throughout.

The next pas de caractère, 'Red Riding-Hood and the Wolf,' is a scurrying staccato movement in G minor, which admirably portrays its dramatic story. Then follow two further pas de caractère which are normally omitted in the Royal Ballet production, that of Hop o' my Thumb, his brothers, and the Ogre, and that of Cinderella and Prince

Fortune. Next comes the great 'adagio' in C for Aurora and the Prince, one of Tchaikovsky's most majestic and expansive movements, with its broadly flowing melody and rich orchestration. There follows a variation for the Prince—this is not used in the Royal Ballet production, one of the 'Florestan' variations being substituted—and then one for Aurora, the latter with a solo violin part, marked 'staccato e grazioso,' which is very typical of Tchaikovsky. The coda music of this pas de deux is used for the dance of the Three Ivans, a vigorous 'allegro vivace' in E. The next dance, a sarabande, is normally cut, and the ballet ends with a 'Finale and Apotheosis' in the form of an extended mazurka, culminating in an 'andante molto maestoso' in G minor, the modal harmonies of which enhance the dignity of the ending.

The score of *La Belle au Bois Dormant* is slightly larger than that of some ballets, containing a piccolo in addition to two flutes, a cor anglais as well as two oboes, and two cornets as well as two trumpets. The ballet has always remained a favourite in Russia, and is a prominent feature of the Moscow Bolshoi Theatre Ballet's repertoire to-day. Its first important production outside Russia was that staged by Diaghilev at the Alhambra Theatre, London, on 2 November 1921, under the title of *The Sleeping Princess*. The choreography was based on notes made by Sergeyev, who had been a producer at the Maryinsky Theatre and knew the original production. In addition some dances were choreographed by Bronislava Nijinska, and Bakst and Stravinsky also co-operated in the production, which was on an extremely lavish scale. Unfortunately it was not greatly successful. Diaghilev had himself steered balletomanes' taste in the preceding years away from the old-fashioned romantic type of ballet and towards more experimental types of work, and the revival seemed a step backwards to many people. In this production, as in the present Royal Ballet version, the 'Hop o' my Thumb' and 'Cinderella' dances were omitted in the last act. Instead Diaghilev inserted some numbers from *Casse-Noisette* and elsewhere. The choreography of the Royal Ballet version is based, like Diaghilev's, on Sergeyev's reconstruction of Petipa's original production. It has been a continuous success, and was in fact used for the reopening night of Covent Garden after the war in 1946.

On the occasion of the 1921 production of *The Sleeping Princess* Stravinsky wrote in an open letter to Diaghilev: 'Tchaikovsky possessed the power of melody, centre of gravity in every symphony, opera, or ballet composed by him. It is absolutely indifferent to me that the quality of his melody was sometimes unequal. The fact is that he was a creator of melody, which is an extremely rare and precious gift. Among us Glinka too possessed it. And that is something which is not German. The Germans manufactured, and manufactured music with themes and leitmotive, which they substituted for melodies.' And certainly Tchaikovsky's outstanding gift of melody explains a great deal of his success as a ballet composer; for it is melody and rhythm which are essential to all ballet music, and no amount of ingenious contrapuntal development or devices of orchestration can make up for the lack of them.

Before leaving *La Belle au Bois Dormant* we should mention a one-act ballet, *Aurora's Wedding,* which is based on its music and contains some of its characters. This was danced in the 1930's by Colonel de Basil's Ballets Russes, a company which contained many dancers who had previously been with Diaghilev, and has since been taken up by other companies with some variants. The music is mainly taken from the last act of *La Belle au Bois Dormant,* though some numbers from *Casse-Noisette* are also interpolated. It begins with the 'andantino' introduction from Act III of *La Belle au Bois Dormant,* followed by the polonaise from the same act. Then comes the pas de six from the 'Prologue,' followed by the 'Sugar Plum Fairy' from *Casse-Noisette.* We then return to Act II of *La Belle au Bois Dormant* for the dances of the Duchesses and Countesses (and in some versions also the Marquises) and the farandole. Next comes a pas de quatre (or in some versions the pas de trois of Florestan and his sisters from Act III), followed by the pas de caractères of 'Red Riding Hood and the Wolf,' and the 'Blue Bird' pas de deux. Next the 'Chinese Dance' from *Casse-Noisette* is interpolated, followed by the 'Three Ivans' from *La Belle au Bois Dormant,* Act III, and the ballet ends with the final pas de deux, mazurka, 'Finale and Apotheosis' from the same act. It will be seen that this ballet is somewhat of a hotchpotch, but it has proved effective in cases where it has not been possible to mount the full-length version of *La Belle au Bois Dormant.*

Tchaikovsky's last full-length ballet, *Casse-Noisette,* was written in 1891-2 in response to a commission from the Imperial Opera at St. Petersburg, and was produced at the Maryinsky Theatre on 5/17 December 1892 together with Tchaikovsky's one-act opera *Iolanthe,* which had been commissioned for the same occasion. *Casse-Noisette* is therefore really a two-act ballet, though on occasion it has been divided into three. The scenario is based on E. T. A. Hoffmann's 'Nutcracker and Mouse-King,' from his *Serapionsbrüder.* The choreography was begun by Petipa, who later handed it over to Ivanov, and the latter's name is now universally quoted as the choreographer. The suite drawn from this ballet has become world-famous on the concert platform, and the 'Miniature Overture' with which the suite begins is also the overture to the ballet. Here the bass instruments are omitted and the cheerful atmosphere of a children's party is immediately evoked. Act I, which is divided into two tableaux, begins with a piece which accompanies the lighting and adorning of the Christmas tree. It is in D major, 'allegro non troppo' with a more sustained middle section. This leads directly into the 'March,' familiar from the concert suite. Next comes a 'Galop and Entrance of the New Guests,' bringing presents for the Christmas tree. There follows a 'Dance Scene' in which the music becomes more descriptive, here depicting the arrival of the Councellor Drosselmeyer who brings a number of gifts, including mechanical dolls and a little wooden nutcracker. The dolls dance. The following 'Scene' and 'Grossvatertanz' are again mainly descriptive. Clara wants the nutcracker for herself, but Fritz also wants it and breaks it in their struggle. The 'Grossvatertanz,' familiar to us from Schumann's *Carnaval* and *Papillons,* is a solid German folk theme which is associated with family parties of this kind. Then follow two further 'Scenes' which are linked together; they depict the departure of the guests. Then Clara, who has been sent to bed, comes down in her nightgown to look for her nutcracker, but falls asleep among the toys. An army of mice appears, and there is a tremendous battle between them and the Ginger Cake soldiers, the former being led by their king and the latter by the nutcracker. Clara, in her dream, fears that the mice will be victorious, and throws her slipper at the Mouse King. His subjects disappear, and the nutcracker is transformed into a Prince. The music of these two scenes is dramatically developed, though at some length, and as a result they are often cut. They also need first-class orchestral playing. But they are worth preserving, as apart from their musical value they do provide the centre of the story of the ballet, such as it is.

The Prince now invites Clara to accompany him to the Kingdom of Sweets, and their journey is shown in the second tableau of Act I. First there is a 'Scene' in which the toys come down from the Christmas tree to honour the Prince and Clara. The music is a continuation of that of the previous scene, in a somewhat similar style. Then comes the 'Waltz of the Snowflakes,' a large-scale symphonic waltz in Tchaikovsky's best vein. It ends with a brilliant 'presto' Coda in which much use is made of the semiquaver figure which is an integral part of the waltz itself.

The second act is set in the magic castle on the Sugar Mountain, otherwise the Kingdom of Sweets. First comes an overture, and then the entrance of Clara and the Nutcracker Prince together with the court of the Sugar Plum Fairy. Then follows a divertissement which contains many of the dances which were included in the concert suite. The first is a Spanish dance called 'Chocolate'—this is not in the concert suite—followed by the 'Arab Dance,' representing Coffee. Next comes the 'Chinese Dance,' representing Tea, and then the exciting 'Russian

Dance,' or Trepak. The final pair of dances are the 'Dance of the Reed Pipes,' with its delicious passages for three flutes, and 'Mother Gigogne and the Clowns'—the latter is normally omitted nowadays. Next comes the big 'Waltz of the Flowers,' which ends the concert suite, and then a pas de deux for the Prince and the Sugar Plum Fairy which is perhaps the finest music in the whole ballet. This consists of an intrada, 'andante maestoso,' with a broad and flowing melody richly scored and symphonically developed, and two variations—a tarantella and the well-known 'Dance of the Sugar Plum Fairy,' with its ingenious passages for bass clarinet and celesta. Tchaikovsky had heard the latter instrument in Paris in 1891, and here introduced it into Russia for the first time: its limpid tones are exactly right for the atmosphere which he wished to evoke here. The last part of the pas de deux is a coda, 'vivace assai,' and the ballet ends with a waltz-finale and apotheosis.

Though *Casse-Noisette* has never quite achieved the popularity of its two famous companions—perhaps its rather naïve scenario and also the fact that it does not really fill an evening are somewhat to blame for this—it contains a good deal of Tchaikovsky's most delightful and skilful music, and it has remained in the repertoire of many ballet companies, either as a whole or as a one-act divertissement: the Sadler's Wells Ballet produced it complete as long ago as 1934. Apart from the dance numbers in his operas . . . a good deal of Tchaikovsky's other music has also of course been drawn upon by modern choreographers: some notable examples are his fifth symphony (*Les Présages*—Massine), his second piano concerto (*Ballet Imperial*—Balanchine), the variations from the Suite in G, the Serenade for strings, and various smaller works (*Hamlet*—Helpmann). . . . Stravinsky also drew heavily on Tchaikovsky in his ballet *Le Baiser de la Fée.* The use of these other works of Tchaikovsky for ballet purposes has met with varying success. Certainly his large-scale symphonic works are not really suitable for ballet purposes. Although Tchaikovsky himself was worried about his methods of symphonic construction, his symphonies and concertos are in fact worked out in a broad symphonic style—even if this differs from those of Beethoven or Brahms—which is not very suitable to being cut up into individual dance numbers, and Massine, for instance, when preparing *Les Présages* was compelled to make very considerable cuts in the score. Tchaikovsky in fact differentiated quite strongly between his dance music and his symphonic works, and always tried to see that each was suitable for its intended purpose. Those works of his which are divided up into short sections, such as the variations from the Suite in G, are naturally much more suitable for ballet, and a dramatic symphonic poem like *Hamlet* also lends itself fairly easily to balletic treatment: but the ballets based on concertos and symphonies have shown a somewhat uneasy alliance between dance and music—the natural forms of the one do not really correspond to those of the other.

As an example of the type of collaboration which existed between Tchaikovsky and his choreographer, we may append here Petipa's instructions for the first scene of *Casse-Noisette.* Petipa, as an experienced choreographer, knew exactly what he wanted in the way of music, and tried to ensure that his composers would produce this. He asked for:

1. Soft music. Sixty-four bars.
2. The lighting of the tree. Sparkling music, eight bars.
3. The entry of the children. Noisy and joyous music, twenty-four bars.
4. The moment of astonishment and admiration. A tremolo for some bars.
5. March, sixty-four bars.
6. Entry of the Incroyables. Sixteen bars rococo, minuet tempo.
7. Galop.
8. The entry of Drosselmeyer. The music slightly frightening and comic at the same time. A broad section, sixteen to twenty-four bars.
   The music gradually changes in character, twenty-four bars. It becomes less mournful, brighter and ends in gaiety.
   Fairly solemn music, eight bars and pause.
   Repeat the same eight bars and pause.
   Four bars with chords of astonishment.
9. Eight bars mazurka tempo.
   Eight different bars mazurka tempo.
   Sixteen bars mazurka.
10. Waltz—sharp, jerky, and very rhythmic. Forty-eight bars.

This may appear to be putting the composer very much in a strait-jacket, and so in a way it is. On the other hand a good professional composer ought to be able to make something interesting even out of exact limits of this kind, as Tchaikovsky certainly did. It is always better if the choreographer, composer and designer can work together in close collaboration of this kind, and if the choreographer can indicate his exact wishes before the music is even written, it will clearly help the unity of the ballet. It is after all the choreographer who is the final creator of the ballet, and it is much better if his wishes can be realized as closely as possible, provided that he and his collaborators are temperamentally suited to each other and to the theme of the ballet. . . .

After the death of Tchaikovsky Petipa was forced to seek rather less distinguished composers for his ballets, the only one of any real importance being Alexander Glazounov, who lived from 1865 to 1936. Glazounov had been brought up very much in the nationalist Russian school of Rimsky-Korsakov and Borodin, and his earlier works, written before he was thirty, such as the symphonic poem *Stenka Razin,* have a definitely Russian flavour which contrasts with the more cosmopolitan style of Tchaikovsky. He was precociously brilliant at an early age—when only seventeen he wrote a symphony which won general commendation—but unfortunately his style became less distinguished and distinctive as he grew older, and his ballet music all dates from the period when this decline was beginning to set in. His ballet *Raymonda,* with choreography by Petipa, was first produced at the Maryinsky Theatre on 7/19 January 1898. The story is set in the Middle Ages and includes troubadours, a Saracen knight, and a statue which descends from its pedestal and plays an important part in the action—together with lute playing, sword play, elves, and goblins. These differing elements should have given Glazuonov a good deal of scope for musical characterization, but he did not profit by them, and most of the music could fit any story and any age just as well. It is competent in the late nineteenth-century manner, opulent, pleasantly scored, and completely undistinguished. However, *Raymonda* remains in the repertoire of the Bolshoi Theatre Ballet and is mentioned here for that reason, and occasionally excerpts from it do appear in concert programmes.

Much the same may be said of Glazounov's other ballet scores, *Les Saisons* and *Les Ruses d'Amour*. The former was produced at the Maryinsky Theatre on 7/20 February 1900, again with choreography by Petipa. Here, as also in his *Scènes de Ballet,* there is no story, and the seasons of the year are presented in the form of a straight divertissement. In the first scene Winter is shown with his friends Hoar-Frost, Ice, Hail, and Snow. In the second comes Spring, with birds and flowers. Summer is enriched with Fauns, Satyrs, and Naiads, the latter wearing azure veils. Autumn is given over to the Bacchantes, and at the end the previous Seasons return for solo variations. Here again there is no attempt to give the atmosphere of the different scenes, and we are left with a string of more or less effective dances, some of which are heard from time to time in concert programmes. Music of this kind is much better used as a background to purely abstract dancing, and this has been excellently done by Frederick Ashton, who used music from Glazounov's ballets, as well as his 'Valse de Concert No. 1' and a piano mazurka orchestrated by Robert Irving, for his *Birthday Offering,* presented at Covent Garden on 5 May 1956 in honour of the twenty-fifth birthday of the Sadler's Wells Ballet. Here the series of solo dances fits admirably with the music: there is no story, and the only characterization is that inherent in the personalities of the solo dancers for whom the dances were created.

QUESTIONS

1. What is the origin of the word "ballet?" Look up the terms *prima ballerina, pas de deux, choreography, divertissement.* Discuss the meanings of these words and their use by ballet people.
2. Can you suggest reasons why the ballet has been virtually a monopoly of the French and Russians?
3. Look up the names of Fokine, Diaghilev, Pavlova. What were their contributions to the development of the ballet? Can you discover the names of their present-day counterparts?
4. Many people who have difficulty enjoying symphonic music nevertheless find much enjoyment in ballet music. Can you suggest reasons for this?
5. Listen to the ballet music of any of the ballets whose story is outlined in the essay. Can you follow the story line while listening? Is it necessary to know the story to enjoy the music? Give your reasons.

MUSIC FOR THE CHURCH / 1

The subject of music in the church is a vast and complex one. In one sense it covers not only church music but primitive and ancient music as well. Music in the Western church, as we know, did not spring up full bloom, but was rather a gradual development of all the music that preceded the formation of the church. It is not possible to know thoroughly Protestant church music without having a substantial knowledge of Catholic church music; and it is not possible to know Catholic church music without a substantial knowledge of the music from which it is derived. In this essay Edward Dickinson, late Professor of the History of Music at Oberlin Conservatory of Music, surveys almost two thousand years of the history of the liturgical music of the Catholic Church.

The Ritual Chant of / the Catholic Church

EDWARD DICKINSON

IN READING THE WORDS OF THE CATHOLIC LITURGY from the Missal we must remember that they were written to be sung, and in a certain limited degree acted, and that we cannot receive their real force except when musically rendered and in connection with the ceremonies appropriated to them. For the Catholic liturgy is in conception and history a musical liturgy; word and tone are inseparably bound together. The immediate action of music upon the emotion supplements and reinforces the action of the text and the dogmatic teaching upon the understanding, and the ceremony at the altar makes the impression still more direct by means of visible representation. All the faculties are therefore held in the grasp of this composite agency of language, music, and bodily motion; neither is at any point independent of the others, for they are all alike constituent parts of the poetic whole, in which action becomes prayer and prayer becomes action.

The music of the Catholic Church as it exists today is the result of a long process of evolution. Although this process has been continuous, it has three times culminated in special forms, all of them coincident with three comprehensive ideas of musical expression which have succeeded each other chronologically, and which divide the whole history of modern music into clearly marked epochs. These epochs are those (1) of the unison chant, (2) of unaccompanied chorus music, and (3) of mixed solo and chorus with instrumental accompaniment.

(1) The period in which the unison chant was the only form of church music extends from the founding of the congregation of Rome to about the year 1100, and coincides with the centuries of missionary labor among the Northern and Western nations, when the Roman liturgy was triumphantly asserting its authority over the various local uses.

(2) The period of the unaccompanied contrapuntal chorus, based on the mediaeval key and melodic systems, covers the era of the European sovereignty of the Catholic Church, including also the period of the Counter-Reformation of the sixteenth century. This phase of art, culminating in the works of Palestrina in Rome, Orlandus Lassus in Munich, and the Gabrielis in Venice, suffered no decline, and gave way at last to a style in sharp contrast with it only when it had gained an impregnable historic position.

THE RITUAL CHANT OF THE CATHOLIC CHURCH from *Music in the History of the Western Church* by Edward Dickinson; Scribner and Sons; 1925.

(3) The style now dominant in the choir music of the Catholic Church, *viz.*, mixed solo and chorus music with free instrumental accompaniment, based on the modern transposing scales, arose in the seventeenth century as an outcome of the Renaissance secularization of art. It was taken up by the Catholic, Lutheran, and Anglican Churches, and was moulded into its present types under the influence of new demands upon musical expression which had already brought forth the dramatic and concert styles.

The unison chant, although confined in the vast majority of congregations to the portions of the liturgy that are sung by the priest, is still the one officially recognized form of liturgic music. Although in the historic development of musical art representatives of the later phases of music have been admitted into the Church, they exist there only, we might say, by sufferance—the chant still remains the legal basis of the whole scheme of worship music. The chant melodies are no mere musical accompaniment; they are the very life breath of the words. The text is so exalted in diction and import, partaking of the sanctity of the sacrificial function to which it ministers, that it must be uttered in tones especially consecrated to it. So that in process of time these two elements have become amalgamated into a union so complete that no dissolution is possible even in thought. There is no question that the chant melodies as they exist today are only modifications, in most cases but slight modifications, of those that were originally associated with the several portions of the liturgy. At the moment when any form of words was given a place in the Missal or Breviary, its proper melody was then and there wedded to it. This fact makes the Catholic liturgic chant a distinctive church song in a special and peculiar sense. It is not, like most other church music, the artistic creation of individuals, enriching the service with contributions from without, and imparting to them a quality drawn from the composer's personal feeling and artistic methods. It is rather a sort of religious folk-song, proceeding from the inner shrine of religion. It is abstract, impersonal; its style is strictly ecclesiastical, both in its inherent solemnity and its ancient association, and it bears, like the ritual itself, the sanction of unimpeachable authority. The reverence paid by the Church to the liturgic chant as a peculiarly sacred form of utterance is plainly indicated by the fact that while there is no restraint upon the license of choice on the part of the choir, no other form of song has ever been heard, or can ever be permitted to be heard, from the priest in the performance of his ministrations at the altar.

If we enter a Catholic church during High Mass or Vespers we notice that the words of the priest are delivered in musical tones. This song at once strikes us as different in many respects from any other form of music with which we are acquainted. At first it seems monotonous, strange, almost barbaric, but when we have become accustomed to it the effect is very solemn and impressive. Many who are not instructed in the matter imagine that the priest extemporizes these cadences, but nothing could be further from the truth. Certain portions of this chant are very plain, long series of words being recited on a single note, introduced and ended with very simple melodic inflections; other portions are florid, of wider compass than the simple chant, often with many notes to a syllable. Sometimes the priest sings alone, without response or accompaniment; sometimes his utterances are answered by a choir of boys in the chancel or a mixed choir in the gallery; in certain portions of the service the organ supports the chant with harmonies which seem to be based on a different principle of key and scale from that which ordinarily obtains in modern chord progression. In its freedom of rhythm it bears some resemblance to dramatic recitative, yet it is far less dramatic or characteristic in color and expression, and at the same time both more severe and more flexible. To one who understands the whole conception and spirit of the Catholic worship there is a singular appropriateness in the employment of this manner of utterance, and when properly rendered it blends most efficiently with the architectural splendors of altar and sanctuary, with incense, lights, vestments, ceremonial action, and all the embellishments that lend distinction and solemnity to the Catholic ritual. This is the celebrated liturgic chant, also called Gregorian chant, Plain Song, or Choral, and is the special and peculiar form of song in which the Catholic Church has clothed its liturgy for certainly fifteen hundred years.

This peculiar and solemn form of song is the musical speech in which the entire ritual of the Catholic Church was originally rendered, and to which a large portion of the ritual is confined at the present day. It is always sung in unison, with or without instrumental accompaniment. It is unmetrical though not unrhythmical; it follows the phrasing, the emphasis, and the natural inflections of the voice in reciting the text, at the same time that it idealizes them. It is a sort of heightened form of speech, a musical declamation, having for its object the intensifying of the emotional powers of ordinary spoken language. It stands to true song or tune in much the same relation as prose to verse, less impassioned, more reflective, yet capable of moving the heart like eloquence.

The chant appears to be the natural and fundamental form of music employed in all liturgical systems the world over, ancient and modern. The sacrificial song of the Egyptians, the Hebrews, and the Greeks was a chant, and this is the form of music adopted by the Eastern Church, the Anglican, and every system in which worship is offered in common and prescribed forms. The chant form is chosen because it does not make an independent artistic impression, but can be held in strict subordination to the sacred words; its sole function is to carry the text over with greater force upon the attention and the emotions. It is in this relationship of text and tone that the chant differs from true melody. The latter obeys musical laws of structure and rhythm; the music is paramount and the text accessory, and in order that the musical flow may not be hampered, the words are often extended or repeated, and may be compared to a flexible framework on which the tonal decoration is displayed. In the chant, on the other hand, this relation of text and tone is reversed; there is no repetition of words, the laws of structure and rhythm are rhetorical laws, and the music never asserts itself to the concealment or subjugation of the meaning of the text. The "jubilations" or "melismas," which are frequent in the choral portions of the Plain Song system, particularly in the richer melodies of the Mass, would seem at first thought to contradict this principle; in these florid melodic phrases the singer would appear to abandon himself to a sort of inspired rapture, giving vent to the emotions aroused in him by the sacred words. Here musical utterance seems for the moment to be set free from dependence upon word and symbol and to assert its own special prerogatives of expression, adopting the conception that underlies modern figurate music. These occasional ebullitions of feeling permitted in the chant are, however, only momentary; they relieve what would otherwise be an unvaried austerity not contemplated in the spirit of Catholic art; they do not violate the general principle of universality and objectiveness as opposed to individual subjective expression—subordination to word and rite rather than purely musical self-assertion—which is the theoretic basis of the liturgic chant system.

Chant is speech-song, probably the earliest form of vocal music; it proceeds from the modulations of impassioned speech; it results from the need of regulating and perpetuating these modulations when certain exigencies require a common and impressive form of utterance, as in religious rites, public rejoicing or mourning, etc. The necessity of filling large spaces almost inevitably involves the use of balanced cadences. Poetic recitation among ancient and primitive peoples is never recited in the ordinary level pitch of voice in speech, but always in musical inflections, controlled by some principle of order. Under the authority of a permanent corporate institution these inflections are reduced to a system, and are imposed upon all whose office it is to administer the public ceremonies of worship. This is the origin of the liturgic chant of ancient peoples, and also, by historic continuation, of the Gregorian melody. The Catholic chant is a projection into modern art of the altar song of Greece, Judaea, and Egypt, and through these nations reaches back to that epoch of unknown remoteness when mankind first began to conceive of invisible powers to be invoked or appeased. A large measure of the impressiveness of the liturgic chant, therefore, is due to its historic religious associations. It forms a connecting link between ancient religion and the Christian, and perpetuates to our own day an ideal of sacred music which is as old as religious music itself. It is a striking fact that only within the last six hundred or seven hundred years, and only within the bounds of Christendom, has an artificial form of worship music arisen in which musical forms have become emancipated from subjection to the rhetorical laws of speech and been built up under the shaping force of inherent musical laws, gaining a more or less free play for the creative impulses of an independent art. The conception which is realized in the Gregorian chant, and which exclusively prevailed until the rise of the modern polyphonic system, is that of music in subjection to rite and liturgy, its own charms merged and, so far as conscious intention goes, lost in the paramount significance of text and action. It is for this reason, together with the historic relation of chant and liturgy, that the rulers of the Catholic Church have always labored so strenuously for uniformity in the liturgic chant as well as for its perpetuity. There are even churchmen at the present time who urge the abandonment of all the modern forms of harmonized music and the restoration of the unison chant to every detail of the service. A notion so ascetic and monastic can never prevail, but one who has fully entered into the spirit of the Plain Song melodies can at least sympathize with the reverence which such a reactionary attitude implies. There is a solemn unearthly sweetness in these tones which appeals irresistibly to those who have become habituated to them. They have maintained for centuries the inevitable comparison with every other form of melody, religious and secular, and there is reason to believe that they will continue to sustain all possible rivalry, until they at last outlive every other form of music now existing.

No one can obtain any proper conception of this magnificent Plain Song system from the examples which one ordinarily hears in Catholic churches, for only a minute part of it is commonly employed at the present day. Only in certain convents and a few churches where monastic ideas prevail, and where priests and choristers are enthusiastic students of the ancient liturgic song, can we hear musical performances which afford us a revelation of the true affluence of this mediaeval treasure. What we customarily hear is only the simpler intonings of the priest at his ministrations and the eight "psalm tones" sung alternately by priest and choir. These "psalm tones" or "Gregorian tones" are plain melodic formulas, with variable endings, and are appointed to be sung to the Latin psalms and canticles. When properly delivered, and supported by an organist who knows the secret of accompanying them, they are exceedingly beautiful. They are but a hint, however, of the rich store of melodies, some of them very elaborate and highly organized, which the chant-books contain, and which are known only to special students. To this great compendium belong the chants anciently assigned to those portions of the liturgy which are now usually sung in modern settings—the *Kyrie, Gloria, Credo, Sanctus, Benedictus, Agnus Dei,* and the variable portions of the Mass, such as the Introits, Graduals, Prefaces, Offertories, Sequences, etc., besides the hymns sung at Vespers and the other canonical hours. Few have ever explored the bulky volumes which contain this unique bequest of the Middle Ages; but one who has even made a beginning of such study, or who has heard the florid chants worthily performed in the traditional style, can easily understand the enthusiasm which these strains arouse in the minds of those who love to penetrate to the innermost shrines of Catholic devotional expression.

The theory and practice of the liturgic chant is a science of large dimensions and much difficulty. In the course of centuries a vast store of chant melodies has been accumulated, and in the nature of the case many variants of the older melodies—those composed before the development of a precise system of notation—have arisen, so that the verification of texts, comparison of authorities, and the application of methods of rendering to the needs of the complex ceremonial make this subject a very important branch of liturgical science.

The Plain Song may be divided into the simple and the ornate chants. In the first class the melodies are to a large extent syllabic (one note to a syllable), rarely with more than two notes to a syllable. The simplest of all are the tones employed in the delivery of certain prayers, the Epistle, Prophecy, and Gospel, technically known as "accents," which vary but little from monotone. The most important of the more melodious simple chants are the "Gregorian tones" already mentioned. The inflections sung to the versicles and responses are also included among the simple chants.

The ornate chants differ greatly in length, compass, and degree of elaboration. Some of these melodies are exceedingly florid and many are of great beauty. They constitute the original settings for all the portions of the Mass not enumerated among the simple chants, *viz.,* the *Kyrie, Gloria,* Introit, Prefaces, Communion, etc., besides the Sequences and hymns. Certain of these chants are so elaborate that they may almost be said to belong to a separate class. Examination of many of these extended melodies will often disclose a decided approach to regularity of form through the recurrence of certain definite melodic figures. "In the Middle Ages," says P. Wagner, "nothing was known of an accompaniment; there was not the slightest need of one. The substance of the musical content, which we today commit to interpretation through harmony, the old musicians laid upon melody. The latter accomplished in itself the complete utterance of the artistically aroused fantasy. In this particular the melismas, which carry the extensions of the tones of the melody, are a necessary means of presentation in mediaeval art; they proceed logically out of the principle of the unison melody. . . . Text repetition is virtually unknown in the unison music of the Middle Age. While modern singers repeat an especially emphatic thought or word, the old melodists repeat a melody or phrase which expresses the ground mood of the text in a striking manner. And they not only repeat it, but they make it unfold, and draw out of it new tones of melody. This method is certainly not less artistic than the later text repetition; it comes nearer, also, to the natural expression of the devotionally inspired heart."

The ritual chant has its special laws of execution which involve long study on the part of one who wishes to master it. Large attention is given in the best seminaries to the purest manner of delivering the chant, and countless treatises have been written upon the subject. The first desideratum is an accurate pronunciation of the Latin, and a facile and distinct articulation. The notes have no fixed and measurable value, and are not intended to give the duration of the tones, but only to guide the modulation of the voice. The length of each tone is determined only by the proper length of the syllable. In this principle lies the very essence of Gregorian chant, and it is the point at which it stands in exact contradiction to the theory of modern measured music. The divisions of the chant are given solely by the text. The rhythm, therefore, is that of speech, of the prose text to which the chant tones are set. The rhythm is a natural rhythm, a succession of syllables combined into expressive groups by means of accent, varied pitch, and prolongations of tone. The fundamental rule for chanting is: "Sing the words with notes as you would speak them without notes." This does not imply that the utterance is stiff and mechanical as in ordinary conversation; there is a heightening of the natural inflection and a grouping of notes, as in impassioned speech or the most refined declamation. Like the notes and divisions, the pauses also are unequal and immeasurable, and are determined only by the sense of the words and the necessity of taking breath.

In the long florid passages often occurring on a single vowel analogous rules are involved. The text and the laws of natural recitation must predominate over melody. The jubilations are not to be conceived simply as musical embellishments, but, on the contrary, their beauty depends upon the melodic accents to which they are joined in a subordinate position. These florid passages are never introduced thoughtlessly or without meaning, but they are strictly for emphasizing the thought with which they are connected; "they make the soul in singing fathom the deeper sense of the words, and to taste of the mysteries hidden within them." The particular figures must be kept apart and distinguished from each other, and brought into union with each other, like the words, clauses, and sentences of an oration. Even these florid passages are dependent upon the influence of the words and their character of prayer.

The principles cited above concern the rhythm of the chant. Other elements of expression must also be taken into account, such as prolonging and shortening tones, crescendos and diminuendos, subtle changes of quality of voice or tone color to suit different sentiments. The manner of singing is also affected by the conditions of time and place, such as the degree of the solemnity of the occasion, and the dimensions and acoustic properties of the edifice in which the ceremony is held.

In the singing of the mediaeval hymn melodies, many beautiful examples of which abound in the Catholic office books, the above rules of rhythm and expression are modified as befits the more regular metrical character which the melodies derive from the verse. They are not so rigid, however, as would be indicated by the bar lines of modern notation, and follow the same laws of rhythm that would obtain in spoken recitation.

The liturgic chant of the Catholic Church has already been alluded to under its more popular title of "Gregorian." Throughout the Middle Ages and down to our own day nothing in history has been more generally received as beyond question than that the Catholic chant is entitled to this appellation from the work performed in its behalf by Pope Gregory I, called the Great. This eminent man, who reigned from 590 to 604, was the ablest of the succession of early pontiffs who formulated the line of policy which converted the barbarians of the North and West, brought about the spiritual and political autonomy of the Roman See, and confirmed its supremacy over all the churches of the West.

In addition to these genuine services historians have generally concurred in ascribing to him a final shaping influence upon the liturgic chant, with which, however, he probably had very little to do. His supposed work in this department has been divided into the following four details:

(1) He freed the church song from the fetters of Greek prosody.

(2) He collected the chants previously existing, added others, provided them with a system of notation, and wrote them down in a book

which was afterwards called the Antiphonary of St. Gregory, which he fastened to the altar of St. Peter's Church, in order that it might serve as an authoritative standard in all cases of doubt in regard to the true form of chant.

(3) He established a singing school in which he gave instruction.

(4) He added four new scales to the four previously existing, thus completing the tonal system of the Church.

The prime authority for these statements is the biography of Gregory I, written by John the Deacon about 872. Detached allusions to this pope as the founder of the liturgic chant appear before John's day, the earliest being in a manuscript addressed by Pope Hadrian I to Charlemagne in the latter part of the eighth century, nearly two hundred years after Gregory's death. The evidences which tend to show that Gregory I could not have had anything to do with this important work of sifting, arranging, and noting the liturgic melodies become strong as soon as they are impartially examined. In Gregory's very voluminous correspondence, which covers every known phase of his restless activity, there is no allusion to any such work in respect to the music of the Church, as there almost certainly would have been if he had undertaken to bring about uniformity in the musical practice of all the churches under his administration. The assertions of John the Deacon are not confirmed by any anterior document. No epitaph of Gregory, no contemporary records, no ancient panegyrics of the pope, touch upon the question. Isidor of Seville, a contemporary of Gregory, and the Venerable Bede in the next century, were especially interested in the liturgic chant and wrote upon it, yet they make no mention of Gregory in connection with it. The documents upon which John bases his assertion, the so-called Gregorian Antiphonary, do not agree with the ecclesiastical calendar of the actual time of Gregory I.

In reply to these objections and others that might be given there is no answer but legend, which John the Deacon incorporated in his work, and which was generally accepted toward the close of the eleventh century. That this legend should have arisen is not strange. It is no uncommon thing in an uncritical age for the achievement of many minds in a whole epoch to be attributed to the most commanding personality in that epoch, and such a personality in the sixth and seventh centuries was Gregory the Great.

What, then, is the origin of the so-called Gregorian chant? There is hardly a more interesting question in the whole history of music, for this chant is the basis of the whole magnificent structure of mediaeval church song, and in a certain sense of all modern music, and it can be traced back unbroken to the earliest years of the Christian Church, the most persistent and fruitful form of art that the modern world has known. The most exhaustive study that has been devoted to this obscure subject has been undertaken by Gevaert, director of the Brussels Conservatory of Music, who has brought forward strong representation to show that the musical system of the early Church of Rome was largely derived from the secular forms of music practiced in the private and social life of the Romans in the time of the empire, and which were brought to Rome from Greece after the conquest of that country B.C. 146. "No one today doubts," says Gevaert, "that the modes and melodies of the Catholic liturgy are a precious remains of antique art." "The Christian chant took its modal scales to the number of four, and its melodic themes, from the musical practice of the Roman empire, and particularly from the song given to the accompaniment of the kithara, the special style of music cultivated in private life. The most ancient monuments of the liturgic chant go back to the boundary of the fourth and fifth centuries, when the forms of worship began to be arrested in their present shape. Like the Latin language, the Greco-Roman music entered in like manner into the Catholic Church. Vocabulary and syntax are the same with the pagan Symmachus and his contemporary St. Ambrose; modes and rules of musical composition are identical in the hymns which Mesomedes addresses to the divinities of paganism and in the cantilenas of the Christian singers." "The compilation and composition of the liturgic songs, which was traditionally ascribed to St. Gregory I, is in truth a work of the Hellenic popes at the end of the seventh and the beginning of the eighth centuries. The Antiphonarium Missarum received its definitive form between 682 and 715; the Antiphonarum Officii was already fixed under Pope Agathon (678-681)." In the fourth century, according to Gevaert, antiphons were already known in the East. St. Ambrose is said to have transplanted them into the West. Pope Celestine I (422-472) has been called the founder of the antiphonal song in the Roman Church. Leo the Great (440-461) gave the song permanence by the establishment of a singing school in the neighborhood of St. Peter's. Thus from the fifth century to the latter part of the seventh grew the treasure of melody, together with the unfolding of the liturgy. The four authentic modes were adaptations of four modes employed by the Greeks. The oldest chants are the simplest, and of those now in existence the antiphons of the Divine Office can be traced farthest back to the transition point from the Greco-Roman practice to that of the Christian Church. The florid chants were of later introduction, and were probably the contribution of the Greek and Syrian Churches.

The Christian chants were, however, no mere reproductions of profane melodies. The groundwork of the chant is allied to the Greek melody; the Christian song is of a much richer melodic movement, bearing in all its forms the evidence of the exuberant spiritual life of which it is the chosen expression. The pagan melody was sung to an instrument; the Christian was unaccompanied, and was therefore free to develop a special rhythmical and melodic character unconditioned by any laws except those involved in pure vocal expression. The fact also that the Christian melodies were set to unmetrical texts, while the Greek melody was wholly confined to verse, marked the emancipation of the liturgic song from the bondage of strict prosody and gave a wider field to melodic and rhythmic development.

It would be too much to say that Gevaert has completely made out his case. The impossibility of verifying the exact primitive form of the oldest chants, and the almost complete disappearance of the Greco-Roman melodies which are supposed to be the antecedent or the suggestion of the early Christian tone formulas, make a positive demonstration in such a case out of the question. Gevaert seems to rely mainly upon the identity of modes or keys which exists between the most ancient church melodies and those most in use in the kithara song. Other explanations, more or less plausible, have been advanced, and it is not impossible that the simpler melodies may have arisen in an idealization of the natural speech accent, with a view to procuring measured and agreeable cadences. Both methods—actual adaptations of older tunes and the spontaneous enunciation of more obvious melodic formulas—may have been allied in the production of the earlier liturgic chants. The laws that have been found valid in the development of all art would make the derivation of the ecclesiastical melodies from elements existing in the environment of the early Church a logical and reasonable supposition, even in the absence of documentary evidence.

There is no proof of the existence of a definite system of notation before the seventh century. The chanters, priests, deacons, and monks, in applying melodies to the text of the office, composed by aid of their memories, and their melodies were transmitted by memory, although probably with the help of arbitrary mnemonic signs. The possibility of this will readily be granted when we consider that special orders of monks made it their sole business to preserve, sing, and teach these melodies. In the confusion and misery following the downfall of the kingdom of the Goths in the middle of the sixth century the Church became a sanctuary of refuge from the evils of the time. With the revival of religious zeal and the accession of strength the Church flourished, basilicas and convents were multiplied, solemnities increased in number and splendor, and with other liturgic elements the chant expanded. A number of popes in the seventh century were enthusiastic lovers of Church music, and gave it the full benefit of their authority.

Among these were Gregory II and Gregory III, one of whom may have inadvertently given his name to the chant.

The system of tonality upon which the music of the Middle Ages was based was the modal or diatonic. The modern system of transposing scales, each major or minor scale containing the same succession of steps and half steps as each of its fellows, dates no further back than the first half of the seventeenth century. The mediaeval system comprises theoretically fourteen, in actual use twelve, distinct modes or keys, known as the ecclesiastical modes or Gregorian modes. These modes are divided into two classes—the "authentic" and "plagal." The compass of each of the authentic modes lies between the keynote, called the "final," and the octave above, and includes the notes represented by the white keys of the pianoforte, excluding sharps and flats. The first authentic mode begins on D, the second on E, and so on. Every authentic mode is connected with a mode known as its plagal, which consists of the last four notes of the authentic mode transposed an octave below, and followed by the first five notes of the authentic, the "final" being the same in the two modes. The modes are sometimes transposed a fifth lower or a fourth higher by means of flatting the B. During the epoch of the foundation of the liturgic chant only the first eight modes (four authentic and four plagal) were in use. The first four authentic modes were popularly attributed to St. Ambrose, bishop of Milan in the fourth century, and the first four plagal to St. Gregory, but there is no historic basis for this tradition. The last two modes are a later addition to the system. The Greek names are those by which the modes are popularly known, and indicate a hypothetical connection with the ancient Greek scale system.

To suppose that the chant in this period was sung exactly as it appears in the office books of the present day would be to ignore a very characteristic and universal usage in the Middle Ages. No privilege was more freely accorded to the mediaeval chanter than that of adding to the melody whatever embellishment he might choose freely to invent on the impulse of the moment. The right claimed by Italian opera singers down to a very recent date to decorate the phrases with trills, cadenzas, etc., even to the extent of altering the written notes themselves, is only the perpetuation of a practice generally prevalent in the mediaeval Church, and which may have come down, for anything we know to the contrary, from remote antiquity. In fact, the requirement of singing the notes exactly as they are written is a modern idea; no such rule was recognized as invariably binding until well into the nineteenth century. It was no uncommon thing in Händel's time and after to introduce free embellishments even into "I know that my Redeemer liveth" in the *Messiah*. In the Middle Ages the singers in church and convent took great merit to themselves for the inventive ability and vocal adroitness by which they were able to sprinkle the plain notes of the chant with improvised embellishments. "Moreover, there existed in the liturgic text a certain number of words upon which the singers had the liberty of dilating according to their fancy. According to an ancient Christian tradition, certain chants were followed by a number of notes sung upon meaningless vowels; these notes, called neumes or *jubili*, rendered, in accordance with a poetic thought, the faith and adoration of the worshipers who appeared to be unable to find words that could express their sentiments. These vocalizations or embroideries were sometimes longer than the chants themselves, and many authors complained of the importance given to these vocal fantasies." (Lemaire, *Le Chant, ses principes et son histoire.*)

Among the mnemonic signs which, before the invention of the staff and notation system, indicated the changes of pitch to be observed by the singer, there were many that unmistakably point to the traditional flourishes which had become an integral element in the Plain Song system. Many of these survived and were carried over into secular music after the method of chanting became more simple and severe. Similar license was also practiced in the later period of part singing, and not only in the rude early counterpoint of the thirteenth and fourteenth centuries, but even in the highly developed and specialized chorus music of the sixteenth century, the embellishments which were reduced to a system and handed down by tradition, gave to this art a style and effect the nature of which has now fallen from the knowledge of men.

Such was the nature of the song which resounded about the altars of Roman basilicas and through convent cloisters in the seventh and eighth centuries, and which has remained the sanctioned official speech of the Catholic Church in her ritual functions to the present day. Nowhere did it suffer any material change or addition until it became the basis of a new harmonic art in Northern Europe in the twelfth and thirteenth centuries. The chant according to the Roman use began to extend itself over Europe in connection with the missionary efforts which emanated from Rome from the time of Gregory the Great. Augustine, the emissary of Gregory, who went to England in 597 to convert the Saxons, carried with him the Roman chant. "The band of monks," says Green, "entered Canterbury bearing before them a silver cross with a picture of Christ and singing in concert the strains of the litany of their church." (Green, *Short History of the English People.*) And although the broad-minded Gregory instructed Augustine not to insist upon supplanting with the Roman use the liturgy already employed in the older British churches if such an attempt would create hostility, yet the Roman chant was adopted both at Canterbury and York.

The Roman chant was accepted eventually throughout the dominions of the Church as an essential element of the Roman liturgy. Both shared the same struggles and the same triumphs. Familiarity with the church song became an indispensable part of the equipment of every clergyman, monastic and secular. No missionary might go forth from Rome who was not adept in it. Monks made dangerous journeys to Rome from the remotest districts in order to learn it. Every monastery founded in the savage forests of Germany, Gaul, or Britain became at once a singing school, and day and night the holy strains went up in unison with the melodies of the far distant sacred city. The Anglo-Saxon monk Winfrid, afterward known as Boniface, the famous missionary to the Germans, planted the Roman liturgy in Thuringia and Hesse and devoted untiring efforts to teaching the Gregorian song to his barbarous proselytes. In Spain, Ildefonso, about 600, is enrolled among the zealous promoters of sacred song according to the use of Rome. Most eminent and most successful of all who labored for the exclusive authority of the Roman chant as against the Milanese, Gallican, and other rival forms was Charlemagne, king of the Franks from 768 to 814, whose persistent efforts to implant the Gregorian song in every church and school in his wide dominions was an important detail of his labor in the interest of liturgic uniformity according to the Roman model.

Among the convent schools which performed such priceless service for civilization in the gloomy period of the early Middle Ages, the monastery of St. Gall in Switzerland holds an especially distinguished place. This convent was established in the seventh century by the Irish monk from whom it took its name, rapidly increased in repute as a center of piety and learning, and during the eighth, ninth, and tenth centuries numbered some of the foremost scholars of the time among its brotherhood. About 790 two monks, versed in all the lore of the liturgic chant, were sent from Rome into the empire of Charlemagne at the monarch's request. One of them, Romanus, was received and entertained by the monks of St. Gall, and was persuaded to remain with them as teacher of church song according to the Antiphonary which he had brought with him from Rome. St. Gall soon became famous as a place where the purest traditions of the Roman chant were taught and practiced. Schubiger, in his extremely interesting work, *Die Sängerschule St. Gallens vom VIII.-XII. Jahrhundert,* has given an extended account of the methods of devotional song in use at St. Gall, which may serve as an illustration of the general practice among the pious monks of the Middle Ages:

In the reign of Charlemagne (803) the Council of Aachen enjoined upon all monasteries the use of the Roman song, and a later capitulary required that the monks should perform this song completely and in proper order at the divine office, in the daytime as well as at night. According to other rescripts during the reign of Louis the Pious (about 820) the monks of St. Gall were required daily to celebrate Mass, and also to perform the service of all the canonical hours. The solemn melodies of the ancient psalmody resounded daily in manifold and precisely ordered responses; at the midnight hour the sound of the *Invitatorium, Venite exultamus Domino,* opened the service of the nocturnal vigils; the prolonged, almost mournful tones of the responses alternated with the intoned recitation of the lessons; in the spaces of the temple on Sundays and festal days, at the close of the nightly worship, there reëchoed the exalted strains of the Ambrosian hymn of praise (*Te Deum laudamus*); at the first dawn of day began the morning adoration, with psalms and antiphons, hymns and prayers; to these succeeded in due order the remaining offices of the diurnal hours. The people were daily invited by the Introit to participate in the holy mysteries; they heard in solemn stillness the tones of the *Kyrie* imploring mercy; on festal days they were inspired by the song once sung by the host of angels; after the Gradual they heard the melodies of the Sequence which glorified the object of the festival in jubilant choral strains, and afterward the simple recitative tones of the Creed; at the *Sanctus* they were summoned to join in the praise of the Thrice Holy, and to implore the mercy of the Lamb who taketh away the sins of the world. These were the songs which, about the middle of the ninth century, arose on festal or ferial days in the cloister church of St. Gall. How much store the fathers of this convent set upon beauty and edification in song appears from the old regulations in which distinct pronunciation of words and uniformity of rendering are enjoined, and hastening or dragging the time sharply rebuked.

Schubiger goes on to say that three styles of performing the chant were employed; *viz.*, a very solemn one for the highest festivals, one less solemn for Sundays and saints' days, and an ordinary one for ferial days. An appropriate character was given to the different chants—*e.g.*, a profound and mournful expression in the office for the dead; an expression of tenderness and sweetness to the hymns, the *Kyrie, Sanctus,* and *Agnus Dei;* and a dignified character (*cantus gravis*) to the antiphons, responses, and alleluia. Anything that could disturb the strict and euphonious rendering of the song was strictly forbidden. Harsh, unmusical voices were not permitted to take part. Distinctness, precise conformity of all the singers in respect to time and purity of intonation were inflexibly demanded.

Special services, with processions and appropriate hymns, were instituted on the occasion of the visit to the monastery of the emperor or other high digntary. All public observances, the founding of a building, the reception of holy relics, the consecration of a bell or altar—even many of the prescribed routine duties of conventual life, such as drawing water, lighting lamps, or kindling fires—each has its special form of song. It was not enthusiasm, but sober truth, that led Ekkehard V to say that the rulers of this convent, "through their songs and melodies, as also through their teachings, filled the Church of God, not only in Germany, but in all lands from one sea to the other, with splendor and joy."

At the convent of St. Gall originated the class of liturgical hymns called Sequences, which includes some of the finest examples of mediaeval hymnody. At a very early period it became the custom to sing the *Alleluia* of the Gradual to a florid chant, the final vowel being extended into an exceedingly elaborate flourish of notes. Notker Balbulus, a notable member of the St. Gall brotherhood in the ninth century, conceived the notion, under the suggestion of a visiting monk, of making a practical use of the long-winded final cadence of the *Alleluia.* He extended and modified these melodious passages and set words to them, thus constructing a brief form of prose hymn. His next step was to invent both notes and text, giving his chants a certain crude form by the occasional repetition of a melodic strain. He preserved a loose connection with the *Alleluia* by retaining the mode and the first few tones. These experiments found great favor in the eyes of the brethren of St. Gall; others followed Notker's example, and the Sequence melodies were given honored places in the ritual on festal days and various solemn occasions. The custom spread; Pope Nicholas I in 860 permitted the adoption of the new style of hymn into the liturgy. The early Sequences were in rhythmic prose, but in the hands of the ecclesiastical poets of the few centuries following they were written in rhymed verse. The Sequence was therefore distinguished from other Latin hymns only by its adoption into the office of the Mass as a regular member of the liturgy on certain festal days. The number increased to such large proportions that a sifting process was deemed necessary, and upon the occasion of the reform of the Missal through Pius V after the Council of Trent only five were retained, *viz., Victimae paschali,* sung on Easter Sunday; *Veni Sancte Spiritus,* appointed for Whit-Sunday; *Lauda Sion,* for Corpus Christi; *Stabat Mater dolorosa,* for Friday of Passion Week; and *Dies Irae,* which forms a portion of the Mass for the Dead.

Many beautiful and touching stories have come down to us, illustrating the passionate love of the monks for their songs, and the devout, even superstitious, reverence with which they regarded them. Among these are the tales of the Armorican monk Hervé, in the sixth century, who, blind from his birth, became the inspirer and teacher of his brethren by means of his improvised songs, and the patron of mendicant singers, who still chant his legend in Breton verse. His mother, so one story goes, went one day to visit him in the cloister, and, as she was approaching, said: "I see a procession of monks advancing, and I hear the voice of my son. God be with you, my son! When, with the help of God, I get to heaven, you shall be warned of it, you shall hear the angels sing." The same evening she died, and her son, while at prayer in his cell, heard the singing of the angels as they welcomed her soul in heaven. According to another legend, told by Gregory of Tours, a mother had taken her only son to a monastery near Lake Geneva, where he became a monk, and especially skilful in chanting the liturgic service. "He fell sick and died; his mother in despair came to bury him, and returned every night to weep and lament over his tomb. One night she saw St. Maurice in a dream attempting to console her, but she answered him, 'No, no; as long as I live I shall always weep for my son, my only child!' 'But,' answered the saint, 'he must not be wept for as if he were dead; he is with us, he rejoices in eternal life, and tomorrow, at Matins, in the monastery, thou shalt hear his voice among the choir of the monks; and not tomorrow only, but every day as long as thou livest.' The mother immediately arose, and waited with impatience the first sound of the bell for Matins, to hasten to the church of the monks. The precentor having intoned the response, when the monks in full choir took up the antiphon, the mother immediately recognized the voice of her child. She gave thanks to God; and every day for the rest of her life, the moment she approached the choir she heard the voice of her well-beloved son mingle in the sweet and holy melody of the liturgic chant."

As centuries went on, and these ancient melodies, gathering such stores of holy memory, were handed down in their integrity from generation to generation of praying monks, it is no wonder that the feeling grew that they too were inspired by the Holy Spirit. The legend long prevailed in the Middle Ages that Gregory the Great one night had a vision in which the Church appeared to him in the form of an angel, magnificently attired, upon whose mantle was written the whole art of music, with all the forms of its melodies and notes. The pope prayed God to give him the power of recollecting all that he saw; and after he awoke a dove appeared, who dictated to him the chants which are ascribed to him. Ambros quotes a mediaeval Latin chronicler, Aurelian Reomensis, who relates that a blind man named Victor, sitting one day before an altar in the Pantheon at Rome, by direct divine inspiration composed the response *Gaude Maria,* and by a second miracle immediately received his sight. Another story from the same source tells how a monk of the convent of St. Victor, while upon a neighboring mountain, heard angels singing the response *Cives Apostolorum,* and after his return to Rome he taught the song to his brethren as he had heard it. (Ambros, *Geschichte der Musik,* vol. ii.)

In order to explain the feeling toward the liturgic chant which is indicated by these legends and the rapturous eulogies of mediaeval and modern writers, we have only to remember that the melody was never separated in thought from the words, that these words were prayer and praise, made especially acceptable to God because wafted to him by means of his own gift of music. To the mediaeval monks prayer was the highest exercise in which man can engage, the most efficacious of all actions, the chief human agency in the salvation of the world. Prayer was the divinely appointed business to which they were set apart. Hence arose the multiplicity of religious services in the convents, the observance of the seven daily hours of prayer, in some monasteries in France, as earlier in Syria and Egypt, extending to the so-called *laus perennis*, in which companies of brethren, relieving each other at stated watches, maintained, like the sacred fire of Vesta, an unbroken office of song by night and day.

Such was the liturgic chant in the ages of faith, before the invention of counterpoint and the first steps in modern musical science suggested new conceptions and methods in worship music. It constitutes today a unique and precious heritage from an era which, in its very ignorance, superstition, barbarism of manners, and ruthlessness of political ambition, furnishes strongest evidence of the divine origin of a faith which could triumph over such antagonisms. To the devout Catholic the chant has a sanctity which transcends even its aesthetic and historic value, but non-Catholic as well as Catholic may reverence it as a direct creation and a token of a mode of thought which, as at no epoch since, conceived prayer and praise as a Christian's most urgent duty, and as an infallible means of gaining the favor of God.

The Catholic liturgic chant, like all other monumental forms of art, has often suffered through the vicissitudes of taste which have beguiled even those whose official responsibilities would seem to constitute them the special custodians of this sacred treasure. Even today there are many clergymen and church musicians who have but a faint conception of the affluence of lovely melody and profound religious expression contained in this vast body of mediaeval music. Where purely aesthetic considerations have for a time prevailed, as they often will even in a Church in which tradition and symbolism exert so strong an influence as they do in the Catholic, this archaic form of melody has been neglected. Like all the older types (the sixteenth century *a capella* chorus and the German rhythmic choral, for example) its austere speech has not been able to prevail against the fascinations of the modern brilliant and emotional style of church music which has emanated from instrumental art and the Italian aria. Under this latter influence, and the survival of the seventeenth-century contempt for everything mediaeval and "Gothic," the chant was long looked upon with disdain as the offspring of a barbarous age, and only maintained at all out of unwilling deference to ecclesiastical authority. In the last few decades, however, probably as a detail of the reawakening in all departments of a study of the great works of older art, there has appeared a reaction in favor of a renewed culture of the Gregorian chant. The tendency toward sensationalism in church music has now begun to subside. The true ideal is seen to be in the past. Together with the new appreciation of Palestrina, Bach, and the older Anglican Church composers, the Catholic chant is coming to its rights, and an enlightened modern taste is beginning to realize the melodious beauty, the liturgic appropriateness, and the edifying power that lie in the ancient unison song. This movement is even now only in its inception; in the majority of church centers there is still apathy, and in consequences corruption of the old forms, crudity and coldness in execution. Much has, however, been already achieved, and in the patient and acute scholarship applied in the field of textual criticism by the monks of Solesmes and the church musicians of Paris, Brussels, and Regensburg, in the enthusiastic zeal shown in many churches and seminaries of Europe and America for the attainment of a pure and expressive style of delivery, and in the restoration of the Plain Song to portions of the ritual from which it has long been banished, we see evidences of a movement which promises to be fruitful, not only in this special sphere, but also, as a direct consequence, in other domains of church music which have been too long neglected.

The historic status of the Gregorian chant as the basis of the magnificent structure of Catholic church music down to 1600, of the Anglican chant, and to a large extent of the German people's hymn-tune or choral, has always been known to scholars. The revived study of it has come from an awakened perception of its liturgic significance and its inherent beauty. The influence drawn from its peculiarly solemn and elevated quality has begun to penetrate the chorus work of the best Catholic composers of the recent time. Protestant church musicians are also beginning to find advantage in the study of the melody, the rhythm, the expression, and even the tonality of the Gregorian song. And every lover of church music will find a new pleasure and uplift in listening to its noble strains. He must, however, listen sympathetically, expelling from his mind all comparison with the modern styles to which he is accustomed, holding in clear view its historic relations and liturgic function. To one who so attunes his mind to its peculiar spirit and purport, the Gregorian Plain Song will seem worthy of the exalted place it holds in the veneration of the most august ecclesiastical institution in history.

QUESTIONS

1. What do you believe distinguishes a religious song from a secular song? Is it the words? the music? Why?
2. Look up in a dictionary the words "sacred," "religious," and "liturgical," and discuss the difference in their meanings. Can you name some musical compositions that illustrate the differences?
3. For whom was Gregorian chant named? What was the chant called previously? What was the founder's contribution to Church music?
4. Name the principal parts of the Mass. From what are the names of these parts derived? What is the English meaning of the Latin names?
5. Look up the "Motu Proprio of Pope Pius X on Sacred Music," in Nicholas Slonimsky's *Music Since 1900,* page 629. Discuss its various points.

MUSIC FOR THE CHURCH / 2

Albert Schweitzer is known throughout the world as a selfless physician, philosopher, and humanitarian. In the musical world, Schweitzer is known as an organist of uncommon feeling and power and an authority on Johann Sebastian Bach. More than fifty years ago Schweitzer wrote a book on Bach that has since influenced all who perform Bach's music. As a first-rate organist, Schweitzer is able to discuss Bach's music authoritatively, and, as a historian, he is able to place Bach in his proper historical context. To deepen further his already profound grasp of church music, Schweitzer went on to study organ building and in 1909 presided over a conference that set up world-wide regulations for organ construction. In this essay Schweitzer traces the early development of the organ and congregational singing in the Protestant service.

The Chorale in the Church Service

ALBERT SCHWEITZER

HOW WAS THE CONGREGATIONAL SONG INTRO-duced into the church service at the time of the Reformation? It is usual to look upon the question as very simple and to suppose that the people had little by little come to sing the melody while the organ played it. Did the sacred instrument really teach the congregation in this way?

We may read through all Luther's writings without finding a single place where he speaks of the organ as the instrument accompanying the congregational singing. Moreover he, the admirer of true church music of every kind, gives no directions as to how the organ is to coöperate in the service. It is really incredible, however, that in the few places where he mentions the organ at all, he speaks of it not enthusiastically but almost scornfully! He does not look upon it as necessary or even desirable in the evangelical service, but at most tolerates it where he finds it already.

His contemporaries shared his view. We need not be astonished that the Reformed Church dealt drastically with the organs and banished them from the churches. In the Lutheran and even in the Catholic churches at that time it fared almost the same. It had always had, indeed, its adversaries. No less a person than St. Thomas Aquinas had declared war on it, not regarding organ music, or indeed instrumental music in general, as calculated to stimulate devotion. In the sixteenth century, however, complaints against it arose on all sides, and the Council of Trent (1545-1563), which dealt with all the doubtful questions relating to the church and its service, was compelled to enact severe regulations against the erroneous and too prevalent employment of the organ in worship. Catholics and Protestants alike at that time imposed on it a term of penance, in order that it might alter its ungodly nature, in default of which the Church would excommunicate it.

It had fully merited this disgrace. The character of the tasks allotted to it may be seen from the *Caeremoniale Episcoporum* issued by Pope Clement VIII in the year 1600. The organ preludised in order to give the tone to the priest or the choir. It further gave out the liturgical songs and hymns in alternation with the choir, one verse being sung and the next played on the organ. It was never used, however, to accompany the choir. The primitive structure of the organs of that time quite forbade this; their heavy keys did not permit of polyphonic play-

---

THE CHORALE IN THE CHURCH SERVICE from *J. S. Bach,* Volume 1, by Albert Schweitzer (translated by Ernest Newman); The Macmillan Company. Reprinted by permission.

ing, while their crude, untempered tuning made it as a rule impossible to play on them in more than one or two keys.

Since therefore they could not coöperate, the choir and the organ functioned in turns. When the organ had completed its verse, the text, in accordance with the above-mentioned regulations of the Pope, was either recited loudly by a chorister, or else sung, which latter was recommended as the better course.

With the organ employed in this independent way, abuses could not fail to creep in. As the organist was unable to play polyphonically on his instrument, he was tempted to amuse himself with quick running passages in his preambles to the verses or during the course of these. Still worse was it when he indulged in well-known secular songs, which seems to have been a wide-spread practice. In 1548 an organist in Strassburg was dismissed from his post for having played French and Italian songs during the offertory.

At a later date the organ unwarrantably deprived the choir of many of the hymns, taking almost everything upon itself. The extent to which this had become prevalent appears from an incident that happened to Luther, which he tells in his best style in the *Table Talk:* "When I was a young monk in Erfurt," he says, "and had to make the rounds of the villages, I came to a certain village and celebrated Mass there. When I had dressed myself and stepped before the altar in my fine attire, the clerk began to strike the *Kyrie eleison* and the *Patrem* on the lute. I could with difficulty keep from laughing, for I was not used to such an organ; I had to make my *Gloria in excelsis* conform to his *Kyrie.*"

It seemed so much a matter of course at that time to substitute the organ for the choir in the liturgy that this clerk, in default of an organ, simply had recourse to the lute!

In the Evangelical church the rôle of the organ had for a long time now been the same as in the Catholic church. It preambled to the hymns of the priest and the choir and alternated with the latter; only now the congregational song is merely an addendum, to which the organ preambles and wherewith it alternates. In Wittenberg it preambled to almost all the vocal pieces, whether of priest, choir, or people, and shared with the choir in the rendering of the *Kyrie,* the *Gloria,* and the *Agnus Dei.* We learn this from Wolfgang Musculus, who in 1536 attended the Concordia conferences at Wittenberg, and described the singing at the service in the Wittenberg parish church on the fifth Sunday after Easter.

This explains the curious injunction which we find in the church ordinances of the fifteenth and sixteenth centuries, namely that the organ "shall *strike* into the song in the churches." It means that certain verses are to be played by the organist alone, the congregation being silent. At the same time the caution is given that this must not happen too often, but at the most two or three times in the one hymn. It is so laid down in the "Strassburg Church-ordinance" of 1598, and, in exactly the same way, in the "Nuremberg Congregation ordinance" of 1606. At first, and for another three generations at least, there was no question of the organ *accompanying* the congregational singing.

How did the choir stand with regard to the congregational chorale? Did it take the place of the organ, guiding and supporting the song of the people? A glance at the earliest hymn books appointed for the service shows us that this solution did not occur to Luther.

The *Erfurt Enchiridion* of Justus Jonas was a hymn-book not for the church but for the home, as, indeed, its title expressly indicates. The melody alone was noted over the poem, so that the father of the household could give it out to the children and the servants. The Strassburg reformer Catharina Zell hoped that "a poor mother should go to sleep, and, if at midnight the crying child had to be rocked, sing it a song of heavenly things"; this would be the right kind of lullaby, and would please God more than all the lullabies played on the organ in the Catholic church.

The *Church chorale book* published at Wittenberg in 1524 by Luther and Walther, while the *Enchiridion* was being printed at Erfurt, makes no reference whatever to congregational singing. It merely consists, in fact, of the vocal parts of chorales written in four and five parts, and the coöperation of the faithful is barred at the outset by the fact that the chorale melody lies in the tenor, not in the soprano. These vocal parts—which were probably engraved by Luther's friend, the painter and wood engraver Lucas Cranach—are those of chorale motets sung by the choir, and therefore having a cantus firmus, as was customary in the religious and secular music of that time.

Luther was not only a reformer but an artist. The logical outcome of his reforming ideas would have been a remodeling of the church service on the lines of the simple home service, in which case the congregational chorale would have been the only music used in the church. This, indeed, is the line we find him pursuing in his first drastic treatise on the service. But, as in most men of genius, there was a fatal side to his greatness that prevented him from thinking out his ideas to their logical conclusion, and made him endow a thing and its antithesis with equal life. He was an admirer of the contrapuntal music of the Netherlands school. He regarded artistic music as one of the most perfect manifestations of the Deity. "When natural music is heightened and polished by art," he said once, "there man first beholds and can with great wonder examine to a certain extent (for it cannot be wholly seized or understood), the great and perfect wisdom of God in His marvellous work of music, in which this is most singular and indeed astonishing, that one man sings a simple tune or tenor (as musicians call it), together with which three, four, or five voices also sing, which as it were play and skip delightedly round this simple tune or tenor, and wonderfully grace and adorn the said tune with manifold devices and sounds, performing as it were a heavenly dance, so that those who at all understand it and are moved by it must be greatly amazed, and believe that there is nothing more extraordinary in the world than such a song adorned with many voices." The wonders of contrapuntal polyphony have never been so admirably described before or since.

His favorite composers were Josquin des Près (1450-1521), the court musician to Louis XII of France, and Heinrich Isaak's pupil Ludwig Senfl (died 1550), who was successively in the service of the courts of Vienna and Munich. His remark upon Josquin is well-known: "He is the master of the notes; they have to do as he wills; other composers have to do as the notes will." On one occasion, when a motet of Senfl's was being performed in his house, he called out: "I could not write such a motet if I were to tear myself to pieces, just as he, for his part, could not preach a sermon like me."

The musician in Luther could not tolerate the banishment of choir and art-song from the church, as many people desired, or the restriction of the choir to leading the congregational singing. "And I am not of the opinion" he says in the preface to Walther's chorale parts of 1524, "that on account of the Gospel all the arts should be crushed out of existence, as some over-religious people pretend, but I would willingly see all the arts, especially music, in the service of Him who has given and created them."

A licence was thus granted to the art in the Lutheran service; it took its place in the ritual as a free and independent power. All the phases of the development of music in general are to be clearly seen in the Lutheran service. Finally, when the motet, under the influence of Italian art, was transformed into the cantata, bringing not only instrumental music but an undisguised opera-style into the church, the service actually came to be interrupted by a sacred concert, which was looked upon as its culminating point. It was at this juncture that Bach came on the scene. On the covers of his scores he writes, not "cantata," but "concerto."

Thus had Luther not been an artist, Bach would never have been able to write his sacred concert-music for church purposes and as part of the church service. Would he nevertheless have written it in any case? What would he have done had he been born in Zürich or in Geneva?

At first, then, the congregational chorale was not supported either by the organ or by the choir, but sung *unisono* without accompaniment, precisely as in the Catholic church at the end of the Middle Ages.

We must not overestimate the number of the congregational chorales that were sung during a service. Where a choir existed, the congregation took little part in the singing, being restricted to the *Credo,* sung between the reading of the Gospel and the sermon, and perhaps a communion hymn. In Wittenberg—so it appears from the account given by Musculus—the congregation as a rule did not sing, but left even the chorales to the choir. In other places—Erfurt, for example—it was customary for the people to sing alternately with the choir between the Epistle and the Gospel, in such a way that the choir sang the sequence and the people joined in with a German chorale appropriate to the time of the year. Five or six chorales in the year sufficed for this, since the same chorale was used on each Sunday during that particular period.

In the churches that had no choir, more importance attached to the congregational singing, since in that case the *Kyrie,* the *Gloria,* and the *Agnus Dei* were sung in the corresponding German chorales. But here again, as a rule, fifteen or at most twenty chorales, which had been laid down, once for all, for their particular Sundays, sufficed for the whole year.

On closer inspection we get the impression that the congregational singing, instead of gaining ground, was in the course of the sixteenth century driven back by the art-singing and by the organ, the pretensions of the latter increasing everywhere, in spite of all ordinances.

There was thus good cause for the attempt that was made, at the end of the first century of the Reformation—not indeed by a musician but by a priest—to improve the position of the chorale. In 1586 the Würtemberg court preacher Lucas Osiander published his *Fünffzig geistliche Lieder und Psalmen, mit vier Stimmen auf kontrapunktweise, für die Kirchen und Schulen im löblichen Fürstentumb Würtemberg, also gesetzet, dass eine gantze christliche Gemein durchaus mitsingen kann* (Fifty sacred songs and psalms, for the churches and schools in the worshipful principality of Würtemberg, set contrapuntally in four parts in such a way that the whole Christian congregation can always join in them). This was the first real chorale book in our sense, except that it was written for the choir instead of for the organ. The fact that Osiander relies only on the choir, not on the organ, for the leading of the congregational singing, proves that the instrument in his time had no concern whatever with the latter.

In his preface he expresses his confidence that he has made things easier by removing the melody from the tenor to the soprano, and thinks that when the laity recognize the tune they will joyfully take part in it.

Was not his confidence misplaced? It was indeed only a half-measure, a false compromise between polyphony and melody. If he wanted polyphony, he should have allowed the whole congregation to sing in chorus in four parts, as was the custom later in Switzerland; on the other hand, if he wished to do without polyphony, he should have let the choir sing in unison, acting, as it were, as precentor, somewhat in the way the village cantors in his day led the chorale without choir or organ, simply by the unison singing of the school children. His desire, however, was to reconcile artistic singing and popular singing, and instead of a solution he achieved only an unstable compromise. For what support could the harmonies of a choir—and the choirs at that time were very weak in numbers—give to a *cantus firmus* sung by a mass of people?

Hans Leo Hassler also tried to make a forward step in this direction, and published, besides his splendid *Cantiones sacrae* and *Sacri concertus* (for performance by the choir only), his *Kirchengesäng, Psalmen und geistliche Lieder auf die gemeinen Melodien mit vier Stimmen simpliciter gesetzet,* which, according to the preface, were so constructed that the ordinary man could sing them in the Christian assembly to figurate music.

It would be wrong, however, to suppose that all the masters of church music who, in the sixteenth and seventeeth centuries, removed the melody to the soprano part, were imitators of Osiander, and that it was for purely practical reasons that they abandoned the earlier system. The real reason is quite different and must be sought in the fact that in the meantime German church music had shaken off the influence of the purely contrapuntal music of the Netherlands school and had fallen under that of the Italians, in which the melodic style began to dominate the contrapuntal. Melchior Vulpius, Seth Calvisius, Michael Praetorius, and Johann Eccard thus follow in their admirable music not so much the lead of the Würtemberg Court preacher as the trend of the art itself.

It was a pure accident that through this change in polyphonic art the possibility was opened to the congregation to join in the *cantus firmus* with the choir. How far it availed itself of it we do not know, for in the history of art, as a rule, we never get to know the things that would be of practical interest to us, for these, being looked upon as matters of daily custom, are not recorded. The fact that at this epoch the term "chorale" begins to be applied to the melodies sung by the congregation throws no light on the question, unless we regard it as proving that by this time the melodies of the church song had ceased to be congregational property and had become the property of the choir.

In any case the composers themselves, in spite of the fine practical suggestions as to congregational singing that they put forward in their prefaces, thought only of the choir when composing, as is shown by their counterpoint, which, with all its simplicity, becomes richer and more and more in the style of the motet. For us these chorale pieces, with their singularly beautiful blending of Italian and German art, are choral works pure and simple, and the idea of trying again the experiment of letting the congregation join in them would not occur to us. But if only we could hear them even as choral works! When will the time come when these treasures are exhibited each Sunday in our church services?

The attempts to have the singing of the congregation led by the choir were made about the end of the sixteenth century and in the first decade of the seventeenth. By the middle of the seventeenth century the question is settled by the organ assuming this rôle. In 1650 appears the *Tablature-book* of Samuel Scheidt, with a hundred chorale harmonizations intended for the accompaniment of the congregational singing.

This was no thought-out experiment, but a solution arising out of the facts, i.e. the progress of organ-building. The sacred instrument had in the meantime been made more practically fitted for polyphonic playing, and endowed with such fulness of tone that it overwhelmed the small and weak choirs of that time. Whereas hitherto it had accompanied the choir, which supported the singing of the congregation, its powerful tone now made it possible for it to assume the lead. But again we cannot be sure of the date at which the organ began to support the choir in the chorale, or when it began to coöperate with the choir in general. This was certainly not the case before the beginning of the seventeenth century. Vulpius, Praetorius, Eccard, and the others appear to know nothing of it. But as early as 1627 Johann Hermann Schein, Cantor of St. Thomas's church in Leipzig, adds a figured bass—intended for "organists, instrumentalists, and lutenists"—to the four, five, and six-part chorale pieces for the choir in his *Cantionale* of that year; and this most probably points to a joint performance by choir and organ.

We must not, however, conceive the organ accompaniment to the chorale, as it was practiced in the second half of the seventeenth century, as a supplanting of the choir by the organ in the chorale. The choir, even in Bach's time, coöperated in the chorale as in earlier times—polyphonically, indeed—although the organ took the lead, as it were a kind of second and stronger choir without words.

This transference of vocal polyphony to the organ by means of chorale accompaniment was of cardinal significance to the art of organ music. The chorale was the teacher of the organists, leading them from the false and fruitless virtuosity of the keyboard to the true, simple organ style. From this moment German organ music severs itself from that of

Italy, France, and the Netherlands, and, always under the control of the chorale, pursues the path along which, in the course of two generations, it was to arrive at perfection. Scheidt, already in possession of the true organ style derived from the chorale, sees that his life-work consists in combating the "colored" organ style of the school of the Dutchman Sweelinck.

It is an illustration of how an idea is, in the end, always stronger than circumstances. Organ music did not come to perfection in Paris or in Venice, where everything seemed to be in its favor, but among the poor cantors and schoolmasters of an impoverished country, as the Germany of the two generations after the Thirty Years' War was. How small Frescobaldi, the organist of St. Peter's in Rome, whose fame among his contemporaries was so great, seems beside a Samuel Scheidt, whose name was unknown on the other side of the Alps!

From the moment when organ, choir, and congregation together gave out the chorale, it was inevitable that the antiphonal method, under which the organ alone performed certain of the verses, should sooner or later fall into disuse. But of the perfection of these independent organ renderings at that time we may judge from Scheidt's *Tablatura nova,* published in 1624. It consists for the most part of a species of variations upon the chorales most generally used—the number of variations corresponding to the number of verses of the song—and upon the hymns of the various seasons of the church year, which at that time were still sung in Halle in Latin, and not, as in other places, in German. In addition there are liturgical pieces, such as the *Kyrie, Gloria, Magnificat,* and the *Psalmus sub communione* "Jesus Christus unser Heiland," which are all treated in the same way.

The Celli Tablature that appeared twenty-three years earlier is on the same lines, except that it also contains the complete "catechism songs."

How long the custom, testified to in all contemporary tablatures, of rendering vocal pieces on the organ alone, still lasted after the process of decay had once set in, can no longer be ascertained. When we consider the extremely numerous arrangements by Bach of the chorale "Allein Gott in der Höh sei Ehr," we are inclined to think that even down to his day there persisted, under certain circumstances, the practice testified to by Scheidt, of the organ responding to the *Gloria* intoned by the priest at the altar.

As to the position of the congregational singing in Bach's time, we have only conjecture to go upon. One thing at any rate had been achieved—the number of the hymns affiliated to the service had considerably increased. Each Gospel had one or more of these allotted to it, so that the same ones were always sung on a particular Sunday. They were called the *Cantica de tempore;* in the hymn-books they formed the first class and were arranged according to the Sundays of the ecclesiastical year. The cantor selected them himself without consulting anyone else. In our day, on the contrary, the hymns are always selected by the clergyman, to tally with the spirit of his sermon.

This use of the *Cantica de tempore* helps us to understand how the organists of the time of Pachelbel and Bach came to write cycles of chorale preludes for each Sunday of the ecclesiastical year.

Whether the congregation took possession of all these hymns and took an active and hearty part in the singing of them is, however, another question. It is well known that Mattheson and the famous Hamburg musicians thought nothing at all of the congregational chorale, and in general refused to recognize singing of this kind as music. From this we may conclude that it did not occupy a prominent place in their churches, and that they, for their part, did nothing to encourage it. It must have been the same in other towns that had celebrated choirs. The cantata—that sacred concert intercalated in the service—absorbed all the interest, and the art-song, as at the beginning of the Reformation, had once more triumphed.

We do not know whether things were better in this respect in Leipzig than in other towns. The truth is that no remark of Bach's has come down to us to show that, in contradistinction to his contemporaries, he felt any particular interest in congregational singing. In his Passions, at any rate, he does not desire its co-operation, in spite of the splendid rôle that he assigns to the chorale in those works. It is highly probable that in Bach's time the singing of the Leipzig congregations was not so good as is commonly supposed.

Not until the concert style of music was banished from the service, in the generation after Bach, and the town choirs that had been allotted to the churches ceased to exist, did congregational singing become the characteristic and sole service-music of the Protestant church. In the epoch of rationalism and pietism the ideal was realized which the Reformation had indeed perceived, but, for conservative and artistic reasons, had not pursued. However barbarously rationalism behaved towards the old hymn, it did good work for congregational singing. Its ultimate aim, of course, was to substitute a new kind of hymn for the old, the diction and the ideas of which had by then become so antiquated as to unfit it for use as a real congregational hymn.

Whether the problem has been really solved by allowing the organ to support the congregational singing is doubtful. The method has established itself, because it is practical. But the ideal is not congregational singing of this kind, directed by, and dependent on, the organ; the true ideal is free and confident unaccompanied singing, as in the congregational singing of the Middle Ages and of the first Reformation period. Perhaps that complete and unfettered cooperation of organ, choir, and worshippers was, in its way, an ideal, towards which we shall some day aspire more than we do now.

QUESTIONS

1. Why has the organ come to be regarded as a "sacred" musical instrument? When did this phenomenon develop? Who was responsible?
2. What does Schweitzer mean when he says, concerning Renaissance organs, "their heavy keys did not permit of polyphonic playing?" What is the meaning of polyphonic?
3. Besides the organ, what other musical instruments have you heard used in church? For what purpose were they used? Do you believe that some instruments can be classed as "religious," and some as "secular?" Which ones? Why?
4. What was Martin Luther's purpose in having the congregation participate in the singing of the church service? Did this affect the musicality of the service? In what ways?
5. Do you think professionally-trained choirs are an asset in the singing of the church service? Discuss the singing in your own church. Is the choir a professional one? Are they paid for their services? Do you think it is ethical to be paid for singing in church?

COMPOSERS IN THEIR TIMES / 1

Middle Ages *The* troubadours *and the* trouvères, *two French minstrel groups, were active from the end of the eleventh century through the thirteenth century. These two groups have provided us with the most important collections of secular monody. Along with the troubadours and the trouvères were the minstrel entertainers and performers known as* jongleurs. *Similar musical groups developed in Germany, where the* Minnesingers *took over from their French counterparts. Wilhelm Langhans (1832-1892), author, composer, and violinist, received his Ph.D. from the University of Heidelberg, where he later taught. He is especially known for his two-volume continuation of Ambros'* History of Music.

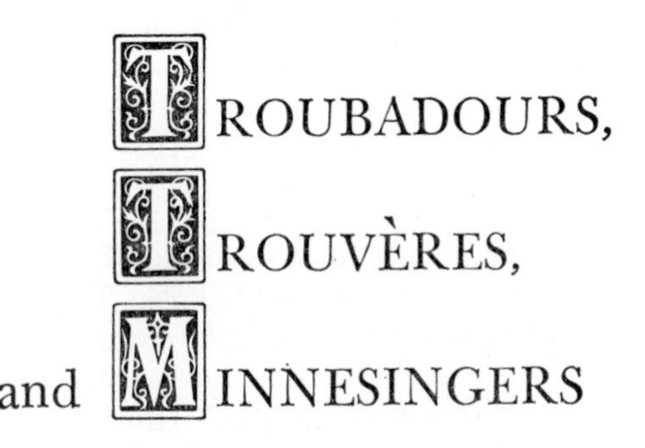

WILHELM LANGHANS

THROUGH THE LABORS OF A HUCBALD, A GUIDO, and a Franco, the soil in which a genuine art-music could grow-up was, indeed, prepared; yet it was a considerable time before the first buds of such a thing ventured to show themselves. The European nations were still too deeply sunken in lethargy and barbarity to allow to art free space for its development; when all at once an event happened which powerfully transformed not only the religious and political situation, but also the collective intellectual life of Europe. And that was the Crusades, beginning in 1096.

It was not only to the members of the religious and knightly orders that the summons of a Peter of Amiens, a Bernard of Clairvaux, for the rescue of the holy sepulchre from the hands of the infidels was addressed; to all who should join the expedition eternal salvation was promised. And in consequence of this, multitudes belonging to the most diverse conditions of life, who were eager for the adventure, took part in the march to Jerusalem, as in a general pilgrimage. For the great majority of the Crusaders, however, the impressions and experiences gained in the East must have had a lasting effect, since . . . the civilization of that country was, even from the reign of the Abassides, especially of the caliph Haroun al Raschid (800 A.D.), who belonged to that dynasty, in every respect superior to that of the West.

Similarly, the singers and instrumental musicians in the retinue of the Crusaders found in the East rich inspiration and nutriment for their art. For, although the Oriental music—like that of the Arabs in Spain—was of its very nature ill-adapted to the solution of ideal art-problems, yet the singing-method of the Orientals, with its characteristic richness of ornamentation, as also their musical instruments (the lute and the guitar), which had been unknown to the Crusaders; moreover the noisy instruments used in the Saracen military music (the drum and the kettle-drum), all these elements, after they had been introduced into the western music, necessarily gave the latter an altered character.

Still more important appears to be the enrichment experienced by the poetry of the West in consequence of the Crusades. The separation—often for years—from home and family brought about a deepening of the emotional life till then unknown; a new species of poetry arises in which the feeling for chivalry and love-service (*Minnedienst*) finds its expression, the so-called "gay science" (*gaya ciencia*), indigenous es-

---

TROUBADOURS, TROUVÈRES, AND MINNESINGERS from *The History of Music in Twelve Lectures* by Wilhelm Langhans; G. Schirmer, Inc.; 1886.

pecially to the soil of Provence, favored as it is by a happy climate and the lively disposition of its inhabitants.

Here the grandees of the land devoted themselves to this science, the first being Count William of Poitiers (1087-1127), afterwards King Thibaut of Navarre (1201-1254), these however, always only as *originators* of songs, whence they were also called *Trouvères* (from the French *trouver*), a word which has become in our English tongue (more identical with the Italian synonym *trovatore*) *Troubadours*. The *execution* of the songs composed by them, as also the instrumental accompaniment of them they handed over to the so-called Minstrels (derived from *ministerialis*, from the Latin *minister*, a "helper"), also called *Jongleurs* (from the Latin *joculator*, "merry-maker"), who belonged to a lower class of society and were often ranked with buffoons, as is seen in a contemporaneous sculpture of the church of St. George at Bocherville near Rouen, representing among a group of instrumental musicians a human figure walking on his hands. [Later studies show that certain troubadours not only composed songs but performed them as well.]

An exceptional position among the troubadours is occupied by Adam de la Hale, called after his deformity and his native place, "the hunchback of Arras," inasmuch as he unites in his person the composer of songs and the executive musician. He was moreover well-versed in the strict art-forms also, so far as they had then been developed, and ranks among the first musicians who undertook to compose four-voiced vocal pieces. His *Robin and Marian* (a dramatic pastoral), the subject of which is the naïve description of a rustic love affair, was performed in 1282 at the court of Robert the second, of Artois, at Naples; it is therefore the oldest example of dramatic art in France, for which reason Adam de la Hale is rightfully indicated in the history of French literature as the founder of comic opera.

The same intellectual current that in the case of the Roman peoples had called into existence the art of the troubadours, expressed itself among the ancient Germans who had remained unmixed in Germany, in the form of erotic poetry called, in their tongue, *Minnegesang*. The "minnesinger" differed, however, from the troubadour in that he himself sang his songs and accompanied them on an instrument, usually a small three-cornered harp. Such an instrument is often seen depicted in ancient manuscripts, among others in that of Godfrey of Strassberg's *Tristan and Isolde,* belonging to the first half of the 13th century, and found in the court library at Munich.

Moreover the minnesingers did not belong, as the troubadours did, exclusively to the knightly order. Of the singers participating in the *Sängerkrieg auf der Wartburg* (contest of singers on the Wartburg), in 1207, under landgrave Herrmann of Thuringia, Wolfram of Eschenbach, Walter of the Vogelweide, Heinrich Schreiber, and Heinrich of Zwetzschin were, as the chronicler puts it, "knightly men"; on the other hand, Biterolf was "one of the landgrave's household servants," and Heinrich of Ofterdingen, a burgess of Eisenach. The musical difference of the German minnegesang, or love song, from the song of the troubadours consisted in this: that the latter made the text subservient to the melody, whereas with the former the poetry becomes the principal thing, and the characteristic song-melody is supplanted by the recitative style of the ecclesiastical chant.

This predominance of the poetical over the musical element is exhibited also in the songs of the mastersingers, who undertook the care of art after it had passed over from the knightly singers to the burghers and respectable artisans. According to F. H. von der Hagen (*The Minnesingers and Song-poets of the 13th, 14th and 15th Centuries*, Leipzig, 1838), by the so-called "tones" of the mastersingers are meant not only the song-melodies themselves, but also the metrical schemes; hence they have special reference to the poetry.

Concerning the interior economy of these singing societies organized after the manner of a guild, we find copious information in Wagenseil's book, *Von der Meistersinger holdseligen Kunst* ("Of the delightful art of the Mastersingers"), published in Nuremberg, 1697. In our own time Richard Wagner has renewed the memory of the mastersingers in his poem bearing that title. In these works we are made acquainted, in the first place, with the Tablature, by which is meant the whole body of laws for the government of the guild. The members are divided into three classes: Whoever has learned the various tones is a "singer"; a higher degree, the rank of "poet," is attained by him who composes a new and suitable text to one of the tones; but to acquire the dignity of "master," the union of both faculties, the poetical and the musical, is requisite.

> The poet who, with brain so witty,
> To words and rhymes, by himself prepared,
> Can shape from the tones a new strain or ditty,
> He is a Mastersinger declared.

The conscientiousness and the zeal shown by the members of the guild, in the observance of their laws, can serve as a gratifying testimony to the feeling for art entertained by the German burgherdom, even though the artistic results of those efforts have only extremely little value. The melodies of the mastersingers were like the church psalmody: monotonous and lacking in expression, although they were embellished at the cadencing sections with all kinds of ornamentation. The relation of their music to poetry was as good as none at all; as a rule the tune was not determined by the text, but vice-versa, the text by the tune;

frequently the tune was composed first, and after it was found to be free of faults the author was required to make a suitable text to it, upon a determined biblical or spiritual subject. With this homely manner of art-education, which moreover is manifested in the strange names given to the tunes—there was, for instance, "an Over-short evening-red tune," a "Black ink tune," a "Short monkey tune," a "Gormandizer-in-secret tune," etc.—neither poetry nor music could especially thrive. Yet the mastersinger schools had unquestionably a good effect on the morality of their members, and much as we may feel repelled by the pedantry inherent in their artistic efforts, yet on the other hand the tendency of these simple natures, aiming at the ideal in the midst of all the worry of common-place life, deserves the warmest recognition. This view is taken by Richard Wagner also when he makes his mastersinger Hans Sachs (1495-1576) answer as follows the question as to the rules of the Guild: "By what man were they first devised?"

By certain sorely troubled masters,
Their hearts oppressed by life's disasters;
By suffering overweighted,
A model they created,
That they might take it,
And ever make it
A memory of youthful love,
In which the soul of Spring should move.

The schools of the mastersingers fell, after the Thirty Years' War, more and more into decay; only those of Nuremberg and Strasburg maintained, up to the close of the preceding century, a certain importance. The German mastersong did not actually come to an end before 1839, when the last surviving members of the School at Ulm handed over their corporation badges to the Liederkranz of that city, and thereby dissolved their guild. The mastersingers were, moreover, of advantage to the music of their time because, taking their example, the instrumental musicians also united in corporations organized like guilds, gave up the wandering life which they had previously led, and took up a permanent abode in the cities.

Thus arose, as early as 1288, in Vienna, a society under the name of the *Nicolai-Bruderschaft,* and in 1330 in Paris the *Confrérie de St. Julien des Ménestriers* (Minstrels), these latter under a director with the title *Roi des violons* ("King of the violins"), whose rule continued till the 17th century when it was terminated by Louis XIV, after the last director, Dumanoir II, had arrogated the jurisdiction over all the musicians of Paris, including the organists, and thus brought on himself his downfall.

Side by side with the minnesong and the mastersong (but independent of each other) the folk-song had, in the last centuries of the Middle Ages, been developed. The so-called Limburg Chronicle, edited by the scribe Johannes (1317-1402), gives the earliest details concerning the nature of the folk-songs, and of the contemporaneous instrumental music ("pipe-playing," as it calls it). But unfortunately there are no musical specimens; these, however, are found in great number in a manuscript of the 15th century, called, after the place where it originated, the *Lochheim Songbook.* The melodies therein given are remarkable not only for the significant voice-leading and the skilfully organized rhythms, but also for the fidelity with which they reproduce the subject-matter of the poetry and give expression to that which language is unable of itself, alone, to utter.

QUESTIONS

1. Look up the names of Hucbald, Guido, and Franco. What were their contributions to music?
2. Who are the present-day counterparts of the troubadours and jongleurs? Can you name any of them? Discuss your selections.
3. What, exactly, is the difference between a troubadour and a jongleur?
4. Look up the story of the Wagner opera that deals with the Mastersingers. How would you "modernize" the plot? Can it be done? Give your reasons.
5. In what Gilbert and Sullivan operetta do we find a "wandering minstrel?" In what period is this operetta laid? Does this minstrel have any relation to the minstrels mentioned in the essay? In what ways?

COMPOSERS IN THEIR TIMES / 2

Renaissance *Orlande de Lassus (1532?-1594) was one of the greatest and most important of the Renaissance composers. Apparently equally at home with sacred and with secular music, he is generally regarded as a master of polyphonic composition. His fame during his lifetime was so widespread and his musical talent so well established that he was variously known as "The Belgian Orpheus" and "The Prince of Music." He was among the most prolific composers of the Renaissance, creating a staggering total of some two thousand compositions. In her especially lucid essay on a difficult subject, Edna Richolson Sollitt manages to show us a portrait of one Renaissance man.*

Orlande de Lassus

EDNA RICHOLSON SOLLITT

ORLANDE DE LASSUS WAS BORN AT MONS, HAInault, in 1532; this date is established by an inscription on the portrait by Johan Sadeler painted in 1593, "at the age of sixty-one," and by his epitaph, which shows the agreement of his heirs with this date. This must be considered decisive, although Samuel Quickelberg, who was acquainted with Lassus in Munich in 1565, and who wrote the oldest biographical notice concerning him, places the date at 1530.

Many musical historians have made Lassus the object of special study and research; among these may be mentioned Delmotte, Bäumker, Declève, Destouches, Mathieu, Mantovani, Sandberger, Van der Straeten, and Van den Borren; the last named has published the most recent as well as the fullest and most exact study of the master and his work. [But see Gustave Reese's *Music in the Renaissance,* 1954.]

In common with other biographers of Lassus, Van den Borren attacks the ancient piece of misinformation which makes the renowned artist the son of a counterfeiter; his paragraphs on this matter are conclusive: they do not merely attack the libel; they demolish it. Orlande de Lassus is generally known in Belgium as Roland de Lattre, and the form Lassus is considered as a Latinization. This is an error, based on the statement of the Hainault annalist, Vinchant, according to which statement the master changed his original name of de Lattre to escape the shame of the family disgrace. It is true that a Jehan de Lassus was condemned at Mons for counterfeiting in 1550; but there is no remotest particle of evidence connecting this man with the great musician; the name is very common in that part of the country. This would seem enough, but Van den Borren goes on to mention an argument which has escaped others. The name of the criminal was de Lassus, not de Lattre; there would be no object in changing from the latter to the former, from a name with no odium attached to it to one so burdened! The two names are, besides, utterly without connection: de Lassus derives from de-là-dessus; de Lattre from de l'Atre. Thus is this piece of mediaeval gossip effectively countered.

Vinchant tells us that Lassus was born in the "rue dicte Gerlande" (de la guirlande), and that he was a choirboy in the Church of St. Nicolas in the Rue Havré. Quickelberg relates that the young Orlande

---

ORLANDE DE LASSUS from *Dufay to Sweelinck* by Edna Richolson Sollitt; Ives, Washburn; 1933.

commenced his studies at seven years of age, and was taught the first principles of music at eight and a half years.

His voice was so beautiful that he was three times stolen from the school where he lived with the other choir-boys. We may recall in this connection the "frantic search," mentioned by Van der Straeten, which was made in the Netherlands for high voices of good quality by agents of the various princes throughout Europe. On the first two occasions the boy Orlande was recovered by his parents; on the third he consented to follow his abductor into the service of Fernand de Gonzaga, Viceroy of Sicily, who was at that time commanding the forces of Charles V at the siege of St. Dizier. This siege took place between the 8th of July and the 7th of August, 1544, when Orlande was about twelve years old.

After the peace of Crespy in September of that year, which peace cut short a march on Paris, Gonzaga set out to return to his estates in Sicily, taking the boy with him. They arrived in Sicily in November of the following year, being delayed for some reason not known to us.

The transfer of Gonzaga to Milan occurred the next May, and again Orlande went with him. In Milan the boy enjoyed the first quiet existence which he had known since his abduction. The maestro di capella at Milan was at that time a Netherlander, Verecore, and Orlande was placed in his choir. When his voice changed he was taken to Naples, where he lived for three years with the Marquis de la Terza. This nobleman was himself a poet, a man of distinguished taste and real accomplishment in the arts. Naples had already enjoyed the musical influence of Tinctoris and Diego Ortiz, and the environment was an excellent one for the young musician.

From Naples Lassus went to Rome; after six months as guest of the Archbishop Altoviti, as Quickelberg relates, he was named director of the choir at San Giovanni Laterano. No documents have come to light relative to this activity. What a contrast was the environment at Rome to that of Naples! From princely luxury and worldly gaiety to the quietude of a sanctuary; from villanelles to masses. The young Palestrina was becoming known in Rome for his work as master of the boys at the Julian Chapel, and his devout and genial efforts, emphasized by his success, made a deep impression on Lassus. Palestrina was about twenty-eight years old and Lassus twenty-one when the latter arrived in Rome.

After two years in Rome, Lassus was recalled to the Netherlands by the grave illness of his parents. The journey was long; he arrived to find them already dead. Some writers state that the composer then went upon a journey to England in the company of a noble Italian amateur, Cesare Brancaccio, whose acquaintance he probably made at Naples; Brancaccio had a diplomatic mission to fulfill in England; there are records concerning its failure and his deportation to France. It is far from certain that Lassus made this trip to England or accompanied Brancaccio to France. What is certain concerning this period is that Lassus was settled in Antwerp late in 1554 or early in 1555. This is fixed by a dedication of his first book of madrigals, villanelles, etc., dated May 13, 1555, when he had been already some months in Antwerp.

The Antwerp of that period was a delightful place of residence for a talented young musician. The musical and artistic life was highly developed, and the city was able to sustain this life, being a center of world commerce. The great firms of every country had offices and representatives there. One of the most important of these was that of Fugger, the banking family of Germany, the richest family of that age. The name of Fugger is encountered in every sort of commercial and cultural history of northern Europe for many years.

Such commercial princes as these have at various times had a strong influence on art development. When they are enlightened and cultivated, and their influence is active in behalf of worthy artists, they are benefactors indeed; when, as sometimes happens, they are merely eager for prominence, desirous of being considered lovers of art yet unable to place their patronage with discrimination, such families can hinder or destroy much that is of value, by the negative process of aiding what is mediocre or worse. For it is as impossible for artistic excellence to thrive surrounded by an encouraged mediocrity as it is impossible for delicate flowers to flourish in a bed where weeds are given careful tendance.

Very fortunately the Fuggers were a family of cultivated artistic amateurs; and there were other families of wealthy and discriminating art-lovers in the Netherlands at that time, several of them in Antwerp. These were happy to welcome with enthusiasm an artist so eminently gifted as Lassus. He remained two years in Antwerp, and they must have been two of the pleasantest years of his life.

The reputation of the young musician was made in these years, and his first published works appeared here and in Venice simultaneously. We have already mentioned the book of madrigals and villanelles; this was published by Tielman Susato in 1555. The same year Gardano placed on sale in Venice the first book of Lassus' five-part madrigals. In the next year appeared the first book of the composer's motets, which were issued by Jean de Laet, afterwards the partner of Waelrant.

Established thus in the midst of powerful friends and admirers, and already known as the composer of varied and interesting works published in far separated countries, it is certain that Lassus had a reputation commensurate with his abilities. Albert V, Duke of Bavaria, learned that Antwerp possessed a musician of this distinction, and was desirous of acquiring his services for the ducal chapel. Orlande was invited to Munich in 1556.

The Bavarian Court Chapel had been established since the fourteenth century; the eminent Swiss musician, Senfl, had been active in its service for a number of years previous to the arrival of Lassus, and the reigning duke had increased the personnel of the chapel. From the autumn of 1556 we have constant mention of Lassus in the chapel records and those of the Bavarian court. These records make plain the importance of the eminent musician in his new environment. Not that he was given a high office at once; on the contrary, he entered as a simple singer, modestly taking his place without comment. But his genius made itself felt from the beginning.

In 1560 the Duke sent him on an important musical mission to the Netherlands; he was to engage singers and choirboys for the chapel. This we learn from a letter of Margaret of Parma, Regent of the Netherlands. She calls Lassus "maître de chapelle du Duc de Bavière." The Bavarian records make no mention at this time of a change in the status of Lassus; Sandberger believes that the advancement came to him in 1563. Whatever his title, however, it is plain that Lassus had in 1560 the confidence and respect of his patron and was invested with a very real power in the chapel.

The first work of the composer to be published in Germany was issued in Nuremberg in 1562 and was dedicated to the Duke. In October of that year Lassus accompanied the Duke on his journey to the coronation of Maximilian II at Frankfort; they visited Prague, Bamberg, and Wurzburg, also.

Van den Borren mentions the preparation in 1563 of a codex which contains the Penitential Psalms of Lassus; the two volumes have each a portrait of Lassus "by the court painter, Hans Muelich." We have already been told by Van Aerde that a codex containing works by de Rore had been prepared for Albert by "Johan Mielich, the court painter"; also Ambros, in the third volume of his history, uses this version of the name. The portrait of Lassus shows, says Van den Borren, "a large forehead, somewhat receding, the hair close-cut, the arch of the eyebrow well defined. The eyes are large, and have a rather vague expression, traducing the strength and finesse of Lassus' intelligence. The nose, 'd'aspect flaireur' (an untranslatable description, this) seems to prolong the receding line of the forehead. The mouth is sensual; the beard is short and cut in a round. The whole appearance of the artist is unusual rather than attractive."

In 1564 and 1565 occurred the first French publication of an entire volume of Lassus' work, by the firm of LeRoy and Ballard; previously these editors had included single pieces in their collections. In 1562 and

1567 Lassus visited Italy to engage singers and players of instruments. During the latter journey occurred the regrettable incident concerning the Duke of Ferrara; to a courteous dedication of a work by Lassus the Duke responded with so niggardly a recognition that "a diplomatic question was avoided only by his supplementing this in an indirect manner." Lassus remained but a short time in Ferrara and returned to Munich.

In the "Discorsi" of Troiano are found descriptions of the many festivities organized and conducted by Lassus in 1568 on the occasion of the wedding of the young Duke William with Renée of Lorraine; in these descriptions Orlande is praised for his polished and modest manners. The festivities, remarks Van den Borren dryly, were of a variety and were given under conditions calculated to astonish those who still labor under the delusion that the sixteenth century was devoted entirely to a cappella polyphony. Many works were performed entirely by instruments, many by instruments and voices, in addition to those for voices alone.

We learn that in these festivities Lassus took part also in a comedy improvised for the occasion; his rôle was that of Lorenzo Magnifico, and "he appeared on the stage wearing a mask which at first sight raised a shout of laughter."

In 1570 Lassus was given a patent of nobility, valid for his descendants as well as for himself; this was bestowed by Maximilian II. In 1571 he made a long-desired journey to Paris. He was received with honor and acclaim; Charles IX showed him every attention, and the publisher, LeRoy, arranged the introduction of everyone of note in Paris at the time. Orlande "returned to Munich loaded with honors and money."

Many letters of Lassus to the young Duke William about this period show us the humor, gaiety, and wit of the composer. These letters are written in "a mosaic of French, Latin, and German, following and interlarding each other with burlesque vivacity, giving them a flavor of frolicsome roguery worthy of a college youth in delirium." This gaiety was but one side of the nature of Lassus, however; it was a surface covering a character deeply religious and most sensitive. He was at times melancholy, and always introspective. The Penitential Psalms were composed in a sincere outpouring of belief and feeling.

In 1574 Lassus went again to Italy. Interesting letters tell us of his experiences in the Tyrol, experiences which the traveller of today finds unchanged to a startling degree. Arrived in Rome, Lassus was received in audience by Pope Gregory XII, who greatly enjoyed meeting the composer, we are told, and who conferred upon him the honorary title of Chevalier de St. Pierre. This Italian voyage of Lassus was not highly successful; only four singers were engaged, with "a viol-player and some dancers." The Duke was not pleased; the journey had been costly; it was not until some months later that serenity was restored between Lassus and his patron.

Magnificent offers were made to Lassus in 1574 by the King of France. Large sums of money and honorable titles were promised him in an invitation sent through his publisher, LeRoy, who doubtless would have been happy to see the great musician established in Paris. As Lassus had already planned his journey to Italy before receiving this invitation, we know that his voyage was not "a start toward Paris, interrupted by news of the death of the French King." This piece of misinformation has been incorporated as fact into some musical histories; but the full correspondence of Lassus, available now, shows clearly that he returned to Munich before May 5th, and the king did not die until May 30th. Another myth concerning Charles IX is that Lassus composed the Penitential Psalms to assuage the King's remorse for the events of St. Bartholomew's Eve; as we know, these Psalms were written thirteen years before that date and were for the private use of the Duke of Bavaria.

The letters of Lassus to Duke William are particularly frequent and intimate in the years from 1574 to 1578. These missives speak of little dinners, of gardening, of musical jests, and a thousand other trifles in the lives of friends. In 1579 the composer signed an agreement to remain throughout his life at the Bavarian court. Shortly after this Duke Albert died, leaving gigantic state debts to be immediately faced by his son and successor, the genial, light-hearted William.

The first things to be sacrificed to the pressing necessity of the ducal position were the artistic luxuries of Albert; the chapel was reduced at one blow from 44 members to 22; two years later it was further reduced. The payment of wages to Lassus was faithfully carried out, but the musician found himself hampered in all his plans by the small number of performers; he had long been accustomed to having at his command a body of singers and players without parallel in Europe.

Lassus remained faithfully attached to the Bavarian house. He offered to release his claims to funds which he had received from Albert and re-loaned at interest; William, however, would not hear of his sacrificing this part of his earnings. The entire episode is greatly to the credit of both William and Lassus. The Duke, now weighted with cares of State and overwhelmed with debt, changed from the gay young man who had exchanged sprightly letters with Lassus to a careworn, serious ruler. He became deeply religious, and Munich grew to be a stronghold of Catholicism. This was well suited to the true nature and feelings of Lassus, as we know; he was the loyal friend of the Jesuits at Munich; their Seminary there has a portrait of him. This is a contrast to the former portrait; here the composer is graver, more dignified, and somewhat melancholy.

Lassus went to Italy for the last time in 1585. He made a pilgrimage to Loreto, and afterward visited Ferrara. This time he was received there with the greatest honor. The court of the art-loving Alfonso II enjoyed one of the earliest and most complete orchestras of Europe; remembering the delight of Lassus in using the instrumental facilities at his disposal in Munich, we may imagine his deep pleasure in the performances at Ferrara.

Returning to Munich Lassus became more and more subject to melancholia. His physician was one of his best friends; the relations with the ducal family were all that could be wished, and Lassus was given every honor and privilege which the Duke was able to bestow; there was no true cause for the gloom which clouded the days of the master. It was disease and not reality which tormented him. He passed from his suffering to death in 1594. His heirs erected a monument the following year; it is now in the Bavarian National Museum. But no monument is needed to Orlande de Lassus. His own work is the most glorious of monuments.

The compositions of Orlande de Lassus may be divided into eight groups: motets; Masses; Magnificats; Passions; madrigals; villanelles, moresques, and miscellaneous pieces; French songs; German lieder.

The motets form the most important group of his works, both from the point of view of musical value and that of numerical preponderance. The sons of Lassus, Ferdinand and Rodolphe, issued in 1604 a collection as complete as possible, calling it "Magnum opus musicum." This collection contains one hundred motets for four voices, 24 for two voices, 24 for three, 167 for five, 159 for six, 11 for seven, 24 for eight, two for nine, three for ten, and two for twelve voices.

Among the motets must be included the Penitential Psalms, which were composed for Duke Albert and not published until 1584, five years after the Duke's death. These Psalms are for five voices, but various sections of single numbers are for two, three, or four voices. Also among the motets are: the "Lectiones," in two parts, one with text from Job, and one concerning the Nativity; Offices, five in number; the Stabat Mater; and Lamentations (five voices).

The Magnificats were published complete by Rodolphe de Lassus in 1619. This edition included the Nuremberg collection, those of the Patrocinium of 1576 and of 1587, and sixteen posthumous works.

The Passions are four in number; one was included in the Patrocinium of 1575.

The madrigals of Lassus comprise the second, fourth, sixth, eighth, and tenth volumes of the magnificent Breitkopf and Härtel edition of the complete works, which edition was begun in 1894 to commemorate the 300th anniversary of his death. The eighty-nine madrigals for five voices appeared in a half-dozen volumes published between 1555 and 1587, and in a series of collections issued at different dates. There are forty-one four-voice madrigals; thirteen of these were published prior to 1560, the rest between that date and 1587. The six-voice pieces were all published after 1578. There are two madrigals for seven voices, and three for ten.

The villanelles, songs concerning the loves of peasants and shepherds, are souvenirs of the Neapolitan period of Lassus; they are written principally to texts in the Neapolitan dialect and are eighteen in number. The moresques are dialogues, serenades, etc., concerning Giorgia, Lucia, Cathalina, Zanni, and other figures; the patois of the Moorish-Italian lower classes is used for the texts of most of these pieces. They show an aspect of the composer which reflects his observations of the tumultuous and teeming life of Naples' streets. They are, on occasion, far from edifying.

The French songs number 146; they form the twelfth, fourteenth, and sixteenth volumes of the complete works. There are 67 for four voices, 58 for five, one for three, four for six, and five for eight.

The German lieder are 93 in number; 25 for three voices, 17 for four, 41 for five, nine for six, and one for eight.

QUESTIONS

1. Why is Lassus considered an important composer? What were his particular contributions to music?
2. Can you suggest reasons why the general public is unfamiliar with the work of Lassus? Can you name some other Renaissance composers?
3. Name some contemporaries of Lassus living in other countries. Are they generally familiar names? Why? Is Shakespeare a contemporary? What accounts for his fame?
4. Look up the name of Fugger. Compare the contribution of the Fugger family to music with that of the Esterhazys, the family discussed in the essay on Haydn.
5. Look up the words, "madrigal," "villanelle," and "motet." What do they have in common? Do you know whether composers still compose pieces with similar titles? Can you find some examples?

COMPOSERS IN THEIR TIMES / 3

Baroque *Musicians, music critics, historians may disagree about the significance of one composer or another. But about Johann Sebastian Bach (1685-1750) there is no question. Along with Mozart and Beethoven, Bach is justly considered one of the undeniably great composers of the past three hundred years. Born into the most important musical family in history, Bach was known in his lifetime as an extraordinary organist, but a composer of church music whose skill was spent on archaic and academic forms; his star was pale beside that of a Handel, a Telemann, or even a K.P.E. Bach. Richard Anthony Leonard, author and music historian, shows us in an exceptionally well-constructed essay the middle and late period's of Bach's life.*

RICHARD ANTHONY LEONARD

SHORTLY AFTER HIS SECOND MARRIAGE A RIFT began to appear in the placid relations of Bach and his patron. The prince also married and his bride caused a decided change in the order of things at Cöthen. She was a light-minded and flighty young person, described as caring only for "balls and fireworks." Her appreciation of music was adolescent. In the playing of her husband's Kapelle, and particularly in the weighty music of its director, she had no interest whatever. Bach termed her an "*amusa*" and, realizing that the prince's interests were diverted from his music, he began to look about for another post. For a long time the urge seems to have been strong in him to get back into church music, to a post which would put a choir and an organ once again at his disposal. In 1723 he got what he wanted.

In Leipzig there was a famous school for boys, St. Thomas's, a venerable institution that had been founded in the thirteenth century. Bach heard that the cantorship was vacant, so he applied for the post. The duties of the cantor included teaching singing and Latin to some fifty boys between the ages of fourteen and twenty-one, and acting as music director of the two churches with which the school was connected —St. Thomas's and St. Nicholas's. It was the latter phase of the cantor's duties which attracted Bach, for it meant that he had to provide an elaborate program of music in one of the two churches every Sunday and on certain feast days.

Early in 1723, Bach underwent the trials for the appointment, and on Good Friday of that year he conducted his hastily composed *St. John Passion* in St. Thomas's Church, as proof of his ability. A few months later he was formally appointed. The leave-taking from Cöthen was under unforeseen and tragic circumstances. Nine days before Bach and his family departed the *amusa* died. Two years later the prince married again; but in 1728, five years after Bach left his service, he too was dead. Bach's affection for the young nobleman who had treated him so kindly is shown by his journey to Cöthen to attend the prince's funeral and to provide music for the memorial service.

The Leipzig post was Bach's last. He remained there for twenty-seven years until his death in 1750. He went to Leipzig in his thirty-eighth year, an artist with almost two decades of very great accomplishment behind him. All this, however, was in reality only the prelude to what was to come. The music of the Leipzig period is difficult to

---

appraise, because in physical bulk alone it is gigantic. Bach was a busy man much of the time, occupied with the routine tasks of his cantorship; yet during these years he composed the *St. Matthew Passion* and the colossal Mass in B minor, which are his greatest works; the *Magnificat,* six motets, a series of organ pieces that crown his entire accomplishment for that instrument, more superlative works for the clavier, and a vast series of church cantatas. Not only is this music enormous in physical bulk, but some of it is on a scale of architectonic design that is mountainous, and inspired beyond any music composed before its time or since.

Viewing these accomplishments, it is hard to believe that the cantorship of St. Thomas's was a sorry disappointment to the composer. The existing record of his office is a long recital of misunderstanding and petty bickering, quarrels with associates who tried to cheat him out of his perquisites, with church authorities who treated him like a hack, and with narrow-minded rectors who had no sympathy with his music and no realization of his stature as an artist. When Bach went there in 1723 he found that the school was badly run down, in the hands of an old rector who was tottering and senile. The boys were an undisciplined gang of young ruffians, morally weakened by having to beg in the streets of Leipzig for donations to the school, and often ill and miserable from undernourishment and neglect. Their musical education was poor and their voices were wretched. Moreover, the older singers and instrumentalists who were hired from the town to fill out the choir and the orchestra were also inadequate. When Bach complained about these conditions he only got himself on bad terms with the rector and the town council.

With the death of the old rector in 1729 a new one named Gesner was appointed, and for the next five years improvement and order reigned at St. Thomas's. Gesner was young, a good organizer, and a scholar, and his regard for Bach's music and attainments was marked. But Gesner was followed in 1734 by one Johann August Ernesti, a hardheaded bigot who became one of Bach's worst persecutors. He hated music, disparaged its importance even in front of the boys, and did his best to humiliate the cantor. Bach was something of a match for him. Always proud when his dignity was affronted, and pugnacious when the rights of his office were at stake, the composer stood by his guns to the bitter end. One of his worst encounters with Ernesti would be essentially comic if it did not involve the personal feelings of one of the world's greatest geniuses. It began when the boys of the choir, unruly because Bach was a poor disciplinarian, behaved in a scandalous manner during a wedding. This led to a quarrel between Bach and Ernesti over the right to appoint a prefect. The battle lasted for two years, during which time both cantor and rector bombarded the council with petitions, charges, and countercharges. It did not end until Bach at last petitioned the King of Saxony. His majesty resolved the matter by a compromise, with Bach on the long end of the stick.

Bach and his family lived in one of the wings of the school building itself. When they first came to St. Thomas's the ancient structure was overcrowded and badly in need of repair. It housed the family of the rector, the schoolrooms and dormitories of the boys, and the family of the cantor. The crowded and unsanitary conditions are blamed by Professor Terry for the depressing record of mortality among Bach's children during his early years in Leipzig. Of the first eight children born to Anna Magdalena only two survived, one of whom was an imbecile. The other six children died at ages ranging from one day to five years. After Bach had been there eight years the building was enlarged and renovated. Of the five Bach children born thereafter four were healthy and survived their father many years. Among them was Johann Christian (1735-1782), one of the most illustrious of the sons. Through his successes as a composer in London he became known as the "English" Bach.

In the gloomy, congested quarters of the cantor one room was reserved for his study. It was small and narrow, lighted by a single window. A thin whitewashed partition separated it from one of the classrooms, and from it could be heard the sound of a near-by mill wheel. This was Bach's workroom for many years.

The composer's regular salary at St. Thomas's was small, but it was increased by special fees which he earned at funerals and weddings, so that his income amounted to about five hundred dollars a year. To this were added allowances for corn, firewood, and wine. Bach once remarked that in certain years his income from funerals was a disappointment, because the air of the town of Leipzig was good and therefore deaths were fewer.

The most important of Bach's duties as cantor was the composition of music for the church services. Anyone wishing to trace reasons for the slow decline of Protestantism since the eighteenth century might do well to examine the regular Sunday service which took place in St. Thomas's and St. Nicholas's during Bach's tenure. It was a mixture of worship, preaching, and music of appalling length. It began at seven in the morning and lasted until nearly noon. The discomforts to the congregation resulting from such a stupefying ritual can only be imagined. Some slight relief was afforded the boys in the choir: if the church got so cold that they could no longer endure it, they were marched back to the school to listen to a sermon. The only respite for adult worshipers occurred about midway in the eighteen-part service, when (on alternate Sundays) the choir would perform a cantata, accompanied by organ and orchestra. The cantata was an elaborate collection of solos, recitatives, duets, and choruses, with occasional orchestral interludes. It lasted about half an hour.

The cantata as a musical form occupied Bach's attention over a space of forty years. He wrote his first in 1704 when he was the boy organist at Arnstadt, and his last in Leipzig in 1744. The sum total is two hundred and ninety-five cantatas, but the great majority belong to the Leipzig period. There, in the space of about twenty years, he composed about two hundred and sixty-five cantatas, an average of one a month. About two-thirds of these are extant. It is true that there were other cantors of his time who were even more prolific than Bach in the production of these works, but his achievement remains monumental. What in other hands was simply a routine and hack production, he maintained at the level of great art.

The cantata was in reality a sacred concert which had gradually grown up in the Lutheran service. It was customary for the cantata to be linked with the particular Gospel of the day; in fact it was a kind of musical exposition of the Gospel text. For the words of some of his early cantatas at Weimar Bach went directly to the Bible, piecing together various verses to suit his purpose. Thereafter he began using librettos which had been prepared by various religious writers and which were in common use throughout Germany. These librettos provided the composer with a ready-made framework for his music. There were rhymed stanzas, portions of blank verse, excerpts taken directly from the Bible text, and generally as a conclusion a stanza from one of the old Lutheran hymns—all bearing directly on the day's Gospel.

Bach's treatment of the words of his cantatas was identical with his procedure in his organ chorale preludes. He sought always to make his music express as vividly as possible the ideas conveyed by the words. He painted pictures, imitated sounds, portrayed emotions, often with complete realism. The musical symbols that he used were the same as those he evolved for the chorale preludes, a tonal language that anticipated the speech of many of the nineteenth-century song composers.

In a number of his last cantatas Bach dispensed with librettos entirely and evolved the so-called "chorale cantatas." Just as the organ chorale preludes are a polyphonic expansion of the simple old hymns, so the chorale cantatas are an even more elaborate and extended glorification of these same sacred songs. Using both the words and music of some chorale as his basic thematic idea, Bach constructed recitatives, ariosos, duets, choruses—weaving a spreading polyphonic fabric out of a single slender thread. Only at the end of the cantata was the basic hymn tune heard in its original form, when the choir, proclaiming it simply but with Bach's incomparable harmonization, was probably joined by the congregation.

Even though his immense collection of cantatas comprises by far the greater bulk of Bach's entire output, it remains the least known of all his work. The reason lies partly in the fact that the cantata as part of church worship is long since obsolete. It had passed from the liturgy of many churches even during Bach's lifetime. In modern times few countries have had musical organizations with the training and the traditional background necessary for adequate performances of Bach's cantatas. These works require soloists of exceptional talent and intelligence, first-rate instrumentalists, and choruses equipped to sing in a musical style of great difficulty—in short, a group as perfectly trained and organized as a modern symphony orchestra. In America, where virtuoso orchestras are common, choruses of the same caliber are comparatively non-existent. Public interest in choral music is as low as that in symphonic music is high and widespread. Until some revival of interest takes place in the field of choral music, that vital part of Bach's art represented by his cantatas must remain virtually unknown in this country—like a gallery of great paintings locked from the public gaze.

On the afternoon of Good Friday, 1729, the congregation of St. Thomas's assembled according to an ancient custom to hear a presentation of the Passion of our Lord in musical form. In this particular year the biblical account was to be that contained in the Gospel according to St. Matthew. Bach was ready with a newly composed work, and around him in the organ loft he had assembled an exceptionally large group of singers and instrumentalists. In addition to his regular chorus there was a second chorus made up of singers who did not usually perform at the church; organists were ready at both organs; and there were two orchestras, the usual group being augmented by players from the town, the school, and a local university. This impressive band of performers must have indicated to the congregation that the cantor had prepared something of an exceptional order.

One of Bach's pupils who was present at this first performance of the *St. Matthew Passion* recorded that the congregation was confused by what it heard and left unappreciative. "Some high officials and well-born ladies in one of the galleries began to sing the first chorale with great devotion from their books. But as the theatrical music proceeded, they were thrown into the greatest wonderment, saying to each other, 'What does it all mean?' while one old lady, a widow, exclaimed, 'God help us! 'Tis surely an opera-comedy!' " It is doubtful if the cantor himself, retiring to his home in the Lenten twilight after his strenuous labors, had any realization of the magnitude of his accomplishment.

Representations of the Passion of Jesus Christ, both musical and dramatic, are as old as the Church itself. Medieval mystery plays, oratorios, and musical Passions all stemmed from the same impulse—a desire to illustrate and act out the stories of the Bible, so that they could be made clear and vivid to the masses who no longer understood the Latin tongue of the Catholic service. The Passion as a musical form had begun in the early centuries of the Church as a simple dramatic recitation. Through the Middle Ages it had been joined to music, with the parts of the Evangelist, the Saviour, and the Disciples intoned in plainsong instead of merely recited. With the gradual enrichment of the art of music the Passion evolved into an elaborate and extended form, employing soloists, chorus, and instrumentalists.

The exact number of Passions which Bach wrote is in doubt, despite exhaustive research by Bach experts. Only two are extant—the *St. John Passion,* which he composed hurriedly for his examination as cantor, and the *St. Matthew*. It is known that he composed a *St. Mark Passion,* which is lost. There is a strong possibility that he composed a fourth, also lost. However, it is certain that of all these works it was the *St. Matthew* which received his most mature inspiration, that it was the most elaborately conceived and the most carefully wrought. Thus we are fortunate in having Bach's masterpiece in the Passion form, and the greatest work of its kind in existence.

The literary framework of the *St. Matthew Passion* indicates the process of evolution that must have gone on through the centuries which preceded it. Composers obviously had grown tired of repetitions of the same words from the Gospels describing the Passion; they sought to vary and to enrich the scenario itself. Bach's work indicates how this was done. The main burden of the story is taken directly from the Bible—from Chapters XXVI and XXVII of St. Matthew. These biblical verses are set to music by Bach in the form of recitatives, with the words of the Evangelist sung by a tenor and those of Jesus by a bass. Interspersed between these verses are short poems, not from the Bible but from the pen of Picander, a religious writer of the period. Bach set these in the form of arias and choruses with orchestral accompaniment; and in essence they are a sympathetic commentary, like that of the chorus in the Greek drama, upon the biblical story as it unfolds. Finally, several of the old Lutheran chorales are also set between the recitatives and arias. These were sung by the chorus, joined probably by the congregation.

The framework of a Passion was thus a piece of literary joining which required considerable skill. The man who made Bach's libretto was one Christian Friedrich Henrici, who wrote under the pen name of Picander. He was a post-office official and tax collector. On the side he amused himself by writing satirical verse, some of it scandalously vulgar. Quite incongruously he turned to religious poetry, writing one of the most popular sets of cantata texts. Bach knew Picander well, and most of his Leipzig cantatas are to this writer's words.

Like the church cantata, the Passion was a dying form when Bach produced his masterpiece. It did not disappear from the liturgy of the churches as rapidly as the cantata, but it was definitely on the way out. In reality Bach said the last word, for in the whole history of religious music there is nothing to compare with his portrayal of the Passion of Jesus Christ. This work stands at the end of a long evolution of devotional music; it is modern in complexity and scope, but its mystical fervor, its emotional ecstasy, its passionate absorption in the divine epic of the Christian faith—all this is medieval in spirit. That spirit was soon to vanish from music, just as a century before Bach's time it had begun to disappear from the art of painting.

For Bach the Passion of Jesus Christ was no mere religious allegory; it was a drama of reality, and its poignancy touched the deepest chords of his nature and his lifelong faith. In the *St. Matthew Passion* he is first of all a tonal dramatist, striving to bring to life with all the power and vividness at his command the personal portrait as well as the epic tragedy of the Man of Sorrows. He took full advantage of the tragic and dramatic side of the story; in fact it is astonishing how nearly operatic in the modern sense many of his devices are. But the focal point of the entire work remains always the portrait of the Saviour. Through the long and complex score—the swirling masses of choral polyphony; the arias with their incredible richness of texture, and their adorning obbligatos of violin, oboe, and flute; the devotional chorales, strewn through the score (in Terry's phrase) "like jewels of price"—through all this gorgeousness it is nevertheless the music accompanying the words of Jesus which achieves the inspirational apex of the entire score. By the simplest means Bach attains his ends. When the Evangelist relates his story it is fairly simple recitative, accompanied by sparse chords from the orchestra. When the voice of Jesus is heard it is always to the accompaniment of soft string passages. No more moving music has ever been written for the human voice. The brooding sadness, the infinite compassion of the Saviour are limned in these vocal lines; while around Him, in the superb harmonies of the strings, glows the nimbus of divinity. In this portrait Bach is like a Rembrandt of the tonal art. He had seen in his own heart the piercing vision of the man he was portraying; he had enveloped his subject with his own boundless sympathy.

The *St. Matthew Passion* had a few performances in the Leipzig churches while Bach was still alive, but it seems to have made no special impression. After the composer's death it lay silent and forgotten for more than three quarters of a century. On Good Friday, 1829, exactly a century after its premiere, Mendelssohn revived it with a performance in Berlin. With that event began the resurrection of Bach's music for the modern world.

Great as it is, the *St. Matthew Passion* does not stand alone in Bach's catalogue. One other work, the Mass in B minor, must be ranked with it as a summation of the composer's art.

In July 1733, Bach's oldest son, Wilhelm Friedemann, was installed as organist in a church in Dresden, and his father went along as his sponsor. While there Bach took the opportunity to ask a favor of his sovereign, Augustus III of Saxony. He wanted an appointment as court composer, an honor which was finally conferred three years later. To pay homage he sent Augustus the manuscript of the *Kyrie* and *Gloria* of a Mass in B minor, together with a letter in which the composer referred to the work as a "trifling example of my skill in Musique."

Sometime during the next few years (no one knows exactly how or when) the composer added to the Mass by constructing a *Credo, Sanctus,* and *Agnus Dei.* Much controversial ink has been shed on the question of how Bach, a stanch Lutheran, came to write a Roman Catholic Mass. Terry's explanation seems to be the most logical. The original *Kyrie* and *Gloria,* he points out, were in reality part of the Lutheran church service. When Bach expanded the work with a *Credo, Sanctus,* and *Agnus Dei* he did not create a purely Roman Catholic Mass. For one thing the work is far too long for a church service, and it departs in a number of instances from the strict letter and order of the Roman liturgy. Terry believes that "the Mass is neither Roman nor Lutheran in intention and outlook, but the expression of a catholic Christianity. . . . Bach's genius was Teutonic in its inclination to complete a design" . . . and "in the compulsion to express himself in an art form which he had studied deeply."

The final Mass is gigantic in size. It consists of twenty-four movements, for chorus, orchestra, and five solo voices. Fifteen of the movements are for chorus, with six solos and three duets. A complete performance requires almost three hours. The work was not entirely original; the composer borrowed and adapted about one third of the movements from his other works—chiefly from his church cantatas. Bach appears to have worked at the Mass over a period of five years, and the adaptations of the old sections as well as the composition of the new were done with extreme care, so that the vast architectural scheme could be satisfying in every detail.

The Mass in B minor contrasts strongly with the *St. Matthew Passion.* The latter work is far more personal, both in style and approach. It relates a biblical story, first translated into the German language and then into illuminating and deeply expressive music. The Mass in B minor has, of course, no story to tell. It expounds in music the tenets of a great faith. Its text is in general the Ordinary of the Roman Mass. Bach takes those Latin words, phrase by phrase, and builds them into lengthy movements. The result is a series of stupendous murals, each affirming a phase of the beliefs which are the foundation stones of Christianity. In his *St. Matthew Passion* Bach had worked with the deeply human perceptions of a Rembrandt, and at times the mystical insight of a Leonardo; in the Mass in B minor he is a Michelangelo, the painter of colossal frescoes. His vision sweeps across vast distances, spanning heaven and earth.

The main burden of this structure is carried by the choruses. The arias and duets between them, though bearing the thread of literary continuity, are in reality moments of respite from the weight and impact of the choral masses. It is true that some of them fall below the inspirational level of the greatest arias in the *St. Matthew Passion,* perhaps because the words of the liturgy are often dogmatic abstractions which almost defy musical setting. The best of them is the pathetic *Agnus Dei* for contralto.

The choruses dwarf everything else by comparison. All but one are in five vocal parts, with the orchestra adding a contrapuntal web of its own. The dimensions of the Mass, its exalted mood, the majesty of its subject, are all set in the first four measures of the *Kyrie eleison* which open the work. There follows a long and stunning exposition, developed fugally, the vocal lines interweaving and overlapping in a bewildering pattern of sound as they proclaim again and again a powerful basic theme. The inspirational level is high, but Bach maintains and even surpasses it in the fourteen choral movements that follow. Some are exultations of the most brilliant sort, like the *Gloria in excelsis Deo,* or the dazzling fugue *Cum sancto spiritu.* Others are solid, broadly developed affirmations of dogmatic faith; for example, the *Credo,* which is based on a theme intoned in the church for more than fifteen hundred years. Still others are poignant and sorrowful—like the second *Kyrie eleison,* the *Qui tollis,* and the *Et incarnatus*—movements which are saturated with pathos and tenderness.

The *Crucifixus* stands alone in the entire range of musical expression. Bach's portrayal of the tragedy of Calvary exemplifies the enigma in which his art remains eternally wrapped, defying analysis and dissection. For this supreme moment in the history of mankind the composer had first to decide upon a musical form commensurate with the idea. He chose a passacaglia. A desolate falling theme in the bass, four measures long, is repeated, note for note, thirteen times, while above it the chorus intones its grief-stricken vision of the dying Saviour. Thus the basic structure of this music, which is unplumbed in emotional depth, is found to be a problem in pure musical mathematics.

In the nineteenth movement, the *Confiteor,* there is an adagio of twenty-six measures, to the words *"Et expecto resurrectionem mortuorum."* Here Bach paints the prophecy of the great Resurrection. All contrapuntal movement suddenly slows down; the music evolves through a long series of harmonic progressions which are a hundred years ahead of the composer's time in their daring modernity. The dead rise from their tombs for the Last Judgment.

The climax of the entire Mass (and of the composer's whole creative effort) is reached with the *Sanctus.* In a six-part chorus the scene of paradise and the Almighty unfolds. "Holy, holy, holy, Lord God of Hosts. Heaven and earth are full of Thy glory." We behold the adoration of the heavenly hosts, with the higher voices of the chorus simulating the antiphony of the seraphim and the quiring angels, while the basses intone a vast theme that strides in octaves—gigantic pillars of tone upon which the nave of heaven rests. The movement is one great rolling thunder of music that seems to echo to the last boundaries of a limitless creation.

When Bach finished the Mass in B minor he was close to fifty years old and entering the last phase of his life. He never again attempted anything of such dimensions, and the swift current of his production began to abate somewhat. However, there was not the slightest sign of a flagging inspiration. He maintained his standard to the last days of his life.

After years of not composing for the organ he returned to that instrument, making several collections of his chorale preludes for publication. A number of these were based on the Lutheran Catechism hymns. They contain some of his weightiest music and are massive specimens of his mature organ style. Two works especially tower above the rest—*Aus tiefer Noth* [In Deepest Need], a gloomy and ascetic monument in six-part harmony with double pedal; and the incredible *Kyrie, Gott heiliger Geist* [Kyrie, Thou Spirit Divine]. Bach himself never surpassed the latter work, either in the development of a mountainous structure of tone from a few notes, or in the building of dramatic climax.

In this last period of his life the composer also returned to the clavier. His most notable work was Part II of *The Well-Tempered Clavier,* which appeared in 1744. This second set of twenty-four preludes and fugues is one of those rare species of the arts—a sequel which actually surpasses the original.

The so-called *Goldberg Variations,* published in 1743, were written to order. The Russian envoy to the Dresden court was a certain Count Kayserling, who was tortured by chronic insomnia. He hired a clavicenist named Goldberg, a young pupil of Bach's, to play for him at night when he could not sleep. He also commissioned Bach to compose something that would soothe his nerves during the long wakeful hours. The fee was a generous one—a snuffbox containing one hundred louis d'or. Bach responded with a set of thirty variations, a work of such amplitude and quality that the count certainly got his money's worth.

Goldberg must have been a performer of unusual ability, for these variations bristle with technical difficulties. Until recently they were seldom performed in public, because they were originally written for harpsichord with two keyboards, which permitted the hands to cross each other in a manner impossible on the modern piano keyboard. Modern editors have found ways to surmount these difficulties and today the *Variations* are frequently played, despite their great length.

The main theme which Bach used for his thirty-room structure is a charming Aria in G major, ornate with grace notes. The variations grow out of this central stem in a bewildering variety of melodic and rhythmic ideas. However, they are far from being simply variations. Digging under the surface of this luxuriantly blooming plant, one finds the real roots of the composer's ideas. The piece is actually a kind of passacaglia. A bass line of thirty-two notes governs the entire piece. It is not strictly adhered to, but nevertheless it forms the basis of all growth. Even that is not the end of the technical design. At every third variation a canon is introduced, that is, a strict imitation of the particular theme of the movement in another voice. There are nine of these canonic movements in all, each at a different interval, beginning with the unison and ending with the ninth. Moreover, there are movements in the form of a fughetta, a French overture, and a quodlibet, the last being an ancient form in which the theme is combined contrapuntally with folk tunes. In this case Bach used two popular German songs.

From this elaborate structural framework it would be easy to infer that in the *Goldberg Variations* the old cantor was chiefly bent on showing off his technical wizardry, like a pedagogue compiling a dry textbook of mathematical problems and their solutions. The *Variations* could in fact be used as an instructional work for the use of ornamentation, variation, passacaglia, and canon. If that were their main virtue they would be dead these many years, instead of holding their place among the most beautiful works in keyboard literature. They prove again the paradoxical fact of Bach's creative processes—that mathematical problems were far from shackling his imagination; that actually they stimulated the flow of his ideas, with the result that many of his works which are most rigidly bound in technical fetters are the most poetic, emotional, and humanly expressive of all.

Sometime during the last decade of his life Bach rounded off his organ works in the prelude-and-fugue style with four famous specimens. They are the preludes and fugues in E♭ major, C major, E minor (the "Wedge" Fugue), and B minor. All are big works, representing the accumulated thought and the technical mastery of the composer's lifetime at his favorite instrument. The B minor Prelude and Fugue is probably the ripest of all. Its key, it is worth noting, was obviously a favorite of Bach's; he used it for many of his finest works. The E♭ Fugue, popularly known as the "St. Anne" Fugue, is most frequently played. Speaking of this piece, and of the final entry of the main theme in the pedals—a thrilling, roaring declamation—Harvey Grace quotes an old English musician who said that it sounded "as if it ought to be fired off with cannon!"

In the spring of 1747, when Bach had reached the age of sixty-two he enjoyed a unique personal triumph, on the occasion of his visit to the young King of Prussia, later to be known as Frederick the Great. This is one of the few episodes in the composer's life which is documented in some detail.

Bach went to Potsdam to see his son, Karl Philipp Emanuel, who was harpsichordist in Frederick's court orchestra. The King, who later became the arch-Prussian war lord, was passionately fond of music. He had studied the flute from childhood (to the disgust of his tyrannical father, Frederick William I), and he tried seriously to become a composer. The story is told that one evening Frederick stood, flute in hand, before his orchestra, ready to play a concerto. The list of visitors to the court was handed to him. Suddenly he exclaimed, "Gentlemen, old Bach is here!" The composer was quickly summoned from his son's house. He had no time to change from his traveling clothes, a detail which embarrassed him in the presence of the King.

Frederick gave over the flute concerto and took the old man through his palace, showing him the new Silberman claviers with hammer actions—forerunners of the modern piano. Bach asked the King for a fugue subject upon which he might extemporize, and Frederick wrote one out for him. Bach's improvisation astonished the King, but the composer still held something in reserve. The next day he returned to the palace, and this time on a subject of his own he imrovised a six-part fugue. Several times Frederick cried out in amazement, "There is only one Bach!"

A few months later the composer repaid the King with a graceful tribute. He sent Frederick *The Musical Offering,* in which he used the

King's theme as a subject of two fugues and a number of canons, adding for good measure a trio for flute, violin, and clavier.

The journey to Potsdam was Bach's last. He was an old man now, and the body that had borne such a heavy burden of labor for so many years began at last to fail. Even so, he was not ready to stop. He set to work upon *Die Kunst der Fuge* [The Art of Fugue], a study which would demonstrate with finality his mastery of the old form. The resulting work is one of the most unusual in music; it is a puzzle which remains unsolved because the composer died before its completion, leaving doubt about certain of his purposes.

One phase of the work is perfectly clear. By taking a single theme and treating it in a great variety of ways, developing it through all the devices known to fugal and canonic procedure, from the simplest to the most astonishingly intricate, Bach intended to expose, as it were, the mechanism of his art as a writer of fugue. However, when the work was published there was nothing to indicate for what instrument or instruments it might be intended. It was long believed, therefore, that *The Art of Fugue* was not intended to be played at all, but was instead a tremendous abstraction, aimed chiefly to instruct and to inform. Even Schweitzer found no aesthetic purpose in the work. He wrote, "It introduces us to a still and serious world, deserted and rigid, without color, without light, without motion; it does not gladden, does not distract; yet we cannot break away from it."

Various modern editors have sought to prove that the piece is much more than cold theory. Some of them have scored it for instruments, and worked out completions of the final fugue left unfinished by Bach. The best proof that *The Art of Fugue* is suited to actual performance and is music in its fullest sense was an arrangement for chamber orchestra made in 1927 by Wolfgang Gräser, a young Swiss genius of music (and of mathematics, physics, and oriental languages), who killed himself in 1928 at the age of twenty-two. Convincing as his arrangement is, Gräser's is clearly not the last word on the subject, and *The Art of Fugue* is likely to fascinate and mystify students of music and Bach arrangers in particular for generations to come.

Bach did not complete *The Art of Fugue* because his eyesight began to fail. He was finally persuaded to consult an English oculist, Chevalier John Taylor, who was then visiting and practicing in Germany. Early in 1750, Taylor performed an operation of some kind on Bach's eyes. The operation failed and Bach emerged totally blind. The excruciating pain of the ordeal and the long confinement that followed broke down the composer's physical strength. This same Taylor, a few years later, performed a similar operation on Handel. The results led Edward

MacDowell to remark that Bach and Handel were in every way different, "except that they were born in the same year, and killed by the same doctor."

For weeks Bach lay in his bed, a broken man. During the year preceding the operation he had turned for the last time to his beloved chorale preludes, and in moments when his eyes would permit was copying and revising eighteen of them for the engraver. Contained in this collection are some of his finest examples in the form, among them the exquisite *Schmücke dich* [Deck Thyself, My Soul, with Gladness]. Almost a century later Robert Schumann heard this work performed by Mendelssohn, to whom he afterwards wrote, saying that around the old chorale hymn "hung winding wreaths of golden leaves, and such blissfulness was breathed from within it, that you yourself avowed that if life was bereft of all hope and faith, this one chorale would renew them for you. I was silent and went away dazed into God's acre, feeling acutely pained that I could lay no flower on his urn."

The last of the collection, *Wenn wir in höchsten Nöthen sein* [When We are in Deepest Need]," remained unfinished during the last days when the blind composer lay waiting for death. Making his last effort, he dictated to his son-in-law the completion of this work, changing its title to that of another hymn on the same tune, *Vor deinen Thron tret' ich allhier* [Before Thy Throne I Come].

Ten days later, on the twenty-eighth day of July 1750, Bach died. He was buried in the ancient graveyard of St. John's Church in Leipzig.

Neglect of Bach's music began almost with the instant of his death. Public interest in it was so small that when Karl Philipp Emanuel published *The Art of Fugue* only a handful of copies were purchased, and he finally sold the plates for the value of the metal. The oldest son, Wilhelm Friedemann (who later became an alcoholic), cared so little for his father's work that he lost a number of the manuscripts of the cantatas which had been willed to him. The sons did not even care for their stepmother. Anna Magdalena died ten years later in poverty. Gradually the manuscripts and published works of the father dropped from sight; soon the place of his grave was forgotten. During the next seventy-five years the name "Bach" meant not Johann Sebastian but Karl Philipp Emanuel.

It would be wrong to assume that the age which neglected Bach's music must be accused of a lack of aesthetic perception. Bach belonged to the baroque era, and he arrived on the scene in time to sum up that style in music. Long before he had finished, the baroque had begun to fade. The younger composers found they could no longer express themselves in the formulas which a century of usage had worked dry. They wanted no more of fugues and chorale preludes, of toccatas, passacaglias, and chaconnes. They were as sick of them as churchgoers were tired of cantatas and Passions.

In France the baroque age had passed into the rococo, impelled by the enormous personal force of Louis XIV. Art, music, and architecture all reflected the spirit of a new age that was to rule Europe. The baroque had been ornamental and florid, with its lush, decorative exterior covering a platform of massive strength. It had aimed to impress, to glorify, to move deeply. The rococo was also decorative; but it was delicate, refined, poetic, with an elegant charm that was essentially shallow. Its purpose was to entertain, to beguile.

The German composers could not help but be impressed by these changes, but their own version of the rococo was a much more sober product than the French. Theirs was chiefly a rationalizing process, and part of it took the form of simplification. New ideas and procedures had to be sought and explored. Polyphony, which had ruled musical thought for a thousand years, began to crumble. Bach himself had exhausted the possibilities of contrapuntal science; no one could follow his purely mathematical skill. The New Music with which his sons were experimenting would be based instead on homophony, a musical pattern built upon a single line of melody instead of several. The great new form which arose was the sonata; soon the symphonic orchestra would appear, and the string quartet. For the next century the best creative minds would be engaged in the development and exploitation of these new concepts of musical form and medium. The opera would flourish as never before, while music for the church would rapidly decline.

In this evolution Bach's music had nothing to offer. It belonged to a vanished past whose ideas and methods the newer composers were trying to avoid and to forget. Moreover, only a small portion of it had been published in the composer's lifetime, so that it could influence little even those whose predilections might be toward the music of the past.

Almost a century had to pass before the wheel would turn full circle. When composers like Chopin, Mendelssohn, Schumann, and Liszt, all romantic emotionalists, discovered Bach and the emotion that lay under his technique, they regarded him with amazement and adoration. Schumann declared that music owed him a debt as great as religion owed to its founder; for Wagner he was "the most stupendous miracle in all music." With Mendelssohn's revival of the *St. Matthew Passion* in 1829 the Bach resurrection began, and all through the rest of the nineteenth century the work of discovery and compilation and editing went on. It was not until 1894, after long search, that the composer's bones were found and identified in St. John's graveyard. By that time he needed no epitaph but his name.

The history of mankind has recorded no greater achievement than his, in that entire realm of human endeavor which is called art.

QUESTIONS

1. Leonard points out that church authorities treated Bach "like a hack," and rectors "had no sympathy with his music." Can you suggest reasons for this apparent unconcern with Bach's music?
2. What sort of composition is Bach's *Well-Tempered Clavier?* In a music dictionary look up "clavier." What is its meaning? How does it differ from "clavichord?"
3. Bach has been considered by many as one of the greatest composers of religious music for the Protestant church. Yet today, in most churches, his music is relatively infrequently performed. Can you suggest reasons for this?
4. How many cantatas did Bach compose? What is a cantata? How many "Passions" did Bach compose? What is a "Passion?"
5. Explain how Bach, a Lutheran composer, was able to compose his *Mass in B minor,* when the Mass belongs to the Catholic liturgy. What do you believe was Bach's intention in composing this work?

COMPOSERS IN THEIR TIMES / 4

Classical *Wolfgang Amadeus Mozart was born in Salzburg in 1756 and died in Vienna in 1791. His life has been the subject for countless biographers and his music the subject for countless analysists. The most exhaustive and definitive biography has been the four-volume work of Otto Jahn, originally published in Germany between 1856 and 1859. For the past one hundred years Jahn's work has been a standard Mozart reference book. In the following essay Nicolas Slonimsky, composer, musicologist, giant among twentieth century lexicographers, and editor of the newly revised* Baker's Biographical Dictionary of Musicians, *shows how it is possible for error to creep into the work of some of the world's great scholars.*

The Weather at Mozart's Funeral

NICOLAS SLONIMSKY

THE STORY OF MOZARTS EARLY DEATH AND HIS burial in a mass grave fills some of the most poignant pages of history. The last chapter of virtually every biography of Mozart contains a melancholy description of the funeral itself during a raging December storm.

In his basic biography of Mozart, Otto Jahn writes:

> At 3 o'clock in the afternoon of December 6, Mozart's body received the benediction at St. Stephen's Church . . . A heavy storm of snow and rain was raging, and the few friends who had assembled for the funeral procession stood with umbrellas around the bier, which was then carried through the Schulerstrasse to the Cemetery of St. Mark. As the storm grew still worse, the mourners decided to turn back at the gate, so that not a friend stood by when the body was lowered into the grave.

Subsequent biographies and entries in musical dictionaries reproduced Jahn's description of the funeral with only slight variations. Here are some quotations:

> On the day of the burial the weather was so bad that even the few friends who followed the coffin turned back at the gate.
>
> (Eitner, *Quellen-Lexikon*)

> His few friends accompanied the coffin only halfway owing to bad weather.
>
> (Riemann, *Musiklexikon,* 11th ed.)

> On the 6th December the plain coffin was carried through the streets on the shoulders of two men, followed by the faithful Süssmayr. At St. Stephen's Church a few others joined the procession, including, it is thought, Albrechtsberger, Lange, Schikaneder, Van Swieten, and Salieri; but the appalling weather —it was a day of storm and heavy snow—soon drove them all home.
>
> (Ernest Newman, *Stories of the Great Operas,* N. Y., 1928, p. 315)

> Mozart's burial took place on the afternoon of December 6. It was a third-class funeral at the cost of 8 gulden and 36 kreuzer plus 3 gulden for the hearse. The plain pinewood coffin was consecrated in the Church of St. Stephen. A few friends . . . followed the bier with umbrellas to the gate. Then the mournful procession was scattered. Stormy December weather drove even the last of the faithful back to town. Not a single friend reached the cemetery of St. Mark to throw a handful of earth on the grave of the dead master.
>
> (Bernhard Paumgartner, *Mozart,* Vienna, 4th ed., 1945, p. 466)

> At 3 o'clock in the afternoon of the 6th his body was removed to St. Stephen's; the service was held in the open air, as was the custom with the poorest class of funeral, and Van Swieten, Süssmayr, Salieri, Deiner, Roser and Orsler stood

---

round the bier. They followed as far as the city gates and then turned back, as a violent storm was raging, and the hearse went its way, unaccompanied, to the church-yard of St. Marx [*sic*].

(*Grove,* 5th ed., 1954; essentially identical with the first edition, 1880)

A small group joined the funeral procession; of the family there were the brothers-in-law Hofer and Lange, while the ailing Constanze was absent; further, the friends Van Swieten, Salieri, Albrechtsberger, Roser von Reiter, Orsler, Süssmayr, and Deiner. Schikaneder had excused himself. Inclement weather, with driving snow and rain, forced these few to disperse at the gate.

(Erich Schenk, *W. A. Mozart,* Vienna, 1955, p. 784)

In his semi-fictional biography, *Mozart, Genius und Mensch* (Hamburg, 1955), Adolf Goldschmitt gives this vivid description of Mozart's burial (p. 346):

The storm roars and howls through the Stubentor in the faces of the mourners. They struggle through up to the gate. Then opens a vast expanse, filled with dancing, galloping snowflakes . . . "How long still to go?" howls the storm. The snow mutters, "How long still to go?" as it crunches under the feet of the marchers. Then from its nests in the hats, in the furs, and in the crape, the snow begins to melt and drip, and to ask: "Does it make any sense?" . . . In this dreadful storm, in this whirling, crackling snow, in which their feet keep slipping, which makes all thought uncertain and questionable, is not this effort, this struggle senseless? The first who begins to understand is the Baron van Swieten. He speaks to Salieri, who marches next to him, but in the storm his words are blown away . . . One after another, the others follow him with mourning hearts.

An "entr'acte" contributed by Sir George Grove to the program book of the 6th concert of the Glasgow Choral Union, of December 8, 1874, gives a definitive summation of facts and fancies regarding Mozart's funeral, to which little was added later:

Van Swieten undertook to arrange for the hearse and coffin—it would have been more to the purpose if he had also volunteered to pay for them. The undertaker's charge was 8 florins 36 kreuzers, and the hearse 3 florins, in all but some 25 shillings—the mere price of an opera box at one of the performances of *Don Juan* at Vienna, but a heavy charge on a widow's purse. And these two were the only visitors. Schikaneder, the Manager, for whom Mozart had written his *Zauberflöte,* and who had made money enough by that and Mozart's other pieces to rebuild the largest theatre in the city—he, irredeemable snob as he must have been, never came near the house, but contented himself with running about the town in tears, saying that Mozart's ghost was pursuing him, and leaving the poor widowed Constance in her penniless misery and trouble . . . For that they were very poor, there can be no doubt . . . No wonder, therefore, that it was late in the day before the arrangements for the funeral of such a pauper could be made. It was three in the afternoon of the 6th before the coffin was deposited in one of the chapels on the north side of St. Stephen's. Van Swieten, Salieri, Süssmayr, and two other musicians named Roser and Orsler, appear to have been the only persons present, besides the officiating priest and the bearers of the coffin. It was a terribly inclement day; rain and sleet coming down fast; and an eye-witness describes how the little band of mourners stood shivering round the hearse with their umbrellas up as it left the door of the church. It was then far on in the dark cold December afternoon, and the evening was fast closing in before the solitary hearse had passed the Stubenthor, and reached the distant graveyard of St. Mark, in which, amongst the "third class," the great composer of the "Jupiter" Symphony and the Requiem found his resting place. By this time the weather had proved too much for all the mourners; they had dropped off one by one, and Mozart's body was accompanied only by the driver of the carriage.

In all these accounts there is complete unanimity as to the stormy weather raging on the day of Mozart's funeral. Yet the early biographers of Mozart make no mention of the storm. There is nothing about it in Schlichtegroll's *Nekrolog* for the year 1791, nothing in Niemtschek's biography (Prague, 1798), and, significantly enough, nothing in Nissen's account of Mozart's life and death, first published at Leipzig in 1828. Nissen, who married Mozart's widow, was most anxious to explain her position at Mozart's death. He writes:

Baron van Swieten came immediately after his death, so as to weep with the widow, who had lain in the bed of her dead husband in order to catch his disease and die with him. In order to prevent her from surrendering herself to her despair, she was taken to Herr Bauernfeld, an associate of Schikaneder, and later to Herr Goldhahn. [p. 572]

Stricken by Mozart's death, the widow herself fell severely ill, so that Baron van Swieten had to take care of the burial of Mozart's body. Since he had to observe the greatest possible economy for the family, the coffin was put in a common grave and all other expenditures were also avoided. [p. 576]

Mozart's widow and his sister-in-law Sophie Haibl contributed to the posthumous publication of Nissen's book, and it is inconceivable that they should have omitted from their account of Mozart's death and funeral the dramatic phenomenon of a heavy storm. Besides, stormy weather at the funeral would have offered an extenuating circumstance for the widow's absence. And of course it is most unlikely that Mozart's closest intimates should have simply forgotten the weather.

No mention of the storm is found in the *Nouvelle Biographie de Mozart* by Oulibicheff (Moscow, 1843) or in the *Life of Mozart* by Edward Holmes (London, 1845). In fact, no biography before Otto Jahn's has any reference to the subject.

Where did Jahn find his information? The answer is provided in an inconspicuous footnote in Vol. 4, p. 688, of Jahn's biography of Mozart, published at Leipzig in 1859. The footnote cites No. 28 of the *Wiener Morgen-Post* of the centennial year 1856, but vouchsafes no direct quotation from that journal. Subsequent biographers have dropped this bibliographical reference, relying entirely on the authority of Jahn for the authenticity of the report.

This all-important article, the source of the information about the storm, was published anonymously in the *Wiener Morgen-Post* on

January 28, 1856, as a contribution by "one of the people," and the implication is plain that this supposed eye-witness account was being published for the first time. Here are the essential parts:

> Mozart's body received benediction at St. Stephen's on December 7, [An error, corrected in all Mozart biographies. That the funeral took place on December 6 is established by the parish entry at St. Stephen's.] at 3 o'clock in the afternoon . . . The burial was of the third class, costing 8 florins, 36 kreuzer. Besides, the hearse cost 3 florins. The night of Mozart's death was dark and stormy. Also at the benediction it began to blow and storm. Rain and snow fell together, as though nature wished to show its anger with the great musician's contemporaries who came to his funeral in such small numbers. Only a few friends and three women followed the body. Mozart's wife was not present. These few people stood with umbrellas around the bier, which was afterwards conducted through the Schulerstrasse to the cemetery of St. Mark's. As the storm grew still heavier, even those few friends decided to turn back at the gates, and betook themselves to the tavern of the Silver Serpent.

Thus we find that the legend of Mozart's sad funeral in a forbidding blizzard rests on the account of the only one of the participants to record the event. Unfortunately, this witness, who remains anonymous, tells his story sixty-four years after the event took place. Since it is quite unlikely that a child would have attended the funeral of a musician, we are in addition dealing with a very old man—or perhaps with a Romantic steeped in Jean Paul and E. T. A. Hoffmann. Can the deposition of such a witness—and as we have seen, there are no others—be accepted? Furthermore, the opportune publication of this story in January 1856, exactly a hundred years after Mozart's birth, and never previously, raises the suspicion that it was composed *ad hoc*. We had better rely on the testimony of science itself, for science, too, keeps a diary. Moreover, this diary is impersonal, factual, and not subject to the vagaries of *Empfindsamkeit*.

Such testimony is offered by the records of the Vienna meteorological bureau, which go back into the 18th century. I sent an inquiry to the Zentralanstalt für Meteoroligie und Geodynamik of Vienna, and to my amazement and delight received a prompt answer from Professor F. Steinhauser, dated July 9, 1959. He reports the following entry in the records of the Vienna Observatory under the date of December 6, 1791:

	8 a.m.	3 p.m.	10 p.m.
Barometric pressure	27″ 7½‴	27″ 7‴	27″ 8‴
Temperature	+2.6° R	+3.0° R	+3.0° R
Wind	weak east wind at all these times of the day.		

The barometric pressure is given here in Vienna inches and Vienna lines (12 Vienna lines equal one Vienna inch; one Vienna line equals 2.195 mm.). In English measure, the average barometric pressure of 27″ 7½‴ equals about 28.5 inches. The temperature, here given in the

Réaumur thermometric scale, varied from 37.9 to 38.8 degrees Fahrenheit.

Professor Steinhauser adds to his report another precious document: an entry in the diaries of Count Karl Zinzendorf, kept in the Austrian State Archives, in which the weather conditions of the period are punctiliously noted. In Vol. 36 (year 1791), p. 287, of the diary, under the date of December 6, is found the following observation: "Temps doux et brouillard fréquent."

Mild weather and frequent drizzle or mist! Zinzendorf's observation corresponds well with the weather report, the virtual absence of wind, and temperature above the freezing point at all times of the day, ruling out the possibility of snow.

Certainly an intermittent drizzle could not be regarded as deterring Mozart's friends from following the coffin to the grave. And, as we have found, Mozart's family never claimed that the weather was inclement. Professor Steinhauser advances the explanation that in the 18th century it was customary to accompany the body to the grave only when the cemetery was situated in the immediate vicinity of the church. St. Mark's, where Mozart was buried, was about half an hour's march from St. Stephen's Cathedral. Women rarely, if ever, attended funerals at the time and this may well account for Constanze's absence. It should be observed, also, that Nissen does not seek to excuse her absence in the funeral procession, but only her inability to make arrangements for the burial.

Who were the mourners? Nissen and other early biographers are silent on the subject. Otto Jahn lists the following: Baron van Swieten, Salieri, Süssmayr, Joseph Deiner (who was summoned from the Silver Serpent to dress Mozart's body), the 'cellist Orsler, and the Kapellmeister Roser. Whether Emanuel Schikaneder, Mozart's librettist and intimate friend, was present, will never be known. Some biographers add to this list the names of Mozart's brothers-in-law, Lange and Hofer, and also Albrechtsberger.

Most interesting is the inclusion of Salieri among the mourners, in view of the rumor that spread soon after Mozart's death accusing Salieri of poisoning him. It was Anselm Hüttenbrenner, a pupil of Salieri, who was the first to claim that Salieri attended Mozart's funeral. In his obituary article on his teacher, in the *Allgemeine musikalische Zeitung* of November 1825, he wrote: "Salieri spoke of Mozart always with exceptional respect. . . . He visited Mozart two days before Mozart died, and was one of the few who accompanied the body." Hüttenbrenner was not yet born when Mozart died, and his testimony may be accepted at best as a remembrance of what Salieri himself told him;

but Hüttenbrenner does not make even that claim. The assertion that Salieri was present at the funeral therefore rests on a very flimsy foundation.

No one has yet suggested that Salieri attended Mozart's funeral to look at the result of his "dreadful deed" and to make sure that Mozart, whom he was supposed to have poisoned, was indeed dead.

The rumor of poisoning found literary expression in Pushkin's play *Mozart and Salieri,* written in 1830—that is, only five years after Salieri's death. Among Pushkin's papers was found a note relating to this play:

> "During the first performance of *Don Giovanni,* while the entire audience, which included great connoisseurs, silently admired Mozart's harmony, a hiss was heard. Everyone turned to its source in amazement and indignation, and the celebrated Salieri left the theater in a rage, consumed by envy. Some German periodicals report that on his deathbed he admitted a dreadful deed, the poisoning of great Mozart. An envious rival who could hiss *Don Giovanni* was capable of poisoning its creator."

Even the most vicious detractors of Salieri never claimed that he had ever demonstrated in public his hostility to Mozart and his lack of appreciation of Mozart's music. On the other hand, we know that Salieri attended a performance of *Die Zauberflöte* on October 13, 1791, that Mozart himself took Salieri in a carriage to the theater, and that Salieri was so entranced with the music that "from the overture to the last chorus there was not a single number that did not call forth from him a bravo! or bello!"

Among fantastic tales regarding Salieri's guilt was this: In 1822 Rossini asked Salieri to introduce him to Beethoven. Salieri obliged, and took Rossini to Beethoven's house in Vienna. When Beethoven caught sight of Salieri, he turned to Rossini and cried out: "How dare you come to my house with Mozart's poisoner?" Salieri hastily retreated, and was so shaken by the encounter that he suffered a mental collapse leading to complete insanity. The tale is hardly worth refuting, for Beethoven proudly acknowledged that Salieri was his teacher and dedicated to him several works, all this, of course, many years after Mozart's death.

That Salieri died nearly insane is true. His friend Rochlitz wrote in the June 1825 number of the *Allgemeine musikalische Zeitung:* "Salieri lost himself in dark delusions . . . He imagined that his reputation was ruined, and sometimes accused himself of dreadful crimes."

Edward Holmes, in his *Life of Mozart* (New York, 1845, p. 360, note), makes Salieri's self-accusation specific:

> Mozart's notion that he had been poisoned was always treated by those about him as a fantastic idea . . . The tale of poisoning, however, having transpired, Salieri, the known inveterate foe of Mozart, was fixed upon as the imaginary

criminal. It is a singular fact that Salieri, who died in the public hospital of Vienna, thought fit on his deathbed to make a solemn deposition of his innocence before witnesses, and that the document thus duly signed and attested was made public.

No such document has ever come to light, or has been mentioned in the literature on Salieri. But the Soviet musicologist Igor Boelza, in his book *Mozart and Salieri,* published in Russian in 1953, asserts that Guido Adler discovered in the Vienna archives a communication from Salieri's father confessor to the Archbishop of Vienna reporting that on his deathbed Salieri not only admitted poisoning Mozart but also explained in detail how he administered the slowly working venom. According to Boelza, Adler had no time to publish the document, but spoke about his findings to the Soviet music scholar Boris Asafiev. However, Asafiev never referred to the story in any of his published writings. Since both Adler and Asafiev are dead, the *onus probandi* of the existence of Salieri's confession rests with Boelza, who has so far not corroborated his original report.

The calumny grew as rapidly and as luxuriantly as the one in the famous aria of Don Basilio in *The Barber of Seville.* Voices for the defense were barely audible in the noise. One of the most determined among Salieri's defenders was the Austrian composer Sigismund Neukomm, whose communication on the subject appeared in an English translation in the *Quarterly Musical Magazine* of London, 1826, pp. 336-38:

> The public papers persist in repeating that Salieri has confessed himself the cause of Mozart's untimely end, but none of them have mentioned the source of this horrible report, which defames the memory of one, who for fifty-eight years has engaged the universal attention of Vienna.
>
> It is the duty of every honourable man, when an unfounded report is current, by which the memory of a celebrated artist will be dishonoured, to relate all that he knows . . . Mozart and Salieri entertained for each other a mutual esteem, without any intimate friendship, for they were accustomed at Vienna, each to acknowledge the other's distinguished merit. No one could impute to Salieri any jealousy of Mozart's talents, and whoever was acquainted with him (as I was) will agree with me, that this man led, for eight and fifty years, an unblemished life, employing himself simply in his art, and taking every opportunity of doing good to his neighbours. Such an one, I think, could be no murderer—a man who, during the four and thirty years that have passed since Mozart's death, has preserved that delightful flow of spirits which has rendered his society so attractive.
>
> Even if it were proved that Salieri declared himself when dying the perpetrator of this dreadful crime, one ought surely not so easily to receive as truth, and promulgate as such, the words which escape from an unhappy dying old man of seventy-four, worn out by ceaseless pain, when it is known how much his intellects had decayed for months before his decease.

The tale of Salieri's murderous crime was revived in Nazi Germany by Mathilde Ludendorff, M.D., in a book entitled *Mozarts Leben und gewaltsamer Tod,* published by a Ludendorff family printing press (Ludendorffs Verlag) at Munich in 1936. She develops the thesis that Mozart was murdered by the Freemasons, among whom were Salieri, van Swieten, and the mysterious messenger who commissioned the Requiem. Taking advantage of their proximity to Mozart and his trust in them, they slowly poisoned him. Nissen, also a Mason, covered up the crime in his biography of Mozart. Constanze was innocent, and knew nothing about the plot. Mozart's crime, in the view of the murderers, was the revelation of secret Masonic rites that he made in *Die Zauberflöte.* True, Mathilde Ludendorff admits, Mozart himself was a Mason, but he was drawn into the Masonic Order through his racial and personal simplicity. At first, he failed to understand the sinister nature of the Order. When his eyes were finally opened, he decided to expose the misdeeds of the Freemasons, thus sealing his death warrant, immediately upon the production of *Die Zauberflöte.*

Mathilde Ludendorff dismisses the fact that all these people were Catholics in good standing by claiming that the official religion was for them nothing but a cloak to cover their true intentions and beliefs. She also offers a brilliant solution to the psychological puzzle presented by the actions of Baron van Swieten, a rich man who let Mozart be buried in a pauper's grave. It seems that according to the Masonic laws, the body of the transgressor must be cursed, that its skull should be removed so as to prevent decent burial, and that his grave should be unmarked. The thesis thus accepts the long discredited story, possibly based on the known fate of Haydn's cranium, that Mozart's skull was detached from the body and hidden, and it also advances the notion that Constanze was kept away from the cemetery by van Swieten under the pretext of safeguarding her health. In all fairness, it should be noted that Mathilde Ludendorff herself concedes that some people might regard her as mad. Her book certainly justifies that supposition.

To sum up: Mozart's pusillanimous friends, colleagues, patrons, competitors—even his alleged murderer—who stayed away from his funeral could not blame the atmospheric conditions. The tale of Mozart's funeral was a product of the Romantic age. Melodramatically inclined biographers could not very well have Mozart dying, racked with fever, surrounded by friends while exhaling his last immortal melody (as pictured in a well-known 19th-century painting), and so had to be content with a storm-tossed funeral. The Victorians could not stomach the heartless unconcern of the rich Baron van Swieten, who carefully reduced the costs of the funeral to fit the family's depleted purse, but such a realistic attitude was quite in keeping with the unromantic spirit of the time. Even Nissen speaks of the necessity of "holding down expenditures," which explains the third-class funeral. But meteorological records, with relentless objectivity, demolish the Romantic picture, for they inform us that though the funeral took place in the dead of winter, it happened that December 6, 1791, was a relatively mild day that could have prevented no one from marching all the way to St. Mark's Cemetery and throwing a handful of earth on Mozart's grave—if he so wished.

Some thirty-five years later another great Viennese musician, Ludwig van Beethoven, was laid to rest, but he was accorded a grand funeral worthy of his fame, and his grave was well identified. *Mirabile dictu*, the famous thunderstorm at the time of Beethoven's death, reported by all Beethoven biographers, actually did occur! Dr. Steinhauser not only supplied the report on the Vienna weather during Mozart's funeral but also was kind enough to communicate to me a complete account of the meteorological conditions on the day of Beethoven's death, March 26, 1827. At three 'clock in the afternoon stormy weather began, and at four o'clock lightning and thunder struck, with strong winds.

As for Beethoven's defiant gesture with a clenched fist at the "powers of evil," as the peals of thunder filled the air, this story owes its origin to the selfsame Anselm Hüttenbrenner who was responsible for the highly dubious details of Salieri's presence at Mozart's funeral, and must be regarded as another example of musico-biographical folklore.

QUESTIONS

1. How is it possible for a false or misleading biographical item to appear in the work of one authority after another? Discuss the meanings of "primary" and "secondary" sources.
2. Do you think Slonimsky's research on the weather has any special value? In what way? How does it contribute to music?
3. Go to the library and select a Mozart biography. Find the account of Mozart's funeral and compare the information given with the information in Slonimsky's essay.
4. Look up the name of Salieri. How important was he in his time? Can you suggest why today Mozart's name is known the world over while Salieri's name is relatively unknown?
5. What does Slonimsky mean when, concerning the 18th century, he speaks of "the unromantic spirit of the time." And that "the tale of Mozart's funeral was a product of the Romantic age." Discuss what is meant by "the spirit" of a given time.

COMPOSERS IN THEIR TIMES / 5

Romantic *As we move away from a man's life, it becomes increasingly difficult to discover the truth about him, his life and work. Thus, the biographer turns, whenever he can, to letters, documents, sketches, and other writings by writers who knew the man personally. This is not to say that these writings are more factual than later writings; often contemporaries are moved by personal feelings. Nonetheless, their writings are valuable and interesting because they are based on first-hand experience, if not knowledge. Of the four contemporaries included here, W. C. Müller was a tutor and teacher in the city of Bremen; Wenzel Tomaschek was a composer; Karl von Bursy a physician at the Salzburg Johannis Hospital; the last was a journalist for the Stuttgart* Morning Blade *in 1823.*

BEETHOVEN

and His Contemporaries

LUDWIG NOHL, Editor

OUR FIRST SKETCH IS BY THE PHILOLOGIST, DR. W. C. Müller, of Bremen, to whose meeting with Beethoven we shall presently refer, and who immediately after the master's death wrote "Something about Ludwig van Beethoven" in the Leipsig *Allegemeine Musikalische Zeitung*. Although neither exhaustive nor thoroughly accurate, this account gives a clear idea of the unhappiness of his boyhood, and is, therefore, worth preserving.

Beethoven's Boyhood

W. C. Müller

WITHIN the last few weeks the newspapers have contained much that is interesting about this celebrated composer, details about his illness, the assistance sent from England, his death and funeral. To the lovers of art, and even to the world in general, the fullest particulars concerning this extraordinary genius are valuable. The following brief sketch may, therefore, not be out of place. It is a faithful one, for we have, for several years, corresponded with Beethoven and his most intimate friends, and in 1820 we made his personal acquaintance.

We learn from the church register that Beethoven was born at Bonn, December 17, 1770, not 1772 as has been generally stated. On this point he was himself mistaken: time passed unheeded by him; in the tone-world in which he lived, periods flowed on without divisions of days and years. His father was tenor singer in the chapel of the Elector of Cologne, Maximilian Franz, one of the brothers of the Emperor Joseph II. Like all the children of the Empress Maria Theresa, the Elector was a warm lover of music and had one of the most perfect bands of the time. Some relatives of the celebrated Romberg were members of it; two of them are still living—Ries the elder, father of the famous pianist, and Beethoven's best pupil, and Simrock, music publisher at Bonn. These are our chief authorities for particulars about Beethoven's youth.

He received from his father, in early childhood, his first lessons on the piano and violin; and not being compelled to attend to anything else, both wrote and spelt badly. When a boy he had an ungainly figure; as a youth his appearance was not more graceful, nor in his fiftieth year

---

BEETHOVEN AND HIS CONTEMPORARIES, from *Beethoven and His Contemporaries*, Ludwig Nohl, editor, W. Reeves; 1880.

do we in this respect find any change in him. What a striking contrast to Mozart!

Ludwig led a very retired life and was under strict orders from his father to remain constantly in his room practicing; he did not, therefore, feel the loss of society. He was shy, and in what little intercourse he had with others would answer in monosyllables; but he thought and observed a great deal, abandoning himself to the emotions and brooding fancies awakened first by music and afterwards by the poets. Mozart, on the contrary, was taken into society when only seven years of age; whence his pliant, affable, sympathetic, and kindly disposition, his early skill in composition, and the perfect regularity and universally pleasing character of his cosmopolitan music. Beethoven when a boy did not think of preserving his fancies for himself or for others, by committing them to paper; he early began to indulge his imagination on the piano, and more especially on the violin, and was so absorbed and absent-minded that he had many a scolding from his mother for not heeding the dinner-hour.

After giving up the violin, he pursued his beloved art on the piano. It is highly probable that in his twelfth year, he was acquainted with all the forms used by the contemporary composers, Haydn, Mozart, Sterkel, for they appear in his three sonatas which the father published in Ludwig's eleventh (thirteenth) year, and dedicated to the Elector of Cologne. They clearly indicate the young beginner, and how much of them is original cannot be determined, for they are not distinguishable from the style of the day; the figures are borrowed from the above-named masters, and the phrases are deficient in roundness and rhythm. Very opposite is the character of the pianoforte trios, known as his first works. Not only is the form very different, but each trio contains a tone-picture capable of being conceived in the imagination and plastically represented. In his fourteenth year, he was cembalist in the orchestra, that is he accompanied with the double bass in the symphonies; in his sixteenth year, he became organist to the Elector.

While in this position he once incurred the displeasure of his kind patron. To humiliate a confident and boastful Italian singer, who despised all German music, Beethoven was persuaded by his colleagues to put him out in the tune and time of a certain aria. The attempt succeeded to the satisfaction of the band; but as the disturbance occurred during mass, Beethoven received a sharp reprimand; he did not, however, betray the instigators of the trick.

Hitherto his style of playing had been powerful, but rough, although very rich in new forms of fancy. He was universally admired, but being simple, modest, and unpretending, was not envied. In his eighteenth year, some of his companions took him with them to Mayence, that he might appear there as a virtuoso. They were fortunate enough to receive an invitation from the Abbé Sterkel, intendant of the band, a well-known pianist, whom Beethoven much wished to hear. The Abbé played one of his sonatas with great delicacy of execution. Beethoven stood in a corner listening intently; such refined playing he had never heard. Then he was asked to play. Persistently refusing, his companions led him to the piano by force; he began timidly, but soon forgot his surroundings, and launched forth into an improvisation which the Abbé could not sufficiently praise. He was asked to perform his published variations on "Vieni Amore"; but as he did not know them all by heart, he played seven new ones which were still finer. His friends were amazed at the refinement of his playing, which had become as delicate as the Abbé's. We cannot attribute this to a desire of annoying his patron, as has been suggested.

A Pianoforte Competition

Wenzel Tomaschek

OPINIONS differ as to their relative superiority, but the majority incline towards Wölffl. I will endeavour to describe the peculiarities of both, without showing preference to either artist. Beethoven's playing is more brilliant, but less delicate, and fails sometimes in clearness. He appears to most advantage in improvisation, and it is indeed marvellous to see how easily and logically he will extemporise on any given theme, not merely by varying the figures (as many virtuosi do with much success—and bluster), but by a real development of the idea. Since the death of Mozart, who was to my mind the *non plus ultra* of players, no one has given me so much pleasure as Beethoven. Wölffl is, in this respect, inferior; his claim to superiority is that in addition to his thorough musical knowledge and excellence in composition, he performs passages which really appear impossible of execution, with astonishing ease, clearness, and precision. Of course, the size of his hand is a great help to him. He always plays with taste, and in the *Adagii* especially is so pleasing, so equally removed from coldness and exaggeration, that he not only excites admiration, but gives pleasure. Wölffl's unassuming and amiable behaviour naturally contrasts favourably with the somewhat haughty manners of Beethoven.

Beethoven had already attracted public notice by various compositions, and passed in Vienna for a pianist of the first rank, when in the latter years in the last century, a rival arose in the person of Wölffl. Then was in a manner repeated the Parisian feud of the Gluckists and Piccinists; and the numerous lovers of art in the Imperial city divided themselves into two parties. At the head of Beethoven's admirers was the amiable Prince von Lichnowsky; among the most zealous defenders of Wölffl was Freiherr Raymund von Wetzlar. This highly cultured gentleman, with true British hospitality, used to keep open house during the summer, at his pleasant villa at Grünberg, near the Imperial castle of Schönbrunn, for foreign and native artists, to whom it was a resort as agreeable as it was desirable. The interesting competition between the two *virtuosi* was a source of endless enjoyment to the select party assembled there; each artist produced his latest work, or gave free play to the momentary inspirations of his fancy, or they would improvise at two pianos alternately, on each other's themes; and the duet *capriccii* which they thus composed would doubtless have been well worthy of preservation.

For mechanical dexterity it would have been difficult, perhaps impossible, to have awarded the palm to either of the combatants; kind nature had been more liberal towards Wölffl in providing him with a gigantic hand, which made tenths as easy to him as octaves were to others, and enabled him to play successive passages of these intervals with the speed of lightning. In improvisation, Beethoven already displayed his inclination towards the dismal and gloomy; while luxuriating in the boundless tone-world, he was emancipated from everything earthly, the spirit broke its fetters, shook off the yoke of bondage, and soared triumphantly into aetherial realms; now his playing would be like a wild foaming cataract, and the enchanter would force from the instrument astounding effects, almost beyond its possibilities; then sink exhausted, murmuring soft complainings, dissolving in melancholy; then the soul rose again, triumphant over earthly sorrows, turning heavenward with devotional strains, and finding soothing consolation in the innocent bosom of holy nature. But who can fathom the depths of the sea? Beethoven's improvisation was like the sacred Sanscrit language, whose hieroglyphics the initiated alone can decipher. Wölffl, on the other hand, trained in the school of Mozart, was always equal, never dull, and being invariably clear, was more accessible to the majority; art served him merely as a means to an end; he never made it a pompous show-piece of dry learning; and he never failed to excite and sustain interest by a well-arranged succession of ideas. Any one who has heard Hummel will understand what this means.

An unprejudiced and impartial observer derived a great deal of pleasure from watching the two Macenates, seeing with what anxious attention and approving looks they followed the performances of their *protegés,* and then with true chivalrous courtesy how each yielded the palm to his rival.

But of this the *protegés* themselves took little account; they were best able to appreciate each other's merits, and accordingly entertained a mutual esteem. As upright, honest Germans, they proceeded on the praiseworthy principle that the path of art was broad enough for all.

Wölffl showed his respect for Beethoven's genius by dedicating to him his Pianoforte Sonata, Op. 7, which appeared about this time. He soon disappeared from public life, for he died early. He was wanting in that strong, enduring, intellectual energy and ideality which sustained our master in the most troubled circumstances, causing him ever to rise with renewed strength from every sorrow and misfortune. This competition increased his fame as it added to his knowledge.

A Visit in the Year 1816

Karl von Bursy

MUST I not note and commemorate the day on which I made the acquaintance of Beethoven? I went to see him yesterday, but could not find him, as Herr Riedl (music publisher) had given me a wrong address. He lives at No. 1056 in the Seilerstadt, and not as Madame Nanette Streicher wrote to me, No. 1055. I always had the idea that Beethoven must live in a princely palace, and under the protection of a Maecenas of his noble art. How great, then, was my astonishment when a herring-seller directed me to the next-door house, saying, "I think Herr van Beethoven lives there, for I have often seen him go in." I inquired on the ground-floor, and learned that Beethoven lived on the third story, up three flights of stairs. What a contrast to my expectations! A wretched house, and the third floor! A narrow stone staircase led to the room where a Beethoven creates and works. I confess I felt overpowered, as if going into the presence of the sublime. It was, indeed, no everyday sight I was to see, no everyday man with whom I *hoped* to speak; for I could not be sure that I actually should. A small door at which I rang led me into a little vestibule, opening into the kitchen and children's room. I was received by a servant who, with his family, seems to belong to Beethoven's household. He wanted to admit me at once, but I gave him my letter from Amenda and waited anxiously for an answer. The servant at last returned, saying, "Have the kindness to walk in"; and I stepped behind a thick woollen curtain into the study. Beethoven entered from an adjoining room. It seemed hard and unnatural only to pay a ceremonious compliment to the master of my art. I should like to have seized his hand and imprinted on it a kiss of deepest reverence.

If Jean Paul was altogether unlike my previous conception, Beethoven fairly corresponded to what I had imagined. He is short, but sturdy looking, with grey hair, which he wears thrown back, rather a red face, and fiery eyes small, but deeply set, and full of intense life. He is very much like Amenda, especially when he laughs. Beethoven inquired after him first thing, and spoke of him with much friendliness. "He is a very good fellow," he said. "I unfortunately live at a distance from my friends, and am left alone in odious Vienna." He asked me to speak loudly, as his hearing was very bad just then. He wished in the summer to go into the country and to Baden for the sake of his health. He has not been well for some time, and has composed nothing new. I asked him about Berg's opera text, and he said it was very good, and with a few alterations should do very well for composition. Hitherto, his illness had prevented him from undertaking such a work, and he wished to write Amenda himself about it. I shouted into his ear that for such a work one must have plenty of time and leisure. "No," he said, "I do not go on continuously. I always work at several things at once, and take up first one, then the other." He often misunderstood me and had to pay the greatest attention to catch what I said. This of course much disconcerted me, and sharing my embarrassment he spoke the more himself and very loudly.

He told me much about Vienna and his life there. He is full of wormwood and gall, dissatisfied and defiant, pouring out cursings against Austria and especially Vienna. He speaks quickly and with great vivacity. He often strikes the piano with his fist so violently that the room resounds again. He is not reserved, for he soon adverted to his personal affairs and told me a great deal about himself and his circumstances. This is exactly the *Signum diagnosticum* of hypochondraism. To me this hypochondraism was very welcome, for I thus heard from his own lips a great deal about his life. He complains of the times, and for many reasons. Art, being no longer so far above the multitude, is not so much esteemed, nor nearly so well paid. Is it creditable that a Beethoven can have cause for a pecuniary complaint? O ye rich! How poor must you be, if you have nothing to spare for Beethoven! He would have abundance, and you would want nothing. Give him a portion of the treasure you squander, and your life will be rich in good deeds. Generations to come will thank you for every care and grief from which you have released Beethoven; for he must be free from earthly anxiety, if he is to give the world its due. His power is so stupendous that he would unceasingly be laying up a rich store for present and future art-honouring people. "Why do you stay in Vienna, when any other court would gladly offer you an appointment?" "Circumstances keep me here, but it is very miserable and wretched," said he, "things could not be worse. One can trust nobody. No one fulfils anything that is not down in black and white. You have to work for a miserly payment, and then do not get what was promised." Beethoven composed an occasional cantata for the congress, but it was never performed. After many cabals he gave a concert at the Redouten Saal. The Emperor of Russia paid 200 ducats for his ticket. Beethoven was particularly pleased that the General Intendant of the Imperial Stage, Count Palfy, received a severe reprimand. He is not at all partial to him.

Beethoven seems very anxious about money; and I must confess this makes him more human, and brings him closer to us. It shows that he is only a dweller in the dust and gives him a kinship with us, for as an artist he does not belong to earth. I felt nearer to him when he thus talked about the chief need of life. Sad enough, but true. I freely admit that the less ideal side of the ideal artist drew me nearer to him. So commonplace is the ordinary man! I did not speak much about music to one so immeasurably my superior. From vanity? No! That the consummate artist might not look into my lowly sphere, that his eye might be spared the mean prospect—such was the cause of my silence.

He was pleased to hear that *Fidelio* had been so frequently well received in Berlin. He lamented the loss of Milder Hauptmann. "Her place is vacant," he said, "none of the singers here can sing as she did. We could not pay her, so she did well to go to Berlin. Music is very much on the decline in Vienna and is quite neglected, and the public will put up with anything.

His brother having died recently, Beethoven has undertaken the education of the orphan son. He talked much about it, and took this opportunity of finding fault with the schools here, to which he had sent the little fellow, but soon removed him. "The boy must be an artist or a *savant,* that he may lead a noble life." He expressed some grand views on life. When he is silent his brow contracts, and his gloomy appearance might inspire fear, did we not know that such a lofty artistic soul must have noble springs. Confidence growing up between us, he allowed me to visit him frequently, for he only went backwards and forwards to Baden; I was to go to him whenever he could be helpful to me. He wrote down my address and parted from me with the friendly words, "I shall fetch you some day."

Thus I saw him whom I have so long esteemed, loved, and honoured. If Beethoven were not so deaf, I should certainly gain his affection and confidence. In spite of his apparent hardness and coldness, he is rendered warm and gentle by the devotion of a spirit not seeking support from his mind. His house, which looks on to the Green Bastion, is cheerful and kept tolerably clean and tidy. On one side of the vestibule is his sleeping apartment, on the other his music room, in which stands a locked piano. I saw but little music; some pieces of music paper lay on the writing table. Two good oil portraits of a man and a woman hung on the wall.

Beethoven was not, like Jean Paul, dressed in rags, but quite in gala costume, confirming what I had already heard about his being vain, which of course renders his deafness still more annoying to him, and accounts for his excuses that he generally heard better than just then. I find, after inquiry, no grounds for the assertion that he is sometimes mad. Herr Riedl assured me that he was not so at all, and only had what is called artist's spleen. On that point everyone thinks differently. Riedl, for example, as a dealer in works of art and publisher of several of Beethoven's works, probably considers the high price which he puts upon his manuscripts as evidence of such spleen; for, indeed, he said to me that Beethoven charged monstrously for his compositions. My ideas of artistic spleen are something like these commercial ones. To a consummate artist like Beethoven, having a high estimate of himself, esteeming people only for what they are, not for their title or appearance, proud towards the proud, and haughty towards the haughty, so infinitely below him—to such a man would I grant that artistic spleen, which indeed raises him in my estimation. If Beethoven did not feel his worth he would not be Beethoven, nor the great artist whom I had hitherto revered.

On the 25th July, I have recorded a visit to Beethoven, at one o'clock. Availing myself of his promise, I went to him with my copy of *Fidelio,* that it might be consecrated by his handwriting as a sacred memorial of the master-singer. He was not at home. The servant showed me into his room, and I wrote my request on a little sheet of paper. I felt quite strange dipping his pen into his ink. The air around seemed like a breath from Parnassus, and the quill as if it had been plucked from the golden wings of Pegasus. While the servant was gone for a minute into the next room, I was seized by a demoniacal desire. For a moment my better sense prevailed, and I withstood the temptation. But the evil spirit triumphed. I was left a little longer alone, and the temptation acquired irresistible force. My weak will was powerless against it, and the deed was done. Like Faust, who could not conceal his compact with the evil one, but was branded by a scar on the left hand, so a black spot on my light coat exactly over the heart testified to the triumph of the demon. Beethoven's much worn pen, corresponding in its form to his characteristic writing, was the enticing fruit with which the serpent allured me. I quickly seized it, and the sin was committed, the theft accomplished. The *corpus delicti* now lies in my desk, and is a constant memorial of a moment of weakness.

I went to Beethoven on July 27th, at seven o'clock in the morning; I found him at home and had a good half-hour's pleasant chat. He said a great deal against Vienna and spoke with much rancour. He wished himself out of the city, but felt obliged to remain on account of his nephew, a boy of ten, whom he would gladly train as a musician, if there be any chance of his becoming eminent. He already plays the piano exceedingly well. Beethoven has now taken him into his house and means to get him a teacher. He was very kind, and the pressure of his hand at parting made me feel of more value in my own eyes, and raised me from the commonplace sphere of everyday life.

I found Beethoven at his writing table, with a sheet of music before him, and a glass machine in which he was making his coffee. Neither of his two pianos were yet open. I asked him about Berg's opera text. "It does not answer to be an opera composer here, for the managers of the theatres do not pay us." He inveighs against the music publishers for making such confusion in his works by their new editions. They give the numbers according to their fancy. Thus, Mollo has recently re-published the Trio Variations in E flat major as Op. 82; but this number properly belongs to four songs and a much earlier one to the variations. It is indeed low roguery. Everything relating to bookselling is marked by the greatest meanness. There is no sincerity shown in this kind of business.

Beethoven's Character

Stuttgart *Morgenblatt*

LUDWIG VAN BEETHOVEN is one of those who are honoured, not only by Vienna and Germany, but by Europe and the whole civilized world. Beethoven, Mozart, and Haydn form an unapproached triumvirate in modern musical art. In spite of Italian "kling-klang," and modern charlatanism, the intellectual depth, unfailing originality, and the ideality of a great spirit command the homage of every true worshipper of the divine Polyhymnia. Let us, however, speak not of his works, but of himself.

Beethoven's life has, as he says, been chiefly a life of thought. The events of the outward world concern him but little; he is quite given up to art. Midnight finds him at his desk, and sunrise calls him to it again; his activity is unceasing. But he dislikes being asked to compose, for he wishes only to give forth the spontaneous fruits of his genius. Art is to him a divine gift, not a means for obtaining fame or money. Despising all that is false, he strives after truth and character in art and in life. The first time *Fidelio* was performed, the overture belonging to it could not be given, and another overture of Beethoven's was substituted. "They clapped," he said, "but I was ashamed; it did not belong to the whole."

He is incapable of deception. If he vouchsafes any opinion on a composition, it is sure to be a true one; and he immediately dissolves connections which he finds inimical to his upright manliness and lofty ideas of honour. He has a strong, decisive will, but he only desires what is right; and, what is rare in our times, he not only commits no injustice, but will suffer none. He shows a delicate respect for women, and his feelings towards them are of virgin purity. He is gentle towards his friends, all of whom have, in some way or other, experienced the kindliness of his disposition.

He possesses a rich fund of humor, and he castigates anything he despises with pungent sarcasm. Verbal communication is, unfortunately, only possible on his side; but art, science, and nature compensate him for the loss of society. He is a great admirer of Goethe, and recalls with pleasure the time he spent with him at Carlsbad (Teplitz). "I heard better then," he said in that gentle tone which, in his happy moments, is so impressive.

He is particularly fond of out-of-door life; even in the worst winter weather, he is not easily kept at home a whole day; and when spending the summer in the country, he is generally out before sunrise in Nature's blooming garden. No wonder, then, that his works are glorious like herself, and that, in the contemplation of them, we are drawn nearer to the spiritual world. He receives daily proofs from all parts of Europe, and even of America, of the recognition of his genius. He has been much troubled by the loss of all his letters during his removal from the country to town, and which was occasioned either through the carelessness or faithlessness of the person entrusted with the transport of his goods. Being so absorbed in his art, he is frequently imposed upon.

One evening when he was taking supper in a restaurant, an English naval captain, hearing the waiter mention his name, came up to him, and expressed the immense gratification which it gave him to see the man whose glorious symphonies he had listened to with pleasure even in the East Indies. The Englishman's simple, unaffected tribute of respect gave him genuine pleasure; but he dislikes merely curious visitors, for his time is very precious. His whole soul is bound up in his art, and in his nephew, Karl, to whom he is a father in the truest sense.

Beethoven's physique indicates intense strength, and his head recalls Ossian's grey-haired bards of Ullin. The portrait of him in the shops is very good. He is quick in his movements and hates slowness. His table is simply but well appointed, and he is particularly fond of game, which he considers most wholesome food. He takes wine with moderation, drinking generally only the red Austrian, as the Hungarian does not agree with him. In the winter, when he is in Vienna, he likes to look through the newspapers over a small cup of coffee in a coffee-house, to smoke a pipe, or to converse with his friends before taking his after-dinner walk. As he works far into the night, and rises very early, it often happens that he takes an hour's nap after his walk. He finds it injurious to live in a house with a northerly aspect, or exposed to strong winds, for he is very subject to rheumatism, to which he attributes his deafness. This last wet summer, which he spent at Hetzendorf, was therefore very bad for his health, and for two months he suffered intense pain in his eyes.

It is remarkable that, although deprived of the sense through means of which he works so powerfully on other minds, he can produce the softest *piano* when he sits down to his instrument, and abandon himself to his fancy. He receives a pension from the Austrian court, and although this by no means covers his expenses, he declined a tempting offer made to him at the time when the French made their ruler an emperor.

He has just finished a Mass, which he is publishing by subscription. His Imperial Highness and Eminence the Archduke Rudolph and Louis XVIII are among the subscribers. A symphony, some quartets, a Biblical oratorio, translated for him into English by the American consul from the United States, and an opera, the libretto written by Grillparzer, may be expected.

QUESTIONS

1. We know that Beethoven, as a boy, was forced by his father to "remain constantly in his room practicing." Do you know of any present-day counterpart to this circumstance? Look up some articles on Van Cliburn in the *Reader's Guide*. What were his practicing habits? What can you discover about the pianist Ruth Slenczynska?
2. Would you say Beethoven had a happy childhood? Why? How did childhood events contribute to his greatness as a composer? Could his greatness have been achieved under other circumstances? How, for example?
3. In previous centuries there seemed to be no clear-cut distinction between composers and performers; that is, one man encompassed both roles. Today these are considered separate roles. Can you name any famous contemporary performers who are also famous composers? Can you suggest what accounts for this situation?
4. Some of Beethoven's great works were composed while he was deaf. Can you suggest how it is possible for a composer to compose music when he is deaf?

COMPOSERS IN THEIR TIMES / 6

Impressionist *Impressionism is a style inspired in part by poets and painters. Taking hold as it did in the latter part of the nineteenth century, it has been variously considered: (1) the last gasps of the Romantic period; (2) a separate period that acted as a transition between the Romantic period and the Modern period; (3) the small birth-cries of the Modern period. In any case, impressionism has had many advocates who, in turn, have had many disciples. The characteristics of the style, having been embraced by many present-day composers of popular music, is still with us. Kurt Pahlen, a graduate of the University of Vienna, teacher, and writer, in the following essay, surveys the principal works of the foremost impressionist composers.*

THE IMPRESSIONISTS

KURT PAHLEN

IT WAS CLAUDE DEBUSSY WHO REPRESENTED MUSICAL impressionism in its purest form. He was born in St. Germain-en-Laye, in France, in the year 1862, and, when he was but twenty-two, won the coveted *Prix de Rome* of the Paris Conservatory. For a moment, public attention was focused on this new and officially proclaimed musical hope of France and accompanied him on his journey to the Eternal City. But the overture which he wrote there and which he submitted to the Paris jury, as was the custom, startled the learned men by its highly individual musical language. Debussy was trying to find a way beyond Wagner by the use of new sound combinations which in their boldness outdid even those of *Tristan*. And that at a time when the work of Wagner had not as yet fully penetrated French understanding! Contrary to every usage, Debussy's overture was not performed, and the young musician's name was shunted aside. Debussy removed himself more and more from the world. For a long time, this picturesque and exceptionally interesting artist lived the life of a recluse, listening to his inward voices and building up a world of tones which was his exclusively. He spent the years from 1892 to 1902 on a single creation, the greatest of his life, the musical drama *Pelléas et Mélisande,* inspired by the lyrics of Maurice Maeterlinck. This work cannot be compared with any other opera. It occupies a unique place in musico-dramatic literature. Perhaps it is the only entirely successful attempt to unite two conflicting worlds: impressionism and the theater. Not even Debussy himself made another such attempt. The other work he wrote for the stage was a sort of medieval mystery play, *The Martyrdom of St. Sebastian,* based on a text by Gabriele d'Annunzio, in which all dramatic action is supplanted by intoxicating and never-before-heard harmonies.

There is a striking similarity between Debussy's art and the ideological world of his impressionistic colleagues of the brush. Their subjects are frequently the same: delicate landscapes—lost as in a fog, clouds, and above all, and over and over again, the water to which Debussy felt mystically attracted. It returns in hundreds of forms in his music, from the spring representing the eternal leitmotif in *Pelléas et Mélisande,* the *Reflets dans l'eau,* and the *Jardins sous la pluie,* to the *Nuages,* the *Sirènes,* the age-old Breton legend of the *Cathédrale engloutie,* and finally to the superb symphonic poem *La Mer*. Again and again, Debussy

---

finds his way back to the water, inventing new tones and shadings for the mysterious element, which once had so powerfully stirred Schubert.

Symphonic art, with the constantly expanding sound possibilities of the modern orchestra, offered to Debussy's impressionism an inexhaustible field of activity. In every one of the following works, a definite picture rises before our eyes: *L'après-midi d'un faune,* written for the famous Russian dancer Nijinsky; the three Nocturnes—*Nuages, Fêtes, Sirènes*—in the last of which the composer added the mysterious effect of an inarticulate humming female chorus; *Ibéria,* full of genuine Spanish life, although the composer had never set foot on that country's soil—neither had Bizet when he wrote *Carmen,* nor the highly gifted Alexis Chabrier (1841-1894) when he composed the fiery tone poem *España*—and finally *La Mer,* the culminating point of Debussy's orchestral art, with its subdivisions: *The Sea from Sunrise to Noon, Play of the Waves,* and *Discourse between Wind and Sea.*

But also in the much more limited realm of the piano, Debussy succeeded in producing entirely new, magical sound effects, as in the *Suite Bergamesque* which contains the wonderful *Clair de lune,* the *Arabesques,* the scintillating *Préludes,* and, finally, the enchanting *Children's Corner* with its rhythmically agitated climactic *Golliwog's Cake-Walk,* in which elements of jazz are already discernible.

The application of the impressionistic style to the Lied form has been accompanied understandably by happy results. Wherever the seemingly floating melody is supported by the verses of a congenial poet, the expression of the most mature and ultimate beauty, of the most delicate coloring, and of the profoundest wisdom of life has been achieved. The new style had been conceived in the art of Duparc, Fauré, and Hahn. Debussy carried it to its ultimate conclusion in *Fêtes galantes* and *Ariettes oubliées*—cycles based on the melancholy verses of Verlaine—*Five Poems by Baudelaire,* and the *Ballads of François Villon.*

In the course of his lonely creative life, Debussy went through many stages of inward development. It seemed as if his soul were forever roaming. It finally found a resting place in a far-off cultural milieu—that of Malay and Indonesia. Not that he ever traveled there in the flesh; but Javanese and other Far-Eastern groups of musicians could be heard in Paris from time to time.

The First World War filled the hearts of all artists with horror. Debussy retired to a quiet villa at the seashore near the Spanish frontier. For days on end, he would let his gaze rest on the waters. Then again, he would start to write feverishly day and night. He, the laborious producer, was tortured by the thought that many, many works were as yet unwritten and that he would not be able to complete them. For he realized that his body was wasting away from day to day. He died in Paris, in March, 1918, while the Germans were bombarding the city.

One of the significant symptoms of modern art is that increasingly it loses its national characteristics. Just as the great cities of our century resemble each other because of a uniformly adopted style of building, so the musical styles of our era, too, quickly adapt themselves to one another. Modern technique with its railways, planes, and radio is largely responsible for that. The outer confines of musical tendencies no longer coincide with national borderlines, as was the case in the romantic century, when a clear distinction could be made between German, Italian, Polish, and Scandinavian music. The line of demarcation separating the various musical styles of the twentieth century runs between individual groups of the same country, so that, for instance, a French impressionist feels much more akin to impressionists in England, Spain, Italy, or Russia than, say, to the verists, expressionists, and neo-classicists of his own country. This development is also influenced by the fact that national characteristics, which to the romanticists were often all-important, are being eliminated by a great many composers as bases of artistic music. It will be shown, however, that these characteristics are once more essentially important in the development of budding American music.

Although it would not do to assert that Debussy had established a school, in the strict sense of the word, since he was too much of an individualist and kept too much to himself, impressionism nevertheless spread all over the world, as if it were the answer to an era's deep yearning.

Russia's contribution to impressionism was largely due to the interesting figure of Alexander Scriabin (1873-1915), but this Slav genius at the same time expanded the idea to the very limits of music itself. His inexhaustibly imaginative spirit, in which mysticism and fanaticism dwelt side by side with the characteristic melancholy and dreaminess of impressionism, was responsible for rather strange productions. *Prometheus* is generally considered his most characteristic work. In it, man is symbolized by the piano, while the orchestra represents the cosmos and a mixed chorus supplies utterances from the primordial depths of humanity. But sound effects alone did not satisfy the composer. His imagination suggested to him a blending of acoustic and visual effects.

He had a "Light and Color Piano" constructed, an instrument which, according to the tones produced, projected light and color effects on a screen. This strange instrument, widely discussed at the time, but never used again except in similar experiments made by Schönberg, plays a part in some of Scriabin's works, which are thus lifted from the realm of pure sound.

Another interesting work by Scriabin is significantly entitled *Poem of Ecstasy*. Here the composer tries to express by all the means at his command and a veritably all-consuming ecstasy that which lies slumbering in the primordial depths of existence, of the earth, and of mankind. Scriabin's piano compositions also reveal his flaming temperament. There are ten sonatas which fill the old form with an entirely new and revolutionary content, as indicated by the very titles of two of them: *The Black Mass* and *The White Mass*. For the first time, secret sciences, occultism, and magic are transposed into tone language. Of his etudes, the *Pathetic* was the one to become most widely known. Today, his works are almost forgotten, neither is there any trace of the considerable influence exerted by him on a following musical generation; on the young Stravinsky, for instance.

Let us return to France where, in the person of Maurice Ravel (1875-1937), we come face to face with not only the most remarkable of Debussy's successors but also with one of the greatest geniuses among the composers of our century. He felt drawn especially to the artistic dance, to the ballet. In partnership with the Russian choreographer, Sergei Diaghilev (1872-1929), he created a number of highly important dance poems. This renewal of a close contact between the two sister arts proved beneficial to both. It may have saved musical impressionism from the danger of ever increasing abstraction and inanimateness by supplying new impulses originating in the realm of rhythm. On the other hand, it induced the dancer to adhere more strictly to certain rules common to both arts and to discard some of the arbitrariness he had displayed for decades, if not longer, toward music, which he had come to regard as a necessary evil.

Thus came into being the enchanting ballet operas *Ma mère l'oye* and *Daphnis et Chloë*. But many others of Ravel's works were also inspired by dance rhythms, such as *La valse,* his portrait of the city of Johann Strauss, and the world-famous *Boléro* in which a simple theme, taken from Spanish folk music, is by the most ingenious use of the art of instrumentation carried from a delicate melody, in a continuous and most exciting crescendo, to a thundering climax. It is characteristic of all modern composers, children of a technical age, that they are masters in the use of the modern orchestra. Ravel was no exception, as proved by his instrumentation of Moussorgsky's *Pictures from an Exhibition.* A wealth of attractive sound effects is revealed in his opera *L'heure espagnole,* while in his many piano compositions, such as *Pavane pour une infante défunte, Valses nobles et sentimentales, Tombeau de Couperin* (an homage to the great clavecinist of the French seventeenth and eighteenth centuries), as well as in his beautiful string quartet and in his songs he continued to walk in the paths of Debussy's impressionism, although he never failed to sound a personal note of his own.

Some French composers plainly belong, at least in certain periods of their creative activity, to the impressionist school. In this group were Erik Satie (1866-1925), a man who somehow presents a connecting link with Stravinsky, and Albert Roussel (1869-1937), a pupil of Vincent d'Indy, who left to the world a number of important works: symphonies, a notable sinfonietta, chamber music, and a great many other compositions. Not least of all, there was Paul Dukas (1865-1935) who, like Debussy, wrote an opera to a text by Maeterlinck, *Ariane et Barbe-Bleu,* and, with his brilliant *Sorcerer's Apprentice,* created a truly inspired musical interpretation of Goethe's ballad as well as one of the most effective modern orchestral works.

Very close to the world of Debussy is an Englishman, Cyril Scott (1879-), whose finely conceived *Poems* for piano are comparable to some of his British contemporaries' aquarelles, with their exquisite coloring and their slightly foggy atmosphere. England! We have not spoken of music since Handel, and that is a matter of a century and a half. Mention should have been made of John Field (1782-1837), whose *Nocturnes* inspired Chopin to write his own. There are in fact some which are almost undistinguishable from those of the great Pole. But although, thanks to the orchestras, the excellent choruses, and the population's general love of music, England's part in the world's musical life never sank to the level of insignificance—proved by the fact that almost all the prominent composers of the romantic century maintained a personal contact with the British Isles—the country did not rejoin the circle of musically creative nations until the turn of the new century. Then came Edward Elgar (1857-1934) and Frederick Delius (1863-1934).

Elgar centered his attention on the large orchestra and the oratorio. For the former he wrote symphonies, symphonic poems (one of which, *Falstaff,* makes one think of Richard Strauss), and above all, the *Enigma Variations,* which has become an established item in the repertory of not only all English but also many North American orchestras. His oratorio, *The Dream of Gerontius,* a form of composition of great interest to the English ever since the days of Handel, is a fine specimen of this category.

Delius was one of the finest impressionists and one of the loneliest creators, lonelier than Debussy or Moussorgsky. To the text of Nietzsche's *Zarathustra* he composed his *Mass of Life.* Among his six operas, *A Village Romeo and Juliet* stands out especially, based on Gottfried Keller's profound novel. But he probably achieved his greatest stature in the idyllic, tender orchestral pieces inspired by nature, called *On Hearing the First Cuckoo in Spring* and *Song before Sunrise.* Ap-

palachia, a series of variations on a North American Negro song, and *Brigg Fair* must also be mentioned. Delius' life is shadowed in tragedy: he was crippled and he became blind. Despite this, the spring of melody always flowed inside him. *A Song of Summer* was written as a hymn to the sun, to light and life. How spiritually poor are men who believe that the artist must actually see and experience whatever he is to portray. The artist's world lies within himself. Self-sufficient, Delius never sought recognition from the outside world. It came to him only shortly before he died.

Elgar and Delius were not solitary figures in England's musical renaissance. They were merely outstanding composers, among a great many others of the period, from today's standpoint. There were, in the years at the turn of the century, such composers as the Irish Charles Villiers Stanford who wrote the *Irish Symphony, Irish Rhapsody,* and several operas; the Scotchman Alexander Mackenzie, who is closest to the late German romantic period and whose *Scottish Pianoforte Concerto,* sponsored by Paderewski, had a great success; the symphonies of Hubert Parry, and the successful composer Ethel Smyth who produced two operas. To write an opera in the England of those years took a large measure of courage since the chances of its being performed were negligible. That situation soon changed, however, and when we return to a consideration of English music we shall find that England has become one of the first countries in the world in the performance of music.

The homeland of Chopin gave us the impressionist Karol Szymanowski (1883-1937), whose work again bears out our contention that the music of our century has lost its national characteristics. While Chopin's music still drew its strength from his native soil, that of his successor was wholly international in its character. Like Chopin, Szymanowski spent the major part of his life outside his country. Most of his works came into being on the idyllic shores of Lake Geneva. Among them are three symphonies (one of them has a tenor solo and chorus), *Song of the Night,* a song cycle with orchestra accompaniment (the individual parts are entitled *The Siren Island, Calypso,* and *Nausikaa*), a string quartet, a great deal of chamber music, and many songs.

Ottorino Respighi (1879-1936) was the first symphonist from the land of opera. While his beautiful symphonic poems unmistakably bear the imprint of Debussy's influence, his melodies are just as unmistakably Italian. His most prominent, and at the same time most impressionistic, works are *The Pines of Rome* and *The Fountains of Rome,* veritable sound paintings depicting in all their glory and splendor the trees and fountains of the Eternal City, the brilliance of the rising sun, and the magic of the deep blue night. The voice of a bird is heard in Respighi's pines. The sweet melody rising above the soft rustle of the trees is so overwhelmingly beautiful that the listener uneasily holds his breath. No man-made instrument this, no human voice. . . . It is—every hearing makes us marvel anew at the simplicity and ingenuity of the idea—a recording of the actual voice of a nightingale. . . .

Manuel de Falla may well be called the greatest genius in the more recent musical history of Spain. True, he had absorbed many traits of Debussy and Ravel, but the essence of his style is nevertheless wholly his own. And strong though the influence of national folklore may be in his work, he has succeeded in imparting to Spanish music a fully artistic form and in raising it to an international level. In all the nervous confusion of our time and its countless stylistic experiments, Falla is a creative genius whose feet were firmly planted on the ground —the ground of his native land.

Manuel de Falla y Matheu was born in Cadiz, on November 22, 1876. His first musical impression was of a strange kind. In an old church of his home town, on every Good Friday, there was a performance of a Haydn string quartet which the Vienna master had dedicated to that house of worship for its exclusive use and to which he had given the title "The Redeemer's Seven Words on the Cross." The wonderful symmetry of the classic work, in which there was "not a single note too many, not one too few," as Falla himself expressed it, made a profound impression on him and instilled into him, subconsciously, that sense of symmetry and artistic economy which today is the possession of but a few. Of decisive importance for his artistic growth were Pedrell's instructions and the seven years of study in Paris. There he became friendly with Debussy, Dukas, Ravel, and Stravinsky and wrote his *Seven Spanish Songs.* The sketch of his piano concerto, *Nights in the Gardens of Spain,* was also completed when the outbreak of hostilities made him return to his native land. Only very slowly did he gain recognition there. The brilliant work of his youth, the ballet *La Vida breve,* has not been performed in his fatherland to this day. His way of composing was exceedingly slow, and he gave full attention to even the minutest detail. He was one of those who do an enormous amount of correcting and polishing before considering a work worthy of being released. In this manner he wrote *El amor brujo,* a ballet with vocal music, whose orgiastic-ritual *Fire Dance* is a well-known piece in today's concert music; *The Three-Cornered Hat,* based on the Corregidor theme, which the hapless Hugo Wolf had treated before him; the extraordinarily strange operatic work *El retablo de Maese Pedro,* a Don Quixote episode, in which living singers as well as marionettes are used; instrumental compositions, like the *Fantasia Baetica* or the *Cembello Concerto,* the first performance of which was given by Falla in the Pleyel Salon in Paris, a few days before that celebrated hall was turned over to a wrecking crew.

In 1939, Falla, whose sensitive artist's soul was profoundly affected by the happenings in Europe, sought peace in the New Continent and settled in the Cordoban Mountains of Argentina. But his health was so weakened that he was able to work but a few hours a day. That was not enough to finish the monumental oratorio *Atlantida,* intended as a hymn to that legendary submerged continent. A few days before he would have reached the age of seventy, Falla died in Alta Gracia, in the Argentine province of Cordoba, on November 15, 1946.

QUESTIONS

1. Is there any connection between Debussy's obvious concern with "water" music and the impressionism that characterises his work? Could you state the connection clearly?
2. Make a list of synonyms for "vague." Do you think the adjectives you have listed are suitable for describing impressionism? In what ways are they satisfactory? In what ways unsatisfactory?
3. Listen to your instructor play Scriabin's favorite chord: a dominant 13th with a flat fifth and major ninth (C F♯ B♭ E A D). How does the sound affect you? Compare and discuss this sound with that of traditional chords.
4. Listen to a piece by Debussy, and another by Ravel. Do you think these pieces could have been written by the same composer? Why? Can you recognize any difference in the musical atmosphere of these pieces? Can you describe what is mean by "musical atmosphere"?
5. If you were a music historian would you consider impressionism the end of the Romantic period or the beginning of the Modern period? Give your reasons.

COMPOSERS IN THEIR TIMES / 7

Twentieth Century *In 1940 the Second World War forced Béla Bartók (1881-1945) to leave his native Hungary and come to America to begin, as Halsey Stevens put it, "a new life in a new country." He remained in America until his death. Few composers since have remained uninfluenced by Bartók's music. Today, Bartók is recognized not only as the foremost Hungarian composer of our time, but also as a composer with unqualified international stature and respect. In the following essay Halsey Stevens, composer and teacher of composition at the University of Southern California, whose own works have been performed by the nation's major orchestras, presents an authoritative picture of Bartók's last years.*

bartók in america

HALSEY STEVENS

A FEW DAYS AFTER THEIR ARRIVAL, THE NEW Friends of Music presented the Bartóks in Town Hall, in the Sonata for Two Pianos and Percussion; three weeks later they gave a duo-piano recital there, playing the Mozart Sonata in D (K. 448), Debussy's *En blanc et noir,* four pieces from *Mikrokosmos,* two contrapuncti from *The Art of Fugue,* and the Brahms F-minor Sonata. On 25 November, Columbia University held a special convocation in the rotunda of Low Memorial Library, at which Bartók was awarded an honorary Doctor of Music degree. Degrees were granted at the same time to Dr. Karl T. Compton, president of the Massachusetts Institute of Technology; Sir Cecil Thomas Carr, English barrister; and Dr. Paul Hazard, member of the Académie Française.

> This was quite a ceremony [Bartók wrote]. As prelude, my measure had to be taken, in yards, feet, and fathoms, the details of my head, shoulder, etc., size to be sent. They dressed all of us in the university toga or cloak; then in pairs we marched solemnly in, amidst the sounding of discreet organ music. The directions were precise: when my name was called, I must stand up; when the chairman addressed me, I must take off the toga; when at last he reached the proper words, I must go up to him so that he might bestow the diploma; on my back would be hung the pink velvet ribbons of the music degree; then I could go back and sit down. That is the way it happened. Fortunately for us and for the ceremony, we didn't have to speak . . .

In conferring the degree upon Bartók, Nicholas Murray Bulter cited him as:

> . . . distinguished teacher and master; internationally recognized authority on the folk music of Hungary, Slovakia, Romania, and Arabia [*sic*]; creator through his composition of a musical style universally acknowledged to be one of the great contributions to the twentieth-century literature of music; a truly outstanding artist who has brought high distinction to the spiritual life of his country.

On 1 December Bartók left for a week in Cleveland, where there was a festive evening in the Hungarian colony, 'with gipsy music and *palotás* (!!). Hungarians here, Hungarians there, Hungarians everywhere, but we could not be very glad of this, because the second generation already uses the language only with difficulty.' Returning to New York, the Bartóks moved into a fifth-floor apartment in Forest Hills, twenty minutes from New York by subway, and began the process of

---

acclimatization before the appointment at Columbia took effect. In his letters Bartók describes the 'Americanization' of their living—'crackled-*wheat* (!)' for breakfast, the necessity of learning multitudes of new words (subway stations, names of streets), of becoming acquainted with complex transportation systems (they once spent three hours in the subway, 'traveling hither and thither in the earth; finally, our time waning and our mission incomplete, we shamefacedly slunk home—of course, entirely underground'). Their luggage, which had been taken from them in Spain on 16 October, reached New York only on Christmas Eve.

Before beginning work at Columbia University, Bartók and his wife made a transcontinental tour, playing recitals in St. Louis, Denver, Provo, San Francisco, and Seattle, and returning through Kansas City and Detroit. In some places he found the public better prepared than in 1928 to appreciate his music; in others there was only a perfunctory response. The works programmed were still mainly his own, though they were somewhat more varied than before, through the inclusion of a number of the pieces from the *Mikrokosmos;* in addition Mrs. Bartók joined him in the performance of duo-piano works.

In March he took up his appointment at Columbia. No restrictions were placed upon him in his choice of work, but Dr. Herzog suggested that he might like to investigate the large collection of records—nearly 2500 double-faced discs—made in Yugoslavia in 1934-35 by Milman Parry, professor of classical philology at Harvard University. No systematic study had been made of these materials, since the collector died shortly after his return. The great majority of the discs are devoted to the heroic epic songs of Yugoslavia; here was where Parry's interests lay, since his purpose in making the study was to discover relationships between the Homeric chants of Greece and present-day Balkan 'men's songs.' But among the others there are more than two hundred discs of Serbo-Croatian 'women's songs,' of lyrical character and musically more grateful; and it was this section that Bartók elected to prepare for publication.

Dr. Herzog placed a room at his disposal, and he worked there entirely without supervision; his time was his own. The Archives of Primitive Music (in the Department of Anthropology) duplicated the original discs to prevent damage in the transcribing process, and the Alice M. Ditson Fund made a further grant of $2500 to subsidize the publication of the study, without any claims upon the royalties which would accrue to Bartók.

Near the end of his first year as Visiting Associate in Music, Bartók described his situation in a letter to Zoltán Kodály:

It was entirely left to me what sort of work I choose to do—I have not to lecture. I chose the transcribing into musical notation of the Parry Collection—I am working now in a wing of the Columbia University, at the phonograph archive of Herzog's. The equipment is excellent. I almost feel as if I were continuing my work at the Hungarian Academy of Science, only in slightly altered conditions. Even the setting resembles its nobility. When I cross the campus in the evening, I feel as if I were passing the historic square of a European city.

Publication of the results of Bartók's study was delayed for several years. Although the preface of this book, *Serbo-Croatian Folk Songs,* is dated February 1943, it was not published until September 1951; another group of notations made during the course of his work have not yet been issued. These latter concern the heroic epic songs in the Parry Collection. Once having begun the study of these materials, Bartók was reluctant to leave it incomplete; in October 1941, as he was planning another trip to the Pacific Coast (for lectures at Palo Alto and Portland, and a conference at the University of Washington), he wrote to Mrs. Creel:

I prefer to *tell* you than to write about all our good- and mishaps (in fact a great deal of mis-, and tiny bits of good-). My intended letter was to be a very long and un-American letter—complaints and complaints (here one *must* always feel fine and excellent even if dying). The only bright spot in my work at Columbia University: studying Serbo-Croatian folk-music material from really unique records . . . But—*hélas*—this is only a temporary job and the work probably must remaine unfinished, so even there is mingled a bitter drop.

Realizing that the Columbia appointment could not be made permanent, Bartók cast about for other work. Concert engagements were difficult to obtain; for the 1941-2 season there were in prospect by late autumn only a single concert with orchestra, three duo-piano recitals, and four 'minor engagements' (solo recital or lecture). Bartók's younger son, Péter, had obtained a visitor's visa to come to the United States, but encountered difficulty in securing transit visas 'through the wild-beasts-land. But I don't know,' Bartók wrote, 'if it would not be more advisable for us to go back than for him to come over—that of course is only a vague idea.' In the meantime he was carrying on negotiations with the University of Washington, in case the Columbia appointment were not renewed; in August he wrote to Carl Paige Wood in Seattle that he hoped his appointment could be extended beyond June 1942, in which case he could come to Washington for the year 1943-4. It was not until the spring of 1942 that he was notified of a further extension of the Ditson grant, which assured him of an income until the end of December, and he notified the University of Washington that he would be available at any time thereafter.

Meanwhile the United States itself had been drawn into the war, and communication between Hungary and America was cut off. Bartók, his visitor's visa expiring, was compelled to go to Montreal and re-enter as a non-quota immigrant. Péter Bartók, somewhere between Budapest and New York, was not heard from for weeks, but finally arrived in Lisbon in February 1942. There were a few concerts, among them a two-piano recital in Chicago, about which Bartók wrote Mrs. Creel:

We plaid rather well, and got very bad criticisms. In fact, 1 was good, 1 rather lukewarm, and [a third?] as bad as I never got in my life. Just as if we were the last of the last pianists. So you see your choice of piano-teacher was a very bad one! . . .

And now the bad knews. Our situation is getting daily worse and worse. All I can say is that never in my life since I earn my livelihood (that is from my 20th year) have I been in such a dreadful situation as I will be probably very soon. To say dreadful is probably exaggerated, but not too much. Mrs. Bartók bears this very valiantly: the worse the happenings, the more energetic, confident and optimistic she is. She tries to do some work, teaching for instance. But how to get pupils or a job . . . I am rather pessimistic, I lost all confidence in people, in countries, in everything. Unfortunately, I know much better the circonstances, than Ditta does, so probably I am right in being pessimistic. Do you remember what I said just one year ago: I wonder if it is not too late (concerning war preparations). Now, I am afraid it *is* too late. And I wish only to be wrong in this my feeling . . .

Until know we had . . . two free pianos, a baby grand and an upright. Just today I got the news the upright will be taken from us. Of course we have no money to hire a second piano. So we will have no possibility to study two-piano works. And each month brings a similar blow. I am wondering and asking myself what next? With these dissonant chords, I finish my letter . . .

But Mrs. Bartók added a postscript to the same letter, saying, 'In spite of all the difficulties, I always am thankful for being here and I am thinking how sad it would be for my husband to be in his own country now . . .'

On 20 April, at the 231st Street subway station in the Bronx, Bartók unexpectedly encountered his son, who had left Budapest four months before. Although he had cabled from Lisbon, the name of his ship had been deleted by the censor. Péter Bartók's arrival was the occasion for a joyful reunion; but other events were far from reassuring. Bartók wrote to Mrs. Creel about his concern for his health,

. . . which is impaired since the beginning of April: since that time I have every day temperature elevation (of about 100°) in the evening, quite regularly and relentlessly! The doctors cann't find out the cause, and as a consequence, cann't even try a treatment. Is not that rather strange? Fortunately, I can do my work; only it may happen for instance this: in Oct. I had a lecture in New York at the Musicological Society. It was aggravated by a dinner and discussions: when I came home, I had 102.

During the whole year he was busy with his work at Columbia University, completing in October the book on Serbo-Croatian folk-songs, and also working on a collection of 2500 Romanian melodies he had amassed earlier, for which he provided an introductory study and notes in the hope of eventual publication. These works were written in English—his first work in that tongue. 'All this was a rather tiresome work (and my struggling with the English language) but very interesting indeed.'

At the end of December 1942, the appointment at Columbia was scheduled for termination, since the Ditson Fund could no longer be drawn upon for this purpose. Bartók was notified of this, and was quite naturally concerned, since the amount of the Ditson grant, small though it was, had made it possible for the Bartóks to live in reasonable security, especially when supplemented with occasional fees for concerts and lectures. Of course, such funds as might have accrued in royalties and performance fees in Hungary, together with the payments on his pension, were cut off with the entrance of the United States into the war. And with the constant threat of a physical collapse, there was cause for apprehension.

At Columbia I am 'dismissed' from Jan. 1 on. They seem to have no more money for me. This is annoying because little more than half of the work (connected with the Parry Collection) could be achieved during these 2 years; and I hate incompleteness. If it ever can be continued, Heaven only knows. But from Febr. on, I am invited to Harvard University to give there a certain number of conferences and lectures during the 1st [*sic*] semester. This gives us a respite until next fall (no possibilities with concertizing or lecturing; we have a 'unique' engagement in Jan. with the New York Philh. Society, but this is a 'family' business, the engagement was made through my friend Fritz Reiner who is guest conductor in some of these concerts. So we are living from half-year to half-year . . .

So, with my books and articles I am gradually advancing to the position of an English writer (I don't mean it seriously, of course); I never had an idea that this will be the end of my career! Otherwise, my career as a composer is as much as finished: the quasi boycott of my works by the leading orchestras continues; no performances either of old works or new ones. It is a shame—not for me of course.

On 21 January 1943, Béla and Ditta Bartók gave the first performance of his Concerto for Two Pianos (the reworked version of the Sonata for Two Pianos and Percussion) in a concert of the New York Philharmonic-Symphony Society. Fritz Reiner conducted. The audience was generally receptive, the critics antagonistic; one went so far as to wish that the concert had stopped at the intermission, so that he would not have had to hear the Concerto. It is curious to find the words 'arid and doctrinaire' applied to this glowing score, especially after the critic has acknowledged its complete sincerity, and admitted that it 'bears [Bartók's] stamp in every measure.'

This was Bartók's last public concert. During the first part of 1943, his health became conspicuously worse. In January and February there was a complete breakdown, with such weakness that he could scarcely walk from one room to another, and a temperature frequently four degrees above normal. He gave three of the scheduled lectures at Harvard, but was completely exhausted by them; and although he had had a continual series of medical examinations, without tangible result,

> . . . the Harvard people . . . persuaded me to go through another examination, led by a doctor highly appreciated by them and at their expenses. This had a certain result as an X-ray showed some trouble in the lungs which they believed to be T.B.C. and greeted with cheers and great joy: 'at last we have the real cause.' (I was less joyful at hearing these news.) I went home, was kept in bed during weeks. Then came the ASCAP which got somehow interested in my case and decided to cure me at their expenses (though I am not a member!). They sent me to their doctors who again took me to a hospital. The new X-rays, however, showed a lesser and lesser degree of lung trouble, it appears to be a very slight one indeed, and maybe not a T.B.C. at all! *It does not account for the high temperatures.* So we have the same story again, doctors don't know the real cause of my illness—and, consequently, can't treat and cure it! They are groping about as in a darkness, try desperately to invent the most extraordinary hypotheses. But all that is of no avail.

From April on there were recurrent periods of lower and higher fever; from May, pain in the joints which made walking almost impossible.

> The only thing on the credit side is that I gained 9 lb. during Apr. and May (having before the ridiculous weight of 87!). Unfortunately, the terribly oppressing New York heat in June took all my appetite, and I lost again 2 of those precious 9. —So you have a succinct picture of my ailments which makes a tedious and unexhilarating reading! —There is no hope of recovery, and it is out of the question to take anywhere a job.

The summer of 1943 was spent at Saranac Lake, in northern New York, at the expense of ASCAP. Before the Bartóks left the city, Serge Koussevitzky came to Bartók's hospital room to offer him a commission of a thousand dollars from the Koussevitzky Foundation, to write an orchestral work in memory of the late Mrs. Koussevitzky. Unknown to Bartók, the suggestion for the commission had come from Szigeti and Reiner; but the circumstances were concealed from him to prevent interpretation as a form of charity. Bartók was reluctant, even so, to accept, with the prospect of his being unable to fulfill the commission, but Koussevitzky left with him a check for half the amount, the remainder to be paid upon completion of the score, and the Bartóks left for the Adirondacks.

Until mid-August he spent his time reading, finding in the local library such things as Motteux's translation of *Don Quixote,* and being pleased because the seventeenth-century English did not give him 'particular difficulties.' As his recurrent fever abated, he found it possible to work 'practically day and night' on the work commissioned by the Koussevitzky Foundation (which he began on 15 August), and brought the score of the Concerto for Orchestra with him when he came to New York in October to hear—for the first time—a performance of his Violin Concerto. Late in November he met Yehudi Menuhin and heard him play the First Violin Sonata in his New York recital.

> He is really a great artist, he played in the same concert Bach's C-major sonata in a grand, classical style. My sonata, too, was excellently done. When there is a real great artist, then the composer's advice and help is not necessary, the performer finds his way quite well, alone. It is alltogether a happy thing that a young artist is interested in contemporary works which draw no public, and likes them, and—performs them *comme il faut.*

Under the sponsorship of ASCAP, Bartók was sent—alone—to Asheville, North Carolina, for the winter of 1943-4, his wife and son remaining in New York. In the meantime, arrangements had been made by Victor Bátor with Columbia University for a resumption of Bartók's appointment there for another six months, with funds partially collected by Joseph Szigeti through solicitation of musical organizations, recording companies, and individuals. But again the details were kept secret from Bartók, who would have felt obliged to decline the appointment as a charity measure. The work was to be done between April and December 1944; Bartók hoped that his Serbo-Croatian study would be published during that period as well. He had given up hope of being able to publish the Romanian and Turkish material, and after the breakdown of negotiations with the New York Public Library, he deposited the manuscripts at Columbia University: 'there they are available to those few persons (very few indeed) who may be interested in them.'

In Asheville, the apparent improvement in his health continued.

> At present I feel in the best of health, no fever, my strength has returned, I take fine walks in the woods and mountains—actually I climb the mountain (of course only with due caution. In March my weight was 87 pounds; now it is 105. I grow fat. I bulge. I explode. You will not recognize me.

With his renewed strength—to which he attributed his ability to complete the Koussevitzky commission 'or vice versa'—Bartók wrote during his Asheville sojourn a Sonata for Solo Violin, commissioned by Menuhin and completed on 14 March 1944. This was the last original score he was to finish. In the same winter he also busied himself with arranging and writing out fair copies of 2000 Walachian folksong texts, about which he wrote to Szigeti:

> I believe that many interesting things will turn up in this . . . For example, that for the girl it is a much greater misfortune to be jilted than for the boy. This of course we knew before, but now it can be proved in black and white with

statistical facts. Further, that girls (or women) are so much more vehement, more wrathful; there are many more texts about girls cursing faithless boys than vice versa. These cursing texts, incidentally, are exceedingly singular: what a Shakespearean fantasy is manifested in them, quite prodigious. Sorry that I can't quote from the Walachian, since you do not understand it. But we Magyars have an abundance of that kind, for example:

May thirteen apothecary's shelves
Empty themselves in thee;
May nine cartloads of hay and straw
Rot in thy bed;
May thy towel throw out flames,
Thy washing water turn to blood.

Or even:

May God smite thee with bread bought with money,
With bread bought with money, and a whore for a wife.

Bread bought with money—this the urban Americans would not understand, for doesn't everyone buy his bread? Quite so, but not the small-propertied peasant: he grows the wheat himself, bakes his own bread, and if the frost has struck his crops, then he has to buy his bread with money, but where does he get the money? . . .

And so these are the things that occupy me now—and I await the end of my exile.

Other things occupied him as well. There was so far little progress to show in the European war, and Bartók was depressed to see the entire civilization he had known still in peril of destruction.

But what most worries me is this lagging and slow procedure on the 'battlefields.' There is no end in sight—and the destroying of Europe (people and works of art) continues without respite and mercy. Personally, I do not know how long I can endure the insecurity of this gipsy life. (But for 1944, at least, my living expenses are secured, no worry about that.) And the destiny of poor Hungary, with the Russian danger in the background—the prospects of the future are rather dark.

During all this time he could learn nothing of his family in Hungary—his son Béla and his wife, his sister Elza and her family; nor of the many friends he had left there, the Kodálys and all the rest. Péter Bartók, having passed his regents' examinations in New York, remained there for a time, but in February 1944 enlisted in the United States Navy and was stationed in Panama, after a six months' training course. And the promise of continued improvement in Bartók's health was not fulfilled:

You said in one of your letters that my recovering was a miracle. This is true only with some reservations: it was only a hemisemidemi-miracle. Of course, that lung-infection disappeared as mysteriously as it came. . . . There are, however—and almost continuously—some minor troubles which probably never can be completely cured and make a regular job or concertizing etc. impossible for me. So for instance, last April my spleen became rebellious. My Asheville doctor mistook it for a pleuresy. He would have quite gallantly treated me against it, but fortunately I had to come back to New York where the mistake was at once discovered, and my spleen punished by a rude X-ray treatment. Then it appeared there is a disorder in my blood-picture, so they poisoned me with arsenic. Shall I continue? I think better not.

A few weeks ago I said, 'Tell me, doctor, exactly what my ailment is! Choose a nice Latin or Greek word and tell me.' After a moment's hesitation he emitted: 'Polycithemia.' There we are again! Only, 2 years ago this meant too many red corpuscles, and now it means too many white ones.

Even with these difficulties, Bartók felt that he could by exercising care still do some work at home, teaching; but there were only occasional pupils, some who had studied with him in Budapest and came to him for a few lessons when they were in New York: among them were Dorothy Parrish Domonkos and Agnes Butcher. The Bartóks' apartment—at 309 West 57th Street in New York, a few blocks from Carnegie Hall—was too small, but with the shortage of housing they felt fortunate to have found even these two rooms.

In November 1944, Menuhin played the Sonata for Solo Violin in his New York recital. Bartók was present and was brought to the stage to acknowledge the applause of an audience that filled the hall to overflowing. The critics had little good to say about the work. Olin Downes reported the enthusiasm of the audience, which 'must have been rewarding to Mr. Bartók, who has had his share of the difficulties of the radical innovator'; but found the work itself 'a test for the ears, the intelligence, the receptiveness of the most learned listener . . . On initial acquaintance, we take none too kindly to the piece.' But Bartók himself was of another opinion:

It was a wonderful performance. [The Sonata] has 4 movements and lasts *ca.* 20 minutes. I was afraid it is too long; imagine: listen to a single violin during 20 minutes. But it was quite all right, at least for me.

A few days later Bartók was present for another triumph: the first performance of the Concerto for Orchestra, which Koussevitzky and the Boston Symphony played on 1 and 2 December.

We went there for the rehearsals and performances—after having obtained the grudgingly granted permission of my doctor for this trip. It was worth while, the performance was excellent. Koussevitzky is very enthusiastic about the piece, and says it is 'the best orchestra piece of the last 25 years' (including the works of his idol Shostakovich!).

This, the largest of Bartók's mature orchestra works, was to play a significant role in at last bringing his music to the eminence it now occupies. In 1948-9, American symphony orchestras played Bartók's music more frequently than that of any other composer of the twentieth century except Strauss and Prokofiev. In that season, American orchestras gave fifty-six performances of eight works by Bartók; there were more performances of Bartók than of such earlier composers as Berlioz, Liszt, Dvořák, Schubert, or Mahler; the level has remained nearly as high in the years since. Side by side with this, and with the cyclical performances of the six string quartets which contributed to the understanding of Bartók's work, came performances of *Duke Bluebeard's Castle, The Wonderful Mandarin,* and the first American performance of the *Cantata profana.* Simultaneously, the demand for his music has led to the recording of almost all the larger works and many of the smaller ones, and the reprinting of most of the out-of-print scores. From being one of the least accessible of twentieth-century composers, Bartók has become one of the best known.

At the end of 1944, Bartók wrote to Mrs. Creel that he was assured of a 'modest living' for the next three years. During that year he had received about $1400 in royalties and performance fees in the United States and Great Britain, as well as some other income; and he had just signed an agreement with Boosey and Hawkes which called for an advance of $1400 annually for the next three years in addition to income from sale and performance. ASCAP was still assuming responsibility for medical expenses.

In December 1944, Ralph Hawkes commissioned a seventh string quartet from Bartók; the following February, at Hawkes's instigation, William Primrose asked him for a viola concerto. Bartók was reluctant to undertake the latter.

> He showed no great enthusiasm [Primrose wrote]; rather he seemed doubtful as to the success of such an undertaking on his part. As he was anxious to get some idea of the technical capacity of the viola [as a solo instrument], we arranged that he should attend a performance of the Walton Viola Concerto which I was to give the following week . . . Unfortunately he was too ill to attend this performance, but he listened to it over the air . . .

There was also a commission for a duo-piano concerto for Bartlett and Robertson; from almost complete obsurity, almost complete neglect on the part of performers, Bartók had suddenly become sought after. Had there been time, a whole series of major works was in prospect. But in March he became ill with pneumonia; thanks to recently-developed antibiotics, this was quickly conquered. Yehudi Menuhin invited the Bartóks to spend the summer in California, and Bartók, with his doctor's approval, gladly accepted, planning to leave New York in mid-June. Early in June, however, he had to write to Menuhin:

> Regretfully I must tell you that we cannot come to California! I am not feeling very well, and—owing to a variety of things—now my wife has been ill for

several weeks and has still not recovered. The whole thing is that we are afraid of such a long journey, which, especially, now, would be attended by all kinds of inconvenience. I hardly know how to say how sorry I am. I had so many plans for music in connection with my sojourn there. Now these have turned to naught . . . We must try next winter somewhere to talk about the final form of the Solo Sonata; the matter is not urgent . . .

Instead of California, the Bartóks went back to Saranac Lake. There at last they received news from Hungary. Zoltán and Emma Kodály were well, though they had lost their home and possessions; Bartók's son Béla and his wife, and his sister Elza and her family, had escaped. Both copies of his thirteen years' work of folksong notation had survived, carefully hidden; his own household goods were almost unscathed. But the situation of the country itself was far from reassuring.

More harm—at least spiritually—was done by the extremely bad news about Hungary. Direct news did not arrive . . . But there are regularly reprinted Budapest newspaper (each copy coming probably through the Russian embassy and reprinted in facsimile by a Hungarian language communist newspaper in N. Y.) There we read about Kodály and other musicians, artists, who seem to be (comparatively) well. Dohnányi is a 'war-criminal'! However, so much damage has been done to the country that Heaven knows if and when it can again somehow recover. The Germans were beasts, but the Russians do not seem to be saints, too.

But the summer was not without its rewards. Péter Bartók was discharged from the Navy and returned to the United States in August, stopping in New York and then going on to Saranac Lake to be with his parents. And Bartók found pleasure in the out-of-doors, watching the 'chickmucks' and calculating the number of vibrations per second of the wings of hummingbirds ('My result is about 90 or 100').

During the summer another commission was proffered; Bartók announced it cryptically: 'A turtle wants to order a 5-minute orchestral work from me. . . . Only it's too bad that the turtle makes no sound, so that it could be worked into the piece.' This is another instance of Bartók's punning: the 'turtle' was Nat Shilkret (*Schildkröte* is the German word for turtle), and the proposal was that Bartók collaborate in the musical symposium called *Genesis,* which ultimately brought together separate movements by such strange bedfellows as Schönberg, Stravinsky, Milhaud, Toch, and Shilkret himself. But Bartók could not agree to undertake the composition of such a work for a year, and in addition, because of his commitment to Boosey and Hawkes found participation in the project beset by complications. In the end (Bartók wrote), 'The turtle proved obstinate, he will do nothing at all.'

As for the summer's composition, Bartók divided his waning energies between the Viola Concerto, intended for William Primrose, and a new—and uncommissioned—Piano Concerto. It had been many years since he had worked simultaneously on two major scores; now his desperate activity seems to have been prompted by a realization of the gravity of his illness. On 8 September he wrote to Primrose:

> I am very glad to be able to tell you that your Viola Concerto is ready in draft, so that only the score has to be written, which means a purely mechanical work, so to speak. If nothing happens I can be through in 5 or 6 weeks, that is, I can send you a copy of the orchestral score in the second half of October, and a few weeks afterwards a copy (or if you wish more copies) of the piano score.
>
> Many interesting problems arose in composing this work. The orchestration will be rather transparent, more transparent than in the Violin Concerto. Also the sombre, more masculine character of your instrument executed some influence on the general character of the work. The highest note I use is 'A,' but I exploit rather frequently the lower registers. It is conceived in a rather virtuoso style. Most pobably some passages will prove to be uncomfortable or unplayable. These we will discuss later, according to your observations.

The Viola Concerto was destined to remain unfinished. When Tibor Serly saw him on the evening of 21 September Bartók was working on the orchestral score of the Third Piano Concerto; Péter Bartók had drawn the measure bars for him, and with the manuscript scattered over his bed he was struggling to fill in the last few measures. Other manuscript pages under a clutter of medicine bottles proved to be the Viola Concerto, the completion of which, Bartók told Serly, was a matter of working out details and scoring. The next day he was taken from the tiny apartment on 57th Street to the West Side Hospital. There, on 26 September, Béla Bartók died.

After the last bar of the Third Piano Concerto, Bartók had written—prematurely—the Hungarian word *vége,* the end. For Bartók the man, this *was* the end: an end such as no man would wish for, in a strange land, far from home, family, friends, all that meant so much to him.

But for Bartók the composer, this was by no means an end. It is callous to say, as some have said, that recognition waited only for his death. Such a point of view implies the half-truth that a great artist creates only for the future, not for his own time. But Bartók created for his own time: the essence of that time is in his music, and there were many who during his life heard it with understanding and keenly perceptive enjoyment. It is tragic that Bartók could not have benefited from the wider acceptance he was able to foresee; when he stood upon the stage of Carnegie Hall on 26 November 1944, acknowledging wave upon wave of applause for a 'difficult' work, and when, a week afterward, he heard the tumultuous reception of his Concerto for Orchestra in Boston, he knew that he had written—and written well—for his own time and for the future as well. In the years since, with increasing opportunity to know Bartók's music, audiences everywhere have come to realize that here is a colossus among men. And in that sense, there is no longer *vége,* the end, but only *kezdete,* the beginning.

QUESTIONS

1. Can you suggest reasons why Bartók had such difficulty in America earning enough money to live on? Do you think what happened to Bartók in 1940 could happen today? Discuss your reasons.
2. Do you think the public ought to distinguish between a man's position as a creative artist and his political beliefs? Would you buy a ticket to a concert of a great pianist, violinist, or conductor if you knew he had been a Nazi or a Fascist in a war against the United States? Give your reasons.
3. In 1940 Bartók's musical compositions were relatively unknown in the United States. Yet today many of his works are recorded and in the standard repertory. Can you suggest reasons for this change?
4. Listen to any composition by Bartók. Do you hear anything that sounds like folk music? How can you tell? Give your reasons.
5. Bartók has been called a Hungarian composer. What makes a man a "Hungarian" composer? a French composer? an American composer? an "international" composer? Discuss this question and give your reasons.

MUSIC OF SHOW BUSINESS / 1

Leonard Bernstein's talent and imagination have brought him to the highest places in at least two musical worlds—the world of the Broadway musical, and the world of the concert stage. His fame on Broadway (to take these worlds alphabetically) has been solidly established by On the Town, *his first successful show, and* West Side Story, *his best. His serious work includes the* Jeremiah *Symphony and the one-act opera,* Trouble in Tahiti. *Bernstein dislikes being called versatile, but, call it what you will, he has further distinguished himself as the permanent conductor of the New York Philharmonic Orchestra and as a popular television music educator without peer. This last distinction, together with his magnetic appeal and his engaging appearance, has given him a reknown usually reserved for home-run kings and movie stars. In his essay he referees a bout between Broadway and the classics.*

Whatever Happened to That ☆Great American Symphony?☆

LEONARD BERNSTEIN

(*The following, not properly a conversation, is an exchange of documents between L. B. and Broadway Producer, henceforth known as B. P., a man who interests himself, curiously enough, in some facets of art generally unknown to his calling. A born gentleman of average producer height; chin framed by a luxurious Persian-lamb collar which adorns his fifty-per-cent-cashmere evening coat; a man with an emerald tie pin and a wise, sweaty look—a man, in short, who carries his five feet two with pride and power.*)

I. Via Western Union

B.P.
HOTEL GORBEDUC
NEW YORK
VERY SORRY CANNOT ACCEPT KIND OFFER SHOW BASED BURTON'S ANATOMY MELANCHOLY SPLENDID IDEA WISH YOU ALL LUCK WITH IT REGRET UNABLE BUT DEEPLY INVOLVED WRITING NEW SYMPHONY GREETINGS

L.B.

II. Via Post

L.B.
Steinway Hall
New York City
Dear L.B.:

My associates and I were very much disappointed to receive your refusal by wire yesterday of our offer to collaborate with us, and with many other artists of outstanding merit and importance, on our new project for this season. I have long felt (and now feel corroborated by my associates in that opinion) that Burton's *Anatomy of Melancholy* would one day serve as the basis of a great work in the musical theater. We think that you are just the man to write the music for it, thereby enriching our stage which this season cries for such a work. Instead you tell us that you are writing a new symphony, a commendable enough

---

WHATEVER HAPPENED TO THAT GREAT AMERICAN SYMPHONY? from *The Joy of Music* by Leonard Bernstein; copyright 1954, 1959 by Leonard Bernstein. Reprinted by permission of Simon and Schuster, Inc.

enterprise. But if you will allow me to take a few minutes of your time, I should like to point out a few facts which you may not have taken into account in making your decision.

I begin with a question: why? Why continue to write symphonies in America for a public which does not care one way or the other about them? Can you honestly name me two or three people in all America who actually *care* whether you or anybody else ever writes another symphony or not? Do not answer this too hastily, or too defensively. The more you consider the question, the clearer will come the answer: that nobody, with the possible exception of some other composers and some critics who live by denouncing or flattering new works, will be any the sorrier if you or any of your symphonic colleagues never writes a symphony again. There seems to me to be no historical necessity for symphonies in our time: perhaps our age does not express itself truly through the symphonic form; I really am not in a position to know. I am a simple man, and know mainly through intuition whatever it is I know. I think I have my fingers on the pulse of the people, and believe me, L.B., it is not a symphonic pulse that I feel.

So there you are, writing music for which there is no historical necessity, probably; for which there is no public demand, certainly; and from which, if you will pardon me, there is no economic gain. Perhaps now you can see more clearly why I asked: why? Now let me ask: why not? Why not give of your talents to that sector of musical art in America where there is hot, live, young blood—the theater? Here you will find the public waiting for you, and you will be complying with the demands of history. All art, in all times, I believe, has been created to meet a public or private demand, whether it be the art of building Gothic cathedrals, or of painting the portrait of a wealthy patron, or of writing a play for the Elizabethan public, or of composing a Mass. Or, if you will again pardon me, the art of writing a symphony. Haydn and Mozart and Brahms surely didn't write their symphonies in a vacuum; their symphonies were expected of them. Nobody today really *expects* a symphony of anybody. Our American composers have an obligation to the theater, which is alive and which needs them. Won't you think seriously about it again?

Faithfully,
B.P.

P.S. How had you planned for this new symphony to feed, clothe and house your charming wife and baby (to whom warmest personal regards)?

III. Via Post

B.P.
Hotel Gorbeduc
New York City
Dear B.P.:

I have read and reread your most interesting letter of yesterday, and I am impressed. I say *impressed* rather than *convinced,* since I cannot honestly report a change of heart as a result. But I have rarely met a producer operating in the Broadway area who has given so much sincere and deeply felt thought to a situation which basically does not concern his immediate livelihood. I am further impressed with your legal style, which is persuasive to a point where, if I were not more closely acquainted than you with the facts of the case (which is only natural), I might yield to your arguments. But the facts stand, and I feel obliged to report them to you.

There has never in history, by statistical record, been so great an interest in the symphony and in the symphony orchestra as is at this moment manifested in the United States. There are orchestras everywhere, in every small city, in every university and high school, in even some of our most provincial areas. How can you speak of "no public demand" when the latest figures of the League of Symphony Orchestras shows xx orchestras of major proportions now operating in the United States, as against xx orchestras of similar size in 19xx? The League further reports xx orchestras of smaller proportions now professionally active. Everywhere there have arisen festivals to which the public flocks in unprecedented numbers—and they are festivals which emphasize contemporary music almost as much as the standard repertory. Summer concerts have become as great an attraction as canoeing once was; and the winter seasons of our major orchestras are enjoying a lively increase in both attendance and interest. Community concert services send out great numbers of artists to cities large and small from coast to coast, where they are heard by audiences that a decade ago would not have dreamed of attending a concert.

I am sorry to bore you with statistics this way, but these facts are a matter of record. And think of all the new works being commissioned by such agencies as the Louisville Orchestra. xx works this year alone! And then think of the prizes, fellowships, awards of various kinds, all of which encourage the writing of concert music. Think of the enormous increase in the sale of records: why, it amounts almost to a craze. No, you cannot say that the public is indifferent to concert music. As to your reference to historical necessity, I simply do not understand you. And when you speak of economic gain, you are right; but economic considerations cannot enter into this area. One is an artist by necessity, and there are other ways of making money.

As you know, I love to write for the theater: I have done it before, and hope to do it often again. But this is a moment when other things come first. Thank you again for having asked me and for having taken the trouble to write.

Sincerely,
L.B.

IV. Via Post

L.B.
Yaddo [An artist's retreat]
Saratoga Springs, New York
Dear L.B.:

Forgive me for breaking into your privacy again, but in the week that has elapsed since I received your letter I have given a lot of thought to the subject we have been discussing, and have even done some reading to back me up. Besides, your letter was so incredibly solemn, and, were it not for its obvious sincerity, so *dull*, if you will pardon me, that I am intrigued. I cannot believe that a young fellow like you, grown up in America, with the sense of fun that you have exhibited in some of your works, can possibly be such a fuddy-duddy. This letter is written partly to find out, and partly to acquaint you with my more recent thoughts about the symphonic form. I have given up the idea of trying to persuade you to do our show with us, and we are now negotiating with another composer. But you have awakened in me, by your refusal and your reasons for refusing, a real interest in this whole subject. I now have what might almost be called a theory. I explained it yesterday to our mutual friend P., who was in town for a day, and he found it silly. But what can you expect of a poet? As you know, he is also up at Yaddo for a month, working on his new volume, *Greaves of Brass*, and that's how I knew where to write you. Please avoid discussing my theory with him when you see him; his sense of historical necessity is appalling, if I can judge by the two poems from *Greaves of Brass* that he showed me yesterday.

Well, then, the theory. All music must begin in the theater, historically speaking. Does that amaze you? Just think about it. The origins of music are mostly folklore, comprising songs and dances of prayer, of work, of celebration, of love. This means that music first arises attached to words and ideas. There is no folk music, to my knowledge, that is abstract. It is music for working to, or for dancing to, or for singing words to. It is always *about* something. Then, as it develops, music becomes more sophisticated, more complicated; but it is still attached to concepts, as it is in the theater. Where music really grew up was in the church, wasn't it? The greatest theater of them all! (If ever there was theater music in the truest and best sense it was simple plain-chant.) Now we find little operas beginning to emerge, in Italy and in Germany and in Austria. The little operas (or masques, or singspiels, or whatever they were) become bigger operas—and we have Mozart. While in the church, little motets have grown into large requiems and cantatas. Now is the moment when the big switch can happen, and not until this moment. Now musical idioms have become familiar; and the procedures of Western music are enough alike so that the music can be *separated* from the words or the ideas or the concepts—that is, from the theater—and can exist for the audience in its own right. Now that there is a Mozart opera, there can also be a Mozart symphony. (But never forget that the symphony, as my books tell me, came from the opera overture!) And now that there are Bach Passions, there can also be Bach preludes and fugues. (But remember that the preludes and fugues were first of all reverie-pieces used in the church service!) In short, the audiences had grown up *with* the music in the theater, and had reached the point where they could relate to the music *without* the theater. Their ears were ready for abstract sound: F-sharps and E-flats had become in themselves interesting and moving, without benefit of words to tell why they ought to be. But it had taken the audience a long time to reach this point.

Does all this sound like nonsense to you? I hope not: I'm banking on that solemnity of yours. But now to the meat of the theory.

The point I want to make with all my might is that America right now seems to me to be, musically, just about where Germany was around the seventeenth century. Deep in the singspiel. (We mustn't talk about present-day church music: that must be traditional, and has all been inherited.) But our secular music is just about where German music was fifty years before Mozart. Only *our* singspiels are called *Oklahoma!* and *Can-Can*. This is a period we must pass through before we can arrive at a real American symphonic form, or a real American style of whatever kind of concert music. It may not be the symphony as we have known it: we may produce something very different. But the musical language it will speak must first be created in our theater; then one day it can be divorced from "meaning" and stand alone, abstract. Do you see what I mean? For all our technical mastery and sophistication we are not really ready yet to produce our own concert music. As a result, all the stuff that is being turned out by the mile every day for concert performance in American halls is really European, and *old* European at that, with perhaps some American spice added by way of cowboy tunes or blues harmonies or jazz rhythms. But the music remains essentially European, because the whole notion of the symphonic form is a German notion, and don't let anybody tell you anything else. All the Russian symphonies are really German ones with vodka substituted for beer; and Franck's is German with some cornets making the difference; and Liszt's are German with nothing making the difference, and so are Elgar's and Grieg's and Dvořák's. Whatever national touches have been added, it's all German deep down, because the line of the symphony is a straight one smack from Mozart to Mahler.

Now here we are, remember, a brand-new country, comparatively speaking, a baby only a hundred and seventy-five years old. Which is nothing at all when you think of the old empires that produced that straight line I just mentioned. And actually we have been writing music in this country for only fifty years, and half of that fifty years the music has been borrowed clean out of the pockets of Brahms and Company. Of course we have the disadvantage here of having been born already grown up, so we don't start with folk dances and prayers for rain. We started with the leavings of the European development, handed to us on an old cracked dish. But then, we have an advantage after all: we have jazz. Which is the beginning of some other straight line which will grow here as certainly as the symphonic line grew out of another folk-strain for about a hundred years in Germany. Whatever jazz is, it's our own folk music, naïve, sophisticated, and exciting. And out of it has been born something we call the musical comedy. Well, 175 years isn't very long for that to have happened (and it really took only the last fifty years) compared to the centuries it took for the singspiel to arrive. And here we are at the point of building that singspiel into real opera—or, in our terms, developing *Pal Joey* into whatever American music is going to become. We are all ready and waiting for the Mozart to come along and just simply do it. That's why I'm in the producing business: I want to be there when it happens, if I live that long. I'm taking bids on the new Mozart. Any comers?

Well, there you have it. Very rough, not really thought out, but as plain as day to me. What I would love to make plain as day to you is the difference that arises out of all this between Europe and America as they relate to concert music. A new Brahms symphony to a Viennese of that period was of consuming interest to him: it caused endless speculation about what it would turn out to be, how it would differ from the last one, and all the rest, just as we speculate now about a forthcoming Rodgers-Hammerstein show. It made table-talk the next morning; it was everybody's concern; it was part of daily living, the air breathed, food taken. As a result, the Viennese or German of today has inherited some of that possessiveness about the Brahms music: it is almost as though he had written it himself. The same is true of the relation between Italians and Italian opera. But in America the listener cannot share these feelings, no matter how wildly he loves the music of Brahms or Verdi, and no matter how much talk he makes about music being a universal language. There will always be the element of the museum about this repertory for him—the revered classic, always slightly remote. It can never be his private property, so to speak. And since he doesn't give a damn about whether anyone is writing new symphonies or not, there is no real vitality for him in our concert life, except the vitality of a visit to the museum. Q.E.D.

This has been a really long one, and I hope you will forgive my going on and on. But I was excited about this when it occurred to me and I wanted you to hear it all right away, even if you are trying to write that long, useless piece up there in your retreat. My best to P., and whatever you do don't let him talk you into setting *Greaves of Brass* to music. You're being abstract now, remember: you're committed.

Faithfully,
B.P.

V. Via Air Mail

B.P.
Hotel Gorbeduc
New York City
Dear B.P.:

It is a month since I had your last long, astonishing letter, and I apologize for my lateness in answering; but I have been to Yaddo and back to New York and then here to Milan all rather quickly. I had to suspend work on my symphony temporarily to fill this engagement conducting at La Scala, and now that the rehearsals and first performance are over I finally have a chance to answer you.

I must admit that I see to some extent what you mean about the sense of possessiveness toward music. Here in Milan people are still spending their time and energy at parties and luncheons arguing loudly about which is the greater opera, *Rigoletto* or *Trovatore*. As though it had all been written yesterday, hot off the presses. These Italians (or at least these Milanese) really own that music; and as you say, they seem to think they have written it all themselves. And you are right when you say that the wildest music-lover in the States can never relate that closely and familiarly to the same music. I am reminded of people at similar parties and luncheons in New York who will talk for hours about the relative merits of two hit musical shows, and even get excited or angry or hurt as they attack or defend them. All that part of your letter is perfectly true.

But I must take issue with your historical survey. It all sounds so easy and slick as you put it; and I admire you enormously for going into books and digging out all those facts and making them into ideas. Perhaps your main idea has some validity, but there are remarkable holes in your reasoning. What of the Frescobaldi *ricercare,* and the whole seventeenth-century school of organ music? What of Froberger and Pachelbel, who preceded Bach? Oh, all right, I'm being solemn and dull again, and I won't go into a lot of boring musicology. But you don't say the most obvious fact: that even if America is now in a period analogous to the singspiel period in Germany, she is at the same time equipped with the foreknowledge of the next 250 years. What a difference that makes, after all! Don't you see that the greatest development of German music was dependent on its very naïveté in its early stages? American composers can never be that naïve now, writing as they are after the world has already known Mozart and Strauss and Debussy and Schönberg. Perhaps they are condemned after all to be epigonous, and to follow in the line handed them by an already overdeveloped Europe. It may not be so exciting to compose now as it must have been in 1850; perhaps this is all very sad, but perhaps it is true. And anyway, what would you have all these serious American composers do? Go *en masse* into the shoe business? They are writing out of some sort of inner necessity, so there must be a real validity to it, whether or not it is explainable by your new theory.

I have a matinee today and so I must leave this and run to the theater. How is your show coming? Have you found a composer yet? I wish you luck and hope that whoever finally writes it will turn out to be your Mozart, in spades.

Sincerely,
L.B.

VI. Via Transatlantic Cable

L.B.
SCALA
MILANO
SHOE BUSINESS GOOD IDEA LETTER FOLLOWS GREETINGS

B.P.

VII. Via Air Mail

Teatro alla Scala
Milano, Italy
Dear L.B.:

Hooray! You are a dead duck! You have obviously been convinced of my theory, and that makes me very happy. Your letter clearly shows that you have no real, sensible rebuttal. Of course what I said was full of holes; what do you expect from a brand-new musicologist? What do I know about Pachelbel and Frescobaldi and that other guy? But what I know I know on all twelves, and at this point I am more certain than ever that I am right. Why, I went to the Philharmonic concert the other night, just to see what is happening in your thrilling concert world. There were empty seats everywhere. People were sleeping on all sides, some noisily, and I do not exclude one or two critics. It was all as dull as it could be, and the applause was polite and seemed intended more as something to start people's circulation going again after their nap than approval of the music. Dull, dull, dull! After the concert the audience shuffled out in a stupor, not talking much about it or about anything; and I shuffled to Sardi's for a double stinger. It was like waking up. The theater, the theater, on all sides: people arguing, recalling scenes and jokes with gales of laughter, people singing snatches of tunes to each other to prove some point, everyone alive. Alive, I tell you!

Sure, there are some American composers who will have to go on writing their symphonies which may get heard twice with indifference. They may even be geniuses. I wish them all the luck in the world, and I hope they make it. But I have a sneaky feeling that they will continue to do symphonies because they *can't* do music for the theater. Don't think it is so easy to be a theater composer! In some ways it's harder: there is a discipline of the stage. You're not your own boss; it is the whole work that counts. A composer of symphonies has all the notes in the rainbow before him: he can choose as he wishes; not the theater composer. He really has to *work!* A great theater composer is a rare thing: he must have the sense of timing of a Duse, a sense of when to go easy and when to lay it on, a preknowledge of what the audience will feel every second of the work. He must have lightness and weight, wit and sentiment, pathos and brilliance. He must know his craft and everyone else's as well. Don't disparage him. I listened to *Tosca* the other day, and what a wallop it gave me! That man knew theater. And that man does not exactly languish in dishonor.

I tell you again: what is alive and young and throbbing with historic current in America is musical theater. And I tell you another thing:

you know it as well as I do! You know in your heart that the real pieces of importance and interest to America now are not X's Fourteenth Symphony and Y's Flute Soliloquy, but *Finian's Rainbow* and *Carousel* and maybe even *Wonderful Town,* though I doubt it, and *South Pacific.* And all your long lists of dead statistics and all your Pachelbels put together cannot make you feel otherwise.

I want to thank you for giving me the push to go out and investigate all this stuff. I have never been so glad or so proud to be a producer of musical theater on Broadway. We are going ahead with our show at full speed, as soon as we find the right composer, and I can't wait to begin. I want to be part of this big new line that is forming to the right in the musical history of America, and I want to watch it take its place in the musical history of the world.

Faithfully,
B.P.

VIII. Via Transatlantic Cable

B.P.
HOTEL GORBEDUC
NEW YORK
PLANS CHANGED HAVE DECIDED ACCEPT YOUR SHOW STILL DISAGREE HEARTILY YOUR THEORY HOME NEXT WEEK WARMEST REGARDS

L.B.

QUESTIONS

1. Can you name any composers, in addition to Leonard Bernstein, capable of writing both a symphony and a musical comedy score? Can you suggest the kind of training and experience necessary to this combination?
2. Do you agree with the statement, "There seems to be no historical necessity for symphonies in our time?" Give your reasons. Do you believe there is, in our time, a historical necessity for musical comedies? What, exactly, is "historical necessity?"
3. If Richard Rodgers is essentially a composer of Broadway musicals, why was he selected to compose the music for the TV documentary *Victory at Sea?* Do you think he needed the money? the prestige? Suggest reasons why Rodgers accepted the assignment.

4. Look up the names of Vladimir Dukelsky, Kurt Weill, and Gunther Schuller. What are their accomplishments? What do these men have in common?
5. What is Bernstein's point in making up these letters? Is there any special significance in having one of the writers be a Broadway producer? Are the questions Bernstein poses controversial? If a composer could earn a good living composing symphonies would B.P. still have an argument with L.B.? Discuss these questions.

MUSIC OF SHOW BUSINESS / 2

Jazz is the comprehensive name for a variety of specific musical styles: New Orleans style, Pre-Swing, Swing, Bop, Cool, Thirdstream, and such regional, self-styled types as Chicago jazz, Kansas City jazz, and West Coast jazz. Jazz is a way of playing, a manner of performance. It is not characterized by song titles. There is no jazz unless there is an attempt by the jazzman at creative improvization; and the quality of the jazz then produced is determined by the degree of creativity. For this reason, there is jazz that is great or mediocre or poor—categories that may also be found in classical music. The jazzman attempts to improvise on a theme that may be melodic, harmonic, rhythmic, or any combination of these. In the following essay from The Anatomy of Jazz, *the author discusses early jazz criticism and its effect on the general reader.*

jazz: some early difficulties

LEROY OSTRANSKY

AS RECENTLY AS TEN YEARS AGO, TECHNICAL jazz analysis had been given little serious or systematic thought. The prime reason for this lack of thoughtful analysis may be found in the analyses and evaluations made by jazz writers who apparently had difficulty in making themselves understood. The language of jazz was coined, for the most part, by jazz musicians with little regard for the written word, or by well-meaning writers with little technical knowledge of music in general, or—and worst of all—by a small but influential school of semiliterate enthusiasts whose main interest seemed to lie not in furthering jazz itself, but in merchandising the adjuncts of jazz: records, horns, bop berets, and tired stock arrangements. Aimed at adolescents and jungle intellects, the language of this last group jangled with nouns and verbs that carried little meaning and adjectives that, while scarcely descriptive, were on the whole redundant. Unable to make even an attempt at straightforward musical analysis (or, for that matter, to write a straightforward sentence), they adopted a gibbering prose calculated to hide the thinness of their analysis and evaluation.

With the establishment in 1934 of *Down Beat*, a jazz magazine, there was hope for serious discussion of the subject, a hope soon betrayed, for the editors aimed their publication at adolescent jazz fans and conceived their function to be that of serving the jazz industry as movie magazines served Hollywood. Until the swing era, there was little mention of jazz in popular magazines of national circulation, and whatever notice jazz received in the daily press was—its scantiness notwithstanding—pejorative and a little absurd. Jazz buffs therefore welcomed the new publication sight unseen, only to find its critical writing a disappointment. Serious jazz students, who had little to choose from among the writing on jazz before *Down Beat*, soon learned not to expect much of *Down Beat* either. Nat Hentoff, a former associate editor of *Down Beat*, summed up the magazine's twenty-five years of publication when he said:

> *Down Beat* is especially shallow and is apparently geared for less advanced high school sophomores. . . . Critical and historical jazz writing does appear to be slowly improving, but fervid amateurism is apt to be predominant for some time, because the fan-writer is well entrenched. As long as *Down Beat* remains

---

JAZZ: SOME EARLY DIFFICULTIES from *The Anatomy of Jazz* by Leroy Ostransky;

the "bible" of the field, the writing will be of a caliber more appropriate to revealed religion than to responsible criticism.

Because of their inability to write on jazz as music, writers for most of the popular jazz journals turned their hands to grinding out deadline record reviews and uncovering sensational biographical data that were then translated into trite but shocking headlines; or they concocted diffuse, sophomoric think-pieces intended to show why the jazz musician is a nice guy or a bad guy or simply a misunderstood guy who never got the breaks until the writer discovered him in a tired but happy moment.

The language problem is one thing, but wrong-headed intolerance is another. For some time now there has been a tendency among jazz writers to look down upon anyone who doesn't "dig" jazz. Their attitude toward the uninitiated layman has often been one of indifference. But their attitude toward classical musicians has been one of intolerance —not just a passive intolerance, but an active one. In its most primitive form, this intolerance manifests itself in simple name-calling; in a somewhat higher form it appears in the condescension apparent in the following items. The first compares the musical intelligence of the classical musician to that of the jazzman.

CAT ON KEYS

New York—Drummer Osie Johnson was telling of the time a group of classical musicians were gathered in a jazzman's home, and the latter put some Charlie Parker records on the phonograph.

After a few seconds, one of the classical men protested: "Come on now, fix the machine. That motor's obviously going too fast. Nobody can play that many notes so fast." The jazzman took great and obvious delight in proving that there was nothing at all wrong with the machine.

The second is a three-column headline of an article on recording studios which reminds its readers: "Classics Recorders Just Discovering Something Jazz Fans Found Out Early."

Square or classical musicians, finding themselves patronized by the self-appointed defenders of jazz, were unlikely to seek to overcome their feeling of alienation from jazz. The tone of *Down Beat* helped cement many of the squares into four-square blocks of antagonism toward all jazz. It is a happy circumstance that many serious musicians are able to disregard the rather obvious insinuations of petty jazz writers who, to retaliate for fancied snubs, attack with their fists flying in the name of defending jazz. There are many first-rate musicians who believe it is possible, and even desirable, to study, understand, and enjoy the work of Mozart as well as the work of Thelonious Monk. Such musicians (and it would seem that jazz has need of many) may be amused at the ineptness of undistinguished jazz reporters, but they are less likely to be amused when a critic of André Hodeir's reputation and sensitivity asks a question such as this: "Isn't it true that those who prefer the Beethoven work [*Ninth Symphony*] confess implicitly their inability to understand Stravinsky's masterpiece [*Le Sacre du Printemps*]?"

If Hodeir means to imply by his question that there are musicians who prefer Beethoven to Stravinsky, or that there are musicians who believe there is something unnatural about any music that is not German, then he should say so. No one will question this. If, however, his question is to be taken at face value, it seems to indicate an inability on Hodeir's part to recognize the distinctions between comprehension, appreciation, and enjoyment. A respectable number of classical musicians understand fully the nature of Stravinsky's work, but nevetheless prefer Beethoven's *Ninth Symphony* to Stravinsky's *Le Sacre*—and if not Beethoven's *Ninth,* then a Bach suite perhaps, or a Mozart divertimento, a Schubert song, a Chopin étude. Moreover, there can be no doubt that many musicians, and laymen as well, not only do not prefer *Le Sacre,* but do not understand it; neither is there any doubt, in my mind at least, that there are a good many who prefer Beethoven's *Ninth* and don't understand *it,* either. The fact remains that it is not necessary to understand a work in order to like it; or, to put it another way: a musician may have a comprehensive understanding and appreciation of a work—jazz or otherwise—without liking it. The failure to understand this principle—perhaps the guiding principle in critical evaluation—is part of the reason for the apparent schism between some well-known jazz critics and contemporary classical musicians who evince an interest in jazz.

Jazz has reached an important stage in its growth. In the past decade it has finally attracted a number of men of literary taste and musical perception, and this favorable climate must be maintained. Jazz needs the aid and interest of historians, theorists, composers, estheticians—anyone willing to lend his support, knowledge, and experience to the task of establishing jazz as a significant part of music. Jazz is an important branch of music, of American music especially; as such, it must be allowed to flourish, cultivated by respectful consideration and intensive study. Much has been done in the past ten years toward this goal: the inauguration of jazz study groups and institutes, for example, and the recognition of jazz as a subject for study in institutions of higher learning. Of the highest significance, also, is the probing look backward by men of appropriate intellectual habits, men who feel the compulsion to take the study of jazz out of the shadows of semiliterateness and anti-intellectualism and place it in the light of serious and searching study.

Jazz has at last become respectable. But in order to understand the origins of its present-day problems—semantic and otherwise—it is necessary to survey, however briefly, early jazz criticism. As long ago as 1946, Winthrop Sargeant wrote: "There has been a great deal of dubious and highly confusing writing around the subject of jazz. Probably no musical movement in history has been made the subject of more leaky speculation. . . ." Many critics have since echoed, in more or less detail, Sargeant's view. In order to show the scope of the work still to be done, I have listed the following representative statements, which, I believe, pose the most important problems faced by present-day jazz writers and theorists. Morroe Berger, a Columbia University fellow in sociology, wrote in 1946:

> The origins of jazz and the story of its spread, as well as the careers of its players, are all subjects about which there is still considerable question. The importance of these matters is, in addition, not limited to music itself, or to the interest of collectors or to the reputation of musicians; they are significant, also, for the problems of the origins and diffusion of culture, and racial interaction, which involve other arts as well as some sciences.

In 1955 Keepnews and Grauer commented on the growing importance and complexities of jazz in America:

> Perhaps the truest measure of the validity of jazz is that it can be all things to all men: a mild form of amusement; an emotional or an intellectual stimulant; an art form; a social commentary; a cult; something to like, love, or even hate for a wide variety of esthetic, emotional or social reasons. Thus jazz is both simple (no more than the combinations of notes you hear) and incredibly complex (as complex as human beings and as the world we inhabit). And thus it is a fit subject for all the analysis, history, biography, criticism, and written what-have-you that has been built up alongside it.

In 1956 Jacques Barzun emphasized the difficulty we are concerned with:

> It [jazz] ranks with sports and philately as the realm of the self-made expert and of the controversialist as well, for musicology has not yet settled all the historical, stylistic, and biographical problems that have been raised about it.

In 1957 Shapiro and Hentoff summed up the question: "Since jazz musicians are notoriously inarticulate verbally, a good deal of analytical and creative writing about jazz during the past three decades has been speculative, fanciful, romantic, and wrong."

Shapiro and Hentoff's statement brings us back to the semantic problem. It is sometimes easy for us to forget how new the language of jazz is, and quite frequently how subjective the meanings are of even its most established terms. "One of the difficulties of describing an elusive music like jazz," Whitney Balliett has said, "is a made-at-home terminology that includes such aimless and largely inscrutable brand names as 'swing,' 'be-bop,' and 'Dixieland.'"

To say nothing of "jazz." Although the word "jazz" was undoubtedly in use for a good many years before 1914, it was not until then, according to Nick La Rocca, founder of the Original Dixieland Jazz Band, that "jazz" appeared in an advertisement. "The Original Dixieland Jazz Band," he wrote to Nicolas Slonimsky, "was the first band in the world to be called a Jazz Band. Our first billing was in the year of 1914, month of March, place Boosters Club, Chicago, Illinois, Manager Harry James." Two years later *Variety* wrote, "Chicago has added another innovation to its list of discoveries in the so-called 'Jazz Bands.'" According to Slonimsky, this may be the first mention of the word "jazz" in print. A year after the *Variety* item appeared, the Victor Company issued their first jazz record (March, 1917), and in 1918 the Columbia Phonograph Company issued its first jazz record, *Darktown Strutters Ball* and *Indiana,* played by the Original Dixieland Jass Band.

Conjecture on the derivation of the word "jazz" (or "jass") has ranged widely. The term has been variously considered as a corruption of "Charles" by way of "Chas," "jass," "jazz"; a diminution of *"jaser,"* that is, to exhilarate; and some linguistic scholars claim to have traced its origins to West Africa. In the early days of jazz writing, it may have seemed more profitable to seek the linguistic origins of jazz than to try to define it. Once it was out of its infancy, however, little could be said of its linguistic origins that had not been said before, and critics—the apt and inept alike—set about defining, or not defining, jazz.

Many of those attempting to define jazz took advantage of the elusiveness of the term by using jazz as a springboard for sociological, psychological, and anthropological speculations, without recognizing that jazz is music; nevertheless, many of these critics have made some contribution to the understanding of jazz. Before we attempt to search out the musical aspects of jazz, it might be well to acknowledge the work of those social critics who had a hand in creating the image of jazz still dominant in the minds of many people. These are the critics who have, in the main, produced the miasmatic atmosphere in which jazzmen often have had to perform. These are the critics who have stamped their opinions and attitudes upon the jazz-uninformed reading public and have made it difficult, and sometimes impossible, to convince the uninitiated of the worth of jazz, or to persuade them to accept the analysis of jazz as a serious and worthy enterprise.

For the social critics of jazz and the people they have influenced, the years between 1920 and 1929 were the crucial years, the years when all good men strode onto the field of Armageddon, pen in hand, to conquer the evil forces of jazz. It is therefore natural to search for the corpus of social criticism of jazz in the writings of Jazz Age critics—not because its critics were unmusical (or, in some cases, not even American), but because their criticism reflects the literate viewpoint of sincere writers and jazz-innocent readers at the time when first impressions of jazz were being formed.

In 1920 Harold Spender, a representative critic of American mores and author of *A Briton in America,* was led to believe that many of the jazz tunes he had heard were African in origin. This caused him painful concern. If we were not careful, American musical tradition might be "submerged by the aboriginal music of the Negro," and, if we insisted on stomping along such "semibarbaric paths," heaven knows where we would end up. But Harold Spender, the Englishman, was a mild fellow indeed compared with a critic whom I shall call "The Amazing American." That author, who preferred to remain nameless, wrote a provocative study ingeniously entitled "The Amazing American," in which—and his lack of comprehension did not deter him a bit—he spoke of jazz, among other evils. The place of America in the future spiritual scheme of things was, he opined, assured. Any nation capable of producing the "nigger minstrel, rag-time music, and the tango dance," was close to the top. His indictment of jazz, however, is spiritless compared to his brilliantly indiscriminating castigation of American culture in general. In 1925 he wrote:

> In deathless page, in song, in art, America has contributed but little to the world's treasury. If that land were to cease to be tomorrow, its most flattering epitaph would be the sign of the dollar chiselled in the stone. . . . It is a land of flesh-pots, with no great national aim speaking through a national art. . . . The general attitude of the American mind is in deadly opposition to culture.

Outbursts of this sort were not uncommon even among authors who signed their work. At about the same time, the distinguished writer Aldous Huxley had a go at us. He said much the same thing as the others, but with more style. Here, in jazz prose, is a sample from his book. *Jesting Pilate: An Intellectual Holiday:*

> Jazz it up, jazz it up. Keep moving. Step on the gas. Say it with dancing. The Charleston, the Baptists. Radios and Revivals. Uplift and Gilda Gray. The pipe organ, the nigger with the saxophone, the Giant Marimbaphone. Hymns and the movies and Irving Berlin. Petting Parties and the First Free United Episcopal Methodist Church. Jazz it up!

If laid end to end, all the jazz-inspired, pointed-finger, stream-of-licentiousness pieces of the twenties on the debilitating effects of wine, women, and jazz would span the distance from New Orleans to New York—by way of Memphis, Kansas City, and Chicago—and back again. Jazz, for critics in the twenties, was a social manifestation, not a musical one. For anyone interested in jazz as music, the critical climate promised little sunshine.

The slow progress in jazz analysis is probably due chiefly to the confusion of jazz with commercial popular music. It is scarcely credible nowadays that certain writers of the Jazz Age were unable to recognize that jazz is a manner of performance rather than a collection of Tin Pan Alley tunes. Nevertheless, such was the case, and this confusion resulted in establishing men like Paul Whiteman, George Gershwin, and Irving Berlin at the top of the jazz hierarchy. By now, of course, their place in jazz is clear; their place in popular music even clearer. But in the twenties the confusion—even in the minds of otherwise acute writers—enabled Whiteman to attain the unchallenged position of King of Jazz. For the general public the songs of Berlin and Gershwin, as played by the Whiteman band, had enough characteristics in common with whatever fragments of jazz they knew to seem to be much the same thing. Those who heard genuine jazz occasionally—the music of Armstrong, say, or Fletcher Henderson—heard these men and their groups play tunes with the same titles used by Whiteman, and they naturally assumed they were hearing a poor version of Whiteman's music. To their conditioned ears, Whiteman's "jazz" was smoother, richer, cleaner, and more civilized. In 1926, at the height of the confusion, Henry O. Osgood wrote *So This Is Jazz,* a book Whitney Balliett has happily described as "a triumphant and fascinating failure." In this work Osgood showed how it was possible to write a book on jazz without actually considering the Negro's position in jazz. Here is the premise on which Osgood's book was based:

> Nowhere have I gone into detail about Negro jazz bands. There are so many good ones, it would be hard to pick out a few for special mention. None of them, however, are as good as the best white bands, and very rarely are their best players as good as the best white virtuosos. Their playing makes up for what it may lack in smoothness and finish by abandon, dash, spirit and warmth. There are fewer trained musicians, consequently more of the improvisations and variations which characterized early jazz.

Osgood was not alone in his beliefs; other, more astute writers than he made the same mistakes. In 1923, Gilbert Seldes, then a brilliant young critic with unrestrained interests and perpetually *au courant,* set about answering another critic who believed that jazz was on the way out. "Jazz, for me," Seldes wrote, in *Dial,* August, 1923, "isn't a last feverish excitement, a spasm of energy before death. It is the normal development of our resources, the expected, and wonderful, arrival of America at a point of creative intensity."

Now, that was an enthusiastic, patriotic, moving, even poetic statement, except for one thing: Seldes had little notion of what jazz was in 1923. He made the fashionable mistake of thinking that certain pieces of sheet music were jazz—good or bad—and others were not; that certain songwriters were better jazz composers than other songwriters; and that the notated melodic, harmonic, and rhythmic structure of a piece of music determined its jazz quality. Seldes is a good man to have on your side in any literary battle, but in 1923 he was not writing about jazz; he was writing about popular music. He was not yet aware that the jazz quality of a piece is determined by the manner in which it is played. Jazz is not a piece called *Tiger Rag, St. Louis Blues, Wang Wang Blues,* or *Yes, We Have No Bananas.* The title determines nothing; Whiteman's recording of *Wang Wang Blues* had about as much to do with jazz as his performances of *Song of India, By the Waters of Minnetonka,* or *Oh Katherina,* with its *Ach Du lieber Augustin* introduction. Seldes, apparently unaware of this, made an extraordinary effort to show that Irving Berlin was a great jazz composer. "Mr. Berlin's masterpieces . . . in jazz," he wrote in the same article, "are *Everybody Step* and *Pack Up Your Sins.*" Other of Seldes' favorites were *I'm Gonna Pin My Medal on the Girl I Left Behind* and *Someone Else May Be There While I'm Gone*; he admired these tunes because they were equally good played slow or fast. "Berlin's work," he added, "is musically interesting, and that means it has a chance to survive. I have no such confidence in *Dardanella* or *Chicago.*"

Seldes then went on to distinguish between white jazz and colored jazz, and it is here that he missed the riverboat entirely. About the future of American music, he wrote, "I say the Negro is not our salvation because with all my feelings for his desirable indifference to our set of conventions about emotional decency, I am on the side of civilization." Words like these from a man of Seldes' unquestionable intellect and sensitivity helped delay the unprejudiced, thoroughgoing analysis of jazz a good many years. As long as critics of Seldes' caliber and repuation continued to write about "emotional decency" and whatever it is that is not "on the side of civilization," jazz continued to seek its laurels along skid road.

In 1929, or shortly before the release of Ellington's *Wall Street Wail,* P. F. Laubenstein, a serious music critic, made an attempt to present the prevailing position of jazz in an essay in the *Musical Quarterly.* Trying manfully to be objective—but not always succeeding—Laubenstein was not especially sympathetic to jazz. His essay did, however, summarize certain significant aspects of jazz and recognized certain problems of the future at a time when many hoped that jazz had no future. Here, from "Jazz—Debit and Credit," is Laubenstein's summation:

> The musical historian of the future will doubtless find his *bête noire* in this inescapable task of evaluating jazz. Indeed, many of its contemporaries there be

who execrate the "stuff" as inebriate, doggerel, degenerate, ghoulish, vulturine, etc. *ad infinitum*—music, or as not music at all, bearing inherent frailties which spell its own ephemerality. Its enthusiastic devotees see in its local generation and popular cultivation the very best attestation of its truly representative American character, and from its study would derive invaluable leadings as to the direction which a national music should take. Those holding a middle ground discover in it some elements of permanent value and certain developments which must be counted as real contributions toward the progress of music.

Critical onslaughts in books, journals, and magazines were, of course, the bulk of jazz criticism. In addition, the daily press, acting as if it were woefully certain that jazz would flourish under any circumstances, offered little sympathy or understanding. Until recently, jazz news consisted mostly of unfavorable criticisms by names in the news and self-styled watch and ward societies. The subject of jazz, with its popular connotations, could usually be counted on to make provocative and lively news copy. What the general reader read in the newspapers about jazz was what he wanted to believe; and what the press published reflected his opinion. He knew nothing about jazz as music, but he had a firm opinion that the men and women of jazz were degenerate and unwholesome. The average reader received (and still receives) great comfort in believing that there were people to whom he could feel superior. And much feature writing was intended to reinforce the reader's opinions. With few exceptions, it is not an easy task to find a news item of the twenties on jazz that does not speak of jazz with tongue in cheek, as a kind of drollery always good for a chuckle, if not a laugh. Overseas items, from France particularly, were always welcome and in the twenties were usually offered with heavyhanded merriment. The following headlines from the *New York Times* reflect the general public's attitude toward jazz in the Jazz Age:

Fails to Stop Jazz, Is Arrested Later [July 7, 1922]

French Police Stop Jazz Band Burial; Dead Man Wanted It in Procession, but the Mourners were Foxtrotting [October 18, 1923]

France Orders Our Jazz Players Expelled [May 31, 1924]

Isadora Duncan Plans Greek Temple for Nice; She is Reported to Have Bought the Theatre Promenade des Anglais, to Fight Jazz [May 1, 1925]

Ford Wars on Jazz; Gives Party for Old Time Dances, Seeking to Revive Their Popularity [July 12, 1925]

American Dancer Jazzing the *Marseillaise* Angers Friendly Audience in Paris Music Hall [January 31, 1926]

Church Jazz Wedding Utilizes Saxophone [November 14, 1926]

Damrosch Assails Jazz [April 17, 1928]

French Find Our Jazz Too Soul-disturbing [February 3, 1929]

From these headlines, it would seem that nobody in the twenties dared say a kind word for jazz. By the thirties, however, the jazz initiate could sense that some changes would be made. The Roosevelt administration's early efforts to lift the nation out of the Great Depression looked as if they would work, and everything, jazz included, suddenly seemed brighter and more useful. Many intellectuals sought, and found, rewards in studying America's popular culture, and folk songs and jazz came in for a good share of the spotlight. In 1933, the repeal of Prohibition and the subsequent opening of many night clubs and dance halls led to the employment of more jazz musicians and to a wider audience for jazz. It is possible also that the general unrest caused by events in Europe helped create a small musical nationalism, much of which may well have been fostered by the reports in the daily press of various actions and pronouncements against jazz in European countries. On March 15, 1933, the National Socialist head of the Berlin Rundfunk forbade the broadcasting of "Negro jazz," and on January 7, 1934, a headline in the *New York Times* read: "Ban against Jazz Sought in Ireland." (A week before, an Irish antijazz group had paraded in Mohall, Ireland, with banners and posters bearing the slogan "Down with Jazz and Paganism." The unruly antijazzists had been aroused by the actions of their finance minister, Sean MacEntee, who had stood by while jazz bands broadcast their wares over the state broadcasting system.) On October 12, 1935, Eugen Hadamowski, director of the German broadcasting system, issued an order banning broadcasts of jazz in order, as he put it, "to do away with the last remnants of the culture-Bolshevistic Jew."

By the time these items appeared in the press, the swing era was under way, and swing—or jazz—was beginning to enjoy unprecedented popularity in the United States, and Hadamowski was no longer talking about the music of a handful of people, but the music of millions. Americans, generally speaking, were not particularly curious about their own culture. As long as they regarded jazz as something they were permitted to take or leave alone, they left it alone—it seemed socially more prudent to do so.

However, once swing as a popular movement surged forward, and they learned that other nations saw jazz as a threat to their way of life, many Americans began to see in jazz a symbol of their own freedom, and foreign pronouncements condemning jazz became something to ridicule and defy. There were no great public refutations or demonstrations, of course (unless one so considers the crowds flocking to the New York Paramount Theater, Randall's Island, and Carnegie Hall swing concerts), and the thought that jazz was a symbol of anything was for the most part left unsaid. Altogether, though, there was increasing public support for jazz as something American. And this was all to the good. Pronouncements like those issued by the Nazis may not have sent anyone into a fit of righteous rage, but perhaps such items made it possible for people—some of them public figures—to feel less queasy about defending jazz, in whatever aspect.

In the late thirties, swing burst forth and reached all parts of the nation. Radio and admen—agencies responsible for much of its growth—were becoming powerful and influential; a shrewd promotion of swing, big white bands in particular (with Benny Goodman's name leading the rest), resulted in making swing a suitable, if controversial, topic for conversation however genteel. Since respected figures occasionally spoke up for swing, tongue-in-cheek press notices diminshed (to increase again after World War II, with Dizzy Gillespie and his early high jinks) and became serious, objective, and sometimes even sympathetic reports. And on May 5, 1937, the *New York Times* reported that "Dr. Carleton Sprague Smith, head of the Music Division of the N.Y. Public Library, championed 'swing' music tonight, terming it an 'appropriate' musical expression which must receive serious consideration."

During this same period, however, the opposite point of view continued to be expressed with varying degrees of violence. The president of the Dancing Teachers Business Association, for example, in a talk to his associates reported by the *New York Times* on July 7, 1938, said that swing music was a "degenerated form of jazz," and its devotees were "unfortunate victims of economic instability." He went on to predict hopefully that "the popularity of swing will fade with the return of economic stability." Furthermore, if people wished to dance, there were plenty of suitable and proper tangos, rumbas, and waltzes. On May 22, 1938, an exhibition of "degenerate music" opened in Düsseldorf. Nazi Germany wished to prevent the spread of jazz and atonal music—"the microbes of musical decomposition"—and to wipe out all music that showed "Marxist, Bolshevistic, Jewish, or any other un-German tendencies." And, finally, Dr. Harry D. Gideonse, then head of the economics and social science department of Barnard College, stated in the *New York Times* of November 2, 1938, "Swing is musical Hitlerism."

Altogether, it is not difficult to understand why so little serious work on jazz was accomplished in the twenties and thirties. Add the confusions, misunderstandings, disagreements, and misconceptions of those sincerely interested in jazz to the rantings and bitterness of those opposed to jazz, and you have the main reason why jazz analysis was delayed until we were well into the swing era. By the middle forties, serious attempts to analyze jazz as music became more frequent. Most critics began to recognize the need for emphasizing proper jazz analysis and evaluation and de-emphasizing the social import of jazz and attempts to tie jazz in with sociology became less and less rewarding. Freed of its social shackles, jazz in the forties finally became a fit subject for serious study, and students of jazz were now able to ask, "What is jazz?"

QUESTIONS

1. What enables "fan" magazines of all kinds—jazz, movies, sports, television—to flourish? Discuss the subject matter of these magazines. On what level are the subjects treated?
2. Clarify the distinctions between "comprehension," "appreciation," and "enjoyment." Relate their meanings to jazz and to classical music.
3. Do you think it is possible for one person to understand and enjoy both jazz and classical music equally? Give your reasons.
4. Do you agree that "Jazz has at last become respectable?" What, exactly, does that statement mean? Was there a time when jazz was not respectable? When? Why?
5. In the history of jazz criticism, why are the years 1920-1929 important? Compare the criticism of that era with present criticism. What are the likenesses? the differences?

INDEX

D

E

F

G

H

T

V

W

A NOTE ON THE TYPE FACES USED IN THIS BOOK

THE TEXT of this book is set in Fairfield, a linotype book face designed in America by Rudolph Ruzicka and introduced in 1939. Fairfield is a modern face which incorporates many of the characteristics of an older face.

The display faces used throughout the book are chosen from a wide variety of styles:

LEROY OSTRANSKY	Champion
P	Ombre ornamental initial
E	Graphique
R	Riccardo
S	Gold Rush
P	Trump-Gravure
E	Stymie Open
C	Chisel Open Extended
T	Egyptian Open Expanded
I	Normandia Outline
V	Umbra No. 3
E	Profil
S	Virtuosa
ON	Allegro
MUSIC	Horizon Medium
TO SONYA	Rondo
FOREWORD	Invitation Shaded
ACKNOWLEDGMENTS	Fortune Extra Bold
TABLE OF CONTENTS	Deepdene italic
HOW WE LISTEN	Century Schoolbook
IMAGE PROCESSES AND CONNOTATION	Twentieth Century Medium italic (also known as Spartan Medium)
THE LANGUAGE OF MUSIC	Orpheus italic
LISTENING TO THE MUSICAL ELEMENTS	Melior italic
THE BEGINNING OF ORCHESTRATION	Trajanus
THE ORCHESTRA & THE CONDUCTOR	French Round Face
PROGRAM MUSIC AND RICHARD STRAUSS	"Program Music" is set in Huxley Vertical; "Richard Strauss" is in Latin Wide. The "and" is Electra.
THE NATIONAL SCHOOLS	Legend (or Legenda)
INTRODUCTION TO FORM	Baskerville No. 2
A DIGEST OF FORM	Bulletin Typewriter
CHAMBER MUSIC	Largo Open

FOUR RUSSIANS CALLED BUDAPEST	"Four Russians Called" is in Bodoni; "Budapest" is set in Russian Bold.
INTRODUCTION TO THE SYMPHONY	Garamont (also known as Garamond)
THE INVENTION OF THE SYMPHONY	Gavotte with "Swing" letters (T, I, f, S). Swing or "swash" letters are flourished italics.
JASCHA HEIFETZ	Stradivarius (sometimes called Sinfonia)
VLADIMIR HOROWITZ	Ultra Bodoni italic
THE AMATEUR PIANIST	Stencil
CHOPIN AT 38	Parisian
THE DAWN OF THE ART	Nueland Inline
TENORS & BARITONES	"Tenors" is set in Onyx; "Baritones" in Cooper Black. The Ampersand (&) is Goudy Old Style italic.
THE HEYDAY OF OPERA	Lilith
THE GRAND ROMANTIC BALLETS	Eve Light
THE RITUAL CHANT OF THE CATHOLIC CHURCH	Americal Uncial
THE CHORALE IN THE CHURCH SERVICE	German Bold
TROUBADOURS, TROUVÈRES AND MINNESINGERS	Baskerville with Ornamental Initials
ORLANDE DE LASSUS	Lydian Cursive
BACH	Bold German Condensed
THE WEATHER AT MOZART'S FUNERAL	Caslon Old Style italic
BEETHOVEN AND HIS CONTEMPORARIES	"Beethoven" is set in Franklin Gothic. "And His Contemporaries" is set in Standard.
THE IMPRESSIONISTS	Shadow
BARTÓK IN AMERICA	News Gothic
WHATEVER HAPPENED TO THAT GREAT AMERICAN SYMPHONY?	P. T. Barnum (also called French Clarendon)
JAZZ: SOME EARLY DIFFICULTIES	Champion
INDEX	Folio Medium Extended